Publish It
on the Web!

2nd Edition

Windows® Version

PUBLISH IT ON THE WEB!

2nd Edition

Windows® Version

Bryan Pfaffenberger

AP PROFESSIONAL

AP PROFESSIONAL is a division of Academic Press

Boston San Diego New York
London Sydney Tokyo Toronto

AP PROFESSIONAL
1300 Boylston Street, Chestnut Hill, MA 02167

An imprint of ACADEMIC PRESS
A division of HARCOURT BRACE & COMPANY

United Kingdom Edition published by
ACADEMIC PRESS LIMITED
24–28 Oval Road, London NW1 7DX

ISBN 0-12-553160-5
ISBN 0-12-553161-3 (CD-ROM)

Printed in the United States of America
97 98 99 00 IP 9 8 7 6 5 4 3 2 1

Contents

Part III   Creating Your Web with HTML   193

Part IV   Producing Dynamic Content   425

Part V   Web Publishing Issues   507

Introduction

T he World Wide Web has hit the big time. Growing far beyond its humble 1989 beginnings as an academic information system, the Web has become the medium of choice for just about everyone who wishes to make information available on the Internet.

Just how big is the Web? It's anyone's guess, but one recent estimate noted that the number of Web servers—programs capable of making documents available on the World Wide Web—is doubling every 53 days. And how many people are using the Web? Because the Web is winning out over all other means of accessing data on the Internet, the number of users out there will steadily grow until it approaches the total number of Internet users. A cautious estimate puts that number currently at 25 million—and it's doubling every year. The Internet, with the Web as its chosen user interface, is well on its way to becoming a mass publishing medium.

What kind of mass publishing medium is the Web going to be? One of the most amazing things about the Web is its democracy—the fact that anyone, ranging from an impoverished college student to a huge corporation, can put up a home page and publish something on the Web. This doesn't mean, of course, that a college student can gain a mass audience of millions of people. Most Web servers can handle only a few dozen simultaneous accesses, called *hits*, before overloading the systems on which they're housed. Servers designed to handle millions of hits per day are high-powered machines, beyond the means of most individuals and small businesses.

Still, the Web is one of the most revolutionary developments to have occurred in a century of communication innovations. What's so remarkable about the Web is that it's the first medium to reach a mass market in which a consumer of information can turn the tables and become the *producer* of information. And that's exactly what's happening on the Web. Of course, the Web isn't absolutely necessary for ordinary individuals to publish information, as the existence of more than 75,000 newsletters attests. But the Web has a huge advantage over newsletters or any other do-it-yourself publishing medium: virtually zero distribution costs. Once you've obtained Internet access and equipped yourself with a reasonably powerful computer and server software, you're ready to publish on the Web and you're putting yourself in touch with an audience that's achieving significant penetration in the English-speaking world.[1]

This is a book for any ordinary person who wants to publish on the Web. Perhaps you're hoping to create a Web page for your church or synagogue, a school or charitable organization, or a small business. You don't have the resources to hire a professional Web designer, and you're not exactly a computer whiz. But that doesn't matter. If you can use a computer, you can publish on the Web. This book is your guide to every facet of Web publishing, beginning with framing your purpose and carrying you all the way through preparing simple but effective graphics. On this book's CD-ROM, you'll find a very powerful toolkit for the Web publishing process, containing many of the programs that Web publishing experts use every day.

---

1. If you're thinking of publishing in a language other than English, you should know that the Internet has a pronounced English tilt at the moment—but that's just an artifact of its birth in the United States. Already, there is significant Internet penetration in France and Germany, as attested by the rise of French- and German-language newsgroups on Usenet, a computer discussion system that's widely distributed via the Internet. Internet service availability is also picking up steam in Latin America, spearheaded by forward-looking Mexico.

WHAT'S SO SPECIAL ABOUT THIS BOOK?

If you're browsing at the bookstore, take a look at the other Web publishing and HTML books that are available. I'll bet they concentrate on the HTML code. That's fine—after all, it helps to know a little HTML even if you plan to let somebody else do all or most of the coding.

But these other books can't help you with the big picture. They're obsessed with the technical details. They don't tell you the one thing you really need to know: Considering the unique characteristics of the Web as a publishing medium, what should you publish? That's a very important question, and one that goes far beyond putting your HTML tags in the right order. As anyone who's worked in professional publishing can tell you, the first and most important step in any publishing effort is to frame your objective.

This is the first book on Web publishing that takes the Web seriously as a radically new publishing medium. Underlying this book is the philosophy that the most successful Web publications begin with a thorough understanding of the Web's technical basis, its novel characteristics as a publishing medium, and the changing demographics of the Web audience. You'll find all the HTML you'll need, to be sure. But you'll also find an approach to Web publishing that's unique among the books on this subject—and it's an approach that's designed to make you a winner in Web publishing.

There's one more thing about this book that makes it especially useful: It's designed specifically for users of Microsoft Windows, Windows 95, and Windows NT. In each chapter, the discussion, tips, and resources are focused squarely on the possibilities of Web publishing the Windows way. You'll also find a ton of useful software on the CD-ROM disc included with this book.

HOW IS THIS BOOK ORGANIZED?

This book comprehensively presents all the information you'll need to embark on a serious Web publishing effort. You'll begin by fully understanding the technical basis of the Web and its unique characteristics as a publishing medium. You'll continue by planning your Web pages, using a time-proven publishing design system, and by learning enough HTML to meet your needs—and that could be very little indeed (Chapter 11 alone teaches everything you'd need to know to put together a decent Web page in short order).

Although this book isn't intended to turn you into a professional multi-media designer, it goes on to fill you in on the basics of producing sounds, graphics, and movies for your Web site. Finally, the book concludes by surveying the fast-breaking developments that will affect the Web's future—and yours, if you get involved in Web publishing.

Part I: The New Opportunities in Web Publishing

In this part of *Publish It on the Web*, you'll fully explore the technical basis of the World Wide Web and learn to grasp its radically new possibilities as a publishing medium. You'll learn how the Internet transmits information, and why it's spreading like wildfire all over the globe. You'll next explore the principles of hypertext (nonsequential writing) that provide the basic information-browsing metaphor for the Web. (In addition, you'll learn that the Web—or something very much like it—has actually been under conceptual and even technical development for almost 20 years.)

Next, you'll examine the Web protocols (standards) that make the Web workable as a worldwide information system, and you'll examine the Web's characteristics as a publishing medium (especially in contrast to broadcast media). Part I concludes with a survey of Web publishing possibilities and an examination of Web server software, which provides the technical basis for Web document distribution.

Part II: Planning Your Web

In any publishing effort, the first and most important steps are to frame your objective and know your audience. Part II begins by examining these steps in detail, and goes on to survey the possibilities for Web content design.

Part III: Creating Your Web with HTML

Part III delves into the nuts and bolts of HTML—but you may only need to read the first chapter, which presents everything you'll need to know to create and publish a nice-looking home page. If you'd like to learn more, Part III is rich in information—and what's more, it's tailored for the Microsoft Windows environment. You'll learn how to exploit the incredible power of HotDog, an HTML editor that's available on the Web. You'll even learn how to implement tables, forms, frames, and multimedia, and—thanks to the cool software on this book's CD-ROM disc—you won't have to learn how to do any computer programming to get these exciting, interactive features to work.

Part IV: Producing Dynamic Content

This section thoroughly surveys subjects that almost all HTML books ignore: The specifics of what goes into the preparation of multimedia material for Web pages. Although Part IV can't tell you everything there is to know about preparing multimedia for the Web—each of these chapters could easily grow into a book of their own—you'll learn the basics of scanning, graphics production, sound recording, movie and animation production, and the use of Adobe Acrobat to prepare richly formatted documents for the Web. Like Part III, this part is tailored to the Windows environment—you'll learn how to use the top Windows programs for multimedia production.

Part V: Web Publishing Issues

As fast as the Web has grown, it's not surprising that some thorny issues have come along with the rapid growth. Who controls the Web's standards processes? What about copyright in an age of digital transmission? What do current technological developments mean for the Web's future as a publishing medium? These questions and more are addressed in Part V of this book.

Where Do I Start?

It depends on how much previous experience you've had with the Internet and the Web. If you're new to the Internet and the Web, start with Chapter 1. If you're a seasoned Internet vet but new to the Web, start with Chapter 2. Web-savvy readers should begin with Chapter 4, which surveys the Web's novel characteristics as a publishing medium.

If you'd just like to learn some quick HTML so you can get your page up in short order, don't miss Chapter 11—it's a great "quick start" and it may very well contain all the HTML you'll ever need. Don't miss the HTML 3.2 Quick Reference at the back of the book!

Special Features of This Book

As you're reading this book, you'll find the following icons, which are intended to point out helpful features:

You're sure to run into some roadblocks on your way to Web mastery. Look here for tips and strategies for overcoming common problems.

 Look for the Treasure Trove icon for pointers to rich repositories of information and resources that are available on the Web—for free.

 Look for the Webmaster icon for practical tips of value to anyone who's thinking about setting up a Web server.

A WORD FROM THE AUTHOR

Web publishing may seem overwhelming at first—there's so much to learn. But you can start small. Get going the Web way, by giving something back to this amazing network that's benefited us all so much. Surely there's something you know about that you can share—for instance, knowledge of a hobby or a place you enjoyed visiting. More seriously, maybe you've been through an experience that you'd like to share with others, such as an illness or a summer that you spent working with a social service organization. After putting your page on the Web, you'll soon find that people are starting to access it, and even to include hyperlinks to it on their own pages. Soon, you'll become aware of other people who have tried to accomplish much the same thing, and all the while your knowledge of the Web—and its amazing publishing possibilities—will grow by leaps and bounds.

File Edit View Favorites Help

Address: http//www

Part I

THE NEW
OPPORTUNITIES IN
WEB PUBLISHING

Chapter

1

The Internet as a Publication Medium

If you want to understand the Web and its possibilities for publication you'd best begin by grasping the Internet. The Internet provides the physical medium for the exchange of information on the Web. It has some characteristics that make it very much *unlike* other information-exchange networks, including other computer networks and (especially) the telephone system.

This chapter introduces the Internet, so it's good to read if you're just getting started with the Internet and the Web. Even if you're already familiar with the Internet's basic concepts, though, you should give this chapter a quick skim. The Internet can be broadly conceptualized as a publication medium, and it has many lessons to teach aspiring Webmasters. Remember, too, that the Web is based on the Internet, and many of the Web's peculiarities—again, from the publishing medium standpoint—are the peculiarities of the Internet in general.

For the Time-Challenged

♦ The Internet allows computers of differing makes and models to communicate and exchange data. That's one reason why it's so phenomenally popular.

♦ The Internet also permits one computer to control another one—for example, by telling it to find and send a file. This is called *interoperability*. Again, it doesn't matter if the two computers are of different makes and models.

♦ This book approaches the Internet in general (and the Web in particular) as a publication medium. Viewed as forms of publication, the various Internet tools—e-mail, mailing lists, Usenet, FTP, Internet Relay Chat, and the Web— each have their own strengths and possibilities. Increasingly, the Web is bringing them together. The most advanced sites offer e-mail, mailing lists, discussion groups, file downloading via FTP, real-time chatting, and active Web presentations.

♦ Community-oriented Internet applications (electronic mail, mailing lists, FTP, Gopher, WAIS, Usenet, and Telnet), as well as the Internet's academic birthplace, have shaped the way people view the Internet. Users know that they work together to build collective information pools. They are accustomed to getting valuable information and software for free or nearly so. They respect people who are considerate of others while online.

♦ Your Internet audience tends to be young, wealthy, English-speaking, and male. But you'd be very wrong to assume that other audiences aren't out there. Many successful Web pages began by defining their audience more specifically and focusing on that audience's needs.

♦ You don't have to publish to the entire world. Within organizations (such as schools, universities, and corporations), there are many possibilities for cost-saving publishing on intranets and extranets (private versions of the Internet).

WHAT'S THE INTERNET?

Physically, the Internet consists of a variety of connecting media. The most basic connecting medium is a home computer linked by a telephone line and modem to an Internet service provider or an online service (such as CompuServe or the Microsoft Network).

Thousands of universities and corporations provide Internet access via local area networks (LANs), which connect dozens, hundreds, or even thousands of desktop computers. Spanning long distances are high-speed data communication networks of every conceivable variety, including densely packed telephone wires, microwave relay stations, fiber optical cables, and even satellites.

But just which wires or cables are used really doesn't matter. The incredible thing about the Internet is that it is more or less oblivious to the connecting media it's using—that's the reason it is growing so rapidly. In brief, the Internet consists of a set of public-domain *protocols* (standards) that enable virtually any two kinds of computers to communicate with each other.

INTRODUCING THE INTERNET PROTOCOLS

The Internet isn't really a physical network. (Physically, it's made up of lots of different kinds of networks and individual computers, which are all linked together in just about every conceivable way.) The Internet is really a set of protocols (standards) by which dissimilar computers can exchange information. These protocols were developed by U.S. government-funded research and were subsequently released to the public domain. Any manufacturer can produce equipment conforming to these protocols without having to pay a licensing fee or risk an infringement lawsuit. This alone partly explains the Internet's popularity.

Another reason for the Internet's popularity lies in the fact that it can connect many different brands of computers. Linked to the Internet are Macintosh users, people using Windows systems, engineers using Sun workstations, graphic artists using NeXT workstations, academics using IBM mainframe computers, and some kid using her dad's Toshiba laptop. And more!

If you've ever tried to swap disks with somebody using a different type of computer system, you'll appreciate just how cool the Internet really is. The Internet protocols (also called the TCP/IP protocols) break down the barriers between computers made by different manufacturers—barriers that in some cases were put there deliberately in an attempt to corner the computer market.

You don't really need to understand how this works—just take it on faith. When you equip your computer with Internet (TCP/IP) software, your computer suddenly knows how to package information so that it can be sent out over the Internet and be received and used by somebody with a completely different computer system.

Information about the Internet

For more information on the Internet and Internet protocols, check out the well-organized Internet Protocols & Standards page at http://netlab.itd.nrl.navy.mil/Internet.html. This page includes a search engine that enables you to search for Internet-related terms.

THE MAGIC OF INTEROPERABILITY

The Internet does more than merely allow various kinds of computers to talk to each other. It also allows them to *control* each other. (Scary, isn't it? Now you know why science fiction authors keep writing all those novels about computers getting together and taking over the Earth.)

One Internet computer can tell another, "Hear and obey. Send me the file named galactor.doc." If the receiving computer has been configured to respond to such requests, it coughs up the file and sends it to the requesting computer.

The ability of one Internet computer to control another, even if the other computer is made by a different manufacturer, is called *interoperability*.

Interoperability and Security

Interoperability is great, but it comes with obvious security risks. Sitting at my computer here in Virginia, I could link to your system, right on your desk—and if you hadn't configured it correctly, I could erase your entire hard disk while you watched, helpless to interfere! But that wouldn't be nice.

Kidding aside, security issues really are a problem on the Internet. If you're planning to set up your own Web server (see Chapter 6), I'll recommend that you set aside a computer to use for Web publishing. Do your important work, and carry on your business, with another machine.

There's very little risk involved in getting on the Internet and browsing the Web, unless you send personal information (such as credit card data) over an insecure link. The risks come only when you set up a server, allowing outsiders to control your computer. So for now, don't let security issues keep you from joining in the fun. Later, you'll learn how you can avoid security problems with servers just by following a few simple rules.

INTERNET PUBLISHING MEDIA

As you are probably already aware, the Internet enables people to communicate in a number of different ways. For example, you can send messages via e-mail, Usenet newsgroups, or Internet Relay Chat (IRC). Here's a quick introduction to the various ways you can use the Internet, conceptualized as publication media.

Electronic Mail (E-mail)

By far the most popular of all Internet media is electronic mail, which enables one person to send a message to any other person with a valid Internet mailing address (according to a recent estimate, approximately 72 million people in 130 countries can be reached by Internet e-mail). But e-mail also enables a person to send messages to more than one person—in other words, it can be conceptualized as a publication medium. You can publish using e-mail in the following ways:

- **Organizational mailing lists** Within organizations (such as a college or university), it's easy to set up a named list of e-mail addresses; when you send a message to the list, everyone receives a copy. Similarly, if a person replies to a message on the list, everyone receives it.

- **Private mailing lists** Mailing lists do not have to be based in a particular geographic setting; they can be international in scope. A private mailing list is typically used to enable people who share a common interest or are working on a common project to communicate with each other. Membership in the list is controlled by the list administrator and the list isn't accessible to the public. Because membership is controlled, the quality of discussion is generally very good.

- **Public mailing lists** Public mailing lists closely resemble a private mailing list, in that they frequently embrace a vast geographical scope and focus on a theme of common interest. However, membership in the list is open to the general public. You subscribe to a mailing list by sending a request to the list server. Because membership is open to the public, discussion may be marred by the immature behavior of some participants.

 **I sent my ad to this mailing list, and now everyone hates me!** You bet they do. Unsolicited advertising via e-mail and mailing lists is deeply resented by Internet users, who pay for

their Internet access and do not see why they should subsidize your advertising campaign. Don't sully your firm's reputation by joining the ranks of sleazeball herbal diet scams and bogus investment pitches that make up so much of the current e-mail advertising crop.

Usenet

Organized into more than 24,000 topically named discussion groups, called *newsgroups*, Usenet is a computer discussion system of worldwide scope. When you contribute a message to Usenet, you publish this message on some 300,000 Usenet servers worldwide, where an estimated 7 to 10 million people can potentially access it. In addition, your post is archived on a number of Usenet search services, which enable World Wide Web users to search for information using keywords.

As a publication medium, Usenet is a very appropriate place to contribute your expertise in a subject-related area, but you must do so in accordance with Usenet's well-established usage norms, called *netiquette*. According to these usage customs, your contribution should not be self-serving; advertising on Usenet is quite common, for example, but it is deeply resented where it is done obnoxiously or inappropriately. It's considered appropriate to mention your product or service if your doing so contributes meaningfully to the topic under discussion and is within the topical focus of the newsgroup.

Without question, the quality of discussion on Usenet has declined in proportion to its expanded audience. Usenet discussion is frequently marred by *spamming* (posting unsolicited advertisements to dozens or hundreds of newsgroups), *trolling* (posting untrue or inflammatory statements in an effort to get people to make fools of themselves by responding), and *flame wars* (protracted, ad hominem arguments that shed very little light on the subject under discussion). Still, you can find (and share) valuable information in a variety of low-key newsgroups that focus on specific technical or recreational areas.

Chat Services

Although the Internet isn't designed for real-time communication, it's possible to engage in conversation with other Internet users by means of computer chatting. The most popular Internet medium for computer chatting is called Internet Relay Chat (IRC). In computer chatting, you join a conversation group (called a *channel*). You see the text that others have typed. You can type your own text, and in this way you can join in the conversation.

Although IRC isn't best conceptualized as a publication medium—it's better described as an amusing pastime—many IRC users have learned how to use advanced IRC tools to exchange graphics files, computer programs, and computer expertise. Furthermore, anyone with the necessary knowledge can create an IRC channel. If you do so and succeed in attracting some participants, you have an opportunity to get your message out or make materials available to others.

FTP

Short for File Transfer Protocol, FTP provides the standard by which Internet computers can exchange files of all types, including program and graphics files. As a publication medium, FTP seems poised to revolutionize the way that software publishers distribute their products. Publishing a program the traditional way (with a bound manual, disks, and a box) is very costly and accounts in large measure for the high price of commercial software. By publishing software using FTP and making documentation available on the Web, a software publisher can greatly reduce these costs, enabling them to cut the price of their product drastically.

Authors of shareware programs were quick to realize the distribution possibilities of FTP. In brief, *shareware* refers to a computer program that is copyrighted, but the author distributes evaluation or demonstration versions without charge. You can use this version for free during the evaluation period. If you wish to keep using the program, you must register it.

Commercial software publishers are experimenting with a variety of business models that would enable them to publish their software on the Internet. Netscape Communications essentially gives away copies of their popular Netscape Navigator browser. Initially, it was hoped that by doing so Netscape could create a huge user base, and this would in turn lead to profitable sales for the company's Web servers. The problem with this model is that there is nothing stopping Netscape's competitors from stepping in to the market and offering competing servers—and that's just what has happened.

FTP is also useful for distributing marketing materials, such as product-related videos, graphics, or databases, that must be downloaded and run on an individual's computer system. Access to these materials can be made available by means of Web pages, thus simplifying the file transfer (download) operation.

World Wide Web (WWW)

Unquestionably, the Web is the Internet's premier publication medium. Anyone with access to a Web server can make Web pages available to an audience of millions of people. This book focuses on the Web as a publication medium.

The World Wide Web is a *hypertext* system. In brief, a hypertext is an information repository in which the information is accessed by clicking *hyperlinks* (also called *anchors*). Hyperlinks (or links, for short) contain the address of the desired information; by clicking on the hyperlink, you access the information for which you're looking. You can continue navigating the information by accessing link after link; this is called *browsing*.

The Web is superficially similar to desktop publishing in that current Web tools enable Web designers to create attractively designed pages that compare favorably with the best practices in magazine design (see Figure 1.1). But it's a very different publication medium, with its own peculiarities. Publishers that approach the Web without fully understanding the medium's unique characteristics are very likely to fail. We'll look at this point more closely in Chapter 4.

One Medium to Rule Them All

The Web is quickly emerging as a master medium, a vehicle for uniting and synthesizing all other methods of communicating and exchanging information via the Internet. Some of the most successful and exciting Web sites combine Web-accessible mail, newsgroups, computer chatting, and Web-based FTP access with complex Web presentations.

By combining Web publishing with interactivity (including e-mail, newsgroups, chat groups, and manuals), you may be able to create a learning environment that's superior to traditional instruction. That's the conclusion of a study published by Jerald Schutted, a professor of applied statistics at California State University (Northridge). Students who learned in a virtual, Web-based classroom performed 20% better than students who received traditional instruction.

One of the problems with Web publishing is that Web users must seek out your site. If they don't, you don't get any visitors. And with millions of pages on the Web, you're facing stiff competition. That's why several firms are experimenting with *content push* applications, which broadcast information to the desktop. A pioneer in this area is Pointcast (http://www.pointcast.com), which has developed a proprietary application for receiving news bulletins on the desktop. The application replaces the standard Windows screen saver.

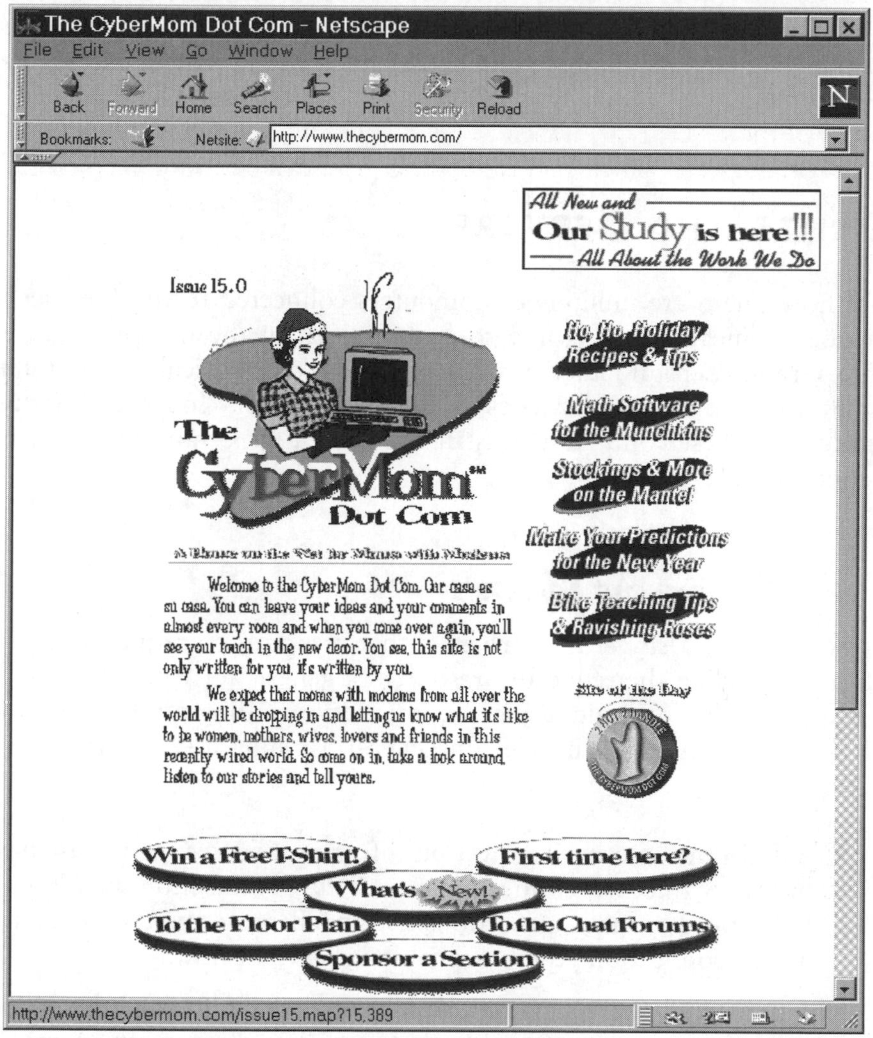

Figure 1.1 This attractive site (www.cybermom.com) has the appeal of a magazine and the interactivity of a computer.

When the screen saver kicks in, you see current news headlines. Pointcast and similar applications can be adapted to distribute information within an organization. Also under development currently is an adaptation of the tried-and-true mailing list, but with a contemporary twist: Today's e-mail programs can receive e-mail in the form of Web pages, so it's now possible to broadcast Web pages to desktops. Expect significant development in this area in the near future.

CLIENTS AND SERVERS

Right now, there are millions of computers connected to the Internet. But that doesn't mean you're going to find yourself in the middle of an electronic Grand Central Station when you log on. Basically, the Internet enables any *two* computers to establish a connection. In order for this to work, one of these computers must function as a *server* and the other must function as a *client*.

Servers: Dishing out the Data

On the Internet, a *server* is a program that responds to requests for information by sending the requested *resource* (a generic term referring to anything that can be transmitted via the Internet, including a file, a graphic, a Web page, a sound, or a movie). In general, running a server requires the following:

- **A full-time Internet connection**   To run a server, you must have a full-time Internet connection—a dialup connection won't cut it. Full-time Internet connections are much more expensive than the dialup connection you're probably using right now.

- **A registered domain name**   A *domain name* is an English version of a numerical Internet address (examples of domain names are *www.microsoft.com* and *altavista.digital.com*). Within large organizations that have dozens of Internet-connected computers, domain names are assigned by local network administrators. If you would like to set up a business with its own domain name, your Internet service provider can help you do this. However, you'll need a permanent Internet connection.

- **Considerable computer and Internet expertise**   Running a server is time-consuming and requires considerable expertise (including computer programming skills for advanced applications).

Clients: Providing Tools to Users

Internet users run programs called *clients*. A client is a program that knows how to interact with servers. For example, an e-mail client knows how to interact with mail servers, while a Web client (also called a *browser*) knows how to interact with Web servers.

Increasingly, users obtain and install just one program—a full-featured browser, such as Microsoft Internet Explorer or Netscape Communicator—to handle multiple client roles. Internet Explorer, for example, includes e-mail, Usenet, IRC, and FTP capabilities as well as advanced Web browsing features.

WHAT TYPE OF CONNECTION DO YOU NEED?

This question boils down to whether you want to run a Web server (see Chapter 6, Choosing a Web Server).

- **If you decide that you'd like to run your own server,** you'll need a permanent—and pricey—Internet connection by means of ISDN or a dedicated line (see Chapter 6 for an explanation of these terms). You'll also need a system sufficiently powerful to deal with lots of incoming requests. This is a good option for a medium-to-large-sized business or nonprofit organization. Unless you already have a permanent Internet connection and a powerful PC, your best bet is the next option.

- **If you decide to use the Web publishing space provided by your Internet service provider,** you can make do with an inexpensive dial-up connection using a modem. This will cost you only about $19.95 per month, at current prices.

DO YOU REALLY NEED TO MAKE IT PUBLIC? (INTRANETS)

The latest wrinkle in Internet publishing involves the use of Internet technology to create private, internal networks (*intranets*). Intranets make use of established Internet technology, including familiar tools such as Web browsers, to create information systems internal to organizations. In virtually every organization there is a need to make information available, such as employee manuals, benefits handbooks, internal telephone books, instructional manuals, and much more. This is currently the fastest-growing area of Internet publishing.

Creating Frequently Asked Questions Pages

Many employees spend a good deal of time answering routine questions, over and over. The solution? Teach them how to create and maintain a Web page that contains a list of "frequently asked questions" (FAQs).

Learn More about Intranets

An excellent source of intranet-related material is The Intranet Journal (http://www.intranetjournal.com). You'll find news and features, interviews, links, FAQs, a chat room, design notes, and information on the latest intranet tools.

An intranet isn't necessarily walled off from the Internet. On some intranets, some or all employees can access the Internet. And the latest wrinkle on the fast-developing intranet scene is the *extranet*, a means of making internal intranet-based information available to strategic partners, customers, and suppliers. This can be done by means of password-based access to an organization's intranet or by means of a *virtual private network (VPN),* a wide-area network that uses Internet technology but doesn't use the same connections that the Internet does.

Here's an example of an extranet in operation: http://www.fedex.com (Figure 1.2). By linking to this site, you can track your FedEx shipment by linking into FedEx's intranet.

Is Web Publishing For You?

The rest of the chapters in Part I are designed to help you answer this question. You'll learn about the special characteristics of hypertext, how the Web works, the nature of the Web as a publication medium, and the type of documents that have already been successfully published on the Web. If you're sure that Web publishing is right for you, Part II introduces you to the fundamentals of Web design, while Part III shows you how to begin creating your pages.

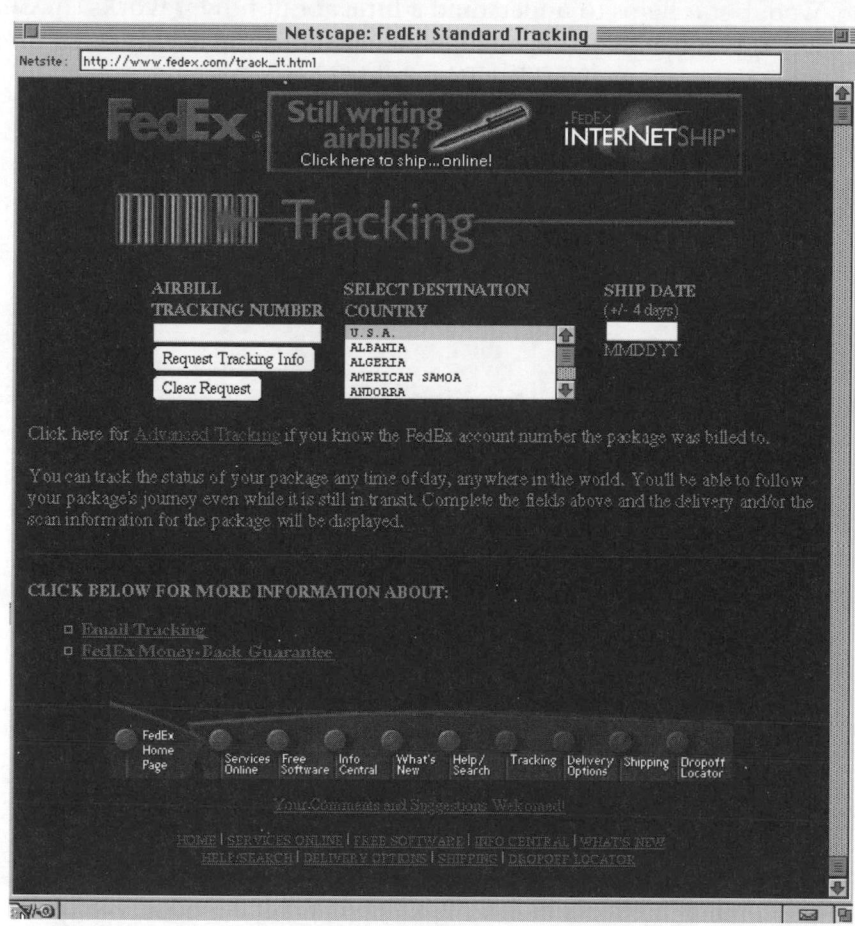

Figure 1.2   FedEx's package-tracking site is a great example of an extranet in action.

FROM HERE

- To publish successfully on the Web, you need to fully understand the concept of hypertext. Check out the next chapter for a complete explanation in plain, simple English.

- You don't need an electrical engineering degree to publish on the Web, but it helps to understand a little about how it works. In Chapter 3, you'll find a thorough explanation of the Web's three fundamental acronyms: HTTP, URL, and HTML.

Chapter 2

Understanding Hypertext

When you publish on the Web, you're publishing in a hypertext medium. Succinctly defined, the Web is a global hypertext system that employs the Internet as its physical medium. Actually, the Web is a *hypermedia* system, one that organizes resources using hypertext but which incorporates multimedia, including graphics, movies, and sounds.

Hypertext is unfamiliar to most people; it isn't taught in high-school English classes (although it soon will be). Due to this lack of familiarity, most of the people now creating Web pages do not fully understand the basic principles of hypertext. That doesn't stop them from putting material on the Web, and sometimes very good material. Still, the most effective Web presentations show full awareness of hypertext principles.

This chapter introduces the basic principles of hypertext, which are very easy to learn. After reading it, you'll know more about the hypertext spirit than most of the people putting up pages on the Web right now. And you'll also know why the Web has some serious deficiencies as a medium for mass publication.

For the Time-Challenged

- ◆ Hypertext is a form of nonsequential writing in which the text of a document is broken down into conceptual chunks. These chunks are then interlinked in a way that permits the reader to access the material in any way he or she pleases. Theodore Holm Nelson first envisioned hypertext in 1965.

- ◆ Some hypertexts contain just one document. Usually, they contain a welcome page (also called a *home page*) and a number of linked documents, called a *web*.

- ◆ A good welcome page lists the available chunks in a web, in decreasing order of importance.

- ◆ To aid browsers in navigating a web, thoughtful authors include navigation buttons.

- ◆ Hypertext systems on standalone computers are time-consuming to create and maintain. A computer network provides the ideal platform for hypertext because the responsibility of creating and maintaining it can be distributed among thousands or even millions of users.

- ◆ In a network-based hypertext system, synergy occurs as authors build on the achievements of other authors. You don't have to reinvent the wheel; you can link to documents that other authors have already contributed.

- ◆ In a network-based hypertext system, the boundaries between authors and readers break down. Readers become authors by incorporating documents that link to existing texts.

- ◆ Nelson's idea of a global hypertext system, called Xanadu, preserves intellectual property rights and grants royalties to authors who publish on the system. The Web's rapid growth vindicates Nelson's conviction that a mass market exists for a networked hypertext system. The Web's deficiencies in protecting intellectual property rights, discussed in the next chapter, also vindicate Nelson's ideas concerning the preservation of intellectual property rights in such a system.

WHAT IS HYPERTEXT?

In 1965, a computer visionary named Theodore Holm ("Ted") Nelson coined the term *hypertext* and described it as the way virtually everyone would write in the future. Nelson says it's simply *nonsequential writing.* Regarding hypertext, Nelson has this to say:

> Ordinary writing is sequential for two reasons. First, it grew out of speech and speech-making, which have to be sequential; and second, because books are not convenient to read except in a sequence. But the structures of ideas are not sequential. They tie together every which-way (Ted Nelson, *Computer Lib/Dream Machines,* rev. ed. [Redmond, Washington: Tempus Books of Microsoft Press, 1987], p. 29).

By this, Nelson doesn't mean that a hypertext is a jumble, all out of order. Rather, a hypertext consists of various *chunks* of text. To prepare a hypertext, you break down all the information you want to present into manageable chunks and then let the reader pick his or her way through the chunks.

For example, suppose you want to present some information about North Carolina's Outer Banks. In no particular order, here are some chunks that came to mind as I was thinking about this subject:

Ecology

Lighthouses

Barrier reefs

Hurricanes and Nor'easters

Vacation rental properties

Investment in vacation rental properties

Beaches

Shopping

Shipwrecks

Windsurfing

Restaurants

The Nature Conservancy

Kayaking

What interests you? (Um, I'm starving and sunburned, I think I'll check out "restaurants.") The neat thing about hypertext is that you can quickly select the topic in which you're interested. A hypertext is organized so that you can pick your own way through the chunks, without necessarily having to follow a sequence dictated by the author. (Note: In Nelson's terminology, each chunk is called a *node*, although terms such as *page*, *card*, and *document* are used synonymously. I prefer *chunk*.)

"I can't let go of my authorial authority!"
This is the biggest problem people run into in writing hypertext effectively. Take the Outer Banks example just mentioned. I'd love to give you a big lecture about the Outer Banks' fragile ecology and the need to protect the barrier islands from overdevelopment. But maybe you're interested in shopping, or just hanging out on the beach. To create an effective Outer Banks hypertext, I've got to let go of my authorial impulse to organize all the material around a theme, like ecology. I must chunk the information and let you, the reader, decide what, if anything, you want to read. I'll put a chunk in about the ecology; it's there if you'd like to read it, but it's *up to you* whether you read it or not. Giving the reader permission to make his or her own decisions is tough for some authors.

What's a good chunk? It's up to you, but the general rule is the smaller the better. For Web presentations, an effective chunk is one screenful of text. (This rule shouldn't be taken so literally that it forbids longer pages; it's just a rule of thumb.)

The chunks of a hypertext are linked by *anchors,* which are underlined (and often shown in a distinctive color) so that you can tell them from ordinary text. (There are two synonyms for anchor: You can also say *hyperlink* or just *link*. Sorry the terminology is so confusing, but that's what happens when you let computer people run around unmuzzled.) Links are put in by people.

You can't really do hypertext in a printed book. You'd have to flip repeatedly to the page where the linked document appears—and that would be very tedious. But the computer is a natural for hypertext: It does the flipping for you. In most compter-based hypertext systems, you activate a link by pointing to it with the mouse and clicking. The computer then displays the requested page.

 **The Hypertext FAQ**
The ultimate hypertext information repository is The Hypertext FAQ, accessible at

http://www.eit.com/reports/ht93/hypertext.faq.txt

UNDERSTANDING HYPERTEXT: AN EXAMPLE

It's hard to convey the look and feel of hypertext in a printed book like this. But let's take a stab.

A hypertext document usually begins with an overview document, called a *welcome page* or a *home page*, such as the following. Note the anchors (links):

> The term **anime** refers to an impressive Japanese tradition of cartoon animation. Based on comic books called **manga**, anime TV shows, videos, and movies attract a wide audience in Japan, where adults as well as children join in the fun. In subtitled **videotapes** and **laserdiscs**, anime is increasingly available in the United States. Try looking for titles such as Akira or Bubblegum Crisis at your **local video store**. For an example of the best in anime, look for **My Neighbor Totoro**, a wonderful children's film that the whole family will enjoy. If you'd like to know more about anime, check out this **more detailed introduction** and read the **reviews** of popular anime films.

To activate one of the anchors, you move the mouse pointer to the anchor and click. Presto! The computer displays the document you want to see.

Suppose you click "My Neighbor Totoro." Here's what you'll see:

> ### My Neighbor Totoro
>
> In this magical film, an artist's heartfelt tribute to the beauty and the customs of the traditional (but disappearing) Japanese countryside, Hayao **Miyazaki** tells the story of two children who discover a magical being, Totoro. Visible only to children, Totoro lives within the base of a gigantic, beautiful camphor tree. The older of the two children, Satsuke,

calls upon Totoro's aid in finding her sister, Mei,
who become lost while trying to visit her hospital-
ized mother. Roger Ebert, one of the thumbs in the
famed Siskel & Ebert duo, says "Very few films come
along that are magical for all ages and are whole-
some, sane, intelligent, and entertaining. 'My Neighbor Totoro' is one of them." The film is available in
an excellent English dub from **Fox Video**.

As this example illustrates, you're not tied to the author's idea of how
you should read the material. You can choose your own path, just as your
interests dictate.

Notice that there are additional anchors on the "My Neighbor Totoro"
page: The "Miyazaki" anchor tells you more about this talented animator,
while the "Fox Video" anchor tells you more about how to order this videotape.

A good hypertext system provides lots of links and cross-links and new
links and who-knows-where-you'll-wind-up links. It invites exploration,
adventure, play, learning. Hypertext is *fun*.

WELCOME TO MY WEB

A really good hypertext system contains lots of links—the more, the mer-
rier. The result is a collection of interlinked documents that enable you to
navigate through them in dozens or even hundreds of different ways. This is
called a *web*.

Figure 2.1 shows the spiderweb-like appearance of a number of documents that are connected in a web. The lines indicate what the links do in
each document. Note that there are multiple pathways through the web.

Many webs begin with a welcome page that succinctly lists the available
topics. For an example, take a look at the University of Virginia's welcome
page (http://www.virginia.edu/), shown in Figure 2.2.

Creating an Effective Welcome Page
Ask yourself, "What do the people accessing my page really
want to know?" Write down the topics that you think would
interest them. Then, put them *in order of decreasing
importance*—the first link on the list should be the topic of
greatest importance to most of your readers. Check out Figure 2.2—UVa's welcome page does a nice job of this.

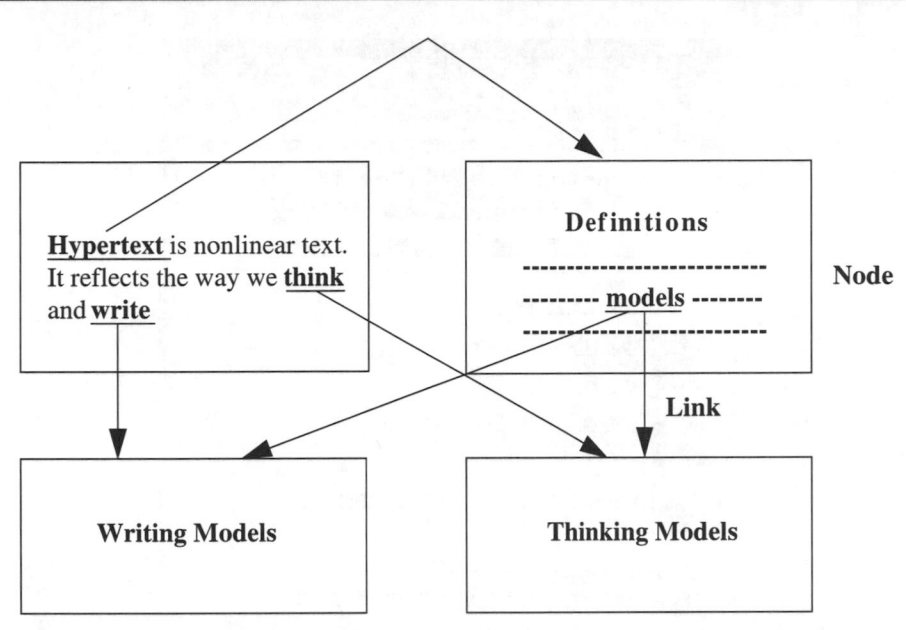

Figure 2.1 Nodes and links in a web. (From V. Balasubramaniam, "State of the Art Review on Hypermedia Issues and Applications," http://www.isg.sfu.ca/ ~duchier/misc/hypertext_review/index.html.)

Help! I'm Lost!

The wonderful thing about hypertext is that you can choose your own way of navigating through the material from dozens or even hundreds of options. That's also the bad thing about hypertext. It's easy to get lost!

Helpful web authors include *navigation buttons*. Minimally, these buttons include a Home button, which lets you go back to the introductory (top level) document. Figure 2.3 shows the navigation buttons used in the Great Lakes Information Management Resource (http://www.cciw.ca/glimr/ intro.html).

 **Creating Informative Navigation Aids**
In the Great Lakes page (Figure 2.3), note how the page's author has provided rich, detailed information about each of the links.

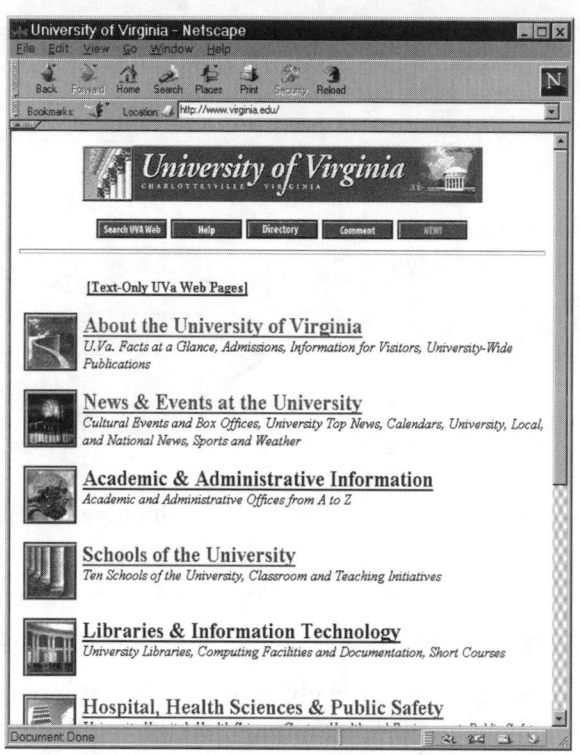

Figure 2.2   University of Virginia welcome page.

IS HYPERTEXT SUITABLE FOR ALL KINDS OF DOCUMENTS?

Hypertext is beautifully suited to any written work in which the material can be broken down into chunks and navigated in the order that the reader prefers. Many kinds of documents are immediately and obviously suited to hypertext, including employee handbooks, catalogs, archives of technical documentation, and much more. But hypertext isn't so hot for fiction, in which sequence really counts. If you found out too soon that Darth Vader is really Luke's father, it sort of spoils the fun. (That said, people are experimenting with hypertext stories that enable you to choose your own plot!)

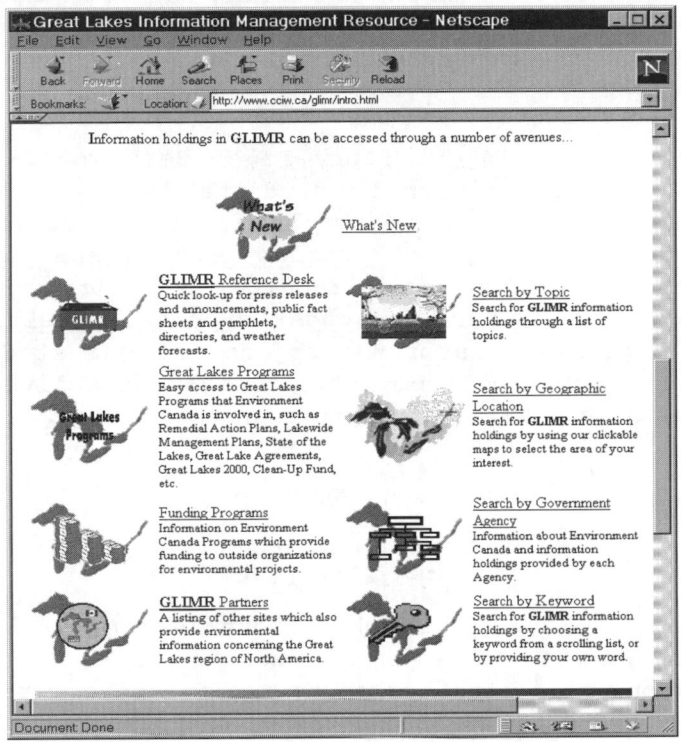

Figure 2.3 Navigation buttons.

Hypertext Fiction

Check out the following page for an introduction to the possibilities of hypertext fiction:

http://www.duke.edu/~mshumate/hyperfic.html

If this subject intrigues you, join the hypertext lit (ht lit) mailing list (http://www.aaln.org/~kmm/ht_lit.html). To subscribe, send e-mail to subscribe@journal.biology.carleton.ca with "subscribe ht_lit" in the body of the message.

For scholars, hypertext provides a wonderful way to annotate literary texts. For a sample, check out the annotated version of Doyle's "The Adventure of the Speckled Band":

http://www.seas.upenn.edu/~dlelong/band.html

Remember, though, that a hypertext system can include ordinary, sequential documents. Here's an example of an opening page of a hypertext system containing ordinary (that is, sequential) short stories:

Short Stories

Welcome to the Short Story Page! Here you'll find short stories written by students in Green Valley University's extension writing program. There are plenty of stories with **science fiction** and **fantasy themes**, a student (and faculty) favorite. You'll also find some chilling **ghost stories**. **Local myths and legends** are favorite subjects of our students, many of whom come from families that have lived and farmed Green Valley for more than two hundred years.

If you click "ghost stories," you'll see this page:

Ghost Stories

There's something spooky about Green Valley—as you'll surely agree after reading some of these! Click on one of the titles to see and read a story.

Alice Bates, "**Spirits of the Night**"

Karen Sawyer, "**Secrets of Dark Water**"

Jim Tantzakis, "**The Unbroken Brooch**"

Clicking one of these anchors brings up an ordinary, sequential document.

In sum, hypertext provides a nonsequential method of navigating through all kinds of information, including types of information that can't be broken down into hypertext documents themselves.

WHAT IS HYPERMEDIA?

Hypermedia is more than the addition of multimedia (sounds, pictures, and movies) to hypertext documents. Far more than mere windows dressing (pardon the pun), it's the use of multimedia as an integral part of the presentation.

By this standard, there are relatively few hypermedia documents, but there are millions of hypertext documents with pretty pictures.

Figure 2.4 shows what true hypermedia looks like. It's the Virtual Frog Dissection Kit, available at http://george.lbl.gov/ITG.hm.pg.docs/dissect/ dissect.html. Try it!

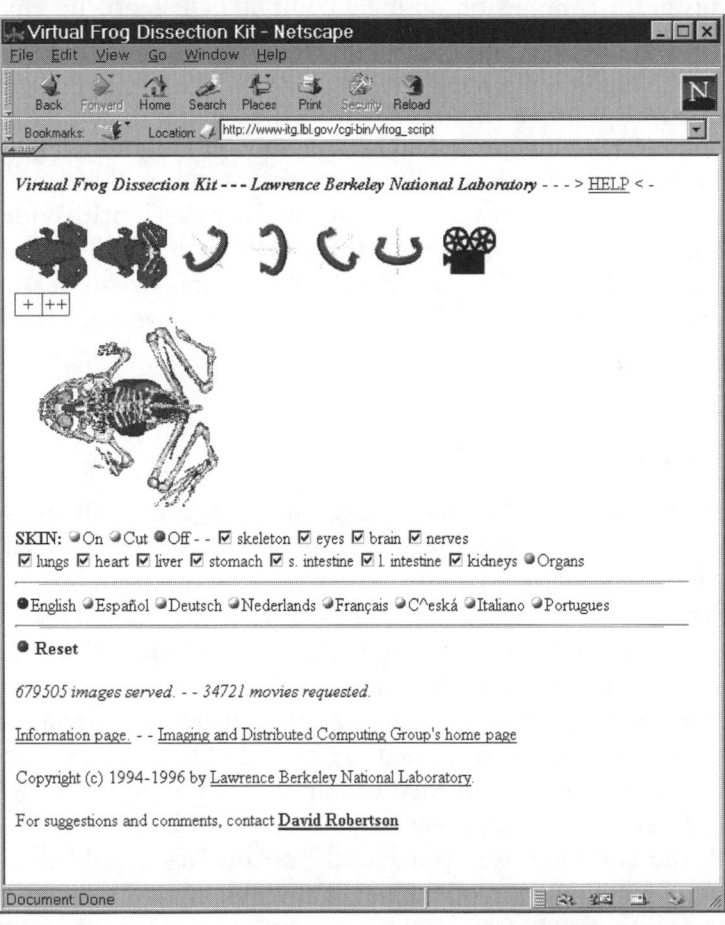

Figure 2.4 Virtual Frog Dissection Kit (http://george.lbl.gov/ITG.hm.pg.docs/ dissect/dissect.html).

Toward a Global Hypertext System (Xanadu)

Nelson first advocated hypertext in 1965. And for a long time, very few people listened. As Nelson beat the hypertext drum, a few hypertext programs were developed, mostly as experiments in instructional technology (yawn). The concept gained wider notice with the mid-1980s release of HyperCard, a file card program (loosely based on hypertext principles) that was included free with every Macintosh computer.

But Nelson saw a much bigger future for hypertext. He didn't see hypertext as a program running on a single computer. Instead, he envisioned a global hypertext system, linking millions of networked computers. Nelson called this system Xanadu, using the name of a magical place described in Coleridge's mystical poem "Kubla Khan."

Nelson has received a great deal of recognition for inventing hypertext, but precious little for envisioning Xanadu. Yet, as you will see in the following paragraphs and the chapter to follow, the way the World Wide Web has developed amounts to nothing less than a total vindication of Nelson's vision. What the Web has become shows that Nelson's vision can excite the imagination of millions. And what the Web lacks shows the need for something very much like Xanadu.

A Brief History of Xanadu

Part of the reason Nelson hasn't received much recognition for Xanadu is that it doesn't exist. His book *Literary Machines*, first published in 1981, describes the features of Xanadu. As initially envisioned, Xanadu would consist of millions of computers, all of them running Xanadu software and linked via modems to regional file servers, which would retrieve documents on request. Nelson did not foresee the Internet.

After working on various prototypes of hypertext software from the period 1960 to 1979, Nelson formed the Xanadu Operating Company, Inc., in 1983. The company was formed to implement the design of Xanadu, as specified in *Literary Machines*.

In 1988, the company was purchased by AutoDesk, publishers of computer-aided design (CAD) software. However, AutoDesk dropped the Xanadu project in 1992 after a new, cost-conscious management team took over the company.

In 1993, Nelson departed for Japan, where he continues work on Xanadu in what he claims to be a more supportive environment.

 **The Ultimate Xanadu Site**
For (a lot) more information on Xanadu, including Nelson's latest writings and opinions, check out http://sensemedia.net/850.

Explorations in Synergy, or, Breaking Down the Author/Reader Distinction

Why did Nelson envision a global hypertext system based on a network of millions of computers? In a word, *synergy*. It's a big job to create an information-rich hypertext system all by oneself. By implementing hypertext on a computer network and encouraging many people to build on what's already there, the system can grow by leaps and bounds. That's synergy—the extra value that occurs when people cooperate instead of working alone.

Let's say you're putting together a document on the history and geography of the Eastern Shore of Virginia, an ecologically and culturally interesting place. As you browse the networked hypertext system, used by millions, you find that many other people have contributed information regarding the Eastern Shore.

Rather than duplicating their efforts, you build on it by including hyperlinks to their documents in your own work. In a networked hypertext system, everyone would be potentially both a consumer *and* a producer of information. And no document would ever exist by itself; it would be linked to, built on, summarized, and otherwise manipulated by readers who are themselves producing information on the system.

Because Xanadu breaks down the distinction between authors and readers, it is far more democratic than any previous publication medium. Authors and readers are considered to be equal. What is more, any author who places a document in Xanadu must concede to others the right to reference that document, to link to it, to comment upon it, to summarize it, and in any other way to use it as a platform for building and extending the database of Xanadu documents—or, as Nelson calls it, the *docuverse*.

Xanadu as a Publication Medium

Although Xanadu radically equalizes the balance between authors and readers, it fully preserves the notion of copyright and includes mechanisms to compensate authors for the use of their documents.

Every time a document is accessed and read by means of a hyperlink, the author would receive a royalty—only a fraction of a cent, to be sure, but fractions of a cent mount up quickly when a document is referenced thousands or millions of times. As Nelson points out, you can sell a few thousand books for $24.95 (with $1 author royalty after all the middlemen take their cut) or have many thousands of readers, maybe millions, on Xanadu, and make the same amount of money. Or more! (If authors wish, they can make their documents available for free.) And anyone who actually downloads or prints the document would have to pay a higher fee.

Advanced features of Xanadu would give authors the right to charge varying fees for different parts of a document. Suppose that Samantha writes a book-long document. She could decide that the abstract will be free, enabling readers to find out what's in her document, but that Chapter 2, which contains a sophisticated data analysis, will be charged at a higher rate than the rest of the document.

What happens when I create a document that includes linked portions from other peoples' work? Suppose, for example, I create a document in which I use Samantha's Chapter 2 instead of writing my own chapter. When people read my document, Xanadu automatically credits part of the royalties to Samantha.

The Inevitability of a Global Hypertext System

Nelson became convinced—correctly, it turns out—that the idea of a global hypertext system is so attractive, and so useful to so many people, that the development of such a system was inevitable. Writing in 1981, Nelson said:

> Forty years from now (if the human species survives) there will be hundreds of thousands of file servers—machines storing and dishing out [hypertext] materials. And there will be hundreds of millions of simultaneous users, able to read from billions of stored documents, with trillions of links among them. All of this is manifest destiny. There is no point in arguing it; either you see it or you don't. Many readers will choke and fling down [this] book, only to have the thought gnaw at them gradually until they see its inevitability.

The meteoric rise of the World Wide Web vindicates Nelson's vision. As you will see in the next chapter, the Web perfectly embodies Nelson's vision of a global hypertext system fueled by synergy, in which the distinction between authors and readers breaks down. What it also vindicates is Nelson's fully developed vision of how intellectual property rights could be protected in such a system. And as you will see in the next chapter, that's where the Web is sadly deficient.

FROM HERE

- As an aspiring Web publisher, you need to understand that the Web has a built-in bias toward academic, nonprofit publication. You also need to understand how the Web implements Nelson's hypertext ideas within the Internet medium. The next chapter gives you the lowdown on both points.

Chapter

3

Introducing the World Wide Web

"A good scientist," says physicist Freeman Dyson, "is a person with original ideas." But a good engineer "is a person with as few original ideas as possible." There is no single quotation that so compellingly sums up the engineering that went into the creation of the World Wide Web (WWW). Basically, the Web drew on four existing ideas: the Internet (Chapter 1), Ted Nelson's conception of a network-based hypertext system (Chapter 2), the idea of workstation-based client programs that interact with server programs capable of dishing out data, and the concept of a *markup language*, which enables Web users to see nicely formatted documents that don't consume a lot of network bandwidth.

This chapter shows how the marriage of these four ideas led to the two fundamental concepts of the Web: the HyperText Transport Protocol (HTTP) with its concept of Universal Resource Locators (URLs), and the

HyperText Markup Language (HTML). You'll also learn about additional Web standards, including Common Gateway Interface (CGI). All of these thorny acronyms are fully introduced in this chapter, with particular attention to their implications for Web publication. This chapter also explains the latest programming standards that enable Web publishers to include active content in their presentations.

"A Culture of Distributed Computing": CERN and the Development of the Web

Not far from Geneva, Switzerland, is one of Europe's leading scientific think tanks, the European Laboratory for Particle Physics. Known by the acronym of its French name (Conseil Europeen pour la Recherche Nucleaire), this lab—called CERN—is the birthplace of the World Wide Web.

Like academic think tanks elsewhere, CERN has some permanent researchers, but most of its scientists visit there on one- or two-year fellowships. These researchers, called fellows, need to keep in contact with local researchers during their visit, as well as colleagues posted at universities worldwide. And after the fellows leave, they need to keep in contact with CERN so that they can keep abreast of fast-breaking developments there.

Understanding their fellows' need for local and long-distance collaboration, the CERN computer services staff see computer networks as a communication medium as well as a means of sharing programs and data. In the early 1980s, CERN experimented with a variety of computer networks, both local area networks (LANs) and wide-area networks (WANs). When CERN staff learned of the Internet, they knew almost immediately that it held the answer to their fellows' collaboration difficulties. By 1988, CERN had established a link to the Internet and, by 1990, became the largest Internet site in Europe.

CERN's early experience with the Internet provided fertile soil for the birth of the Web. Recalls Ben Segal, who was responsible for the introduction of the Internet into CERN, an "entire culture of distributed computing" had been created at CERN; everyone was thinking about ways of spreading computer resources around and creating new, computer-based means for scientific collaboration. By providing electronic mail, mailing lists, and newsgroups, the Internet came with many useful tools.

What it lacked was a user-friendly way of allowing scientists to exchange documents with each other.

For the Time-Challenged

♦ The Web was born in a European think tank (CERN), where computer specialists were searching for ways to enable widely scattered physics researchers to work with reports, notes, databases, computer documentation, and computer help files. Since these researchers used a variety of different computers, the Internet seemed ideally suited. Hypertext promised to provide an easy-to-use mechanism by which these researchers could browse through and obtain the resources they needed.

♦ The Web is based on a client/server model. You run a program called a client on your computer. Under your direction, this program originates requests for information, which are received by server programs running on some other computer. The server program coughs up the requested data, and the client displays it. On the Web, clients are called *browsers*.

♦ CERN's greatest accomplishment was the HyperText Transport Protocol (HTTP), which specifies how a Web client requests information from a Web server. This is done by means of a Universal Resource Locator (URL), which precisely specifies the location of the requested information.

♦ So that the requested documents will look pretty on-screen, the Web development team at CERN added the HyperText Markup Language (HTML) to the emerging Web cocktail. HTML enables people using the Web to see richly formatted documents, replete with nice-looking fonts, emphasis, and text alignment, without requiring all that bulky formatting information to be conveyed over the Internet. With HTML, a Web author tags the parts of a document, such as headings, body text, and extended quotations. The Web browser reads the HTML tags and displays the document using all the font and graphics resources of the user's workstation or PC.

♦ The first successful graphical browser, NCSA Mosaic, was developed at another think tank, the National Center for Supercomputing Applications (NCSA). It, too, was designed for nonprofit academic use.

♦ Growing out of academic cultures in which it is customary to share one's work without expectation of financial gain, the Web lacks one of the key characteristics of Ted Nelson's Xanadu: The Web does not provide any convenient means to compensate copyright holders for use of their work.

Enter Tim Berners-Lee

By the late 1980s, Tim Berners-Lee, a computer specialist at CERN, had drunk deeply from the Internet wellspring; he perfectly understood its nature and possibilities. Segal recalls that Berners-Lee could connect your NeXT workstation to the Internet in a matter of minutes.

But Berners-Lee also understood hypertext. He knew of Nelson's Xanadu project and had himself written a standalone hypertext application. In a brilliant flash of inspiration, Berners-Lee saw that the Internet could provide the basis for an easy-to-use document exchange system based on hypertext principles. In 1989, Berners-Lee and his colleagues began experimenting with these ideas. In November 1990, they proposed a Web development project to CERN's directors.

The Web Proposal

The Web proposal emphasized that, first and foremost, the Web was intended to facilitate access to the types of information that CERN fellows needed. As Berners-Lee put it in the original Web proposal, "[the Web] provides a single user-interface to large classes of information (reports, notes, data-bases, computer documentation and on-line help."

It would also be easy to use. The Web's hypertext foundations would provide an extremely easy-to-use interface: to access a document, you would just point at its hyperlink and click.

In addition, it would make a wide variety of documents accessible. As Chapter 1 noted, the great thing about the Internet is its ability to ensure interoperability among computers that formerly couldn't exchange data with each other. The Web would integrate the many different kinds of hardware at CERN, enabling any two researchers to exchange documents without having to go through a tedious byte-by-byte translation process.

Like to know more about the Web's history?
Check out Ben M. Segal's "A Short History of Internet Protocols at CERN" (http://wwwcn.cern.ch/pdp/ns/ben/ TCPHIST.html).

Clients and Servers, or, Hey! Send Me That Document!

Berners-Lee learned another lesson from the Internet. Many of the Internet's most popular tools, such as FTP, involve two different types of programs, called *clients* and *servers*. The Web has a client/server basis.

Think of a client program as a program that works for *you*. It runs on your computer, taking full advantage of your computer's storage and processing capabilities. It also knows how to present itself (and Internet data) in a way that looks pretty on-screen.

A server program is like a robot that has been programmed to wait for information requests and then dish out the requested document. Clients know how to communicate with servers. The client says, in effect, "Hey, send me document such-and-such." The server receives the requests and says, in effect, "OK," and sends it. The client then displays the requested information on your computer screen.

On the Web, clients are called *browsers*, because they help you to browse for information.

Once Berners-Lee and his colleagues had come up with the idea of marrying the Internet, hypertext, and the client/server model, they could see how it would have to work. Take a look at a sample hypertext document (from the last chapter):

```
The term anime refers to an impressive Japanese tra-
dition of cartoon animation. Based on comic books
called manga, anime TV shows, videos, and movies
attract a wide audience in Japan, where adults as
well as children join in the fun. In subtitled vid-
eotapes and laserdiscs, anime is increasingly avail-
able in the United States. Try looking for titles
such as Akira or Bubblegum Crisis at your local
video store. For an example of the best in anime,
look for My Neighbor Totoro, a wonderful children's
film that the whole family will enjoy. If you'd like
to know more about anime, check out this more
detailed introduction and read the reviews of popu-
lar anime films.
```

Suppose this paragraph of hypertext is being displayed by a browser, running on your computer. You want to click one of these hyperlinks and see the requested document. But the requested document isn't on your computer. It's somewhere on the Internet.

To create the Web, Berners-Lee and his colleagues saw that they needed a *protocol* that would enable a browser to send out a document request via the Internet. So they created the HyperText Transport Protocol (HTTP), the foundation of the Web.

THE HYPERTEXT TRANSPORT PROTOCOL (HTTP)

You don't really need to know much about how HTTP works, except for one thing: HTTP specifies precisely how a given resource can be located and retrieved on the Internet. (A *resource* is anything of value that you can get from another Internet computer, such as a document, a sound, a graphic, an animation, a movie, or a computer program.)

HTTP does this by specifying the form of *uniform resource identifiers*— abbreviated as URI (no relation to the guy who used to go around bending spoons with psychokinetic power). A URI is simply a series of characters (letters, numbers, or punctuation) that identifies the location of an Internet resource.

There are two kinds of URIs: Uniform Resource Locators (URLs) and Relative URLs (RELURLs).

- A URL is used to locate a resource on a computer other than the one on which the client is running.

- A RELURL is used to locate a resource on the same computer.

Let's ignore RELURLs for now; what's important here is the URL, the subject of the next section.

UNIFORM RESOURCE LOCATORS (URLs)

Basically, the Web consists of client programs that send URLs out over the Internet, and server programs that field these requests and cough up the appropriate information (which could be a text document, a sound, a graphic, a movie, a compressed file, a program, or other things). The client program then displays the requested information, if it can.

A Uniform Resource Locator (URL) looks like this:

http://watt.seas.virginia.edu/~bp/parents.html

It has three parts:

1. **Protocol Identifier (*http://*)** This specifies what type of resource the URL accesses. Here, it's a World Wide Web document (http://). It could also be an FTP file (ftp://), a Gopher menu (gopher://), a Usenet newsgroup (news://), a Telnet session (Telnet://), and more.

2. **Domain Name** (*watt.seas.virginia.edu*) This gives the exact Internet address of the computer that houses the resource.

3. **Resource Location** (*/~bp/parents.html*) This specifies the resource's exact location and file name.

In sum, a URL specifies the type of resource, the location of the resource, and the name of the resource. When a Web client sends a URL to a Web server, the Web server responds by locating the resource and sending it back via the Internet.

THE HYPERTEXT MARKUP LANGUAGE (HTML)

The Web is basically a networked hypertext system that enables people to retrieve documents from the Internet. It wouldn't be much fun if the documents didn't look nice, with pretty fonts and graphics.

But there's just one problem. Documents that are formatted with fonts and graphics are *big*—too big to be transferred efficiently via the Internet. The Microsoft Word file containing this chapter, for example, consumes 39K of disk space. And the version I'm writing right now doesn't even contain any graphics—it's just fonts and formatting information. But the text-only version of the same file uses only 16K of storage—less than half!

To reduce the load on the Internet, Berners-Lee and his colleagues decided to compose Web documents using a *markup language*. Unlike a word processing program, a markup language does not attempt to specify precisely how the formatted document should appear. It just identifies the *parts* of the document.

 **HTML: Sorry, but you'll have to learn it**
As Ted Nelson originally envisioned the global hypertext system, it would enable readers to become authors. With the Web, that's possible, but at a cost. You need a pretty good Internet connection, one that gives your computer a permanent address—and that doesn't come cheap. (More on this point in Chapter 6.) In addition, you need to learn at least some HTML. Sure, you've doubtless heard of those easy-to-use HTML editors that do all the coding for you. But here's the bad news. I haven't seen one yet that frees you from knowing at least a little HTML coding. Maybe that will change, but for now, there's some HTML in your future.

An Example

Here's the difference between a word processing program and a markup language. Suppose you're formatting a document title with a word processing program. You type it, and then format it with centering, the Galliard font (18 points), and bold. Here's how it looks:

A Heading

In a markup language, you don't choose the alignment, font, font size, or emphasis. You just use codes, called *tags*, that tell the browser that this text is a certain part of a document—here, a second-level heading. The codes look like this:

```
<H2>A Heading</H2>
```

When people read this document on the Web, their browser looks at the text, and says, "Aha! A second-level heading!" The browser then decides how to format this text. Most browsers give their users at least some control over the way given parts of the document appear. Perhaps Mark has chosen the all-business Avant Garde font, so his heading looks like this:

A Heading

But Sujitha wants something a bit on the informal side, so she chooses Gazelle, and formats the second-level heading flush left:

A Heading

Randi, meanwhile, adds zing by choosing 36-point Marker Felt Wide:

A Heading

As you can see, the good thing about a markup language is that it lets the user choose his or her own formatting preferences. That is also the bad thing about a markup language.

Fair warning: Users may choose bizarre fonts!
As a Web author, you can't control the way your document will look on-screen. You can try, but you're paddling upstream. Most browsers give users options to ignore the

efforts you might make to force a certain kind of formatting, such as a background color.

The HyperText Markup Language and SGML

Berners-Lee and his colleagues didn't invent markup languages. The concept already existed, and so did the *Standard Generalized Markup Language (SGML)*, an international standard that was defined in 1986.

SGML isn't exactly a markup language. Rather, it's a metalanguage that provides the means for formally defining markup languages. With SGML, you can define a *document type definition (DTD)*. This is a formal statement of how a particular markup language identifies the parts of a document. Once the DTD has been created, you can create another program, called a *parser*, that understands this particular document type and knows how to display it on-screen.

The HyperText Markup Language (HTML) is a document type defined by SGML. And Web browsers are also parsers for HTML. Simple, isn't it?

Actually, HTML does more than enable you to add tags defining standard document types such as headings, body text, and quotations. It also lets you create hyperlinks—and hide them so that all the user sees is the underlined text. When you click on the hyperlink, the parser sends the URL out over the network.

GRAPHICAL BROWSERS

The National Center for Supercomputing Applications (NCSA), located at the University of Illinois, Champaign-Urbana, is the birthplace of NCSA Mosaic, the Web's "killer application." Just as Lotus 1-2-3 was a decisive factor in creating a mass market for the IBM PC, Mosaic brought the Web to millions of people who might not otherwise have used it.

Why Browsers Were Created

Opened in 1986, NCSA is one of four government-funded supercomputing research centers. The scientists and researchers who work at NCSA are all involved in what NCSA calls computational science, the attempt to understand natural phenomena by simulating them on high-performance computing systems.

NCSA's Software Development Group (SDG) has been working for years to create software that could enhance scientific visualization. At NCSA, they developed high-performance graphics programs that could display amazing simulations on monitors directly connected to supercomputers. But they recognized that not everyone could afford to come to NCSA. A way needed to be found to make supercomputing resources more widely available.

Enter the Web. A talented young programmer, Marc Andreessen, quickly saw that the Web provided just the distribution and access mechanisms that NCSA was looking for. The program could run animations and videos, so that a researcher in Tuscaloosa, or Tehachapi or Tonapah for that matter, could view much the same patterns that NCSA researchers were seeing. What's more, a researcher in an isolated college or university could upload some data by means of FTP, have the NCSA staff analyze it on a supercomputer, and then view the results on the Web.

Mosaic is a *graphical browser*. At the minimum, this means that the program can parse HTML documents and display them using a computer system's font resources. Graphical browsers can also display *in-line graphics*, the pictures that HTML authors often include with their documents.

Into the Private Sector

Released in 1993, Mosaic took the Internet by storm. However, it quickly became apparent that NCSA got more than it bargained for with its freebie release of X Window/Motif, Macintosh, and Windows versions of the program—a support nightmare. In 1994, NCSA licensed Mosaic to a for-profit spinoff company, Spyglass, which was charged with the task of creating commercial versions of the program. Spyglass did not market these programs directly, but instead resold licensing rights to book publishers (such as O'Reilly and Associates), operating system publishers (Microsoft and IBM), and third-party software vendors (Luckmann Associates). The commercial version of the program is generically known as Enhanced NCSA Mosaic, but it's available under many different names when repackaged by licensees.

Although millions of copies of NCSA Mosaic have been distributed, the real action has shifted to a program called Netscape Navigator, published by Netscape Communications, Inc. Netscape, as the program is often called, was authored by a team led by the same Marc Andreessen who created NCSA Mosaic. Andreessen co-founded Netscape in 1994.

Netscape Navigator has since been published in a number of versions, the most recent of which (version 4.0) is in beta testing at this writing. The program has grown in complexity, adding e-mail, Usenet, collaboration, and other features.

It's also facing stiff competition from Microsoft. Having purchased the rights to a Mosaic spinoff in early 1995, Microsoft released a not-very-impressive product called Microsoft Internet Explorer later that year. The program's second version didn't attract much attention, but by 1996 Microsoft had fully grasped the importance of the Internet. Version 3.0 of Internet Explorer, available for free from Microsoft's server (http://www.microsoft.com), challenged Netscape's dominance for the first time.

 **Getting Your Copy of the Latest Browsers**
To obtain free copies of Netscape Navigator for personal use, access http://home.netscape.com. If you're browsing the Web in a business, you may prefer Microsoft Internet Explorer (http://www.microsoft.com), which is free for all users.

Making Things Happen: CGI

HTML is not a programming language—it's a markup language, one that can describe nothing more than a page's appearance. To transform the Web into an environment with more interactivity than that made possible by hyperlinks, something more was needed.

Forms and CGI: The Two Foundations of Web Interactivity

That "something more" consists of two important innovations:

- **Forms**   The forms tags introduced into HTML version 2.0 enable Web programmers to create documents with interactive features, such as radio buttons, check boxes, pull-down lists, and text entry areas. However, it's very important to understand that these features cannot do anything by themselves. When the user clicks the Submit button (or some other button that completes the action), the client bundles the user's responses into a message that must be directed to a computer program of some kind.

- **Common Gateway Interface (CGI)**   This is a set of standards that describes how browsers should bundle the data that is sent to external programs. Programs that know how to decode and act on this data are said to conform to CGI.

The rise of forms and CGI meant that, for the first time, non-programmers were at something of a disadvantage when it came to creating Web pages. In order to create highly interactive pages using forms and CGI, a Web page designer must know, at the minimum, how to obtain a CGI-compatible program for performing a specific function and how to make it available on the serving system.

Perl

Perl is a scripting language that is widely available on UNIX systems. In consequence, it is frequently used to write CGI programs. Because Perl and CGI are so commonly uttered in the same breath, people tend to assume that they're necessarily related. But that's not true. You can write a CGI program in any computer language, and you can operate a CGI program on any computer that's running a Web server. There are many CGI-compatible programs that have been written for Microsoft Windows systems.

Using Freeware and Shareware Scripts
If you're setting up a Web page for a UNIX system, you may be able to use a public-domain or freeware CGI script to create interactive features for your pages, including database searching, newsgroups, and more. However, you'll need to check with your Web service provider to find out whether CGI programs are tolerated. Often, getting these programs to work is as simple as installing them in the correct directory, setting the file access permissions correctly, and pointing your forms' output to the program. Pretty easy stuff, really. You'll learn more about CGI in Chapter 16, Enabling User Feedback.

I don't want to become a programmer!
Many Web service providers offer custom programming—which might not be as expensive as you'd think. It may involve no more than setting up and configuring a freeware utility.

The Shortcomings of CGI

CGI is a *server-side* solution to the problem of providing Web interactivity. This is CGI's major shortcoming. In order to provide interactivity, you must place a CGI program on the same computer network that's running the Web server. This means you're giving outsiders the ability to run a program on your system whenever they wish. Knowledgeable hackers can use this as a means of intruding into systems or destroying data.

In addition to the security problems, CGI also places a load on the computer system running the CGI program. That's not a problem if your site gets just a few hits each day, but what if it gets thousands? To be sure, there are computer systems out there capable of handling millions of hits a day and executing lots of CGI programs (consider Netscape's home site). But these are very expensive systems, which use multiple processors and heavy-duty equipment. For a small business that can't easily afford to upgrade a computer system, this is something worth thinking about.

TOWARD ACTIVE CONTENT: PLUG-INS, JAVA, JAVASCRIPT, AND ACTIVEX

Owing to the shortcomings of CGI, there are several good reasons to argue for a *client-side* programming language for the Web. Here's how a client-side program would work. Using a specially equipped browser that knows how to read and execute programming language instructions, the user accesses a Web page that contains programming instructions or links to a program. These instructions are then downloaded to the user's computer, which runs the program.

The Advantages of Client-Side Programs

Client-side programs have many advantages, at least from the Web publisher's point of view: They place no burdens on the serving computer, since the programs are executed on the client's computer. In addition, they pose no security threats to the serving system—again, the software is executed on the client's computer, so it can't be used to hack into the server.

The Disadvantages of Client-Side Programs

As you might expect, the disadvantages of client-side programs are all on the user's side (where, one might add, they were deliberately sent). How do you know you're downloading a bona fide program, one that won't do any harm to your computer? There are three solutions to this problem, and none of them is completely satisfactory:

- **Plug-ins**   A plug-in is an accessory program that's designed to blend with a specific browser, adding additional functionality to it. The problem with plug-ins is that they are proprietary. Although Microsoft Internet Explorer 3.0 can run most Netscape plug-ins, for example, it doesn't run them well, and it can't run some of them at all.

- **Downloading mini-programs (applets)**   Another approach is to download a small program (an applet) and equip the browser so that it can carry out (execute) the program's instructions. But what if the program is a prank or a virus? One approach is to run the downloaded program in a specially segregated area of your computer's memory (a "sandbox," in programmer's slang), where the program doesn't have access to file operations. In addition, the programming language can be written so that it doesn't include any instructions that could be used for destructive purposes (such as Erase Whole Disk). The disadvantage of this is that it's very difficult to write a programming language that still does interesting things while posing no danger to your system. This is the approach used by Java.

- **Enclosing downloaded programs in a container**   Another approach is to let the programming language do destructive things—including moving or erasing files. To ensure that users download only virtuous programs, which do not put this destructive power to evil purposes, the program is downloaded in a container that automatically takes care of installation and configuration tasks. In addition, the browser displays a digital certificate prior to downloading (see Figure 3.1). The certificate, signed by an independent verification service, attests that the program really is a genuine program made by a professional software publishing firm, and not some horrible virus masquerading as a bona fide program. This is the approach used by ActiveX. The problem here is that a rogue site could fake the certificate or obtain a valid one under false pretenses (yes, it's happened).

Plug-ins—And Why They're History

Plug-ins are well known among graphics designers, thanks to the availability of plug-ins for programs such as Adobe Photoshop. In brief, a *plug-in* is a program that is designed to extend the capabilities of the host program. The host program must be designed to accomodate these accessories. In

Figure 3.1 This certificate attests that the ActiveX control you are about to download is genuine.

short, the plug-in architecture is *proprietary*. It's structured around the standards established de facto by a particular company.

That's what's wrong with plug-ins, that's why they're history, and that's why you shouldn't use them on your site. If you make your content accessible only to those who have installed and run the correct plug-in, you're turning away the following people:

- Those who have the right browser but don't want to take the time (or use up the disk space) to install the plug-in.

- Those who aren't using the browser for which the plug-in was designed.

For most Web sites, using a plug-in means simply that you're turning too many people away.

Introducing Java

Java, the new programming language created by Sun Microsystems, wasn't originally designed to serve as a client-side programming language for creating active Web content. It was designed to serve as the programming basis for an Internet device connected to a TV set. But Java's designers quickly perceived that it could provide the interactivity that Web page designers were looking for.

In brief, Java is a new version of C++, the object-oriented programming language that is the language of choice in professional programming labs. But it lacks any instructions that could be used to destroy data on the user's system. Designed to run in a sandbox, Java can't be used to create harmful programs—at least, that's the theory.

Although Java is somewhat easier to use than the notoriously difficult C++, it is designed for professional programmers. A finished Java program is an executable file, called an *applet*, that is downloaded along with a Web page. When you access a Java-enhanced page using a Java-capable browser, the browser runs the program, and additional features become available. For example, it's possible to embed a fully functional spreadsheet in a Web page, using Java applets designed for this purpose.

What's good about Java? Plenty. Java is easily learned by professional programmers. What's more, Java is platform-independent: It can run on any computer. I expect Java to become the dominant programming language for Internet applications.

Learn More about Java
One of the best Web sites for learning about Java is Java-World (http://www.javaworld.com). You'll find tutorials, tips, tricks, news, opinions, trends, applets, and much more.

Introducing JavaScript

One problem with Java is that professional programming expertise is required to learn it. Fearing that this would put amateur programmers out of business, Netscape Communications created a simplified version of Java, called JavaScript. The beauty of JavaScript is that you can type JavaScript instructions into a Web page; you don't need to compile the instructions into applets, as Java requires. These instructions (called *scripts*) can add interactivity to your Web presentation with minimal programming investment.

Is there a drawback to JavaScript? You bet. Critics charge that Netscape didn't fully think through all the security issues related to JavaScript. At certain stages in Netscape's product evolution, it was possible to write JavaScript programs that would capture the user's e-mail address without consent, and perform other intrusive or destructive operations. These problems have been addressed in more recent versions of Netscape and JavaScript, but concern remains.

 **Learn More about JavaScript**
For tons of JavaScript resources, including tutorials and scripts you can copy onto your pages, see The JavaScript Resource Center (http://jrc.livesoftware.com). You'll find JavaScript code examples that you can include in your Web pages, JavaScript tutorials, tips, and more.

Introducing ActiveX

Microsoft Corporation has jumped into the active content sweepstakes with its own proprietary container standard, ActiveX. In brief, ActiveX provides a container that enables a Web server to send programs to an ActiveX client. Downloading, configuration, installation, and execution are completely transparent to the user (except for the vital phase of inspecting and approving the certificate). Once installed on your system, the ActiveX program (called a *control*) can take advantage of dynamic data exchange (DDE) to interact with other controls and other programs.

What's good about ActiveX? An ActiveX container can contain a program written in any computer programming language, including Java.

What's bad about ActiveX? Besides the security implications of the container model, which I've already mentioned, you should consider that at present ActiveX runs only on Windows systems. ActiveX can be ported to the Macintosh pretty easily, since the underlying DDE technology is already present in the Mac OS, but it's unlikely that UNIX systems will be able to use ActiveX controls any time soon.

 **clnet's ActiveX Resources**
One of the best places to look for information concerning the ActiveX standard is clnet's activex.com (www.activex.com).

Does Sun have an answer to ActiveX? Yes. It's called JavaBeans. Essentially, JavaBeans is a container technology that's similar to ActiveX in that it can be used to transfer any type of program to a client's computer. However, JavaBeans is a truly cross-platform container—unlike ActiveX, which is currently restricted to the Windows platform.

FROM HERE

- What are the defining characteristics of the Web as a publishing medium? Flip to Chapter 4 to find out.

- Given that the Web isn't Xanadu, what can you publish on the Web? See Chapter 5 for lots of examples.

Chapter

4

The Web as a Publishing Medium

I
f you want to publish on the Web, be forewarned: The Web isn't like any publishing medium that's ever existed. If you think it's anything like a traditional broadcast medium (such as magazines, newspapers, television, or radio), you'll fall flat on your face. Recognizing the peril, big companies are bringing in talented young Web developers to create highly interactive, engaging Web sites for their firms.

But that's not an option for most of the people reading this book—the individual entrepreneurs, owners of small businesses, freelancers, and consultants in today's economy. You'll need to make the break with conventional thinking, and do it fast, if you're going to take full advantage of the Web. To help you accomplish this is the goal of this chapter. It begins by dismissing the *broadcast model* of publishing—a model that's very misleading when applied to the Web. It continues by considering the unique characteristics and possibilities of the Web as a publishing medium and by discussing its very real problems and limitations. As you'll find, though, the limitations are decreasing in importance with each passing month. It seems clear that the Web is destined to become one of modern society's most important media for the distribution of textual and hypermedia-based information.

BROADCAST MODEL? FORGET IT

Let's start by killing off the mind-set that leads to quick, conspicuous failure in Web publishing: thinking that the Web is anything like a broadcast medium.

In a traditional broadcast medium, a firm prepares content (such as an advertisement), selects a medium (such as radio or a magazine), and publishes the content. It's a one-way, one-to-many process, in which consumers are more or less passive consumers of the information the firm puts out.

If you're thinking this way, you're going to have a tough time understanding the Web. Let's look at some of the ways the Web departs radically from the broadcast model.

The Potlatch Factor

Along the northwest coast of what is now British Columbia, Native American peoples developed a unique culture, one that is very different from the cultures of industrialized countries. The central theme: 'Tis nobler to give than to receive. As you'll see, the Web embodies the same spirit.

To be reckoned great, a chief would hold a ceremony called the *potlatch*. The objective of this ceremony was to *give away* hundreds of barrels of fish oil and hundreds of blankets. At the end of the ceremony, his guests— shaken and humiliated by this massive display of generosity—would cart off the goodies, and the chief's name would resound throughout the land. (The chief's house was pretty empty after this, but nobody cared. After all, if you needed some fish oil or blankets, you could always go to some other chief's potlatch.)

You'd think the potlatch values aren't consistent with modern capitalism, but take a look at any university's promotion and tenure system. In universities, you gain professional advancement by publishing the results of your work in scholarly and scientific journals. These journals do *not* compensate you for publishing your work in them. In fact, some of them make you *pay*

For the Time-Challenged

♦ The Web can't be understood if you're thinking of it as a broadcast medium, with content providers involved in a one-way relationship with passive information consumers. Information consumers are becoming information producers, and they're even appropriating advertising!

♦ You don't have to prepare content exhaustively—if somebody else has already contributed something of value on a subject, you can link to it instead of reinventing the wheel.

♦ All the money in the world won't give you any *technical* advantage over a college student when it comes to getting people to access your site. To be sure, the deeper your pockets, the more non-Web publicity you can afford. Still, some of the best Web advertising is word of mouth.

♦ Other characteristics of the Web as a publication medium: Whether you're in New York City or Billings, Montana, you can look forward to zero distance and zero distribution costs, once you've forked over the monthly fees to your Internet service provider. And your Web publication sticks around, 24 hours a day, unless you deliberately alter it or remove it from your site.

♦ Disadvantages of the Web include the difficulty of creating and maintaining Web pages, low control over your documents' look, the difficulty people are going to have locating your site, the lack of audience measurement tools, and the lack of established payment mechanisms. Most of the problems are being resolved, however.

for the privilege of seeing your work appear in such distinguished company. Department chairmen and deans everywhere tell junior faculty, "If you get money for it, it doesn't count." You become famous in academia not by getting rich off your ideas, but by giving them away to low-circulation journals and publication series.

In short, wherever you find academics, there's a potlatch factor. And that's true of the Web. Growing out of two academic think tanks, the Web embodies the potlatch values of academia; it assumes that people will be more than willing to contribute documents to the Web, without the slightest expectation of remuneration.

That works fine in academic environments. Academics are (usually) pretty willing to share information and resources. It also works well for hobbyists. Hobbyists love to share information with each other and don't expect much in return, except friendship and more information.

But will the Web suffice as a mass publication medium, along the lines envisioned by Ted Nelson? Not without some additional means to recompense copyright holders for information they make available on the Web.

As developed at CERN and NCSA, the Web includes only very primitive capabilities for charging people for accessing copyrighted material. This is one of the biggest drawbacks to the Web, at present. That's why they say, "The Web is cool, but it isn't Xanadu."

"Nobody's making money on the Web!"
Don't believe it. To be sure, the Web's academic origins, especially when coupled with the broader noncommercial values of the Internet, make it very difficult to charge for the information you want to make available. But nobody said it's *impossible*. In Chapter 5, you'll see lots of methods that Web authors are using right now to make money on the Web—or to establish a presence that enables them to make money elsewhere.

Why Traditional Publications Fail on the Web
You'll read about it in the *Wall Street Journal*, practically every week. Some well-funded Web publication venture goes under. Why? Chances are you're reading about an attempt to create a traditional magazine on the Web, something that might manage to attract enough hits to justify advertising. But the readers just don't materialize. And neither does the advertising. After an experimental period, everyone's let go and the site folds down. What's wrong here? Lack of awareness of the characteristics of the Web as a publication medium.

CHARACTERISTICS OF THE WEB AS A PUBLISHING MEDIUM

The key to successful publishing on the Web is to realize that the Web isn't *just* a medium for making information available. It's also a *technology* for facilitating community-building and interaction. Successful Web sites begin with clear awareness of their intended audiences.

One of the most striking ways in which the Web differs from traditional broadcast media is that consumers and readers can themselves become content providers. The cost of placing a document on the Web and making it available to others is already very low in comparison to traditional broadcast media—and it's falling. In Figure 4.1, you see a classic low-budget Web production: Equestrian enthusiast Karen Pautz, a journalism student at the University of Missouri–Columbia, created a home page to bring together a number of high-quality horse-related sites on the Web. Her page's name? Hay.net.

The Web is well on its way to a Xanadu-like destruction of the distinction between authors and readers. In Ted Nelson's vision of Xanadu (see Chapter

Figure 4.1 Hay.net (http://www.freerein.com/haynet/).

2), every reader becomes an author almost automatically, in that he or she builds on existing documents by referencing links and adding notes, commentaries, and summaries. The Web isn't there yet—Web browsers provide only minimal facilities for annotation, and annotations aren't accessible by other Web users—but it's on its way. In Figure 4.2, you see a Web document in which hyperlinks to other documents are seamlessly embedded in the text itself, supplementing the presentation and providing branchpoints for exploration. The example is drawn from The Internet Investor, a respected online investment column.

Future HTML editors will do away with the need for programming expertise, both for HTML documents and interactive forms, leading to an explosion of content provision by information consumers themselves.

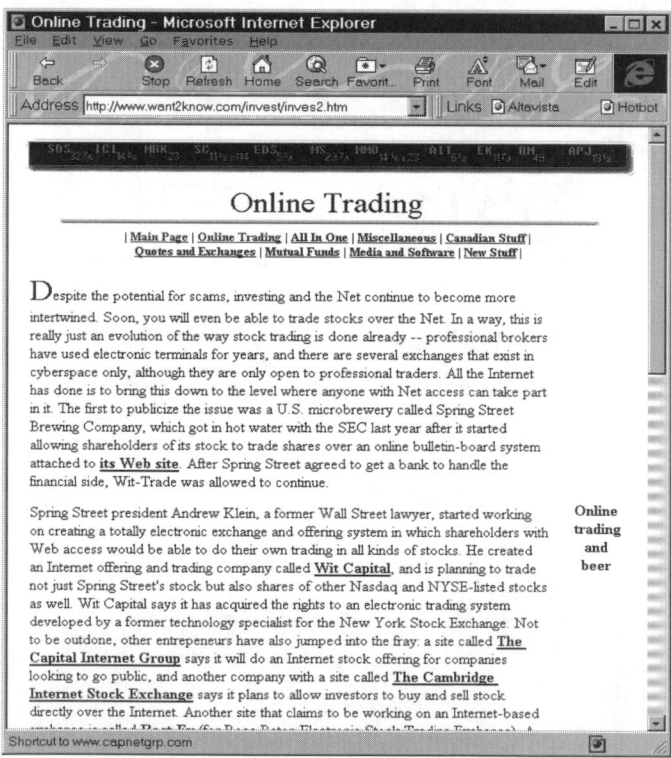

Figure 4.2   Hyperlinks seamlessly embedded in text.
http://www.want2know.com/invest/inves2.htm

If you need any more convincing that the Web radically departs from the previous distinction between information producers and information consumers, here's something else to chew on. In traditional media, firms create advertisements for their products. You can advertise on the Web, but something else is happening too: Consumers are themselves creating Web pages that are concerned, often adoringly, with specific products, including Barbie dolls, Lego toys, and more (for an example, see Figure 4.3). Generally, they do this without asking for permission—and without receiving compensation.

Compared with the content produced by traditional advertisers, consumer "advertising" isn't necessarily the same kind of advertising that a firm would do. Although most consumer advertising is done by product enthusiasts, it's

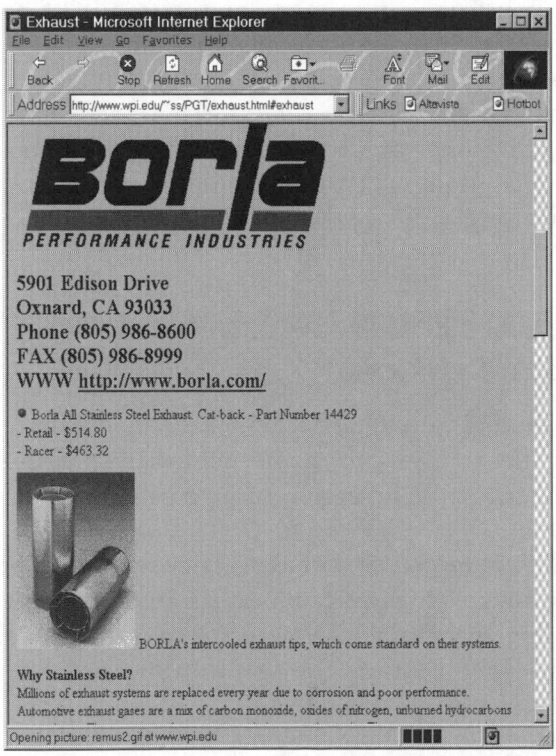

Figure 4.3 Consumer-originated advertisement for high-performance Ford Probe exhaust system (http://www.wpi.edu/~ss/PGT/exhaust.html#exhaust).

likely to come with a good dose of criticism and consumer tips. The Ford Probe page, for example, comes with links to service bulletins, which Probe owners can use to make sure they get the warranty service to which they're entitled.

Synergy (The More the Merrier)

A traditional publishing effort is a solitary thing. It can refer to other publications, perhaps through footnotes or in-text references, but it cannot build on them. The Web, like any hypertext system, is different. In a hypertext document, you can include hyperlinks to other peoples' efforts. You don't have to reinvent the wheel by covering knowledge that's well represented elsewhere on the Web. In time, as a number of people contribute their knowledge and resources in a specific area to the Web, the value and depth of this knowledge grows and grows. The result of this process is an *information community* consisting of as many as thousands of people worldwide who share varying levels of commitment to improving the collaborative information pool.

An example of synergy in action is the remarkable Froggy Page (Figure 4.4), which brings together an astonishing variety of Web resources related to these amphibians—songs, pictures, stories, scientific documents, famous frogs, and even recipes.

All Web Pages Are Equally Accessible (An Information Democracy?)

Let's say that an undergraduate at Virginia Tech invests two hours of time in a home page, while a major magazine publisher spends $125,000 on an extravagantly illustrated Web version of its print-based publication. Which is more accessible?

In strictly technical terms, they're equally accessible. The magazine publisher has more resources to spend on publicizing its site, but the technology doesn't give the big spender any way to make a bigger splash. Compared with virtually any other medium, this feature alone makes the Web an inherently democratic medium.

All the advertising in the world won't do you much good, moreover, if Web users perceive your site to be clueless, Web-wise. To succeed on the Web, you'll need to offer some valuable information or resources for free, you'll need to appeal to the Web user's sense of Web aesthetics (and etiquette), and you'll need to use traditional Web publicizing methods.

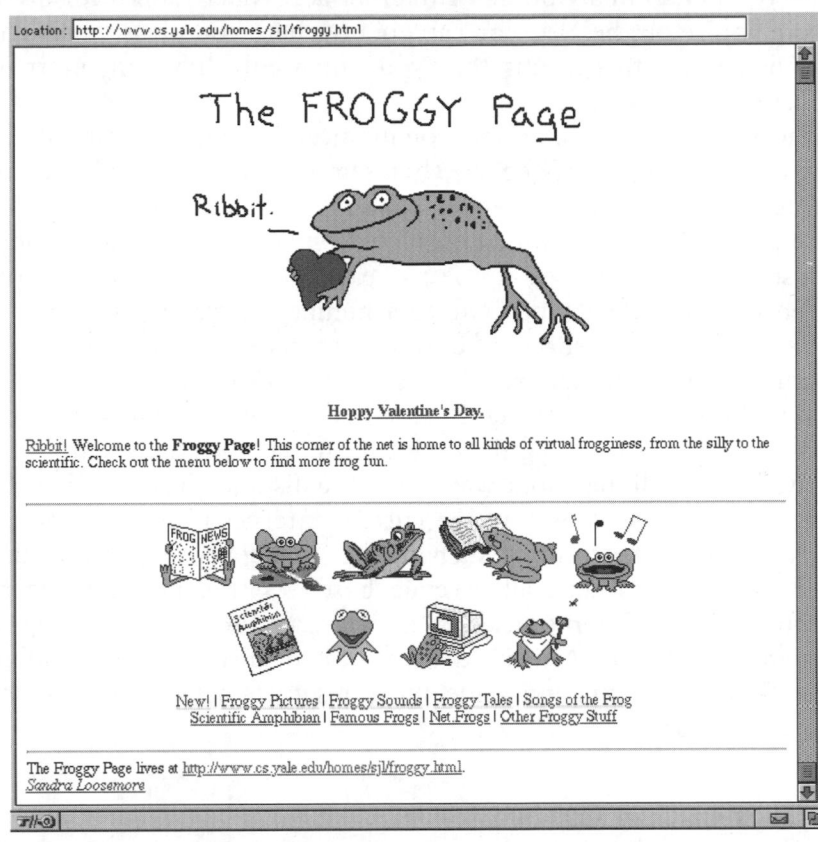

Figure 4.4 The Froggy Page serves as the focus for frog enthusiasts world-wide.

Distance Doesn't Matter (There Are No Long-Distance Charges)

In traditional businesses, as in real estate, the old saying "location, location, location" makes very good sense. Suppose you're setting up a traditional manufacturing business in rural Montana. Good luck—although it's not impossible, you'll have to overcome extraordinary shipping and communication costs attributable to your isolated location.

But that's not true of the Web. Owing to the limitations of the current TCP/IP protocols, which were never designed to permit usage-based billing, most Internet service providers offer Internet access based on a *flat pricing model*—you get so many hours of Internet access per month for a flat fee. And once you're on the Net, you can go anywhere you please. From a publisher's viewpoint, this means that you potentially have an international audience for your work.

Of the various publishing and communications media available in our society, in this respect the Web closely resembles the 800 telephone number service (except that it's international in scope, which 800 services aren't). With an 800 number, you can do business from any state in the Union; from your customers' perspective, it doesn't really matter where you're located. The Web will doubtless contribute to a number of trends that are moving people and jobs out of urban and even suburban centers, raising rural populations and straining meager rural social service resources.

With millions of people using the Internet, service providers are spending billions upgrading their long-distance transmission systems—and not surprisingly, they're talking about ways to create distance-based billing. But it's unlikely they'll succeed. Within the current Internet protocols, there is no technical basis for performing such billing. Moreover, expanding Internet usage is providing additional revenue based on the existing flat billing model. In addition, Internet users are accustomed to the flat billing model and might desert the Net in droves should distance-based billing be imposed. Industry complaints aside, most observers believe that the flat billing model will survive.

Zero Distribution Costs

Once you've placed a document on the Web, it costs you absolutely nothing to distribute it. Every time your document is accessed—this is called a *hit*—a copy of your document is conveyed via the Internet, where it is temporarily stored in the browser's local memory space.

There's one caveat to this point, though. If your Web site becomes very popular, you may find that it's necessary to upgrade your equipment to handle the load! The shareware servers designed to run on Microsoft Windows and Macintosh computers can handle, at most, a few hundred accesses per day; the most popular sites have several UNIX workstations running at high capacities.

High Latency (Documents Stick Around)

The term *latency* refers to the amount of time a message sticks around in a communication medium. Among the various Internet formats, Usenet exemplifies a medium with very low latency: To make room for the dozens of megabytes of new messages coming in daily, system administrators may set the system software to erase posts automatically every 24 hours.

In contrast to Usenet, the Web offers exceptionally high latency—the document remains available, 24 hours a day, until you deliberately remove it. And the longer you let it remain, the more chance there is that somebody else will create a link to your document. And the more people link to your document, the more hits you'll get.

The Web's high latency makes it ideal for creating organizational and corporate *memory structures*, inventories of information that grow over time and eventually constitute an indispensable resource.

 **So who's making money?**
There's a long string of publishing failures on the Web, and an even longer list of commercial site failures. But let's take a look at one of the successes: Amazon.com, an Internet bookstore. Located at www.amazon.com (Figure 4.5), this site takes advantage of the Web's unique capabilities as a publishing medium. Superficially, it's an online bookstore, and a very good one: You can order from a searchable selection of over one million titles. But Amazon.com fully exploits the interactivity and community-building characteristics of the Web. For example, readers and even authors can contribute notes and reviews of the books listed in Amazon.com's database. You can subscribe to mailing lists to receive notice when new books are published in areas of interest to you. If you're thinking about trying to make money in Web publishing, study this site very, very carefully.

DRAWBACKS TO THE WEB AS A PUBLISHING MEDIUM

Compared with the Web, traditional media are more easily accessed, more familiar from a technical standpoint, more susceptible to design control, and easier to find. You'll have little trouble figuring out just who's reading your publication—and how to charge them for the valuable information you're distributing. In all these areas, the Web has shortcomings. The following sections elaborate on these points.

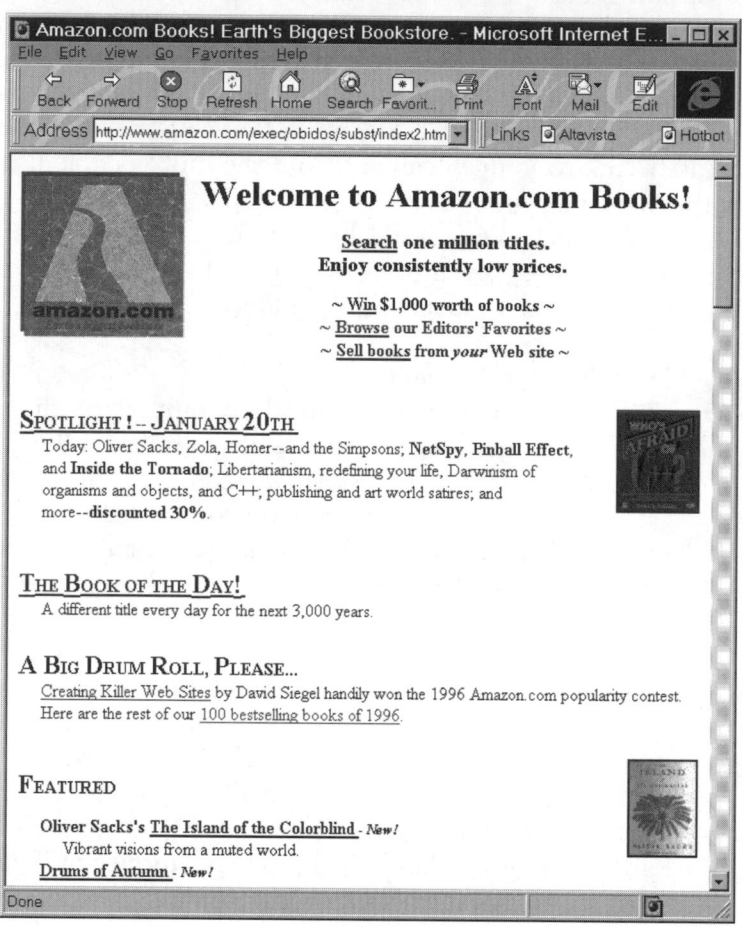

Figure 4.5   Amazon.com has it right.

Technical Barriers to Web Publication

It's pretty easy to find printers who can handle a newsletter, including design, layout, printing, and even mailing and addressing. But would-be Web publishers find several barriers in their path:

- **The relative scarcity of direct Internet connections.** In order to set up a Web site, you need an Internet connection with a permanent IP address. Just a year ago, such connections were a luxury enjoyed only by people working in universities, research centers, think tanks, Internet-savvy corporations, and government agencies. (That's one of the reasons there are so many Web pages authored by college students.) However, new Internet connectivity options, including connections with permanent IP addresses, are now becoming widely available.

- **The technical difficulty of setting up a Web server.** Until 1994, almost all of the available Web servers were UNIX programs that required considerable technical expertise to install (not to mention the fact that they ran on expensive UNIX workstations). However, easy-to-use Web servers are now available for Windows, Windows NT, and Macintosh computers.

- **The need to learn HTML.** To publish on the Web, you need to learn at least a little HTML—and that's still true, despite the arrival of a number of programs that claim to make "HTML programming" unnecessary. To be sure, these programs have reduced the drudgery involved in creating and maintaining HTML documents, but you may need HTML knowledge to add advanced features, such as frames and forms.

Is the Internet running out of IP addresses?
You may have heard of the "IP address crisis" and heard dire warnings of the "impending death of the Net." When the Internet was first designed, a 32-bit address space was thought to be sufficient. This would have been enough to handle billions of computers, but the 32-bit address was broken down into classes (called A, B, and C) to reduce the processing burden on Internet routing equipment. This reduced the number of addresses available and led, ultimately, to the current problem. Only 128 Class A networks are permitted, but each Class A network can have millions of hosts. There can be thousands of Class B networks, and each can have thousands of hosts. There can be millions of Class C networks, but each can have no more than 254 hosts. At current rates of Internet growth, Class B network addresses—by far the most popular choice for networks seeking to link to the Internet—will be exhausted shortly. However, this crisis will be resolved soon. The Internet Engineering Task Force (IETF) has proposed a revision to the Internet Protocol that

will provide a 64-bit address space while retaining compatibility with existing Internet programs and equipment. With a 64-bit address space, there will be sufficient IP addresses for every man, woman, and child on the planet, as well as every single addressable byte of storage in their computer systems. That ought to be enough!

These access barriers are becoming less significant with each passing month. Direct Internet connectivity is becoming widely available, and a new generation of "point-and-click" Web servers will enable virtually anyone to set up a Web site in short order. As for HTML, it's not terribly difficult to learn, and the years to come should see improved HTML editors.

Low Formatting Control

In its original conception, HTML was designed to mark up the parts of Web documents, but it was left up to the *browser* to determine exactly how the documents appear on-screen. This is advantageous in one sense—document downloading proceeds quickly because the formatting information does not have to be transmitted—but very disadvantageous in that a site's author cannot control how a given document will look. For example, it's difficult with HTML to use a corporate font (such as Apple's Garamond Narrow) so that all of your firm's documents have a consistent look. (With HTML 3.2, you can add font definitions to documents, but the fonts won't appear unless they're installed in the user's system.)

There are a number of ways around this problem. For example, you can use tables to create the illusion of newspaper columns (see Figure 4.6 for a good example).

Toward Greater Format Control?
It's clear that the Web is evolving toward giving designers greater control over the layout of their documents. Although layout control is difficult with HTML, it isn't impossible, as the existence of many attractively designed Web pages attests. Microsoft's ActiveX Layout Control, used widely in the Microsoft Network pages, enables Web designers to have what they've long sought: pinpoint, precision control over the exact placement of every page feature, including text and graphics.

Figure 4.6 Controlling layout through the use of tables.

Low Discoverability (Where the Heck Is That Page?)

The Web is making it possible for just about anybody to establish a presence on the Internet—just take a look at all those college students' home pages, which serve no other purpose (apparently) than to gratify egos. With approximately 5 million documents already available on the Web, will yours get lost in the shuffle?

That's a valid concern for any would-be Web publisher. A basic point about the Web is that the technology doesn't thrust your Web pages in peoples' faces—they must deliberately seek you out. And often, that's a tedious and ultimately unsuccessful enterprise.

To be sure, there are search tools available, including *subject trees* (the Web equivalent of a library's subject card catalog) and *search engines* (databases of Web documents that are automatically compiled by programs, called *spiders*, that can detect and index new Web documents). In addition, magazines such as *Internet World* and *NetGuide* report new and interesting sites monthly. Still, many people complain that it's very difficult to locate information on the Web.

Publicity: The Key to an Effective Web Presence
It's not enough just to put your pages on the Web. Sure, they'll be discovered by spiders eventually, and you might attract a few curious surfers. If you want people to visit your site in larger numbers, though, you'll need to devote some time, energy, and possibly money to publicizing your site.

Lack of Audience Measurement Tools

In traditional broadcast media, fairly precise tools exist for measuring both the size and the demographics of the audience. These tools help generate advertising revenue because publishers can describe their audience size with some precision.

On the Web, the only tool that's available for the measurement of audience size is a *hit counter*, a program that records the number of times the page is accessed. However, hit counters can't tell you whether the person accessing the site stuck around to read the material or just surfed through en route to another destination. Worse, a hit counter simply measures how many files have been accessed—and for documents containing a large number of bitmapped graphics, the number might be as high as one or two dozen for a single Web page. *HotWired* magazine records some 600,000 "hits" per day—but estimates that only 6,000 people are accessing the site on a daily basis.

As for demographics, no tools of any kind can automatically detect and record information about what kind of people are accessing a site. However, traditional survey research methods could be adapted to investigate Web usage patterns—and that's exactly what's happening. A.C. Nielsen, the TV ratings company, recently announced a strategic alliance with ASI Market Research and Yankelovich Partners to measure Web site usage, appeal, and impact. Called "ANYwhere Online," the alliance represents "a growing recognition that the World Wide Web and other components of the online world are fast evolving into a major new medium for advertising and commerce."

Like to learn more about Web usage tracking systems? One that's currently under development is called NetCount (http://www.netcount.com). NetCount's objective is to create a Web page rating system that's as accurate—and comprehensible—as the Nielsen TV ratings.

No Established Payment Mechanism

As the previous chapters have explained, Internet and Web users are accustomed to accessing free information. Still, they tell survey researchers that they'd be willing to pay for information that has obvious commercial value. The problem is, how do you collect?

Developed in an academic environment, the HTTP protocols (the standards underlying Web communication) do not include the security and other features required to sell information online. However, a number of Web publishers have developed interim solutions to this problem, and developments in Web security—discussed in Chapter 28—will soon make it possible for your customers to order documents online using Visa and MasterCharge.

One interim solution is to take advantage of the HTTP protocol's authentication standards. In brief, *authentication* is the process of ensuring that a given user, logging on to a site, is in fact the person that he or she claims to be. Most computer systems try to authenticate users by means of a *password*, a string of characters that the user types to identify himself or herself. Most browsers automatically detect the demand for a password and display an appropriate dialog box. One can therefore set up a subscription-based service in which users are charged a monthly fee that enables them to gain access to the system. To be sure, password-based authentication is far from perfect; if users are careless about safeguarding their passwords, others could gain access to your site. Still, password-based authentication is sufficient for many information-vending applications—especially those applications where the information being sold is voluminous and constantly changing, so that an occasional unauthorized access wouldn't cause serious damage.

Pay Mechanisms Are Coming

They're not here yet, but they will be soon. The reason for the delay has to do with the technical difficulties involved, not the lack of a market. Verifone, Inc., the company that makes all those credit-card authorization devices, plans to sell turnkey commercial Web server systems that automatically validate a Web user's credit card information. Other companies are hard at work trying to perfect systems capable of implementing a version of Ted Nelson's "nanobucks" idea: You'd be charged a very small fee, perhaps just a few cents, for viewing a copyrighted document. Information providers would make money if they managed to attract large numbers of viewers.

FROM HERE

- Given the Web's unique characteristics as a publication medium, what can you expect to publish successfully on the Web? Check out the next chapter for a variety of very successful Web publication strategies, ranging from purely voluntary efforts to successful commercial enterprises.

- How does one go about publishing on the Web? See Chapter 6 for a quick introduction to web servers.

Chapter

5

What Can You Publish on the Web?

A s people have gradually understood the Web's unique characteristics as a publication medium, a number of Web publication genres have emerged. (In literature, a *genre* is a particular style or category of writing that emerges as authors try to achieve a certain purpose. As you'll see, the term applies to Web documents as well.)

So that you can fully understand the nature and the potential of the Web as a publishing medium, it's worthwhile to take a look at the Web publishing genres that have emerged thus far. You'll get lots of ideas about what seems to work—and what doesn't—in this unique publishing medium.

This chapter begins with informal Web publishing genres, stressing the efforts of individuals, hobbyists, and volunteers, and moves on to more organized efforts, including corporate presences on the Web. By no means meant to be exhaustive, this chapter surveys some of the more prominent

---

For the Time-Challenged

◆   The unique characteristics of the Web make it ideal for doing the following:

Creating a personal home page
Sharing amateur knowledge
Getting your message out
Organizing political action
Finding an audience for creative work
Creating trailblazer pages
Creating consumer advertising
Creating a stupid Web trick
Creating a zine
Creating an on-line fan club
Supporting communities
Providing documentation
Providing services
Providing self-help support
Sharing your professional knowledge
Educating on the Web
Creating a corporate image
Establishing a marketing presence
Creating advertiser-supported versions of print publications
Creating an on-line shopping catalog
Creating an agent

---

genres of Web publishing activity—but don't be surprised if several new ones have emerged in the year or two following this book's publication!

CREATING A PERSONAL HOME PAGE

ARPAnet, the forerunner of the Internet, was meant to be used solely for technical communication and sharing data related to scientific and military research. To the surprise of the ARPAnet's planners, though, scientists and engineers using the network spent a great deal of time exchanging personal electronic mail and otherwise having fun with the technology newly available to them. The researchers were not content to use the ARPAnet solely as a professional tool; they wanted to make their personalities known to their colleagues. What was intended to be an impersonal, faceless exchange of information became social interaction.

The Web strongly encourages electronic personality sharing. Given the opportunity to share themselves with a potential audience of millions of Web surfers, many people post home pages that feature pictures of themselves and their families, descriptions of professional and hobby interests, and multimedia exhibits, both serious and light.

The best home pages aren't merely monuments to their creators. Good home pages provide useful resources and links to other Web documents. The Web is a project in community authorship, and there's no reason to re-create a resource that's available somewhere else. Make your home page convey your personality, but don't make it the networked equivalent of your vacation slide show. Make it useful to people so they'll want to return again and again. The home page of Meng Weng Wong (Figure 5.1) is a good example.

 Like to see more individuals' home pages? Check out WhoWhere's personal home page directory:

http://homepages.whowhere.com

You can search by keywords or browse by interest area.

SHARING YOUR AMATEUR KNOWLEDGE

Lots of Web pages exist to share hobby and avocational information with the Web community. These pages aren't authoritative resources in the same way, say, that government publications or corporate press releases are, but they're wonderful for hobbyists and casual communities of people with common interests. Usually, the people who post pages containing amateur knowledge aren't certified authorities—how do you certify a kite expert, or an expert stamp collector, anyhow?—but they have some sort of experience that's valuable to others.

The Web lends itself to, among so many other things, swapping information among amateurs. Just as model airplane enthusiasts gather at hobby shops to exchange tips, they can gather online to do the same thing. The Web and the other resources the Internet provides enable practitioners of obscure hobbies, or hobbyists who are geographically far removed from others with similar interests, to participate in communities of hobbyists.

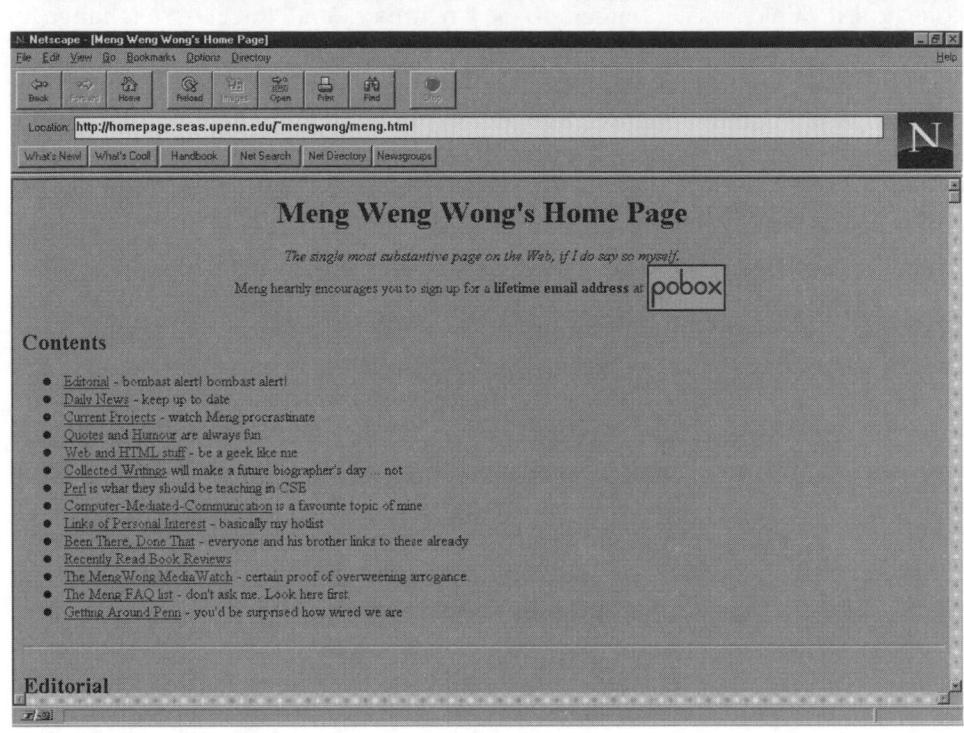

Figure 5.1   Meng Weng Wong's Home Page
http://homepage.seas.upenn.edu/~mengwong/meng.html

The Burrito Page (Figure 5.2) covers burritos, the ever-popular Mexican dish, in depth. It's not likely you'd find burrito information anywhere but on an amateur page.

GETTING YOUR MESSAGE OUT

Give people a soapbox, and they'll think of something to say. Lots of Web sites have to do with people who, regardless of whether anyone agrees with them or even cares, think they have been wronged. There are sites relating to whistleblowers—people who risk their jobs by exposing illegal or unethical situations in their places of work—and criminal defendants who feel

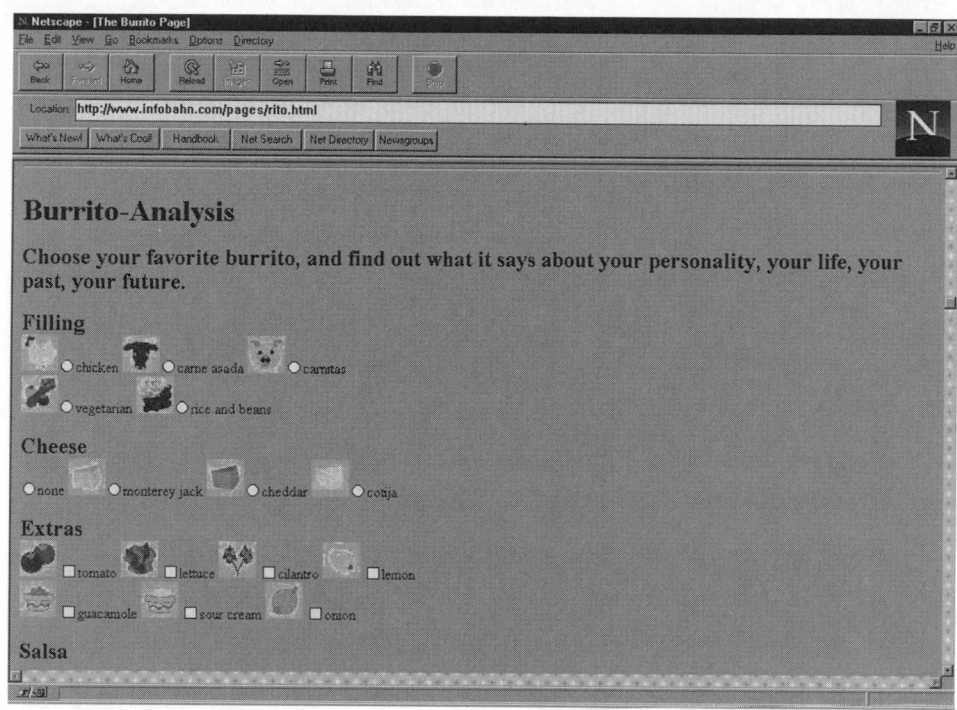

Figure 5.2 The Burrito Page
http://www.infobahn.com/pages/rito.html

they've been wrongly accused. One of the most elaborate sites of this genre is that of the Leonard Peltier Defense Committee, which has worked to free Indian-rights activist Leonard Peltier from prison since he was convicted in 1975 of killing two FBI agents. The Foundation's site (Figure 5.3) features Peltier's account of what happened the day the agents were killed, and calls for surfer support of his cause.

The Web lends itself to the genre of calling for support of a cause. Few of the traditional media of cause champions—handbills and small-press books—can present this kind of information with the professional look of the Web, and certainly no traditional medium offers comparably broad distribution.

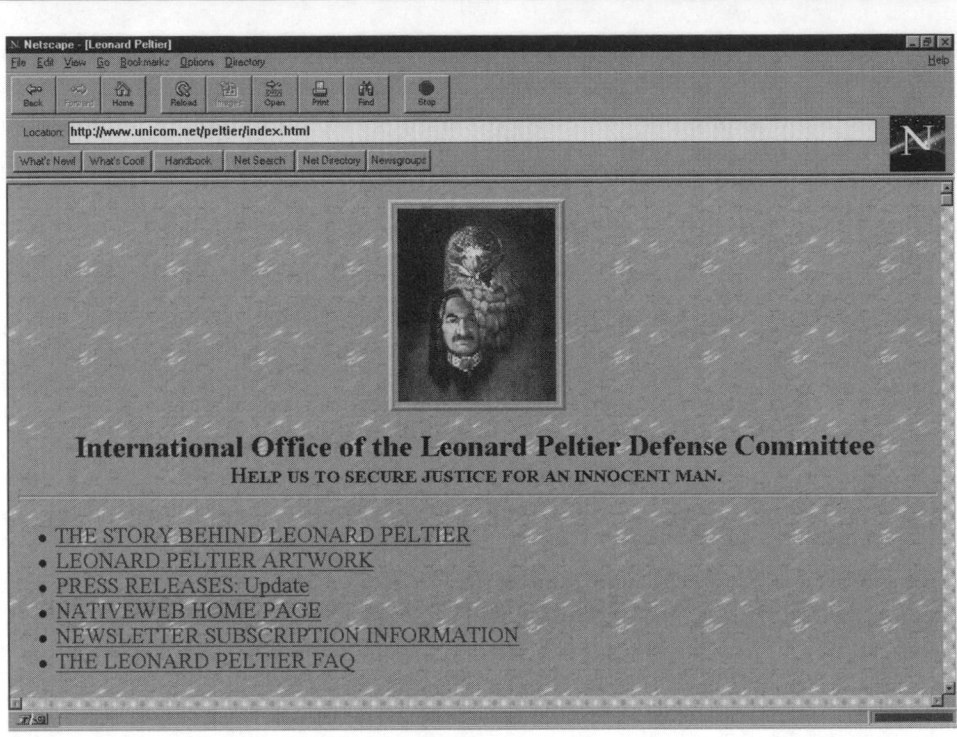

Figure 5.3   The Leonard Peltier Defense Committee Page
http://www.unicom.net/peltier/index.html

The Web gives a professional look and wide distribution to soapbox-type presentations. Whether it garners them any more attention from the general public remains to be seen.

ORGANIZING POLITICAL ACTION

Sites that attempt to organize political activity are different from informational sites in that they try to draw viewers into the cause and get them to act. Though political action may be implicit in sites that get a message out, political action sites call for participation.

The nice thing about organizing political activity on the Web is that you can make a strong logical case for your cause. It's easy to attach supporting documents to your site, to be read at your viewers' leisure. While traditional political organization techniques rely on slogans, brief examples, and high emotional content, a Web political action site can combine those things with rational statements of position.

On the other hand, political action sites lack the charisma factor that fuels traditional political movements. It's hard to rally around a leader when he or she is represented only by a static picture, a thirty-second audio file, and perhaps a video clip. You'll have to weigh both of these characteristics when you incorporate a Web site into a political movement.

Though it's maintained by an individual, the Nature Conservancy site (Figure 5.4) is a good example of a site that promotes a political cause.

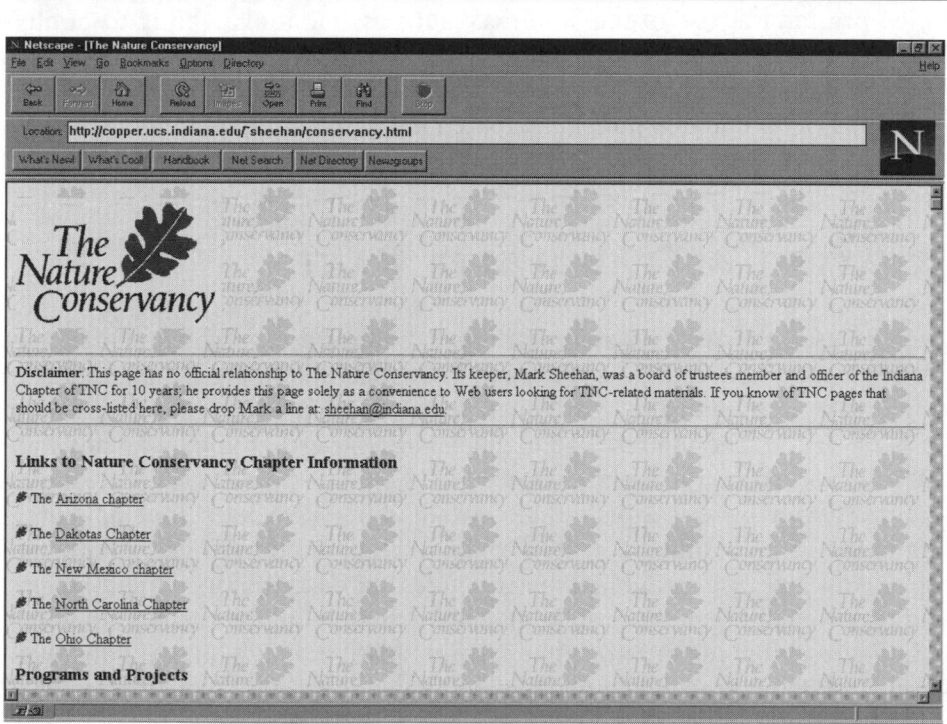

Figure 5.4 The Nature Conservancy
http://copper.ucs.indiana.edu/~sheehan/conservancy.html

FINDING AN AUDIENCE FOR CREATIVE WORK

Once, it was very difficult to publish paintings, photographs, and short sto-ries because there were so few venues for publication. There were maga-zines, but these magazines had a limited number of pages and could contain only so much material in an issue. Outlets for creative work were few, for a very uncreative reason: the limited capabilities of printing presses, paper mills, and broadcast media such as television, radio, and film.

The Web, in some ways, is like a magazine with an unlimited number of pages and free global circulation. If your artwork can be recorded in com-puter-readable form (computers cannot handle some media, such as feature-length film or ballet, easily), you can publish it to an audience that will soon exceed one billion people.

With ease of publication often comes a decline in the quality of what is published. Just as the advent of desktop publishing software meant anybody could put together a font- and clip-art-laden document without paying a skilled printer, the rise of the Web makes it possible for anybody to publish their boring short stories or whangingly melodramatic teenage-angst poems. The best sites, such as SITO (Figure 5.5), have some sort of selection criteria that keeps the quality of published material high.

CREATING A TRAILBLAZER PAGE

If you've used the Web for anything other than random surfing, chances are you've developed a hotlist containing links that likely would be useful to people with interests similar to yours. In the spirit of sharing that exists on the Web, and in the interest of making things easier for you, why not pub-lish your hotlist on a trailblazer page?

A trailblazer page is a page that contains little data itself, but has meta-data in the form of links to other sites or pages that contain useful informa-tion. If you give your trailblazer page a title that describes its subject clearly, your page will appear when someone uses a search engine, such as InfoSeek or Lycos, to hunt for sites on that subject. Also, make a link to your trail-blazer page from your home page, or set your browser to go to it every time you start using the Web.

Nothing says a trailblazer page has to deal with a deadly serious topic. The only requirement is that the page provide lots of links to resources that relate to a particular topic. The Fox Box (Figure 5.6) is one of the best trail-blazer pages on the Web.

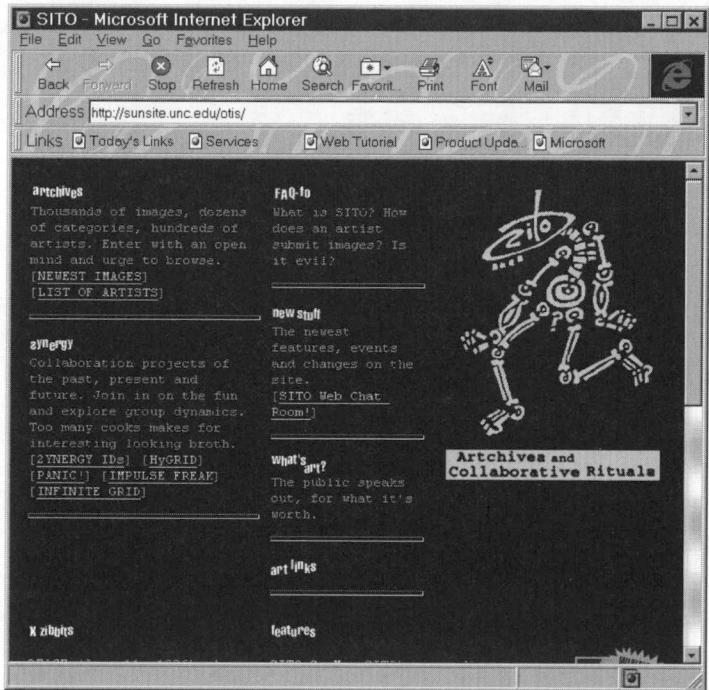

Figure 5.5 SITO
http://sunsite.unc.edu/otis/

CREATING CONSUMER ADVERTISING

Advertising on the Web isn't the same as advertising in a broadcast medium. Not only do consumers reach company propaganda by different means, they can post statements about products themselves. Consumer advertising is a natural—if people really like (or really hate) a product, nothing can stop them from saying so on the Web, as long as they operate within the constraints of copyright and libel law. Consumer advertising on the Web is traditional word-of-mouth advertising taken to a higher level, since instead of being able to speak to a few people in their neighborhoods or at work, Web users can post their opinions of products for millions of people to see.

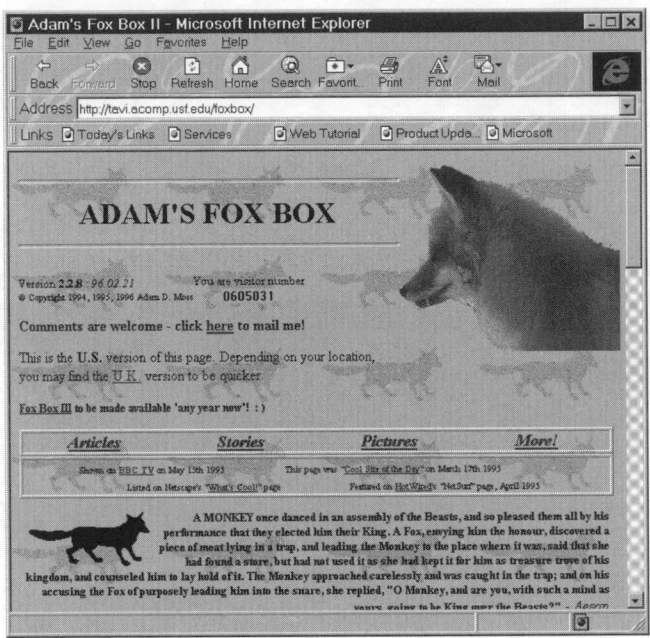

Figure 5.6   The Fox Box
http://tavi.acomp.usf.edu/foxbox/

Barbie dolls, for reasons unknown, are among the products most heavily advertised by consumers on the Web. The Barbie Page (Figure 5.7) praises Barbie, in her various incarnations, to the stars—but the site has no affiliation with Mattel, Barbie's maker.

CREATING A STUPID WEB TRICK

A significant portion of the Web community is composed of college students and computer programmers, which means frivolity is bound to permeate the Web. Plenty of sites exist to entertain Web users, and they often do so in a way that reflects their creator's unique—and technically impressive—skills.

Foam Bath Fish Time (Figure 5.8) is a great example. It's technology for technology's sake, since no one logs onto the Web to check the time. It's

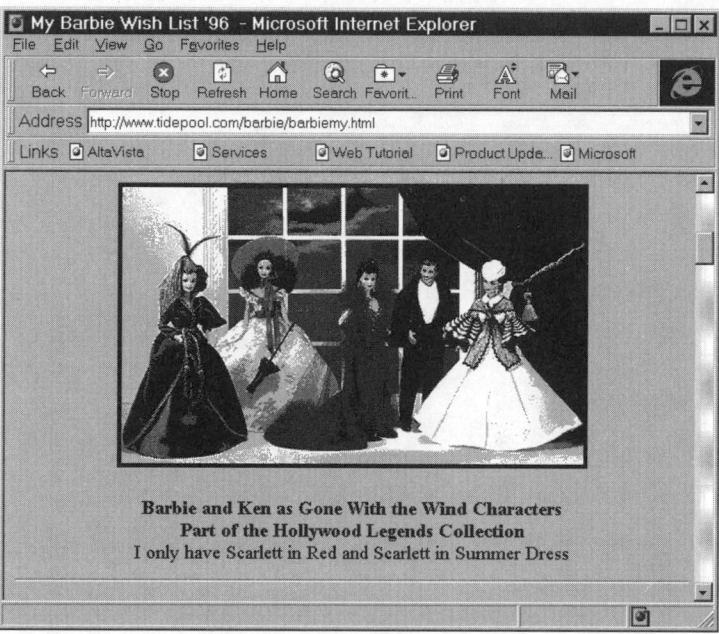

Figure 5.7 My Barbie Collection
http://www.tidepool.com/barbie/barbiemy.html

kind of cool, though, to see how the programmer used a Perl script (his first Perl effort) to combine the time of day with images of kids' bath toys. Sure it's silly, but that's the point.

CREATING A ZINE

Zines are like other outlets for creative work, except that they have a coherent theme and style unto themselves and usually change regularly, like print magazines. Zines combine qualities of amateur information sites with qualities of outlets for creative efforts.

Print zines exist, but even they, noted for their wild content and bizarre illustration, cannot match the level of weirdness of Web zines. Furthermore,

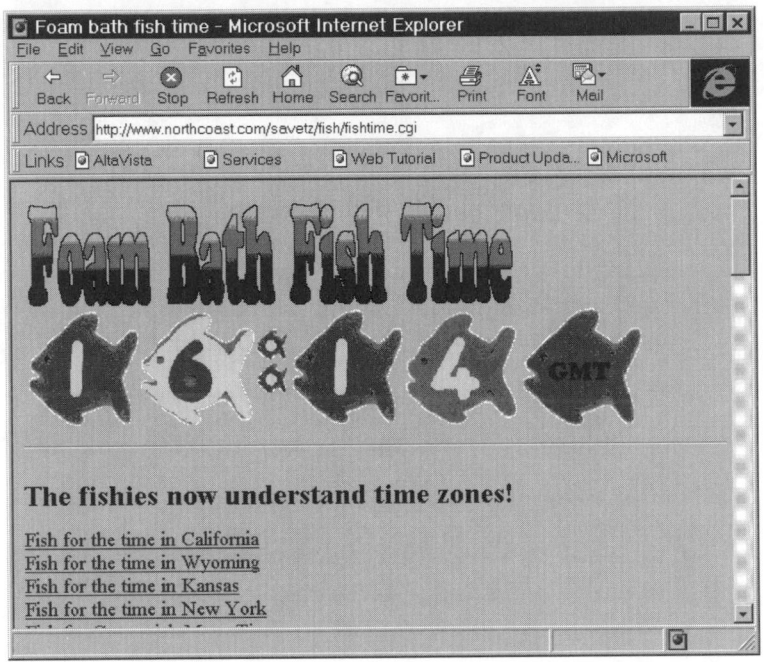

Figure 5.8   Foam Bath Fish Time
http://www.northcoast.com/savetz/fish/fishtime.cgi

print zines come out infrequently, as their often financially strapped publishers struggle to put out each issue.

The Web's free global circulation and virtually zero startup costs guarantee Web zine publishers an advantage over their print counterparts. The best zines, such as Word (Figure 5.9) are edited carefully, just like print publications. Some Web zines are truly odd—there seems to be sort of a competition among zine publishers to see who can put out the strangest publication and embrace the weirdest genre of literature.

Thinking about making money with a zine? You'd best be aware that very few online magazines have managed to attract advertising. A number of well-funded Web magazine ventures have gone under, with heavy losses, because they were unable to interest advertisers.

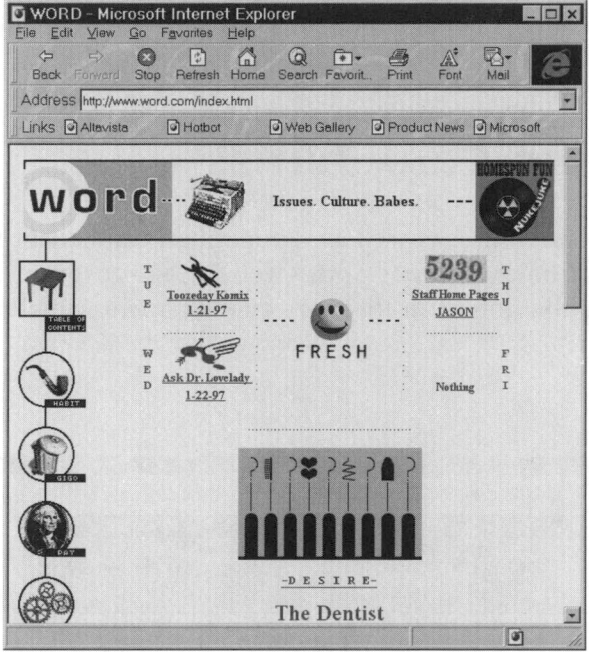

Figure 5.9 Word
http://www.word.com

CREATING AN ONLINE FAN CLUB

The trouble with being a fan of a little-loved actor or musician is that there are few people with whom to share your passion—and even fewer of them live near you. In the past you had to spend money on a small-circulation fan zine, or go to fan conventions and incur large travel and time costs.

Fan clubs exploded on the Web because it amplifies the good parts of clubs—access to such items as bootleg recordings and information about performances—while reducing the effort involved. There's no longer a need to travel to real-life meetings when the exchange that occurs at such meeting happens every day on the Web. More fans can become involved in the club and a community can be maintained, not just formed and quickly dissolved as fan-club communities often are.

Pete Lambie's Bruce Springsteen Page (Figure 5.10), like others devoted to Springsteen's music, enables an online fan community to share information and enjoy each other's personalities without traveling.

SUPPORTING COMMUNITIES

Geographic communities, as well as virtual ones, can benefit from the information-distribution capabilities of the Web. Unlike government-access cable television or public notices in local print newspapers, which are not access-

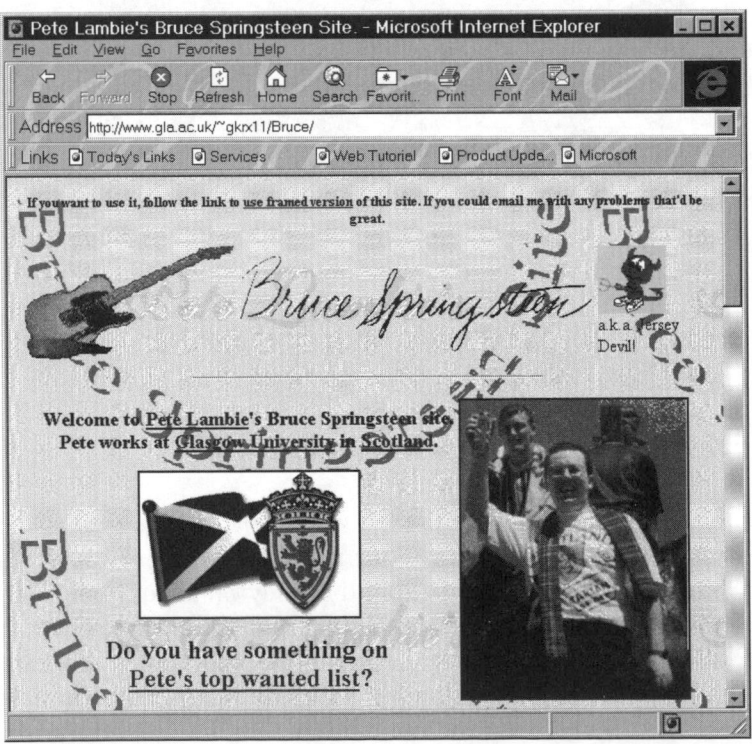

Figure 5.10   Pete Lambie's Bruce Springsteen Page
http://www.gla.ac.uk/~gkrx11/Bruce/

on-demand systems, the Web offers the citizens of a town or city ready access to government information whenever they need it. Tax information, city council agendas, and school data, when posted to the Web, can be had whenever citizens need them.

Community Web pages grew out of the desire of communities to provide information effectively, but also sprang from the same spirit of boosterism that inspired towns in the American midwest to build grand hotels and railroad stations in the last decades of the nineteenth century. A town with a slick, information-rich Web site has bragging rights that less-wired communities lack. The town of Blacksburg, Virginia, has received international attention for its Web site (Figure 5.11).

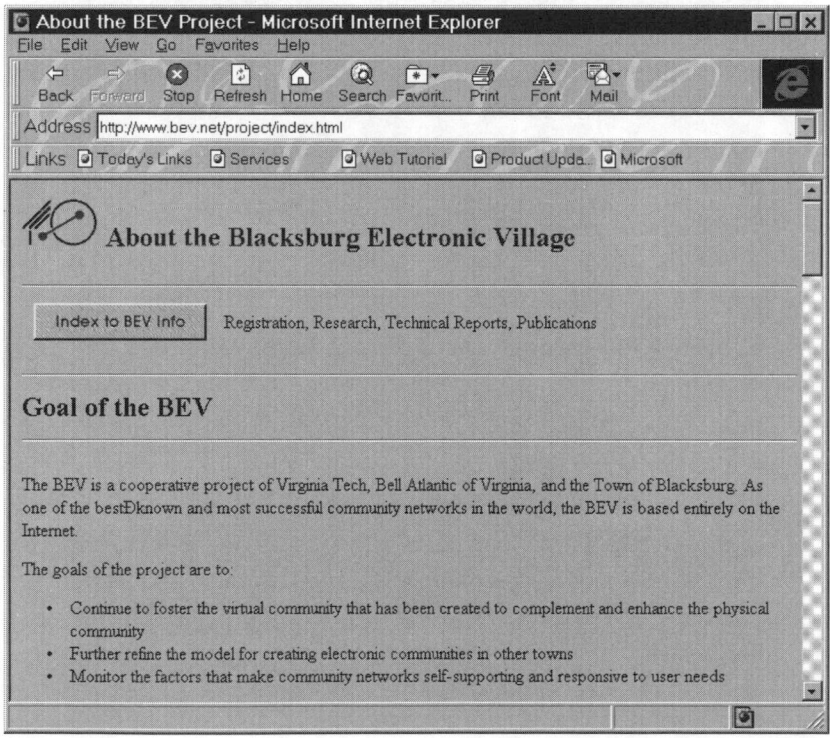

Figure 5.11 Blacksburg Electronic Village Home Page
http://www.bev.net/

PROVIDING DOCUMENTATION

The Web, though its composition is changing, is made up largely of computer experts. Many people who use the Web write software for a living—and for fun—and some of their efforts get published as shareware or public domain software. The Web is a natural place to provide documentation (the manuals and other information that—in theory, anyway—help you use software) and support (answers to questions and solutions to problems) for software.

Documentation sites aren't just for small-time computer hobbyists, either. Microsoft has a giant archive of software that includes bug fixes and extensions for its many popular programs. Popular programming languages, such as Perl, have support sites on the Web, too (Figure 5.12).

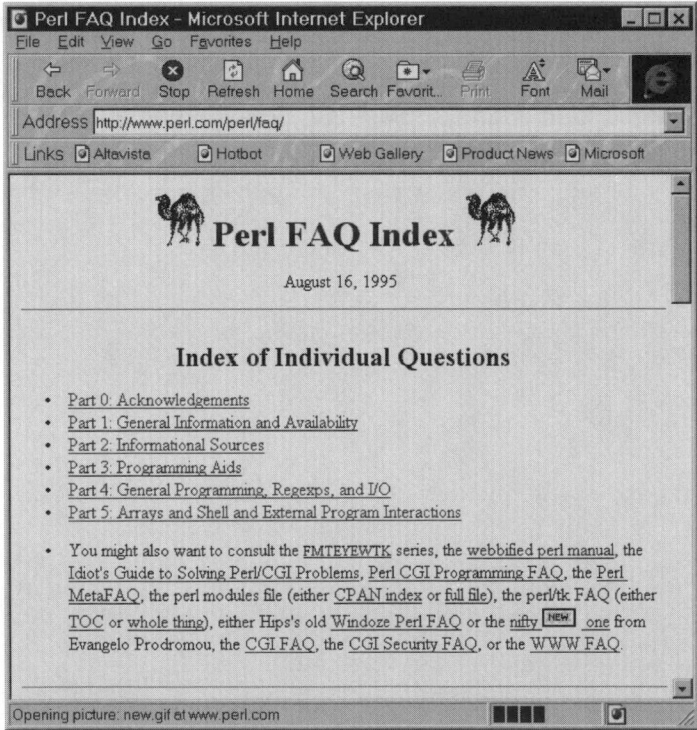

Figure 5.12   The Perl FAQ
http://www.perl.com/

If you want to get information out to computer users, there's no better way to do it than publication on the biggest computer network in the world.

PROVIDING SERVICES

The real-time capabilities of the Web make it useful to companies that want to provide better service to their customers. Companies who have traditionally used toll-free telephone lines and dozens of attendants have turned to the Web to take some of the load off their customer service departments and give customers a sense that the company is on the leading edge of customer-service thinking.

The best service sites are no-frills deals; there's often little to them except a search engine and a very simple interface. At the Federal Express site (Figure 5.13), for example, you can enter a package tracking number and see where a package is en route to its destination.

PROVIDING SELF-HELP SUPPORT

Sometimes, people are drawn together by something less frivolous than love of a band or other celebrity. Dozens of Web sites have sprung up to support people with a common experience, such as an illness or handicapping condition.

These sites have developed for the same reason as fan club sites, but perhaps the motivations are even stronger. While fans of a musician may not care enough about being a fan to travel to a convention and thus miss out on some interesting talk and good companionship, people who cannot, for medical or financial reasons, participate in a support group may miss life-saving information or medically valuable support.

The best community support sites provide lots of data—such as vendors of special equipment or lists of doctors with particular specialties—and encourage interaction among community members. Often, such sites are affiliated with a mailing list, Usenet newsgroup, or other discussion facilitation device. The alt.support.stop-smoking Home Page (Figure 5.14) is associated with the Usenet newsgroup alt.support.stop-smoking.

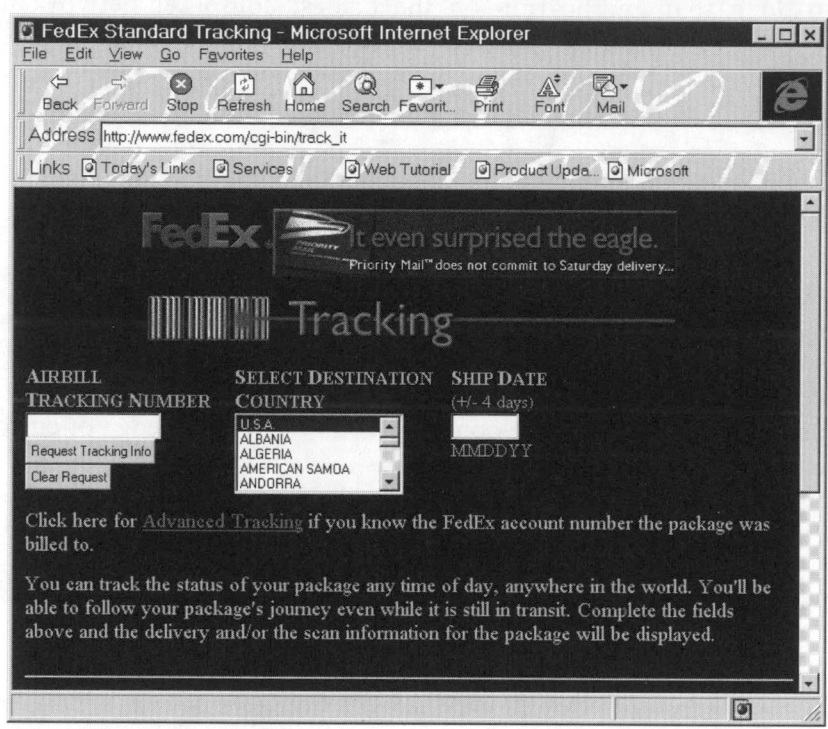

Figure 5.13   FedEx tracking
http://www.fedex.com/cgi-bin/track_it

SHARING YOUR PROFESSIONAL KNOWLEDGE

For now, anyway, many people who use the Web have valuable professional knowledge. The Web was created to provide a way for nuclear physicists to share information, and it came of age in academic institutions, where professors and students posted information they felt would be useful to others.

The Web, with its spirit of sharing and free access to information, encourages people to give of themselves online. Even if yours is an arcane discipline like chinchilla genetics (Figure 5.15), somebody may appreciate that you posted some of your knowledge to the Web.

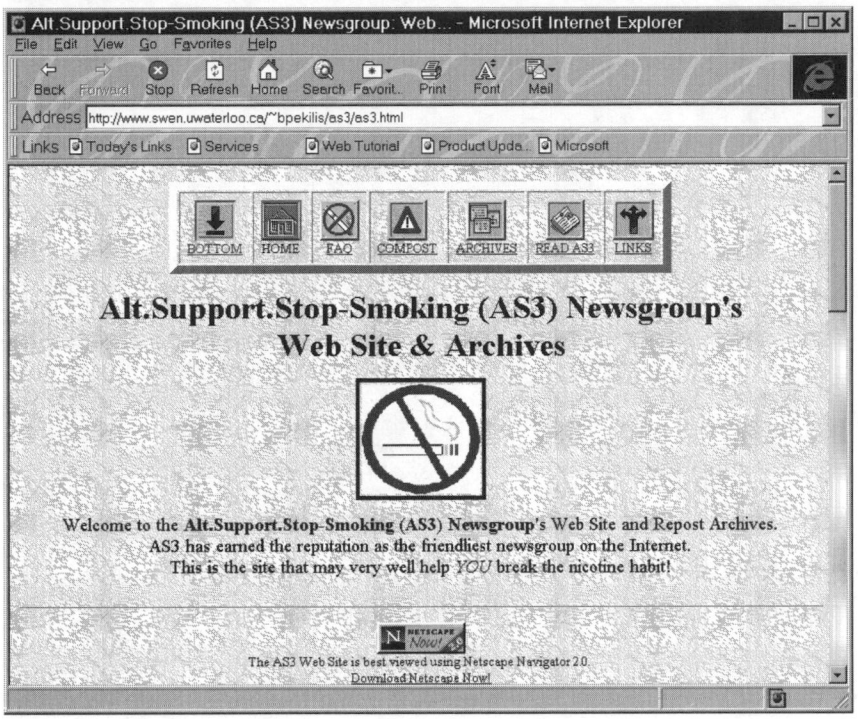

Figure 5.14 The alt.support.stop-smoking Home Page
http://www.swen.uwaterloo.ca/~bpekilis/as3/as3.html

EDUCATING ON THE WEB

Sharing professional information is what education is all about, so it makes sense that instructors at all levels and in all specialties have employed the Web as an instructional tool—sort of a high-tech blackboard. Since the Web is available to far more college professors and students than elementary and secondary students, most use of the Web as a teaching device is at the college and university level. Professors typically post pages containing links to sites they consider useful to their classes, and often include reference information such as syllabi and grading standards.

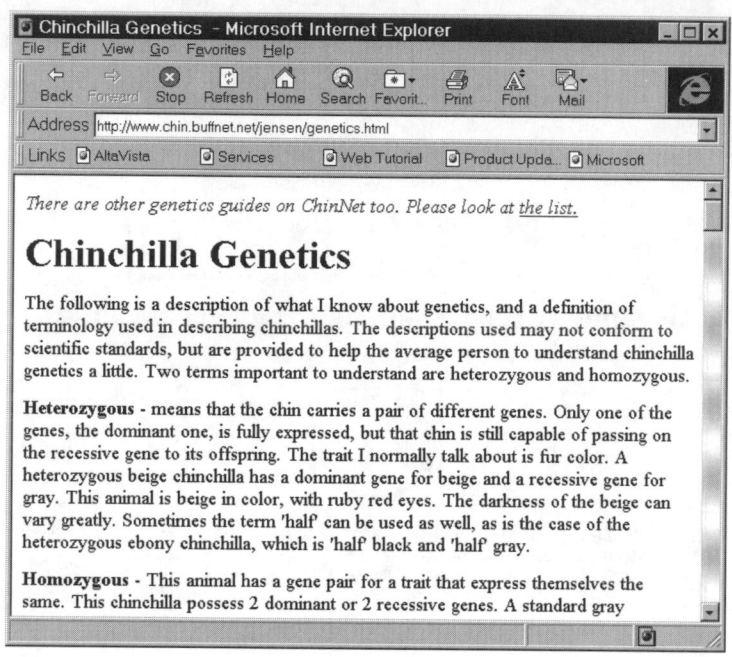

Figure 5.15   Chinchilla Genetics
http://www.chin.buffnet.net/jensen.genetic.html

Professor John Unsworth of the Institute for Advanced Technology in the Humanities at the University of Virginia used a Web page (Figure 5.16) as part of his class "Engineering the Self in the Late Twentieth Century."

CREATING A CORPORATE IMAGE

The Web is still sufficiently avante garde that companies with sites are considered by many people to be technologically savvy. By investing some money in a site that doesn't try to sell a particular product but instead projects a high-tech corporate image, a company can claim to be participating in a hot new medium and show itself to be willing to embrace new technology. Sites that attempt to create a corporate image likely will soon be

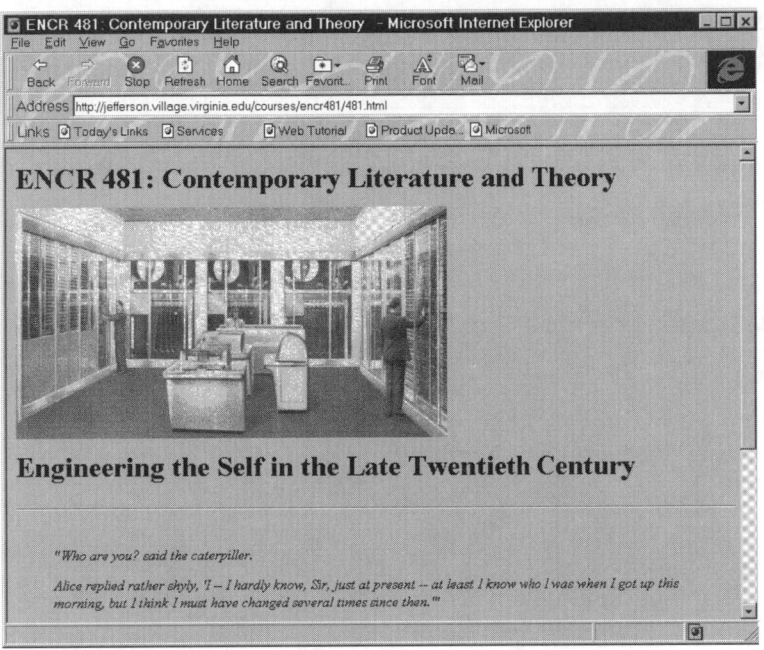

Figure 5.16 Engineering the Self in the Late Twentieth Century
http://jefferson.village.virginia.edu/courses/encr481/481.html

combined with sites that serve a marketing function by providing product information and purchase opportunities.

AT&T doesn't try to sell particular goods or services at its site (Figure 5.17), but it tries to show AT&T as a high-tech, growing company.

ESTABLISHING A MARKETING PRESENCE

Marketing presences appeared on the Web when corporations, particularly sellers of hardware and software, found that the Web was populated by people who had a great deal of influence over their organizations' purchasing decisions. Companies put information about their products online in

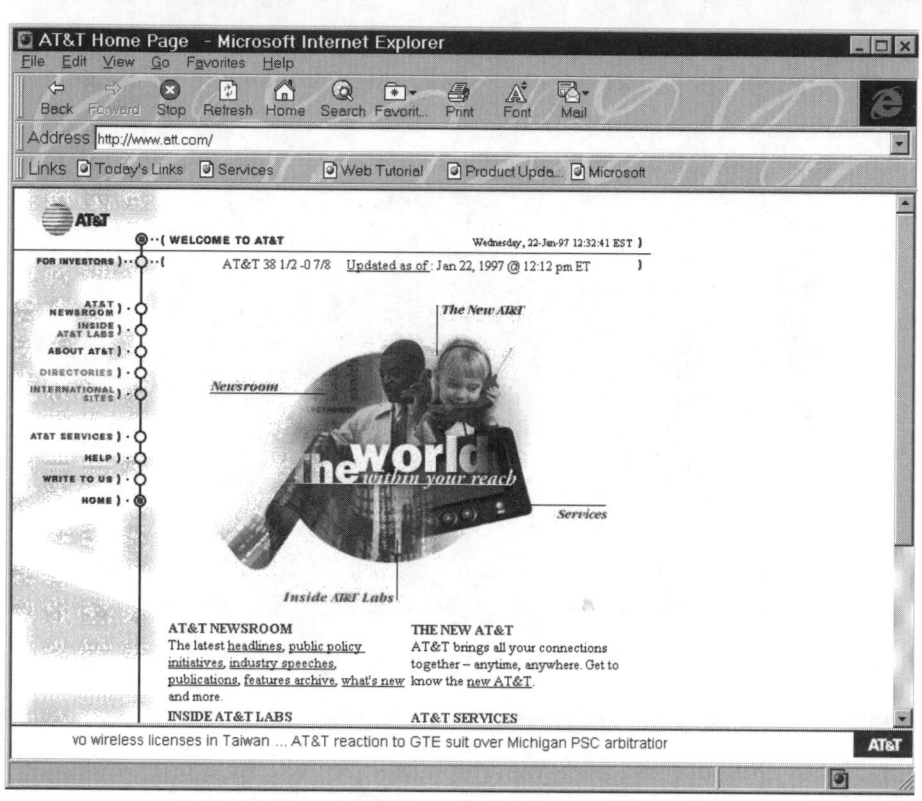

Figure 5.17   AT&T Home Page
http://www.att.com/

hopes that professionals, when preparing to make purchases, would think of products they saw advertised on the Web.

Unlike AT&T's site, Sun Microsystems' site (Figure 5.18) includes lots of product information and instructions on how to order hardware and software. It's an active pitch, instead of a passive display.

With the forms capabilities of today's graphical browsers, it's possible to create interactive Web documents that solicit user opinion. Firms can ask for feedback on products, policies, service, and more. The result won't be scientific—the Web-browsing population has its own unique characteristics—but the information could prove of value as long as it's kept in perspective.

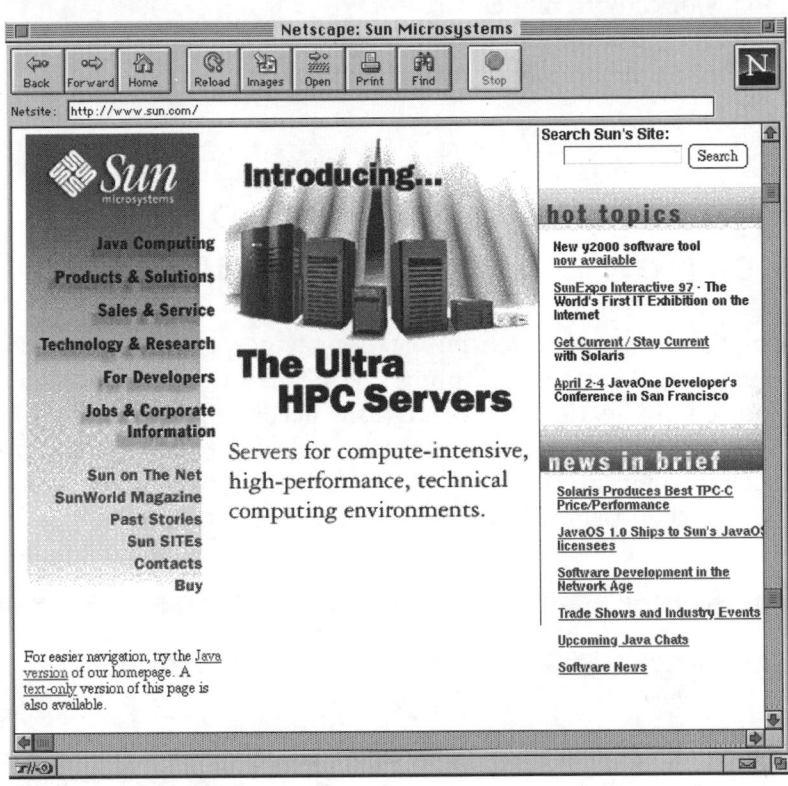

Figure 5.18 Sun Microsystems' home page
http://www.sun.com

CREATING DIGITAL VERSIONS OF PRINT PUBLICATIONS: ADVERTISER-SUPPORTED

The Web has attracted lots of attention from publishers who have been successful in print publications and want to project their influence and expertise into the Web environment. Some magazines and newspapers have created better-looking and more popular Web editions than others.

Advertiser-supported Web publications exist for two reasons. First, it is (or, at least, was, before the question of accurately measuring site visits arose) fairly easy to sell advertisers on the idea of putting an ad where millions of people could see it. Second, it took some time for Web design techniques to allow the construction of subscription-based pages that allowed publishers to collect money directly from their readers.

People Magazine's online edition (Figure 5.19) had ads for Purina and Women's Wire at the bottom of its welcome page.

CREATING DIGITAL VERSIONS OF PRINT PUBLICATIONS: SUBSCRIBER-SUPPORTED

The alternative to unsupported publications (zines, generally) and advertising-supported publications is support by means of subscription. Subscription-supported publications grew out of the needs of publishers who wanted to take advantage of the distribution potential of the Web but did not want to put out information, such as financial tables or real estate listings, that might cut into their print-edition sales and revenue stream.

Figure 5.19 *People Magazine*
http://www.pathfinder.com/people/

The Money and Investing Update (Figure 5.20), an online publication of the *Wall Street Journal,* gives free access to some features, but restricts others to the use of people who have paid a subscription fee. The site also offers a free trial subscription to those who want to try before they buy.

CREATING DIGITAL VERSIONS OF PRINT PUBLICATIONS: INTRANETS

One of the hottest growth areas in Web publishing involves migrating print-based corporate publications to the Web. In many companies, a huge amount of money is expended to write, edit, and publish print-based manuals (including phone directories, employee manuals, technical manuals, directories, internal catalogs, and much more). Huge savings can be realized by moving these documents to the Web. What's more, the material is more

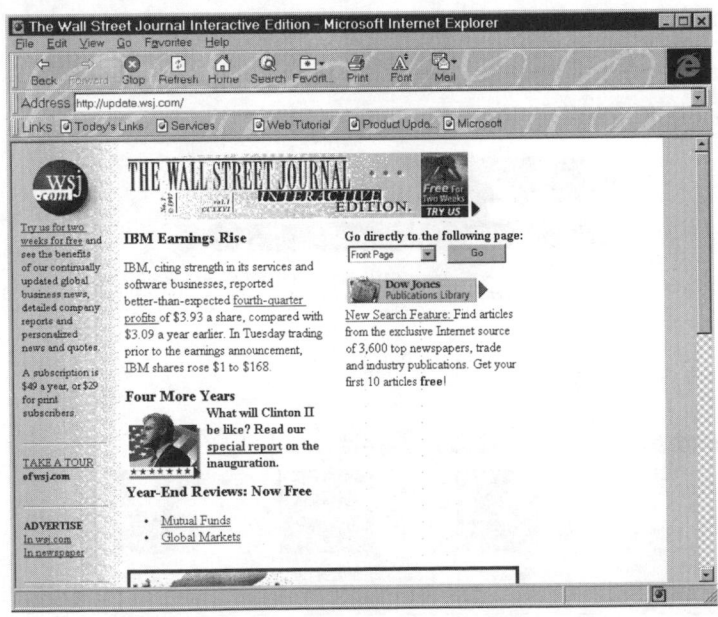

Figure 5.20   Money and Investing Update
http://update.wsj.com/

up-to-date, since changes can be made on the fly (without requiring republication of the entire manual).

CREATING AN ONLINE SHOPPING CATALOG

Shopping catalogs sprang up on the Web when entrepreneurs saw a way to offer products to consumers without investing a lot of money in a physical store or inventory. By creating a few pages that listed goods for sale and providing a toll-free telephone number or secure Net connection, business people could sell things and incur little cost except to cover server access and time.

Some of the most popular shopping catalogs contain listings of recorded music—records, tapes, and compact discs for sale. Sites like CDNow (Figure 5.21) have search engines that give prices and availability for thousands of recordings.

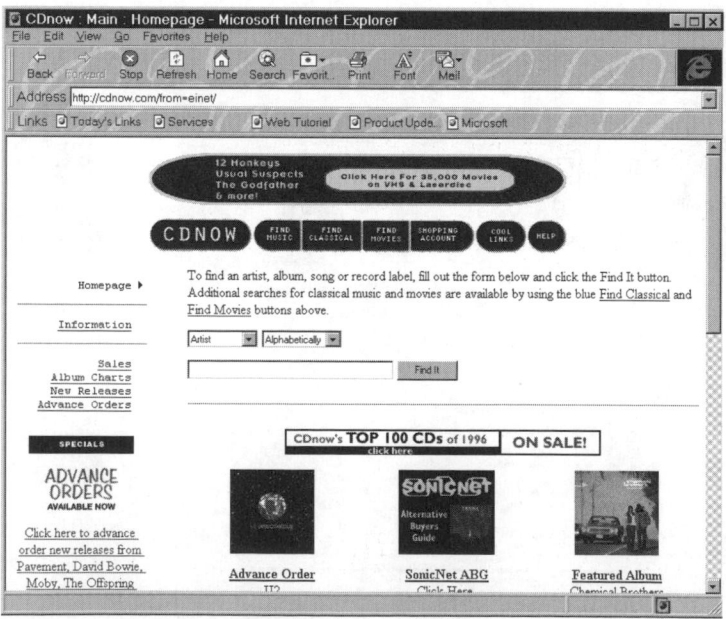

Figure 5.21   CDNow
http://cdnow.com/from=einet/

Shopping catalogs will have to adapt—in favor of the consumer—to accommodate agents.

CREATING AN AGENT

Agents take Web commerce to a higher level. Instead of merely offering something and charging for it, agent sites include search routines that hunt for a particular item of information or product and find the best price. Agents throw a wrench into the plans of Web merchants who counted on using advertising or links to high-traffic sites such as search engines to help ensure their sites' success.

Agents, like Andersen Consulting's BargainFinder (Figure 5.22), have two of the Web's core characteristics. They promote free access to information, in that they make the best price on a given product or item of information

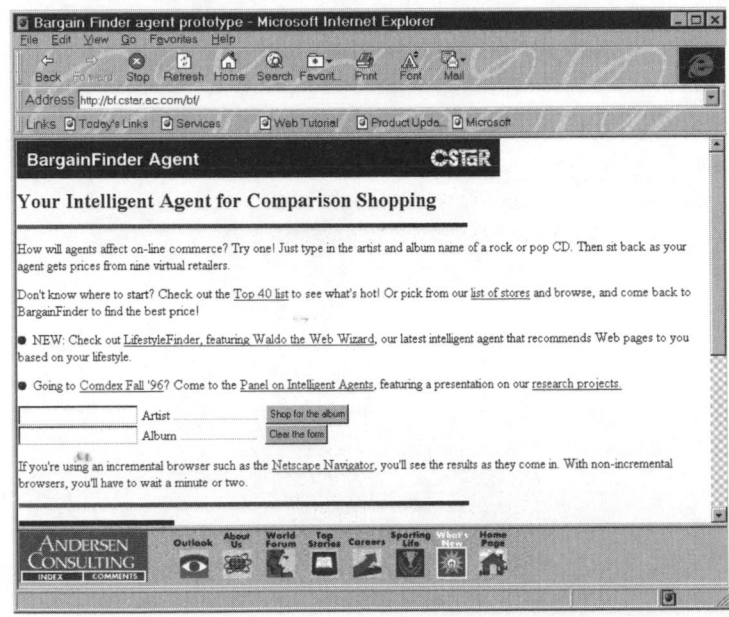

Figure 5.22 Andersen Consulting BargainFinder Agent
http://bf.cstar.ac.com/bf/

available to people who aren't willing to hunt for it on their own. Also, they are essentially hacks—really cool programming tricks that accomplish a task in a novel way.

From Here

- Like to know more about what it takes to publish on the Web? Check out Chapter 6.

- To get started on designing your Web site, flip to Part II.

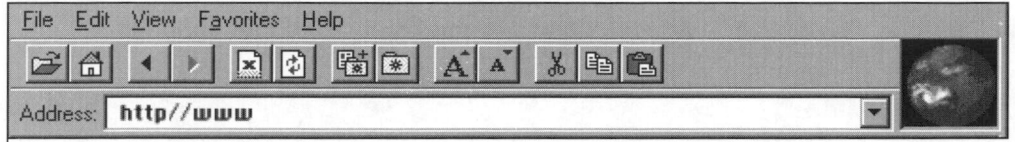

File Edit View Favorites Help

Address: http//www

Part II

DESIGNING

YOUR WEB

Chapter

6

Choosing a Web Server

I n previous chapters, you've learned what makes the Web a distinctive publishing medium. To understand your Web publishing options fully, there's one more important chunk of information that you need to grasp: the technical basis by which Web pages are made accessible to people using Web browsers. In order to make your Web pages accessible, you'll need to place them on an Internet-connected computer that's running a *Web server*, a program that fields browsers' requests for information and doles out the requested documents.

The subject of this chapter is technical, but it doesn't require any technical expertise to read and understand. Its goal is to orient you, not to drag you through every last detail concerning Web servers. And once you've finished reading it, you'll know what you're up against when you want to make your Web pages accessible to others.

♦   Web servers receive browsers' requests for information, run scripts, ensure security, and provide statistics on access.

♦   You'll need to decide whether to run your own Web server or obtain space on a system where Web server software is already installed (a commercial system, or one at school or work).

♦   To run your own Web server, you'll need an Internet connection with a permanent IP address.

♦   Windows 95 is Microsoft's entry-level operating system. Not a true 32-bit operating system, it is designed to run existing 16-bit Windows programs. However, it also contains all the resources necessary to run 32-bit Windows programs, with advanced multithreading capabilities. Designed with excellent Internet support built in, Windows 95 is an excellent choice for a Web server platform.

WHAT WEB SERVERS DO

A Web server is a program that fields requests for information from Web browsers, runs scripts, and provides a variety of additional functions, including the vital one of ensuring the security of the host system.

Dishing Out Documents

The most important function of a Web browser is to intercept requests from Web browsers and deliver electronic copies of the requested documents—or an error message, if the requested document is not available. Such requests are made using the HTTP protocol.

Web servers are *stateless programs*. This means simply that the server software does not remember anything about previous transactions with a server. In the course of downloading a document, a server must establish a distinct connection for *each part* of a retrieved document—the text, each in-line graphic, each multimedia object. This design enables the server to field requests from dozens, or even hundreds, of browsers simultaneously.

The stateless design of Web servers ensures that many browsers can access the server simultaneously, but it also means that Web servers consume big chunks of computer system resources (memory and processing time). Just think about it—a request comes in over the network for a document or graphic, which are stored on disk. The document or graphic must be read from the disk and transferred to the network. That adds up to a lot of byte crunching. You can draw one conclusion from this right now: If you're thinking about running Web server software, you'd better be prepared to set the computer aside for exclusive use as a Web server.

 Don't be misled by claims that such-and-such a page has received several hundred thousand or millions of hits per day—that doesn't mean that huge numbers of people are accessing the page. To download a relatively complex document that has dozens of inline images, the browser and server may establish dozens of completely independent connections, each of which will be recorded as a hit. There's still no reliable *technical* way to estimate how many distinct individuals are accessing a given Web site. That's why Nielsen and other media assessment firms are developing surveys and other techniques for measuring the popularity of Web sites.

Any Web server can dish out a document, but servers vary in their capacity to handle the fine points of this function. For example, CERN's HTTPD cannot send certain error messages unless a programmed script is provided. Some shareware and freeware servers do not automatically respond to a browser's request to send a document only if it has not been modified since a certain date (this is a very desirable feature; without it, the browser will download the document from the network rather than loading it from the disk cache, which is considerably faster).

Running Scripts

Web servers also provide another important function, running *scripts*. A script is a short computer program that is needed to support the interactive features of HTML, such as fill-in forms and searches.

As you will learn in Part III of this book, it's relatively easy to insert HTML tags for interactive features, such as option buttons, drop-down list boxes, and fill-in text boxes. However, these features do not *do* anything in the absence of scripts. When someone using one of your pages fills in a form and clicks the Submit button, nothing will happen unless you have provided a script that is specifically designed to deal with this action.

When you access a Web page that contains an interactive element, such as a fill-in form, you'll see a Submit button (or an equivalent). When you click this button, the page originates a message, which is basically a URL: It points to the exact location of the script. The server intercepts the message, locates the script, and executes it. The script performs the requested action and generates a new Web page, which is sent to the server; finally, the browser displays the new page. All scripts work in this manner.

With most servers, scripts can be written in any programming language—preferably, one that's suited to the type of computer on which the server software is runnning. On Windows systems, for example, the scripting language of choice is Visual Basic, while Perl is the preferred choice for UNIX systems. Some servers (such as MacHTTP) require a specific language (MacHTTP requires AppleScript).

Can a nonprogrammer learn to write scripts? If you've got some time, the answer is almost certainly yes. For most computers, you can obtain scripts that are ready to use after minor modification. To be sure, you'll need to learn some of the basics of the programming language in which the script is written. If you don't have the time to write scripts, you can find programmers who can do it—but be prepared to pay a hefty price for this service, which is very much in demand.

Ensuring Security

A third vital function of Web servers is ensuring security. Web servers vary considerably in the number and quality of security options that they offer. More than any other single factor, security features distinguish commercial server software from freeware and shareware efforts.

The following list details the ways in which Web server software protects the host system as well as the people accessing the host system by means of Web browsers:

- **Password authentication**   The server demands a login name and password from people attempting to access the system.

- **Prohibited access**   The server excludes accesses from certain IP addresses or domain names. Some servers can be set up to restrict access so that no one outside an organization, community, state, or country can log in to the site.

- **File security**   The server ensures that outsiders cannot access files in any directories other than those set aside for Web documents.

- **Confidentiality** The server accepts encrypted data using the S-HTTP or SSL security protocols, or both (see Chapter 28). This feature ensures that people using secure browsers (such as Netscape Navigator) can upload credit card information without fear of its being intercepted en route.

Logging

A fourth function of Web servers is to provide access statistics. Often, it's necessary to install additional software to provide these statistics, but it's well worth doing so; without statistics, you have no way of knowing how often your site is being accessed and which documents people access the most. Increasingly, this vital function is being built into server software. Here's what logging software can tell you:

- Which browsers people are using.

- How often your site is accessed each day, broken down by the hour.

- Which documents people are accessing the most.

- How many new accesses you're receiving each day.

- Which countries are accessing your site.

SHOULD YOU RUN YOUR OWN SERVER?

Anyone interested in Web publishing is faced with this question—and it shouldn't be taken lightly. Your choices boil down to the following:

- **Setting up your own server** You'll need a fast Internet connection, a Web server program, a PC or workstation that you can set aside for Web publishing, and time to configure and maintain the system.

- **Using a server at school or work** If you're attending a school or working for an organization that has a Web server, you may be able to install your presentation on the same computer (or one that's networked to this computer). Chances are that the server is running on a reasonably potent UNIX workstation or minicomputer—and what's more, there's probably somebody around who knows how to configure the server and perhaps do a little scripting, too. But you'd better find out what your organization's policy is with respect to acceptable uses. If your Web presentation is closely related to your organization's mission, you might be able to place it on the server— but you may be asked to create the presentation in line with your organization's established guidelines for Web design.

- **Using the Web publishing space provided by your Internet service provider**   Most ISPs give you some Web storage space (typically, 5 MB). When you upload HTML documents to this space via FTP, these documents are made available to other Web users by your ISP's server.

- **Leasing space from a commercial service provider**   Pricing and service options vary, but you should be able to find a service provider that will place your presentation on a fast UNIX workstation for a flat monthly fee. If you want the service provider's help in implementing interactive features, expect to pay programmer's fees.

WEB SERVER CONNECTIVITY OPTIONS

If you're thinking about setting up a computer system to run Web server software, you need to understand one important point: Web servers require a much better Internet connection than Web browsers do. With a Web browser, you can make do with a SLIP or PPP dialup account, in which your computer is assigned a temporary Internet address (called an *IP address*) every time you log on. However, this won't do for a Web server. In order for people to access your documents, your server needs to be located at a permanent IP address. Only in this way can people locate your documents.

Does your computer system already have a permanent IP address? Here are some things to think about:

- If your personal computer is connected to the Internet via a local area network (LAN), it probably does have a permanent IP address—ask your network administrator.

- If you connect via a dialup SLIP, CSLIP, or PPP connection, however, your computer probably doesn't have a permanent IP address. You can set up and run a server, but it won't do you any good—people won't have a permanent address where they can locate your documents. That's because most dialup connections use dynamically assigned IP addresses—your system is given a temporary IP address, which is good for the current session. But that particular address might be assigned to someone else's computer after you log off. And consider, too, that people won't be able to access your site when you're not logged on. To make your documents available on the Web, you need a computer that's permanently connected to the Internet.

WEB SERVERS AND OPERATING SYSTEMS

For anyone contemplating setting up a Web server, the most important consideration isn't so much which program to buy, but on which *operating system* to run the server. Web servers are available for Windows 3.1, Windows 95, Windows NT, OS/2, the Macintosh OS, and UNIX. The following sections detail what's at stake when you choose one operating system over another. Since this book is designed for Windows users, I'm assuming you'll run your server on a Windows system, so we'll examine Windows 3.1, Windows 95, and Windows NT.

Windows 3.1

Still in use on millions of IBM PCs and PC compatibles worldwide, Windows 3.1 and Windows for Workgroups 3.1 can run Web server programs, but these systems are a good choice only if you're expecting relatively light loads. The reason? These 16-bit operating systems do not provide sufficient system-level support for *multithreading*, in which a program can carry out more than one task simultaneously. This translates into sharp restrictions on the number of simultaneous accesses—with most servers, you're limited to two dozen or less. That's OK for a site that receives only a few hundred hits a day, but if you're hoping for a bigger audience, look beyond Windows 3.1.

On the plus side, Windows 3.1 servers are extremely easy to install, configure, and maintain. What's more, point-and-click shareware programs are available to provide usage statistics (VBSTATS) as well as form support (PolyForm) and real-time, forms-based interactivity (TalkBack). The following sections describe three programs that, taken together, permit nonprogrammers to put together an impressive Windows 3.1 Web site in short order. (Note that VBSTATS, PolyForm, and TalkBack also work with the much more powerful WebSite, a Windows NT and Windows 95-based server that is described in the following section.)

Solutions

Permanent Connection Options

If you've decided to go the do-it-yourself route, you'll need a fast and permanent Internet connection. Here's a quick overview of your options:

28.8/33.6 Kbps modem on a separate phone line   If your Internet service provider offers a dialup service that assigns permanent rather than dynamic IP addresses, you can set aside a separate phone line for Web access. At 28.8 Kbps, you'd be wise to avoid Web presentations that incorporate large graphics. Recently introduced are 33.6 Kbps modems, but relatively few Internet service providers have upgraded their equipment to take advantage of this. In the works are modems with 56 Kbps speeds, but these won't be widely available until the relevant international committees rule on standardization issues.

56 Kbps dedicated line   Most Internet service providers can make arrangements for the installation of a specially conditioned telephone line that is permanently connected to the service provider's computer. Formerly, this service was extremely expensive—on the order of $500 to $1000 per month—effectively restricting this type of access to relatively well-endowed organizations and corporations. However, 56 Kbps access costs are in free fall, especially in competitive metropolitan areas. You may be able to arrange for this type of service for $200 per month or less, but it's an attractive option only if ISDN isn't available.

64/128 Kbps ISDN   Short for Integrated Services Digital Network, this service is finally becoming widely available in North America (it is already well established in Europe and Japan). A standard for digital telephony, ISDN is available in a variety of service configurations, the cheapest of which is called Basic Rate ISDN (BRI). A significant advantage of BRI is that it does not require the installation of expensive digital telephone wiring; a type of analog wiring known as *twisted pair* will suffice. (Most homes, schools, and offices built after 1980 have twisted pair wiring.) With BRI, the monthly service fee gets you three lines, two of which are used for phones or data (the third is reserved for control signals); you can connect your telephone and your computer with just one BRI service contract. For your money, as little as $32 per month in many areas (not including Internet access), you'll get 64 Kbps service on a noise-free digital line. (128 Kbps service is available in some areas.) One drawback: You'll need to invest in a digital telephone, a digital modem, and circuit termination equipment, which can cost as much as $600. But that's a one-time expense, and then you're set—and you'll have better service than a lot of colleges and universities do right now.

Windows HTTPd

This freeware server can handle up to 16 simultaneous connections—enough for an individual's Web server, or perhaps a very small, local business. A well-designed Windows CGI interface enables the program to work with a variety of freeware utilities.

VB-Server

A Web server for Microsoft Windows 3.1 and Windows for Workgroups 3.1, VB-Server can be used by anyone as a simple Web server. However, it's best applied by Visual Basic programmers, who can use the program's Windows CGI interface to write scripts for processing forms, imagemaps, and other active content. The program is shareware. To find out more about VB-Server, access http://wwwdev.com/products/vbserver/.

Windows 95

Unlike Windows 3.1, Windows 95 and Windows NT are 32-bit operating systems—that is, they take full advantage of the 32-bit architecture of Intel microprocessors (486 and Pentium). This translates into somewhat faster performance. More important, Windows 95 and Windows NT offer true multithreading, which enables a program to run many functions simultaneously. In practical terms, this means that Windows 95- and NT-based servers can handle many users simultaneously. WebSite (from O'Reilly and Associates), a 32-bit version of Robert Denny's Win-HTTPD software, can handle 30 requests *per second* on a 90 MHz Pentium.

What's the difference between Windows 95 and Windows NT? Windows 95 is Microsoft's entry-level operating system. Not a true 32-bit operating system, it is designed to run existing 16-bit Windows programs. However, it also contains all the resources necessary to run 32-bit Windows programs, with advanced multithreading capabilities. Designed with good Internet support built in, Windows 95 is a good choice for an individual's Web server platform. Windows NT is a true 32-bit operating system; it can't run 16-bit Windows 3.1 programs. Because it can handle more simulatneous processes than Windows 95, it's the best choice for small businesses.

Microsoft Personal Web Server

Microsoft Personal Web Server for Windows 95 transforms any Windows 95 computer into a Web server. The program is very easy to install and administer, since it is very nicely integrated with Windows 95. Although Personal Web Server isn't designed for sites that will receive heavy use, it's a good choice for a small-scale internal Internet (an intranet) or for testing your Web pages before uploading them to a more powerful server. The program is freeware; you can download your copy from http://www.microsoft.com/windows/software/localize/spaweb.htm.

Netscape FastTrack Server for Windows 95

This server brings much of the functionality of Netscape's highly regarded Windows NT server to Windows 95 users, including client-side certificate authentication, Java, JavaScript, and mail support. When combined with LiveWire and other Netscape server products, FastTrack can be used to set up a complete commercial Web server system for a small business or an Intranet server for a small corporation.

WebSite

A commercial 32-bit version of the freeware Windows HTTPD for Windows 3.1, WebSite is marketed by O'Reilly and Associates—and it's an excellent choice for individuals, corporate computer users, and small-to-medium-sized businesses. Easy to install and configure, WebSite takes full advantage of the easy-to-use Windows interface. Security features go far beyond Win-HTTPD and include password-based authentication (version 1.1 includes support for the SSL and S-HTTP encryption standards). Like Win-HTTPD, WebSite can run Visual Basic scripts for functions such as clickable maps, fill-in forms, and searches. Several point-and-click Visual Basic programs are available that enable you to implement these and other advanced features without programming. A plus: Access control restrictions enable you to make certain documents available only to persons in a particular group, such as members of a department or an organization. WebSite is currently available for $495. For more information, check out http://www.ora.com.

Windows NT

Although you can set up a Web server with a Windows 95 system, professional uses require Windows NT, which can handle many more simultaneous connections. On a powerful Windows NT system, an NT server can compete with servers running on UNIX workstations.

Solutions

Getting Your Own Domain Name

One difference between a professional-sounding site and one that seems amateurish is the *domain name,* the part of the site's URL that identifies the computer on which your pages are stored. If you've chosen to upload your pages to an ISP's server, your URLs will probably look something like this fictitious example:

http://www.netserv.com/~pfaffey/welcome.html

Here, the server is is provided by NetServ, a fictitious ISP, and the page is located within the user's directory (pfaffey). The tilde is a dead giveaway that this isn't a real Web site.

To get started, you first need to understand the various parts of a domain name. The first part specifies the name of a specific computer within a domain (in www.pfaffey.com, "www" is the name of the computer that's running the Web server). The first part might consist of more than one word, as in watt.seas.virginia.edu. The next-to-last part, called the *second-level domain name,* is the important one. This is the name that's used for domain name registration purposes. In www.pfaffey.com, the second-level domain name is "pfaffey." In watt.seas.virginia.edu, the second-level domain name is "virginia."

In order to register my domain name, I need to know whether someone else has already taken my prospective second-level name. To find out, access the interNIC domain name database at http://rs.internic.net/cgi-bin/whois. In the text box, type your prospective second-level domain name, and press Enter.

Once you've established that your domain name isn't taken, you can obtain it in either of the following ways:

- **Create your own Web server with a unique and permanent IP address, and ask your ISP to obtain a domain name for you.** You'll need to obtain your permanent connection (by means of a dedicated line or ISDN) from a local ISP. As part of the package of services that most ISPs offer, you can ask them to obtain the domain name for you. If you prefer, you can obtain the domain name yourself, directly from the interNIC (http://rs.internic.net/).

- **Ask your ISP to set up a virtual domain.** A *virtual domain* is a named domain that's located within an ISP's computer. In essence, this is a way of transforming a URL such as www.netserv.com/~pfaffey into www.pfaffey.com, but without having to set up your own Web server. You'll pay a fee for this service (as little as $20 per month with some ISPs). Typically included in this service are as many as 20 mailboxes with the same domain name (such as bryan@pfaffey.com).

Microsoft Internet Information Server

This freeware server for Microsoft Windows NT is easy to install, configure, and maintain. If you're already running Windows NT (and you've purchased and installed the Windows NT Server, a $995 product), this server offers excellent performance, SSL security for credit-card transactions, and interfaces for CGI scripts. The server doesn't support Java, however. For more information and to download a copy, access http://www.microsoft.com.

Netscape Enterprise Server

This is Netscape's heavy-duty server for professional Web sites. SSL security and certification for credit-card ordering and other advanced applications are included. Java and JavaScript are supported. Programmers can write interlinked applications using the Netscape Server Application Programming Interface (NSAPI) in addition to using CGI.

Netscape SuiteSpot

This package includes several programs: the LiveWire Pro development environment, Enterprise Server, Mail Server, News Server, Proxy Server, Catalog Server, and Calendar, Media, and Certificate Servers. It's designed for medium to large corporations that want to create a high-capacity Web site for Internet or intranet access.

For information on Netscape servers, access the Netscape Server Solutions page at

http://merchant.netscape.com/netstore/

FROM HERE

- Whether you've decided to create your own Web server or take advantage of an existing Web server installation, your next task is to think about the design of your web. Check out Chapter 7 for suggestions on getting started with your Web presentation's plan.

- Even if you're planning to use an HTML editor (a program that helps you code HTML), you'll still need to learn the basics. Chapter 11 provides an easy-to-follow tutorial that teaches much of what you'll need to know to create a high-quality Web site.

Chapter 7

Developing a Publishing Plan

Y ou wouldn't try to build a house without a blueprint. Nor would you try to invest money without thinking about your goals, or invite a friend to dinner without first considering the menu. Most things we undertake are much more successful if we first think about what we want to accomplish and then develop a plan for achieving those goals.

The Web is no different. If you want to put together a successful Web site, you have to think about the people you want to use it and how you will make them want to visit your site. What sorts of things interest them? Which of their needs are served by existing Web resources? What do they consider cool, and how can you incorporate those features into your documents?

You have to consider technical factors as much as aesthetic ones. Does your audience have computer equipment to handle the MPEG video clips you want to include, or would they be more inclined to come back if you

For the Time-Challenged

♦ Effective communication begins with a clear understanding of purpose. Examples include personal, social, community, publishing, professional/career, and business purposes.

♦ The Web may not be the right place for your message. You're in competition with 55 million additional documents (currently), there's no guarantee that people will access your web from the welcome page, and you'll miss people who aren't yet on the Web.

♦ Effective Web audience analysis requires segmenting the audience and defining your target, free from stereotypes.

♦ A good approach takes the audience into account by focusing squarely on the audience's concerns.

♦ Your web should begin with an effective hook.

♦ Consider your commitment level before proceeding. An out-of-date page, obviously poorly maintained, could mar your image or that of your organization.

provided stills from the video clips—which require less computing power—instead? Does your audience speak the language in which you want to write your page? How will potential visitors learn about your site in the vastness of the Web?

In this chapter, we'll examine the thought process behind preparing to publish a set of killer Web documents. With examples, the chapter will show that the thinking process that precedes actual HTML coding is the most essential part of publishing on the Web.

KNOW YOUR PURPOSE

To communicate well, you must know your purpose. If you're giving a speech, for instance, you'll do much better if you ask yourself, "Even if my audience forgets everything else I say, what's the *one* idea I hope they'll remember?" Before you design your Web page, you should be able to state your purpose—preferably in one clear sentence.

 Just one purpose? A successful Web presentation may accomplish more than one, but it's best to start with a clear focus. The best pages on the Web have a single, clearly defined purpose that leaps out at you the first time you access the page. If you're successful with your first purpose, you can add more later, but you'll risk confusing your audience if you add too many.

Some of the best webs show a simple, clear purpose, one that's discernible in a one-second glance at the welcome page. Take a look at two excellent examples:

- **54 Ways You Can Help The Homeless** (http://ecosys.drdr.virginia.edu/ways/54.html) Rabbi Charles A. Kroloff publishes this hyperbook (Figure 7.1) to raise peoples' consciousness about the homeless and what ordinary people can do to help. The graphic isn't much to write home about, but it's effective: The house shape and 54 suggests that these 54 ways can put people in homes. The web's organization and contents are instantly clear.

- **Jonathan Tward's Multimedia Medical Reference Library** (http://www.tiac.net/users/jtward/index.html) The Web page (Figure 7.2) of an MD/PhD student at Tufts University is instantly recognizable for what it is: An unbelievably rich resource of medical-related information, which you can search using keywords (try "bubonic plague").

Defining Your Purpose

Chapter 5 introduced some of the genres of Web publishing. Underlying each of these genres is a purpose—which may not be as well defined as it should be. The best Web pages express a clear purpose. This section helps you formulate your purpose by presenting questions you should consider.

Personal Purposes

Here, the focus is on you. But you'd better ask why. What's worth sharing?

- **Sharing information about yourself** Do you think that someone would like to know more about you? If you're a teacher, for example, some of your students might like to get to know you better. What are your hobbies? Your favorite actors and musicians?

Figure 7.1   Clarity of purpose: 54 Ways to Help the Homeless

- **Sharing information about a hobby or avocation**   What have you found out that other hobbyists would like to know?

- **Providing entertainment**   To you, it's funny, or moving, or beautiful. Perhaps others would feel the same way!

Figure 7.2 Clarity of purpose: Multimedia Medical Reference Library

Social Purposes

Flourishing in the midst of a capitalist society isn't stopping the Web from developing a social conscience. The following are examples of pages with a cause:

- **Informing people about a social or political situation that concerns you** What should people know? What's there to lose if they don't?

- **Helping others find Web resources** Do you think other people would like to see what you've discovered? Has anyone else already done this?

- **Providing a tutorial or programmed instruction in a subject you're knowledgeable about, as a service to others** What do people need to learn about this subject?

- **Creating information pools concerning a disability or social problem** How could people contribute their knowledge and resources to make things better?

Community Purposes

The Web's global in scope, but some of the most exciting things are happening in smaller spheres, including towns, counties, and cities.

- **Providing a community focal point for an educational institution or nonprofit organization** What information does the community need?

- **Providing information about local or regional resources and services** What do people need to know? How would this web make accessing these resources or services more convenient?

- **Enabling citizen feedback** What information would you like to have, and how could you use it to improve government services?

Publishing Purposes

The Web has transformed publishing, thanks to the fact that the distribution costs are close to zero. But it's a very different ball game: People want content for free.

- **Publishing a newsletter** Are all or most of the intended recipients online, or will you publish a print-based backup? How will you get compensated for your time?

- **Publishing a zine** A *zine* is an avant-garde newsletter featuring original writing, opinion, flames, and reviews. Is there really an audience for your zine? Will you keep it up? Can you get people to write for you?

- **Providing an online version of a printed magazine or newspaper** How can you use this venture to increase sales of the printed version? How can you justify the costs?

Professional/Career Purposes

In many fields, if you're not on the Web, you're not in the game.

- **Making your résumé available to potential employers**   By what sort of firm do you hope to be hired? What do you think they're looking for?

- **Creating recognition for your professional work**   What would make your accomplishments stand out?

- **Sharing creative work and gaining recognition**   Which of your efforts would you most like people to see?

- **Building a list of client prospects**   What will it take to get people to fill out that form and click Submit?

Business Purposes

Not every business purpose works equally well on the Web. Here's an overview of some of the objectives that have worked particularly well.

- **Marketing your firm's products or services**   What could you do with your web that would create lasting interest and recognition?

- **Testing consumer response to proposed innovations**   What would you most like to know concerning customer reactions to your plans?

- **Improving customer service**   What's the biggest shortcoming of your customer service right now, and how could a Web presence improve it?

- **Recruiting talented employees**   In which areas are you experiencing the greatest difficulty recruiting competent people? How could your web attract them?

- **Creating an intranet for internal communications support**   An *intranet* is a network based on the Internet protocols that is designed to enhance an organization's internal communications. What's the biggest problem with your internal communications at present? How could an intranet resolve them?

- **Generating sales leads**   How could you present your firm's products or services in such a way that people would want to request more information?

- **Reducing internal paper consumption/waste**   How could you provide information on the Web in a way that would cut down on paper use?

- **Providing technical support for your products** What do people most need to know about your products? If you were having problems with one of your products, what would you most like to see when you accessed the support web?

- **Explaining your firm's services** What do people want and need to know about what your firm has to offer?

- **Explaining your company's position on an issue** How will this come across to both friendly and unfriendly audiences?

- **Giving your company a Web presence** How could you design your web so that it creates lasting recognition?

- **Providing a catalog and selling goods or services online** Why should people order from you instead of buying locally or by mail?

- **Providing before-sales technical information about a product** What do people need to know in order to decide whether a product is right for them?

Stating Your Purpose

What do you hope to accomplish by putting your pages on the Web? From the above examples, select one that seems most appropriate—or invent your own.

For example, you might phrase your purpose this way:

> My purpose fits into the social cause category. I want to provide information about adult attention deficit disorder—something I've had to cope with myself. Perhaps I can help people determine whether they need to see a specialist for help.

Is the Web the Right Medium for Your Message?

Before you develop your web, you should consider whether the World Wide Web is really the right vehicle for accomplishing your purpose.

- Millions of people are using the Web, but there's absolutely no guarantee that anyone will access your web, or stay there for more than a few seconds. You're in competition with tens of millions of other Web pages; soon, the number will be in the hundreds of millions.

- If you develop a multiple-page web (and you probably will), there's no guarantee that people will access your web in the way you want (i.e., from your welcome page, which explains your web's meaning and purpose). They might get the wrong idea, or a poor impression, from the one page they do see. Of course, you could try to force people through a certain sequence of pages by providing only one link, but there's nothing to stop them from clicking Home or Back and deserting you completely.

- Not everyone's on the Web. According to current estimates, the Web is available in only 8 percent of U.S. households. That number is sure to rise in the coming years, but this isn't a mass-market medium—yet.

On the plus side, it doesn't cost much to publish on the Web, and your distribution costs are zero (once you've paid your Internet access charges).

KNOW YOUR AUDIENCE

Once you've figured out your purpose, the next step is to define the audience for your Web page. Forget the MBA in marketing--this isn't rocket science. It's simply a matter of understanding what your audience wants.

Start by getting rid of some stereotypes about Web users, as explained in the next section. Once you've gotten beyond the myths about Web audiences, you can get to work. You'll need to segment the Web audience, identifying just the group or groups that are really going to take an interest in what you're planning to do. Then you must get inside their heads. What do they want? What are their concerns?

Top Five Myths about Web Audiences

If you'd like to know who's browsing the Web, you can look at a number of demographic studies—but they won't tell you what you really need to know. It's better to start by debunking some common myths and stereotypes.

1. **It's a male-dominated environment.** Early Web usages surveys showed an 8:1 male–female ratio, but that's an artifact of the early surveys—including the very real prospect that the surveys were designed in such a way that men were more likely to respond. More recent numbers have shown rising numbers of female users, and most experts believe that the sex ratio will even out at 50:50 once the Internet has fully penetrated its market.

2. **If you're not speaking to the 18–34 crowd, you won't have an audience.** It's true that the Web audience is youthful, but that's not the whole story. One of the fastest-growing usage segments is the elderly, who use the Web and the Net for amusement, avocational interests, philanthropy, continued career or professional involvement, and social contact in the retirement years.

3. **For a generation raised on video games, you need blinking text and flashy graphics to catch their attention.** Flat out wrong. Big, pointless graphics anger Web users because they download too slowly. Distracting elements, such as Netscape's notorious <BLINK> tag and the more recent scrolling Java banners may be taken as a sign of crass commercialism, something akin to spamming on Usenet. Web users want fast, supple webs, with lean, functional graphics.

4. **Generation X? They're all slackers, who just want to be entertained.** Dead wrong. Everyone enjoys entertainment, but this stereotype is way off the mark. Gen Xers want to get ahead and they're willing to work just as hard as anyone else, but they're confused by the rapidly changing economy and the conflicting advice they're getting. That's one of the reasons they're on the Net in the first place—they're trying to figure out what's happening.

5. **As in broadcasting, you've got to find the lowest common denominator so you can appeal to massive numbers of people.** Terminally wrong. The webs with mass draws on the Web—the ones that get millions of hits per day—fall into two categories: The home pages of the leading browsers (displayed automatically and mindlessly) and the major search services (search engines and subject trees). You're not going to get those numbers. The only way you're going to get modest numbers of people to visit your web is if you've really thought long and hard about exactly what they want—and then you provide it. The Web is *not* a broadcast medium. It's a first-choice medium. Users can select from millions of options. Why choose yours?

Segmenting the Web Audience

The first and most important rule of Web audience conceptualization is *market segmentation*: defining the portion of the audience that you're trying to reach. Remember, this is a first-choice medium. So who's going to choose you?

In market segmentation, you differentiate among the various types of people accessing the Web, focusing on just the group or groups that you think will take special interest in what you're planning to do.

But market segmentation isn't just setting some people apart. It's also getting inside their heads. Having defined a market segment, you should ask yourself What's on their minds? What's troubling them? Where do they need help, or advice, or resources?

 To find out what's on people's minds, try to find Usenet newsgroups or mailing lists pertinent to your web's proposed topic. Post messages on Usenet asking for peoples' reactions to your proposed web. Ask them what they'd like to see—and whether it's already been done to their liking! To find a mailing list on a given topic, check out the searchable Publicly Accessible Mailing Lists (http://www.neosoft.com/internet/paml/).

The following are examples of well-segmented audience definitions for Web pages:

- Professional women concerned about job advancement in Fortune 500 companies.

- Windows 95 users looking for high-quality shareware programs that they can use to make up for some of the deficiencies in Windows 95's functionality.

- Small business owners concerned about whether they need to keep occupational safety and health records and, if so, how they should do it.

Take a look at the following Web pages:

- **CyberMom Dot Com** (http://www.cybermom.com/) Here's a page beautifully targeted to women juggling their interests in computers with their roles as "mothers, wives, lovers, and friends" in this "recently wired world" (see Figure 1.1). Excellent!

- **Children's Literature Web Guide** (http://www.ucalgary.ca/~dkbrown/index.html) This page is targeted to teachers and parents who are looking for children's literature resources on the Internet, including the lists of Newberry and Caldecott Award winners, links to online children's texts, and the latest bestseller lists.

- **A World of Tea** (http://www.teleport.com/~tea) This page is aimed squarely at tea lovers, and not just any tea lovers—it's aimed at those special tea lovers who are willing to go the extra mile to find high-quality tea. There's a gentleness to tea and a gentleness of spirit to those who love tea, and it's captured here. It's sponsored by the Stash Tea Company. You'll find plenty of fun content and no hard-sell tactics.

Defining Your Audience

When you're ready to state your audience definition, do so in the following way: Write a one- or two-sentence description of the type of people who would be most likely to access your web and feel rewarded by the content they'll find there. Then explain *why*.

The following states the audience for the ADD page envisioned earlier in this chapter:

> Many adults suffer from attention deficit disorder (ADD) without realizing it. Other people think they're disorganized, even though adult ADD sufferers are often very intelligent. Most victims have no idea that they suffer from a recognize and treatable disorder.

DEVELOP AN APPROACH

Professional communicators know that it's not enough to define your purpose and know your audience. You must also devise an *approach*. With the right approach, your audience takes interest in what you're saying. With the wrong approach? Forget it.

Just think of all those times you asked your mom for the car keys. Remember? You said, "If you don't let me borrow your car, I won't be able to see my friends at the mall, and I'll retaliate by not eating my broccoli!" Didn't get the keys, huh?

You should have developed an approach. Try this one: "Mom, you've got too many chores to do today. If you lend me the keys, I can get my shopping done at the mall, and I'll have time to swing by the nursery and pick up those chrysanthemums you ordered." You're on your way, baby!

The Secret to a Good Approach

Coming up with an effective approach isn't difficult. Actually, it's ridiculously simple. You focus on your audience's concerns, not your own.

Admittedly, not everyone finds this easy to do. It requires taking attention away from yourself—and that takes a certain amount of maturity. (This goes a long way toward explaining why we never thought of asking for the car keys the right way.)

 You can tell instantly whether a Web author has put any thought into developing an approach. Just look at the pronouns on the web's welcome page. If you see lots of "I" and "me" (or, for companies, "we"), chances are the author hasn't gotten beyond the narcissistic stage. A well-crafted approach emphasizes "you."

Honing Your Approach

Once you've decided to take the "I" or "we" out of your page and put the "you" in, you're on your way. But there are two very, very important questions to ask:

- **What's your audience's *most important concern*?** They're busy folks. When I asked for the keys the *right* way, I go straight to the heart of my poor, frazzled mom's concerns: "Mom, you've got too many errands to run today."

- **What additional topics *follow* from my audience's most important concern?** Two specific anxieties follow from my poor mom's harried schedule—how the heck is she going to take me shopping, and how is she going to get her mums home. Adroitly, I hit them one-two ("I can get my shopping done alone at the mall, and I'll have time to swing by the nursery and pick up those chrysanthemums you ordered").

Here's How the Masters Do It

So how does all of this translate into excellence in Web page design? Let's take a look at a flat-out perfect example: the Walt Disney World home page (http://www2.disney.com/DisneyWorld/index.html), shown in Figure 7.3.

Consider the text: "Mickey has packed all of the magic and wonder of Walt Disney World into his suitcase to help your vacation dreams come true." Hats off to this brilliant Web page's authors! Rather than all the vainglorious things that could be said about Walt Disney World, this web

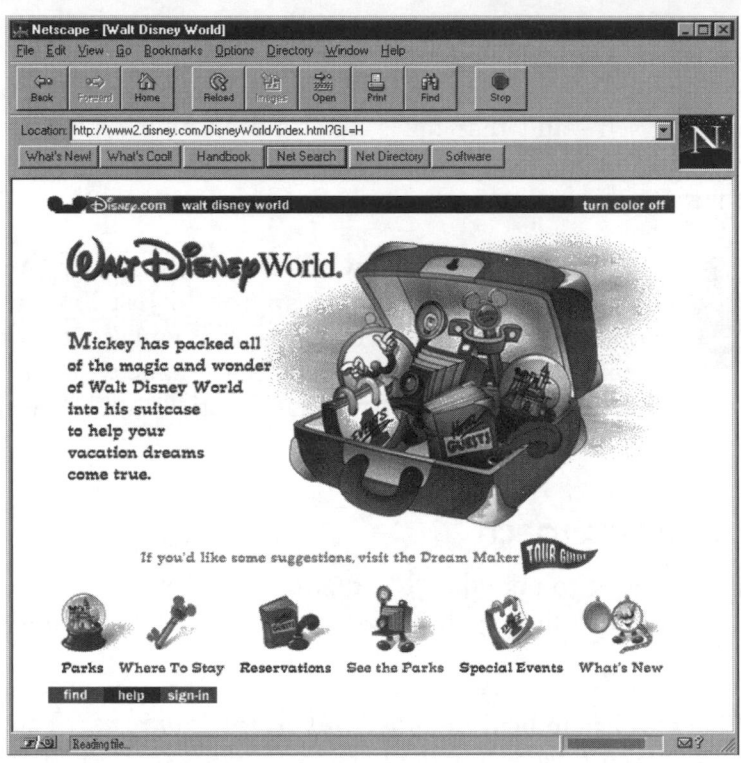

Figure 7.3   Excellent approach: Walt Disney World

chooses to focus squarely on the *most important thing* that the page's reader is thinking: "Gee, I'd love to visit Walt Disney World, but how?"

The following outlines what goes on in a reader's mind after accessing this web:

1. The graphic—an open suitcase, stuffed to the brim with magical things from Disney's world—tells me everything I need to know, in a one-second glance: We're *packing*. We've already decided to go— hey, why else would we have accessed this web? And here are lots of useful things to help my dream vacation come true.

2. What's all that stuff in the suitcase? We're taking wonderful things with us!

3. Hey! The stuff in the suitcase is a bunch of icons, and they're repeated at the bottom of the page!

4. Wow! All those icons represent pages that speak to my concerns and interests about this vacation!

I *told* you this page is good.

This page illustrates something that this book stresses later about graphics. You don't include graphics because it's cool to have a picture on your page or because they look pretty. You include graphics so that you can get a "flash" of cognitive discovery and awareness, a flash that comes from suddenly seeing a connection between the graphic and the page's fundamental message. That's the basic secret of those million-dollar advertising firms, incidentally. Just take a look at any reasonably sophisticated newspaper or magazine, such as the *Wall Street Journal* or the *New Yorker*, and you'll see the pattern immediately. Easy trick, actually.

Develop a Hook

Now that you know these simple secrets, it's a cinch to frame your approach. Just ask yourself, "What's the most important thing on my readers' minds?" and speak to it directly and graphically. Then you ask, "What follows from this concern of theirs?"—and you show that you've packed your web with information that's dead-on-center.

To sum up this chapter, what we're talking about here is developing a *hook*. It's easy to do, once you've got your audience in clear focus. For example, adult ADD sufferers are constantly being berated for being disorganized, and it's murder on their self-esteem. The page ought to open with text or graphics that speak directly to this concern and then open up a world of possibilities. Here's a possible hook; write yours down in the same way.

Do people tell you that you're disorganized? Do you have trouble meeting deadlines and let people down? Is this murdering your self-esteem?

If so, take heart—you're not alone, and there's help. You may be suffering from adult attention deficit disorder (ADD) that's never been diagnosed. And here's the good news: You can overcome your disability, and reach your *full potential*.

Ideally, this hook would segue directly into navigation icons that link to pages explaining what adult ADD is, where to get a professional diagnosis, strategies for overcoming ADD's disabilities, and much, much, more.

DETERMINE YOUR COMMITMENT LEVEL

The Web is full of out-of-date, unmaintained pages. They don't speak well for their authors or the organizations to which they belong. You shouldn't publish on the Web unless you're ready to keep your page up-to-date.

Before you rush off to develop your content, you should take a moment to consider how much time your web will consume. To estimate how much time your Web publishing efforts will take, you'll need to consider whether you know HTML, where you'll keep your pages (on somebody else's server or your own), how much time and effort you're willing to put into publicizing your page, how often you'll update your pages, whether you'll process forms, and how much time you'll need to answer the e-mail that your web will generate (believe me, it will).

How Much Time Will This Take?

Publishing on the Web could amount to a minimal effort, requiring only a few hours of your time per month. Or it could become an all-consuming, eight-hour-per-day task requiring the full attention of as many as a dozen people.

Do You Know HTML?

If you haven't yet learned HTML, be aware that it's not quite as easy as it looks. To be sure, it's simple enough to create your first page, but creating a complex web loaded with lots of internal links and graphics isn't a trivial affair. For someone with good computer background, you can count on at least one solid week of training and practice to learn HTML well.

Bear in mind, too, that knowing HTML isn't enough to create a winning Web presentation these days. If you want to do everything yourself, you'll need a scanner and graphics software, such as Adobe Photoshop, to digitize eye-catching graphics—and you'll need to learn how to use these tools. If you want to offer original sounds and movies, you'll need lots of additional hardware and the expertise that goes along with using these tools well. To create your own Java applets, the mini-programs creaetd with Sun Microsystem's Java programming language, you'll find it very helpful to have considerable background programming in C++.

Most Web authors lack the skills to create a full-featured web, replete with original Java programs, Macromedia animations, and high-fidelity sounds. Increasingly, it's necessary to hire production assistants to prepare these materials.

 Can you dispense with knowing HTML? I don't recommend it. If you do, you'll be dependent on a pricey consultant to fix every little error and make every little change. HTML is the easiest of the hurdles ahead of you; master the HTML and farm out the rest, if necessary.

Where Will You Keep Your Pages?

To determine your level of commitment, begin by thinking through your server options. Holding everything else equal, the server option you choose may require only a few hours every month from you—or an eight-hour day, five days a week.

- **Using free Web space from your Internet service provider** Many Internet service providers (ISPs) give you one or two megabytes' (MB) worth of free Web space—but you'll need to ask whether that's enough. If you plan to provide lots of content, and particularly lots of graphics, you may exceed your disk space quota, and you'll run into additional costs. In addition, you'll need to ask whether the ISP's server can support the interactive features you want, such as CGI scripts, imagemaps, and forms. If the space and server constraints are tolerable, this is by far the easiest and least time-consuming way to put up your pages: Your service provider has to deal with system crashes, outages, and other hassles of keeping a web running.

- **Leasing space from your Internet service provider** If you need more Web publishing space than 1 or 2 MB, your Internet service provider may be able to assist you—for a price, of course. With this choice, you buy time. You won't have to deal with service outages, but you'll still need to put in a few hours per month keeping your page up to date and answering e-mail.

- **Running your own server on a PC with a shareware server** If you have a 24-hour-per-day Internet connection, and if your Internet service provider can get you a fully qualified domain name for this connection, you can set up your own web using an inexpensive shareware program such as Win-HTTPD. These types of programs are suitable for an individual or a small organization that doesn't expect more than a few hundred hits per day, at most. Be aware that you and you alone will need to ensure that the web's up and running; expect to spend several hours a week keeping the server going. Remember, too, that shareware programs aren't very well documented, so you shouldn't attempt this strategy unless you're reasonably knowledgeable about the system you're using. Note: A major advantage of this approach is the availability of an upgrade path; if your web gets too popular for the shareware server to handle, you can upgrade to the commercial version (WebSite is the commercial version of Win-HTTPD, for example).

- **Running your own server on a Windows 95 PC with a commercial server**   This is one step up from the previous option; it enables you to deal with thousands of hits per day, and as many as two dozen simultaneous connections. This is sufficient for an individual's well-patronized page or a small business, but it's not enough for a mid- to large-sized organization. Because you're using commercial software such as WebSite (O'Reilly & Associates), the documentation and technical support are much better, so this choice may actually consume less time than the previous one.

- **Running your own server on a Windows NT system**   Windows NT is a much more powerful operating system than Windows 3.1 or Windows 95, and organizations everywhere are setting up high-capacity servers using Windows NT and the new generation of NT server programs (including Microsoft's freeware server). On the down side, Windows NT is a complicated operating system, and it isn't terribly well documented. Much of the knowlege concerning Windows NT is gained only through experience. If you lack this experience, you may need professional assistance to install and configure your server, but once it's up and running, this option shouldn't consume much more time than the previous one.

- **Running your own server on a UNIX workstation**   For larger organizations expecting tens or hundreds of thousands of hits per day, this is the best choice—but be prepared to spend long hours dealing with UNIX configuration and maintenance tasks. If you're not conversant with the "flavor" of UNIX that your workstation runs, and in particular if you're a nonprogrammer, you may need to hire somebody to keep the web running and to develop the necessary forms-processing hits. This is by far the most time-consuming of the various server options, and can become a full-time job if the web's content changes frequently.

 If you underestimate your usage needs, remember that your users won't appreciate your moving your pages to another server. It's best to start out with more server than you think you're going to need.

How Will You Promote Your Web?

What if they gave a Web page and nobody came? That's the refrain being sung everywhere these days. Although most Web pages are eventually discovered by search engines, there's no guarantee whatsoever that your page will be discovered and patronized. You'll need to do some web promotion, and that's a very expensive and time-consuming business. Here are your options:

- **Do-it-yourself freebie promotion**   Announce your page to the relevant newsgroups and send messages to subject trees (such as Yahoo) and What's New pages, but after that, you rely on word of mouth. Figure on spending a couple of days to get the word out initially.

- **Do-it-yourself freebie promotion with periodic reminders**   Subscribe to mailing lists and read relevant Usenet newsgroups; where appropriate to do so, you reply to relevant messages by reminding people that your page might be useful to them. Figure on spending two to five hours per week on this.

- **Commercial promotion**   If you don't have time to promote your web, several firms will do the job for you—for a price.

How Often Will You Update Your Pages?

Your update frequency—the interval at which you add new material to your pages—is another factor that determines how much time you'll need to set aside for your Web pages. At the minimum, you'll need a couple of hours to perform a minor update to your pages—much more if you're planning to incorporate lots of new material or change the interface.

- **No updates**   This strategy is *not* recommended unless you have compelling reasons. When people come back to your Web page and find that you haven't done anything to it in months, or find an old date at the bottom of the page, they'll dismiss it—and you.

- **Monthly updates**   For most Web pages, this is the minimum update frequency that you should tolerate. Add new material, and call attention to the new material with "New" icons. Make sure you indicate the date of the last update at the bottom of your pages. At the minimum, you'll need a couple of hours to perform a minor update to your pages—much more if you're planning to incorporate lots of new material or change the interface.

- **Weekly updates**   If you want to make the right impression on the Web, try to update your pages at least weekly.

- **Daily updates**   A daily update isn't required unless your material calls for it (for example, an online newspaper), there's a deluge of new material (fast-breaking developments), or you're offering daily content of some sort (such as a quotation of the day or a cartoon). And remember: If you commit to it, you have to do it.

Will You Need To Process Forms?

HTML has several tags that enable users to fill out on-screen interactive forms, including tags for creating text areas, option buttons, check boxes, and pull-down lists. Most browsers can take the forms' output and send it to your server automatically. However, your server can't do anything with this output unless you've created mini-programs, called *scripts*, to deal with the forms. (Some servers, such as WebStar, come with easy-to-use utilities that enable you to set up straightforward forms-processing applications without doing any programming.)

If you're planning a web that includes interactive forms, you'll need to think through how much time you should set aside for dealing with the forms people fill out. Will you need to answer them or process them personally?

How Much Time Will Answering E-mail Require?

When you estimate how much time to set aside for maintaining your web, bear in mind that you'll need to answer your e-mail promptly. Some webs don't generate much mail, while others generate dozens of messages per day. You'll need to estimate how much mail you're likely to get and how much time you need to respond fully to each message. For an average web, you can figure on getting at least five or six messages per week, requiring an hour or two to answer.

 Check your e-mail every day! People expect timely, quick responses to their questions. Set aside a certain time of the day—such as early morning, with your cup of coffee in hand—to answer your messages.

Estimating Your Total Time Commitment

Once you've thought through your commitment options, you're ready to estimate how much time your web will consume.

If you have a very simple one- or two-page presentation on your ISP's system, with no forms, and you update only once a month, your time investment is pretty negligible (perhaps two to five hours per month).

For someone running a fairly serious Web effort, involving a shareware PC server that features a mailing list response form and weekly updates, here's a rough-and-ready estimate of how much time you'll need:

Server maintenance:	3 hours/week
Content maintenance:	3 hours/week
Web promotion:	2 hours/week
Forms processing:	1 hours/week
E-mail replies:	2 hours/week
Total:	**11 hours/week**

A high-capacity UNIX or Windows NT server, daily updates, extensive forms, and heavy volume can quickly grow into a full-time job.

 As any experienced Webmaster will tell you, you should multiply your estimate by at least 1.5. Web presentation development expands to fill all available time—and then some.

FROM HERE

- Once you've devised your purpose statement, you're on your way to crafting a successful web. In the next chapter, you'll take the next step: selecting a web architecture.

Chapter

8

Understanding Web Architecture

Whe building a house, you must first understand the materials with which you're working (your building blocks) and then decide on a basic design scheme to use—is it going to be a ranch, a colonial, or a Buckminster Fuller dome? In this chapter, you'll learn how to develop a list of the Web pages you want to create (by means of *chunking*), and then you'll learn how to select the right architecture for your purposes.

This chapter aims to help you decide among linear and nonlinear methods of presenting information. Consider single Web pages, multipage Web presentations, elaborate semantic nets, and hierarchical structures as you plan your site.

For the Time-Challenged

- Web sites have building blocks and architectures, just like buildings. The building blocks are the pages you've come up with after you've *chunked* your information. A site's architecture is its general design, the way the information the site contains is organized.

- In chunking, you divide your material up into topics that you treat one page at a time. Each page of your web should express and develop one idea only, and it should be able to stand on its own.

- There are four popular Web architectures: the single page, the Web presentation, the semantic net, and the hierarchical web.

- A single page is just that: A single HTML document containing information. Web pages are useful when only a little bit of data is to be published and it's important that the data be viewed in a particular sequence.

- A Web presentation is a series of Web pages that must be viewed in a particular order. Web presentations are useful when a lot of data is to be published and it is important that it be viewed in a particular order. Sales pitches and logical arguments are examples of information that fit into Web presentations.

- A semantic net is composed of lots of little chunks of data, each posted to the Web on its own page. A semantic net architecture makes it easy to navigate among the pieces of data and draw conclusions from them without help from the Web author.

- A hierarchical web employs several distinct levels, enabling users to "tunnel down" in search of more specific information.

- When you've finished your chunking and chosen an architecture, sketch out your ideas using a *storyboard*. A storyboard is a sketch showing the individual pages of your web and how they're connected.

THE ART OF CHUNKING

The basic concept of hypertext writing is that each page of your web should express and develop just one of the ideas you want to express, and it should do so in a way that enables the page to be read independently. Suppose, for example, you're creating a web about historic (and still navigable) canals in Virginia. Your web could consist of the following pages:

Albemarle and Chesapeake Canal
Atlantic Intracoastal Waterway
Dismal Swamp
Dismal Swamp Canal
History of canals in Virginia
Nineteenth-century canal engineering
Norfolk, Virginia
Wilderness areas in Virginia

The term *chunking* refers to segregating the concepts you're dealing with, and developing short, focused documents dealing with each. The more you chunk, the more you'll multiply the possible connections among the documents you're creating.

Page 1: Historic canals of Virginia

The <u>Dismal Swamp Canal</u> and the <u>Albemarle & Chesapeake Canal</u> form alternate routes along the <u>Atlantic Intracoastal Waterway</u> and <u>Albemarle Sound</u>...

Page 2 The Atlantic Intracoastal Waterway

The Atlantic Intracoastal Waterway provides pleasure boaters and commercial shippers with a protected inland channel between <u>Norfolk, Virginia</u> and Miami, Florida...

Page 3: The Dismal Swamp Canal

The Dismal Swamp Canal is misnamed. Far from dismal, the <u>Dismal Swamp</u> is a beautiful wilderness teeming with wildlife. Not far from <u>Norfolk, Virginia</u>, the <u>Dismal Swamp Canal</u> provides an appealing option for voyagers along the <u>Atlantic Intracoastal Waterway</u>...

Page 4: The Albemarle and Chesapeake Canal

The Albemarle and Chesapeake Canal was envisioned as early as 1772, but construction did not begin until 1855. The engineering marvel of its day, the canal required seven steam dredges. The canal's construction consigned the <u>Dismal Swamp Canal</u> to bankruptcy...

Page 5: Dismal Swamp

Virginia's Dismal Swamp, not far from <u>Norfolk, Virginia</u>, may have seemed dismal to early colonists looking for promising agricultural areas, but it's actually a beautiful wilderness, alive with wildlife...

Page 6: Norfolk, Virginia

Home to one of the world's largest and busiest naval bases, Norfolk, Virginia provides the entrance point for <u>Chesapeake</u> boaters planning to navigate the <u>Atlantic Intracoastal Waterway</u> to North Carolina...

These concepts go off in all directions!
Carried to their logical extremes, they embrace the entire world of knowledge. At some point as you're chunking, you must decide where to stop. Which concepts are really important for your message? Perhaps other people have developed pages on a subject that's tangential to your main point. For example, there are many very nicely done pages on Norfolk, Virginia. There's no need to reinvent the wheel by developing a page on a subject that's already well covered elsewhere.

Understanding Your Architectural Options

Now that you've got your building blocks, it's time to figure out which type of structure you're building. On the Web, the following architectural options are commonly chosen: a *single Web page, presentations, semantic nets,* and *hierarchical webs.*

Publishing a Single Page

The fastest and easiest way to publish on the Web is with a Web page—a single HTML document that contains information. A Web page may also contain links to distant pages, but those pages are maintained by someone else. If the page is lengthy, it may contain internal hyperlinks, enabling the user to navigate without becoming lost.

Advantages

Single-page sites offer the advantage of encapsulating all the information they hold into one location on the Web—there's no need to hunt around a complex structure involving dozens of Web pages. Also, when a spider finds your page and lists it in a search engine's database, it's likely that search results will be more useful, since there won't be 15 listings for the same site in a search report. (Imagine running a Lycos search for "Cleveland, Ohio"—the subject of your site, say—and getting back listings for "Sports in Cleveland, Ohio," "Museums in Cleveland, Ohio," and "City Government in Cleveland, Ohio," all of which are pages in the same collection.)

Single Web pages are relatively easy to maintain, since there's only one HTML document to download from the Web server, modify, and upload again. You will probably want to consider a single Web page if you're planning to provide frequently updated information or to alter your page's appearance often.

Web pages also allow you to make a point in a linear fashion, as you learned to do in school. You can treat a Web page like a piece of typing paper by starting with a thesis at the top, explaining some supporting ideas, and wrapping up with a conclusion. If your site's purpose calls for making such a point, you'll probably want to use a single-page architecture.

Disadvantages

The main disadvantage of single Web pages is that they don't exploit the Web's unique ability to break data into small, specific chunks for readers to navigate through as they wish. If you choose to post your data in the form of a single Web page, you should consider the following:

- **People don't like to read on-screen.** They'll do it if they're sufficiently motivated, but they don't like it. If you look at the high-impact webs on the Web, you'll find that most of them limit page length to $1^{1}/_{2}$ to 2 screenfuls of material.

- **Lengthy pages with heterogeneous material tend to disorient readers.** It's easy to get lost in a long, wordy page that covers several unrelated subjects—and that's true even if you provide internal navigation links.

- **Lengthy pages defeat the purpose of hypertext, which is to enable users to choose their own path through the material.** If you find that a page is getting too lengthy, you should consider chunking it further.

Applications

There are two popular kinds of single-page Web sites: home pages and information pages. Home pages are perhaps the oldest genre of Web publication, and by definition they're single-page documents. Even if your home page has hyperlinks to several subsidiary documents, visitors still point their browsers to a particular URL at the beginning of a browsing session.

 If your single-page design is lengthy, include a table of contents at the top and use internal hyperlinks to link each item with the appropriate section. You can do this using the NAME attribute of the <A> tag. For more information, see Chapter 14.

Presentations

If you want to share more information than can easily fit on one page, but don't want to surrender control of the way that information is presented to your readers, a Web presentation may be the best way to organize your information.

A Web presentation, though it is made up of several pages, gives the viewer little flexibility in navigating through the information presented. Typically, the viewer enters the presentation through a welcome page, then proceeds one page at a time through the information, which is presented in the order the site designer wants. A viewer can get out of a Web presentation only by invoking a feature of his or her browser, such as a Hot List item or a URL from a history list.

In some Web presentation designs, viewers have options at different places in the presentation. They may opt to see information about one of several products, for example, instead of having to page through information about products that are uninteresting to them before reaching the product data they want. Typically, Web presentations include navigation aids, such as links back to the welcome page or pages from which others branch, that help viewers quickly find the portion of the presentation that's relevant to them.

A Web presentation architecture is shown in Figure 8.1.

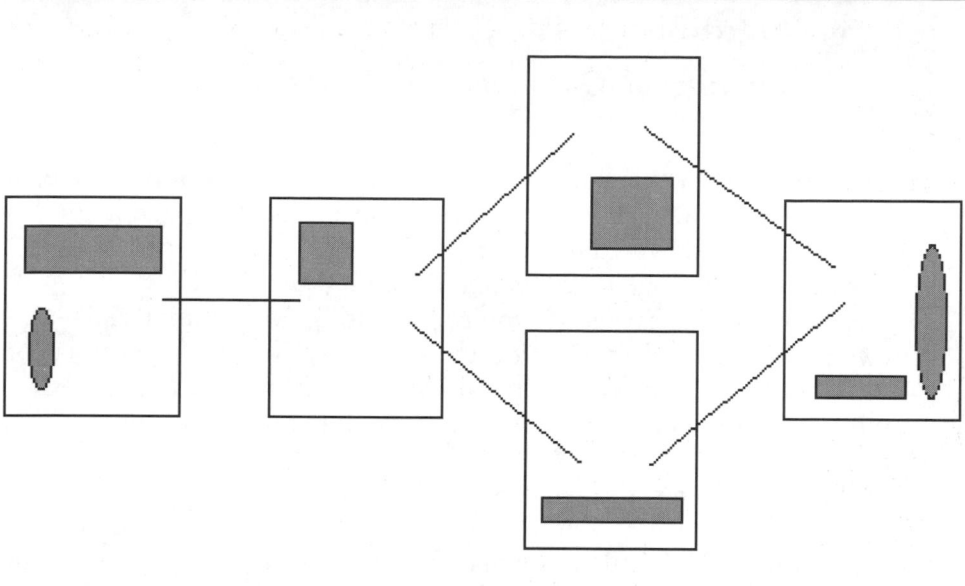

Figure 8.1 A Web presentation architecture.

Advantages

The advantage of Web presentations is that they break large quantities of information into manageable chunks but allow that information to be viewed in an orderly manner. Unlike semantic nets (described next), Web presentations keep control in the hands of the Web designer and surrender very little of it to the person viewing the pages.

Disadvantages

Web presentations are somewhat in violation of the spirit of the Web, where it is considered poor taste to restrict a person's navigation options. If you're going to take away a visitor's freedom of movement, you must be sure that you do so for a good reason and that he or she goes away happy after the presentation.

Web presentations lock your site's viewers into a predetermined routine, something they may not appreciate. If your presentation moves too fast,

Solutions

Finding the Optimum Page Length

Ideally, every page within your web should express and develop a single, unified concept. But how long should you make your pages? If a page is too lengthy, should you chunk down your concepts more? You'll need to consider the problems with excessive page length enumerated on pp. 137–138.

There's one major caveat: If you're presenting unified material—an essay, a news article, a short story—you should always keep this material on one page. Readers accessing this material have already made the decision to read it, and they won't appreciate having to link to the next page every few paragraphs.

There are problems, too, with pages that are just too short. It takes time to download a new page; your readers may get frustrated—and link out—if they're rewarded with little more than a sentence or two. Don't overchunk!

So where's the optimum? Consider the following:

- Every page should express and develop just one concept or topic. Keep overall page length down by making sure that every page deals with just one of the topics treated by your web.

- In general, limit page length to $1^1/_2$ to 2 screenfuls of text. If your pages exceed this amount, consider chunking down your concepts to a more fine-grained level. Don't go under this limit, though, unless you want to irritate your readers.

- Go over the two-page limit if your page contains material that's rhetorically unified, such as a short story, essay, or news article.

- Consider going over the two-page limit if your page contains unified material that's organized according to a clear method of development, such as alphabetical order.

viewers may become intimidated, while if it moves too slow, they may grow bored or conclude that you don't think highly of their intellectual abilities. Either way, they probably won't return and your site will start to earn a bad reputation among users of the Web.

Applications

Certain applications involve too much information for a single page, but do not lend themselves to the chaos of a semantic net. Those applications, which typically involve some kind of linear flow from one idea to another, are good candidates for inclusion in a Web presentation.

The steps involved in a recipe, for example, must be presented in a particular order. If the steps to the recipe won't fit easily on one page—if the recipe is for, say, a home-built aircraft—a Web presentation is an excellent option. The same idea applies to sales pitches. It wouldn't be good if the viewer of your Web site first came to the page that said "Model V: $14,439" and *then* saw the pages that explain why the Model V is such a great machine.

 If you use a Web presentation architecture, be sure to include navigation buttons at the top of each page. One button should be linked to the next page, one to the previous page, and one to the page where the presentation started. Your site's viewers will appreciate being given some extra flexibility in navigation.

Semantic Nets

Semantic nets take advantage of the capabilities of hypertext authoring, but require the creator of a site to surrender navigational control to the reader.

Semantic nets require you to puree your data—you must chop your information into tiny bits and link all the bits together with hyperlinks. There should be only one idea—a paragraph of text, a graphic, or an item of some other medium—on each page. You then provide a point of entry and set the viewer free to explore the information at will. A semantic net architecture is shown in Figure 8.2.

Advantages

Semantic nets are the highest form of hypermedia, since they are freely navigable and offer almost limitless possibilities for interpretation. By organizing your information in a semantic net, you offer your site's visitors great freedom to examine and draw conclusions from data at their leisure. You're not forcing them to look at data in a particular way, and you're not demanding that they conclude certain things from it. Your site's viewers, assuming they have the brain power to absorb data presented in a random

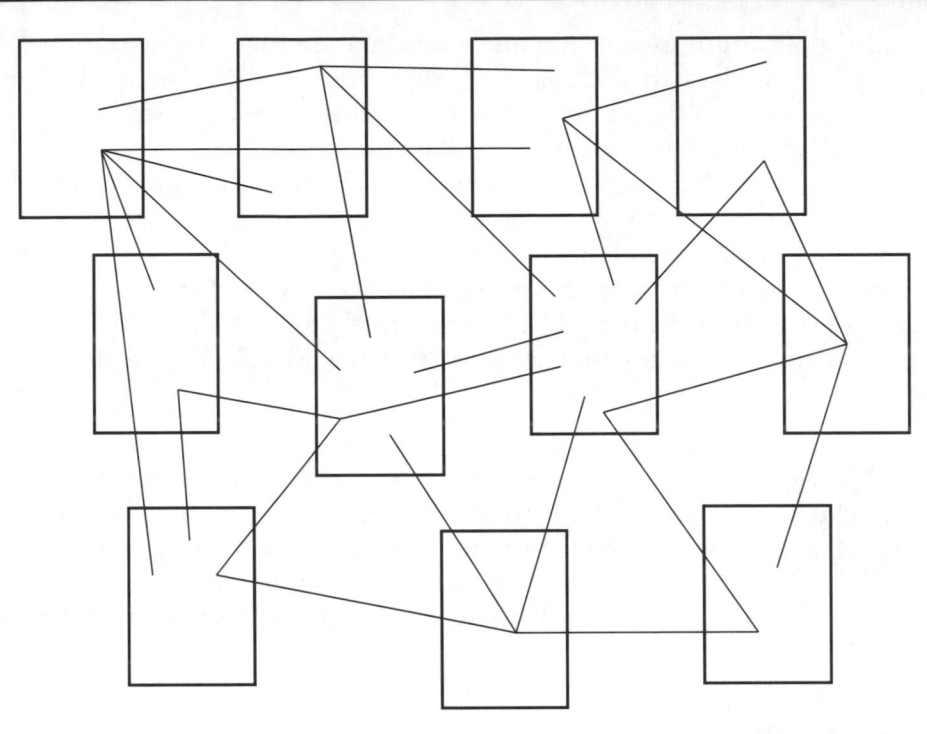

Figure 8.2   A semantic net architecture.

way, will appreciate the fact that you gave them free rein over the data you posted.

Creating a well-done semantic net is rare, and if you succeed at it you'll probably receive considerably more attention than if you post a single page or a Web presentation. The Web community generally rewards hard work and careful design, and a good semantic net requires both.

Disadvantages

Creating a well-implemented semantic net isn't easy. You have to break your information into small pieces, then post all the pieces to the Web. Simply managing the dozens, hundreds, or thousands of HTML documents a semantic net requires is a monumental chore. Then you have to develop a powerful but user-friendly means of moving among the chunks of data, and figure out a way to keep that navigation tool up-to-date when you add new pieces of information.

Basically, ease of use for the site visitor translates into headaches for the site designer and maintainer. If you're willing to spend the time and effort to post and maintain a site based on semantic net architecture, your audience will probably love you for it. On the other hand, you'll probably spend a significant portion of your time maintaining the site and keeping it up-to-date.

Applications

Semantic nets are not suited to applications in which it's important that viewers see certain information before they see other information. You wouldn't want viewers to see the conclusion of your thesis paper before seeing your argument, and you wouldn't want to show viewers a price list before telling them why the thing you're selling is very reliable and is probably worth twice what you ask for it. In such applications, a single Web page architecture or a carefully organized presentation is probably a better bet, as there's less chance of confusing your viewers with a somewhat chaotic presentation of data.

Semantic nets are better suited to applications that involve lots of information of equal importance, such as the rosters of a football team for each of fifty years or biographies of all the middle-level executives in a company. By providing an easy way to navigate from one item of information to any of the other items of information of equal importance, you encourage visitors to your site to choose the information they want to see and ignore the information that doesn't interest them. Semantic nets give Web users a feeling of control—a concept that may be hard for those who are used to dealing with linear media, such as printed text or television, to accept.

HIERARCHICAL WEBS

In a *hierarchical web*, a designer creates two or more distinct levels of specificity. For example, consider the Virginia canals example presented at the beginning of this chapter. This material could be logically organized into the following outline:

Welcome and introduction

Historic canals of Virginia near Norfolk, Virginia

Albemarle and Chesapeake Canal

The Dismal Swamp Canal

The Great Dismal Swamp

Canoeing

Kayaking

Nature trails

In Figure 8.3, you see how this outline could be translated into an architecture with distinct levels.

You could develop additional levels, if you wish. Under canoeing, for example, you could include information about where to rent canoes, where to begin your canoe trip, what to bring, and so forth.

Advantages

The chief advantage of a hierarchical web is that it's capable of storing a great deal of data, but it doesn't throw all this data at the user all at once. On the welcome page, you see only the links to the next level. As you navigate through the web, you "drill down" into lower levels of greater specificity. You only see the complexity of a level when you've drilled down to that level.

Disadvantages

The chief drawback to a hierarchical web is that it's very easy to get lost. You'd be wise to provide good navigation aids, as discussed in the next chapter, as well as an overall index to the pages in your site.

Applications

A hierarchical web is well suited to any Web site that must contain many pages of information. All large-scale sites are organized in this way.

CHOOSING YOUR ARCHITECTURE

The architecture you choose depends on several factors, but, as with nearly every other aspect of Web design, the nature of your audience is the most important. You'll want to pay special attention to such characteristics as their attention span, their skill in navigating among Web documents, and

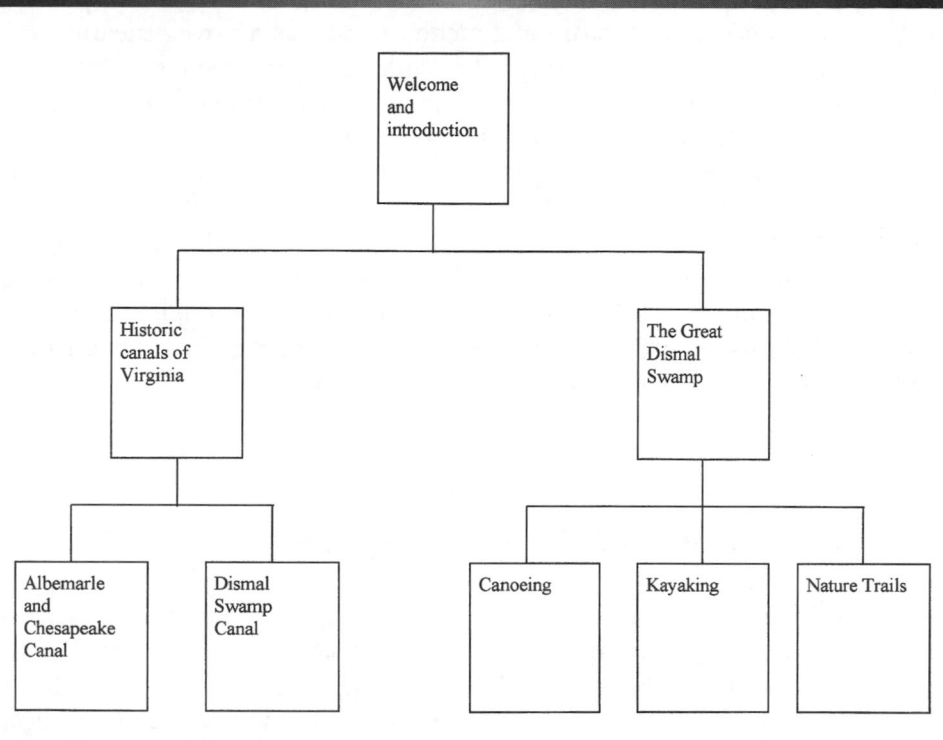

Figure 8.3 A hierarchical web.

whether they need to be led from one topic to another or they can draw conclusions from a generally unorganized collection of data.

You'll also want to consider your goals for the site and think about what Web architecture best suits them. If your goal is to sell a product, for instance, you may need to lead your site's visitors through a presentation one step at a time. If your goal is to provide hobbyists with references and technical information, it might be better to create a site with many small pages—and perhaps a search tool—that would enable hobbyists to quickly find the data they need and move on.

 Consider combining a Web presentation with a hierarchical web, and giving your users the option of which one they'll navigate. For users unfamiliar with your subject, the presentation serves to educate; for users familiar with the subject, the hierarchical web enables them to explore the material as they please.

The prime issue at stake in your Web architecture decision is the question of who is in control. In a traditional medium, such as a novel, the author is in nearly complete control. Though the reader can read the last page of the novel first, it won't make any sense and he or she will have missed the fun of seeing the story develop. That's not the case on the Web.

Web authors can design their sites so the reader has a great deal of control. By giving readers the freedom to move among many different chunks of data at will, the Web author enables them to navigate through the material in their own way and absorb it in the order they wish. Instead of having to offer the reader a more or less linear collection of thoughts and arguments, the publisher of a Web site can give the reader a three-dimensional collection of data to explore in any number of ways.

INCLUDING FUNCTIONAL PAGES

As you're considering your web's architecture, bear in mind that you should include some *functional* pages as well as *content* pages. Functional pages provide information about your Web site and enhance its navigability. Here's a list of the functional pages you'll find in some of the Web's best-developed sites:

Welcome	This is the site's official entry point. For tips on designing your welcome page, see the next chapter.
Info	This page provides information about your site, such as who's responsible for it, how often it's updated, and more. You can include your disclaimer, as well.
Roadmap (Index)	This page lists all the pages in your site, enabling users to find their way if they get confused.
What's New	Previous visitors will appreciate your telling them what you've added since the site was last updated.
What's Cool	Show your users the best you have to offer.
Add a Resource	If your site includes a list of related links, ask users to contribute their own discoveries.
Special Features	List the special or unusual features of your site.

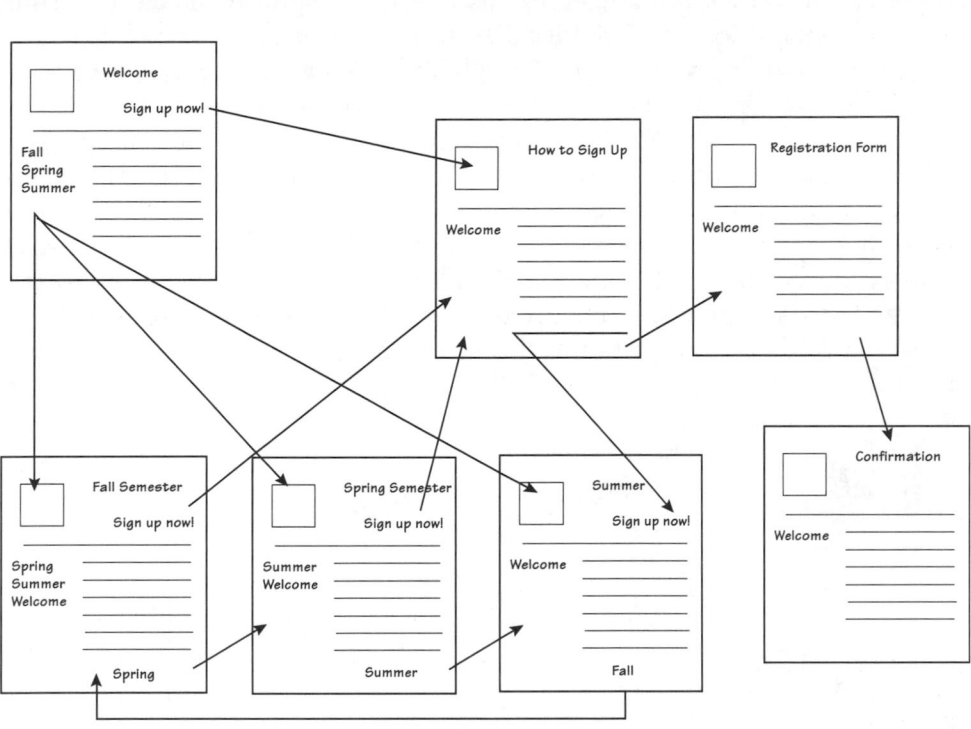

Figure 8.4   In Web design, a storyboard shows the logical relationships among the building blocks in your architecture.

Search	If you plan to make your site searchable, be sure to include a navigation aid that's linked to the search page.
Feedback	Enable your users to send mail to you. You can also use forms to enable richer feedback.

STORYBOARDING

Once you've got some working chunk notes and thought about which functional pages to include, it's time to plan your overall architecture. You may wish to use a forced march, a semantic net, a hierarchical structure, or some combination of these. In any case, you'll find it helpful to sketch out your ideas on paper, using a technique called *storyboarding*.

In storyboarding, you create a rough sketch of what each page of your web will look like, beginning with the welcome page, and you show the relationships among them. In Figure 8.4, you see a sketch of a simple site created to market computer courses at a local computer store. This is a hierarchical web blended with a presentation. From the welcome page, you access links to the fall, spring, and summer course listings; within these, links at the bottom or left margin of the page enable you to move to the next semester's offerings. From any page, you can sign up for classes, which takes you to a mini-presentation that includes the registration form and a confirmation message.

 A storyboard doesn't have to be fancy. Just sketch out your ideas on a large piece of paper (tape some sheets together, if necessary, so you have plenty of room to work).

FROM HERE

- Now that you've determined your Web's architecture, you're ready to start thinking about page design. The next chapter introduces you to the fundamentals of designing effective Web pages.

Chapter
9

The Fundamentals of Web Page Design

I f the last time you attended art class was in junior high, the word "design" can sound pretty intimidating. It tends to make me think of pony-tailed graphics geniuses who produce astonishingly beautiful work but can't for the life of them explain how they did it.

But you don't need to be a design genius to design effective webs. Admittedly, effective graphics design does require some artistic training, or at least some decent artistic sensibilities. But we're talking about Web design here. As you'll see in this chapter, there are four basic principles of effective Web design. They aren't very difficult to grasp, and they're even easier to implement. Once you grasp these principles, you can design a Web site that's going to have people coming back for more.

For the Time-Challenged

♦ On the Web, the four most important design principles are consistency, predictability, accessibility, and navigability.

♦ Consistency ensures that users never have any doubt that they're still within your site. Create consistency by using similar graphics, color, fonts, layout, and other design elements on all pages of your web.

♦ Predictability assures users that they can use the skills they've used throughout your site. Create predictability by using a design grid for all or most of your web's pages.

♦ Accessibility provides users with visual cues to your site's offerings. Achieve accessibility through the use of white space, typography, headings, and other layout elements.

♦ Navigability provides users with supple, responsive means for finding their way. Create navigability by choosing appropriate navigation aids for your web.

♦ A good welcome page anticipates user's needs and provides pathways into your site.

THE FOUR PRINCIPLES OF EFFECTIVE WEB DESIGN

Traditional designers think in terms of concepts such as balance, proportion, and harmony. These are important in Web design—but as you'll see in this section, the Web's a different type of medium than the ones in which designers typically work. When designing for the Web, the top four design principles are consistency, predictability, accessibility, and navigability.

Consistency

In a well-designed web, you never have any doubt whether or not you're still in the web. That's because the design is so distinctive that it says, "You're still here."

Why is this such a big deal on the Web? Consider how easy it is to hyperlink out of a web. Readers may not realize that they have exited your web and entered someone else's—and they might even hold you responsible for that web's content! For this reason, every page of your web should convey a distinctive look, one that firmly demarcates your web from the many external webs that are accessible by means of the hyperlinks you've included. Nothing conveys this message more effectively than consistency in page design.

 Consistency is very important, but don't take it too far. What you're striving for is consistency without monotony. On some of your pages, it's perfectly appropriate to introduce variations on your theme. If you look at the best webs, you'll see that subordinate pages present variations on themes introduced on the welcome page. However, you're always aware that you're at the same web—a very important point when you consider how easily and frequently readers jump from one web to another via hyperlinks.

How to Achieve a Consistent Design

When you create your pages, you have many opportunities for creating a consistent look:

- **Logo**   Many well-designed Web pages feature a logo that's found on each and every page of the web, usually in the same position. Although some Web authors engage professional graphic artists to create logos, others are prepared using tools such as Adobe Photoshop (which enables you to create text with special effects, such as shadowing).

- **Color Theme**   One of the key features that distinguishes professionally designed webs from their amateur counterparts is color awareness. Colors should complement each other, not clash, unless you're trying to make a point with an item that's given a clashing color. If you're not sure what "complement" means, try to stick with consistently "warm" colors (red, orange, brown, yellow) or "cool" colors (blue, green, lavender).

- **Background Color**   Some webs use a distinctive background color to establish an identity, and do so very effectively. For this technique to work, the color must be complemented by harmonious color choices throughout.

- **Text Color** Standard HTML tags enable you to select colors for body text, unviewed hyperlinks, and viewed hyperlinks. These choices apply to the whole document. Thanks to tags introduced by Netscape, it's now possible to choose colors for specific units of text, from one character to many paragraphs. Font colors should be chosen so that they work harmoniously with background and other color choices.

- **Fonts** A web can establish its identify through the use of one or two distinctive fonts. As it stands right now, typography can't be used unless you capture the fonts in graphics—a very inefficient approach, but one that's used effectively at some webs.

- **Background Graphic** Since Netscape introduced the background graphic attribute (BACKGROUND) with version 1.1 of Netscape, amateur Web designers have more than amply demonstrated this tag's drawbacks. They've created Web pages that are almost completely unreadable! Professionally designed pages use very low-key background graphics; they're chosen to blend harmoniously with other color choices and to *enhance* the text's readability.

- **Navigation Aids** Many webs offer a row of navigation buttons or icons, providing yet another opportunity to establish consistency by means of color and graphics.

- **Bullets** In unordered (bulleted) lists, you can use small graphics instead of the default (and unattractive) bullets. Use the same bullet design and color throughout your web.

- **Layout** The term *layout* refers to the overall arrangement of text and graphics on the page. In the hands of a capable designer, layout can be used to establish consistency. For example, some webs use text centering and lots of white space to establish an attractive, consistent look. In particular, tables can be used to pull off formatting tricks that HTML doesn't exactly encourage, such as two-column newsletter layouts.

- **Rules** The default HTML rule (<HR>) is a design cliché that's best avoided. However, you can use graphics as rules, which provides another opportunity to introduce a consistent design element.

Examples of Design Consistency

clnet: The Computer Network (http://www.cnet.com) provides computer-related news and resources of interest to all Web users. Every page of the

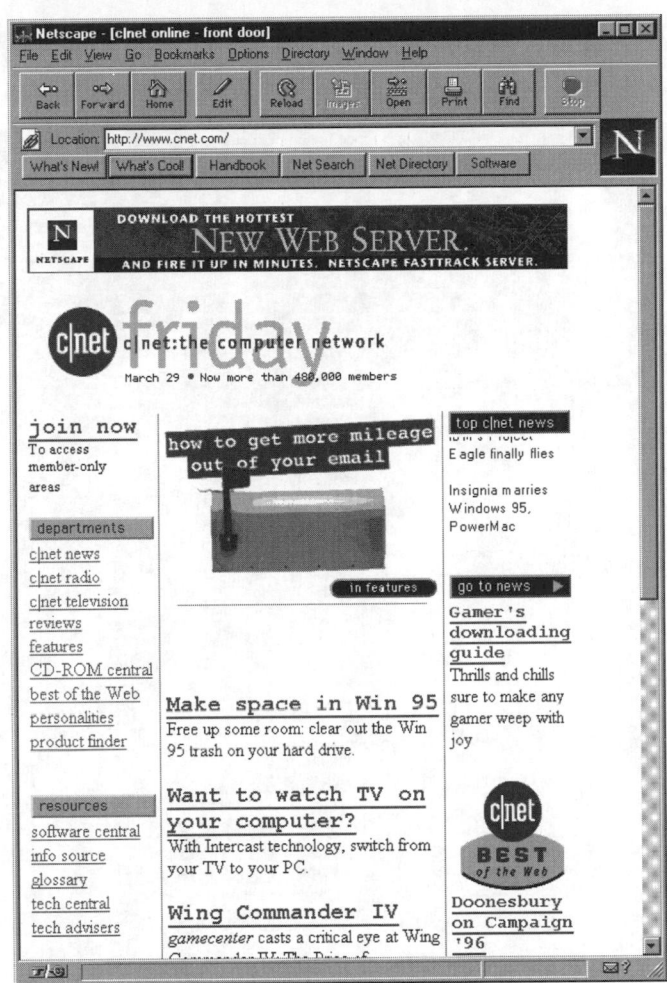

Figure 9.1   clnet achieves consistency through color.

clnet web repeats a set of design themes involving a characteristic logo, an overall color tone, a consistent background color and navigation aids, and the use of a table-based layout to create a consistent page design (see Figure 9.1).

Here's another beautiful example of design consistency: Graphic Communication, an Internet publishing, advertising, and design firm located in

Figure 9.2 Graphic Communication achieves consistency by means of a column layout (created with tables).

Hawaii (see Figure 9.2). The site is located at http://graph.com/. The design achieves consistency by means of an attractive logo, a stylish overall color tone, the use of a pleasingly dark background graphic with light gray text, and a layout featuring what appears to be a newspaper column (for another example, see Figure 9.3). This is done by means of a table.

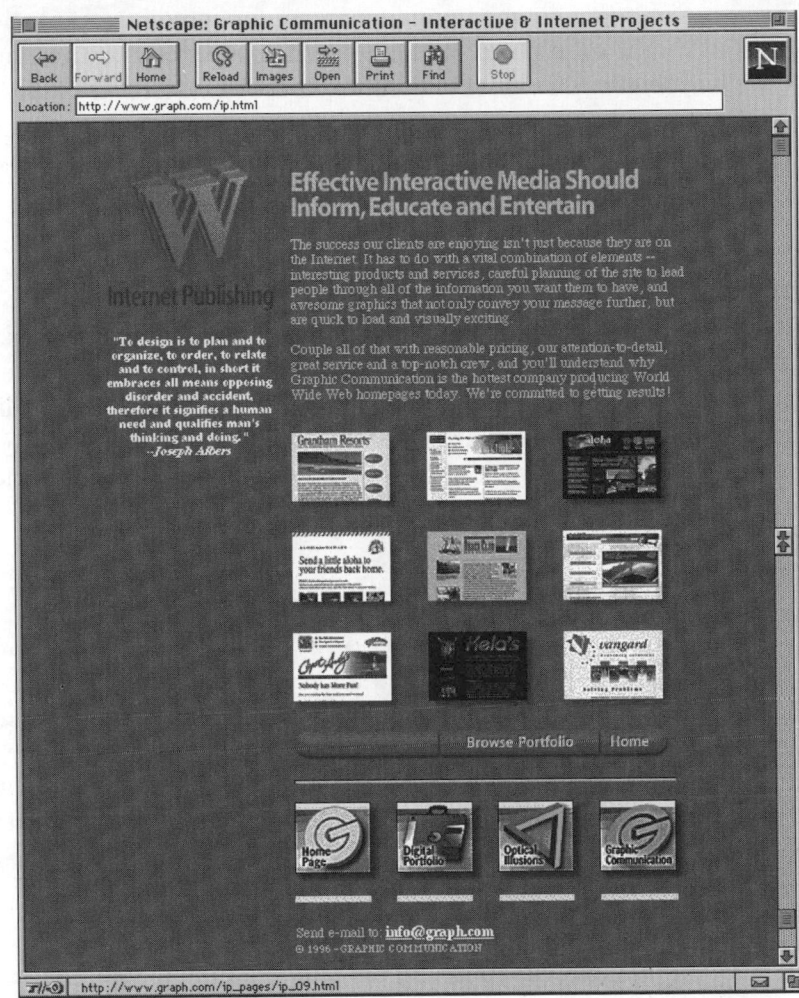

Figure 9.3 In Graphic Communication's site, each page reiterates the basic design themes.

As you can see from these examples, tables can be used to create eye-catching layouts. You'll learn more about the use of tables for layout purposes in Chapter 18.

When you're designing your pages, bear in mind that people don't like to read text on computer screens. Graphic Communication's site shows a keen awareness of this fact. By using a narrow text column, the site's designers make their text more readable. In addition, they keep the text short: There's never more than one screenful per page. You will do very well to study this example carefully.

Predictability

When users access your pages, they want predictability. After a quick look at your welcome page, they want to be able to use the skills they've learned on all the rest of the pages on your web. They want to be able to tell, at a glance, where to look for important information. They want to move effortlessly from page to page. They don't want to learn new skills every time they access a new page.

The Key to Predictability: Repetition of Design Elements

You can ensure predictablity in a number of ways—for example, by providing the same navigation buttons on each and every page of your web—but it's as much a mental attitude as a set of specific suggestions. In Figures 9.4 and 9.5, for example, the page design is simple, pleasing, and clear; what's more, you learn at a glance where to look for the navigation aids (just to the left of the text, positioned at the top of the column). The reader expects to find these aids in the same place on subsequent pages. This site has won a number of awards.

Develop a Design Grid for Your Pages

To ensure consistency and predictability, you'd be wise to do some sketching on paper before you start composing in HTML. Create a design grid that specifies where the most important components of your page design will appear, including your logo and navigation aids. What we're discussing here is the general design grid for your whole web; the welcome page, which has some special characteristics, is discussed later in this chapter.

Figure 9.6 shows a sketch for a design grid. This is a simple, clean design that clearly establishes the web's identity (by means of the logo), provides predictability by placing the navigation aids in the same place on every page, and leaves plenty of room for text. This is a good grid for a web that's loaded with resources and content.

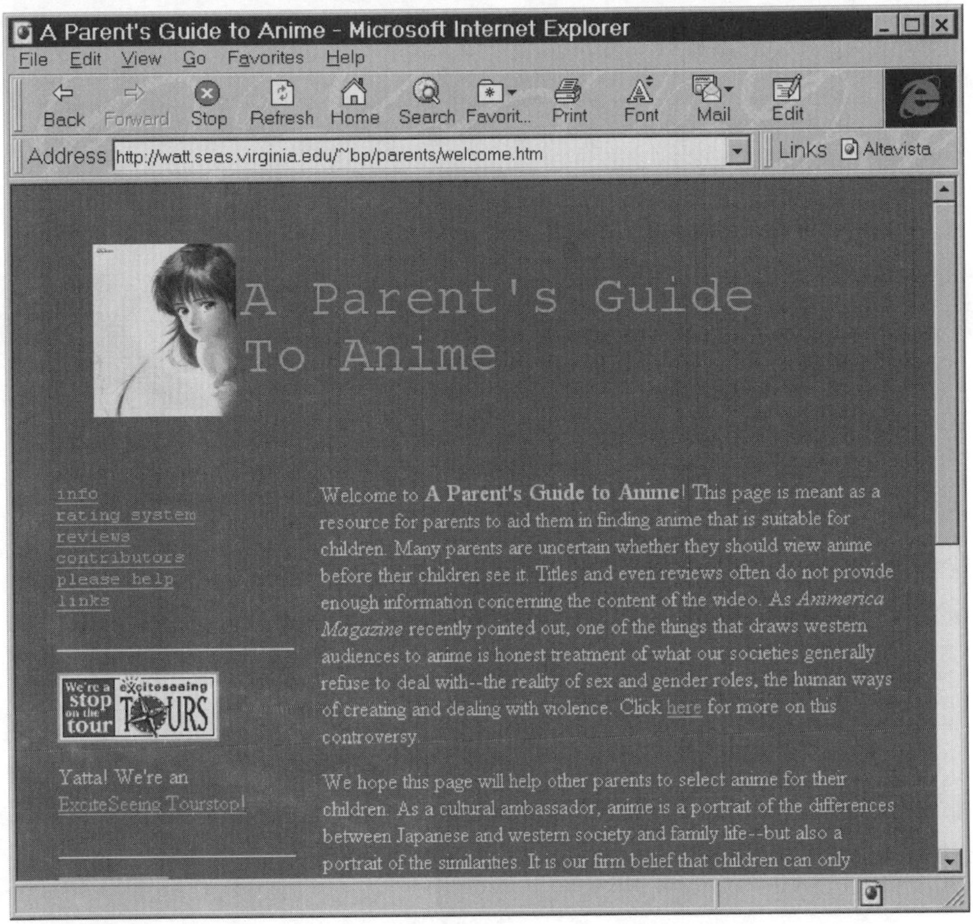

A Parent's Guide to Anime - Microsoft Internet Explorer

File Edit View Go Favorites Help

Back Forward Stop Refresh Home Search Favorit... Print Font Mail Edit

Address http://watt.seas.virginia.edu/~bp/parents/welcome.htm   Links Altavista

A Parent's Guide To Anime

info
rating system
reviews
contributors
please help
links

We're a stop on the tour exciteseeing TOURS

Yatta! We're an
ExciteSeeing Tourstop!

Welcome to **A Parent's Guide to Anime**! This page is meant as a resource for parents to aid them in finding anime that is suitable for children. Many parents are uncertain whether they should view anime before their children see it. Titles and even reviews often do not provide enough information concerning the content of the video. As *Animerica Magazine* recently pointed out, one of the things that draws western audiences to anime is honest treatment of what our societies generally refuse to deal with--the reality of sex and gender roles, the human ways of creating and dealing with violence. Click here for more on this controversy.

We hope this page will help other parents to select anime for their children. As a cultural ambassador, anime is a portrait of the differences between Japanese and western society and family life--but also a portrait of the similarities. It is our firm belief that children can only

Figure 9.4 A simple, clear page design.

In considering your design grid, make sure that you've answered the following questions. Did you:

- Clearly identify the title of your web on each page?
- State the title of each page within your web?

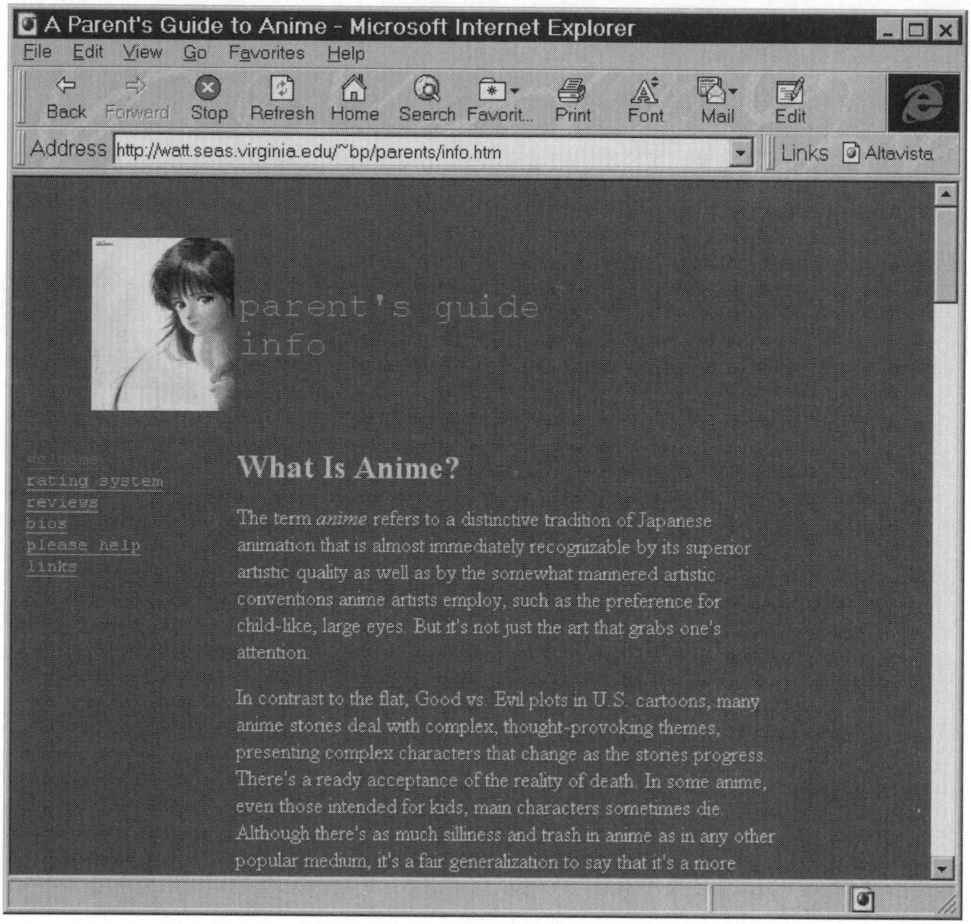

A Parent's Guide to Anime - Microsoft Internet Explorer

File   Edit   View   Go   Favorites   Help

Back   Forward   Stop   Refresh   Home   Search   Favorit...   Print   Font   Mail   Edit

Address http://watt.seas.virginia.edu/~bp/parents/info.htm   Links   Altavista

parent's guide
info

What Is Anime?

The term *anime* refers to a distinctive tradition of Japanese animation that is almost immediately recognizable by its superior artistic quality as well as by the somewhat mannered artistic conventions anime artists employ, such as the preference for child-like, large eyes. But it's not just the art that grabs one's attention.

In contrast to the flat, Good vs. Evil plots in U.S. cartoons, many anime stories deal with complex, thought-provoking themes, presenting complex characters that change as the stories progress. There's a ready acceptance of the reality of death. In some anime, even those intended for kids, main characters sometimes die. Although there's as much silliness and trash in anime as in any other popular medium, it's a fair generalization to say that it's a more

welcome
rating system
reviews
bios
please help
links

Figure 9.5   Page design echoed on subsequent pages to heighten consistency.

- Provide navigation aids in a predictable location?
- Make it easy to locate important material on the page?

Remember that the point of creating a grid is to ensure consistency and predictability, but not to the point of monotony. You can and should vary your design where appropriate.

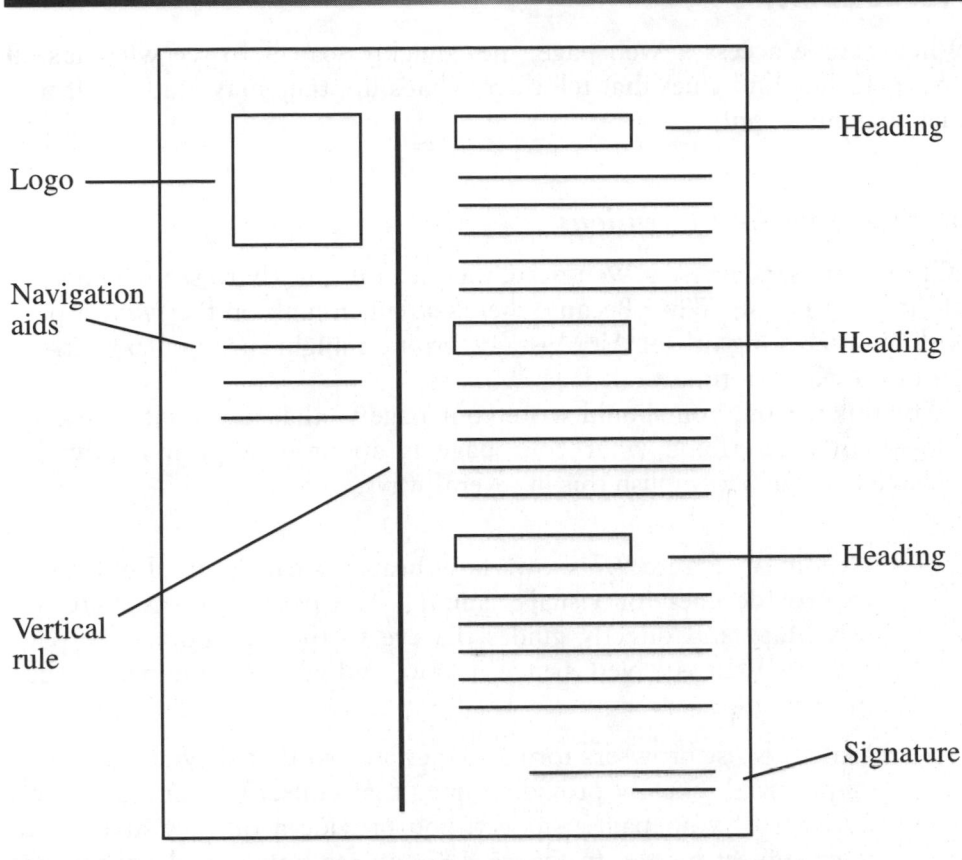

Figure 9.6 Sketch for a design grid.

 When you begin coding your web, create a generic template document that contains your design grid. Save this template using a file name such as "template.html." You can then load this template, add content to it, and save it with a new final name. In this way, you can build your web quickly without having to make the same color and layout choices each time you create a page.

Accessibility

When people access a Web page, they quickly scan it to see what it's all about. If they find clues that tell them what's up, they may read on. If not, they may move on!

Telegraphing Your Intentions

When Web users access a Web page, they scan it quickly to see whether it's of interest to them. Why? Because there's so much junk on the Web. A page with an interesting title or Alta Vista description might turn out to be irrelevant or a waste of time.

For this reason, you should write your page so that key subject descriptors—words describing what your page is about—are prominently displayed. You can accomplish this in several ways:

- **Headings** Figure 9.7 shows how headings can be used effectively to provide cues for visual scanning. The page explains NetCarta WebMap, and directly guides the eye to the two points the page makes: What is a NetCarta WebMap, and what do you need to display one?

- **Links** Most browsers format hyperlinks so that they appear to be emphasized text. By providing links that collectively amount to an abstract of your page's subject, you provide a quick visual cue to your subject matter. In Figure 9.8, you see how a Web author has used a rather lengthy hyperlink—five lines long—to emphasize the page's main point.

- **Pull Quotes** In magazine layout, a *pull quote* is a brief excerpt from the text that's duplicated elsewhere on the page, thus emphasizing a key point or something of special interest. Figure 9.9 shows an effective pull quote from Microsoft's MSNBC.com.

- **Graphics** You can use small graphics with easily perceived meanings to signal your page's intent and subject.

Highlighting What's Important

An effective Web page highlights what's important. You can do this in several ways:

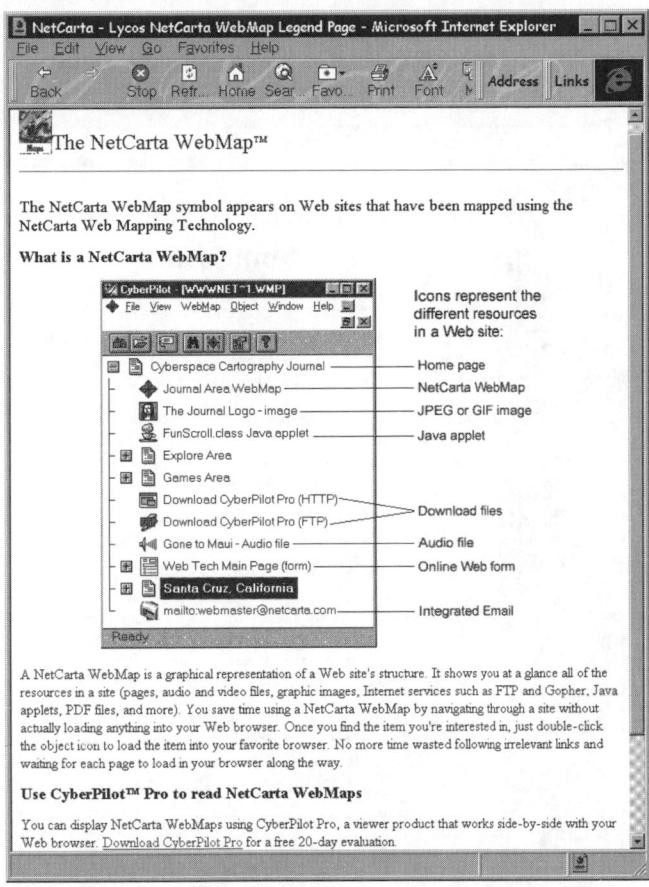

Figure 9.7 Telegraphing intentions with headings.

- **Use a small "New!" graphic**   Unfortunately, this approach has been overused to the point that it has lost effectiveness. At too many sites, items marked "New" turn out to be quite stale, so users have grown accustomed to discounting this method.

- **Put the important material at the top of the page**   Use a method of development that gives primacy to the most recent, the most acces-

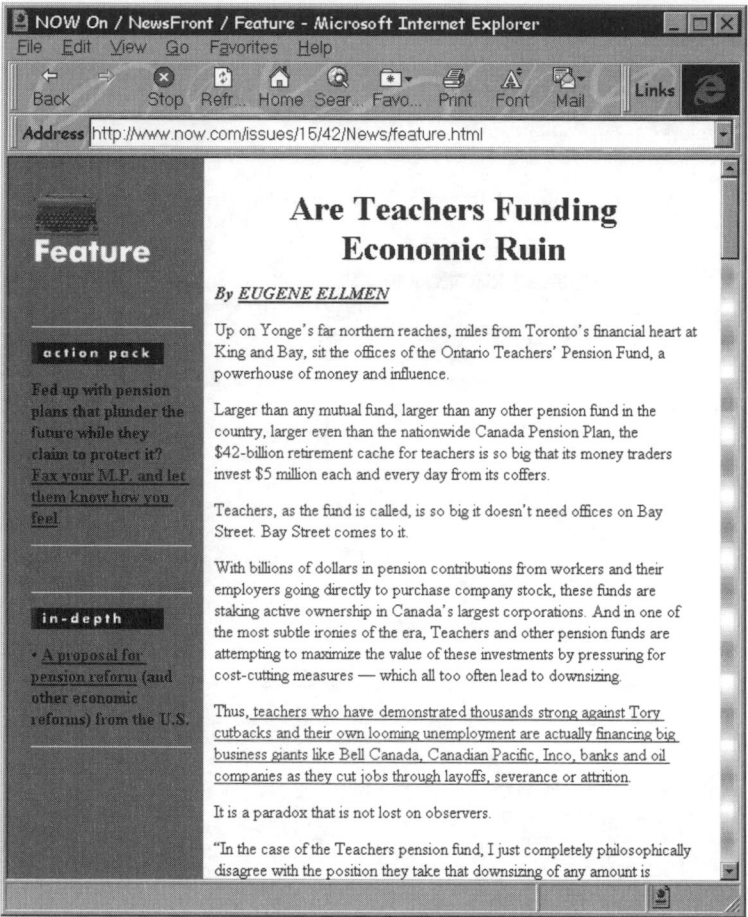

Figure 9.8 Telegraphing intentions with links.

sible, the most frequently accessed, or the most important material
at your site. *Hint:* Studies show that most users first look at the
upper left corner of a Web page.

• **Use animation**   Static pages don't cut it for today's Web audience.
  Animation isn't difficult to produce, as explained in Chapter 23, so
  you should consider adding an animation to highlight what's important at your site.

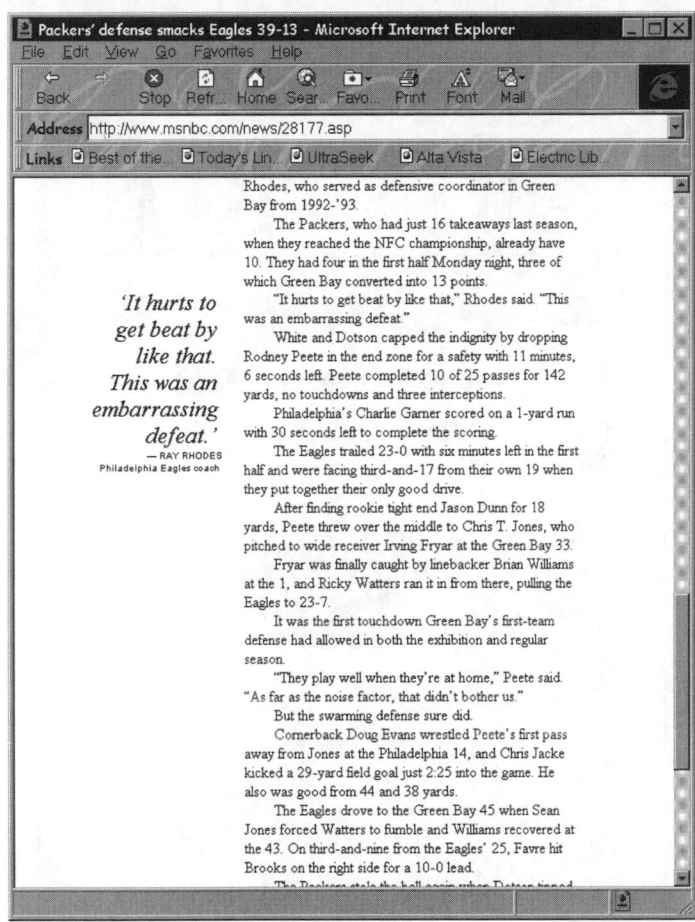

Figure 9.9   Telegraphing intentions with pull quotes (MSNBC).

Using White Space Effectively

Nothing differentiates amateur and professional designers as much as the use of white space. Amateurs tend to crowd too much content into a confined space, creating a pinched, unappealing look. In the hands of a competent designer, a Web page takes on a light, airy feel (see Figure 9.10). The

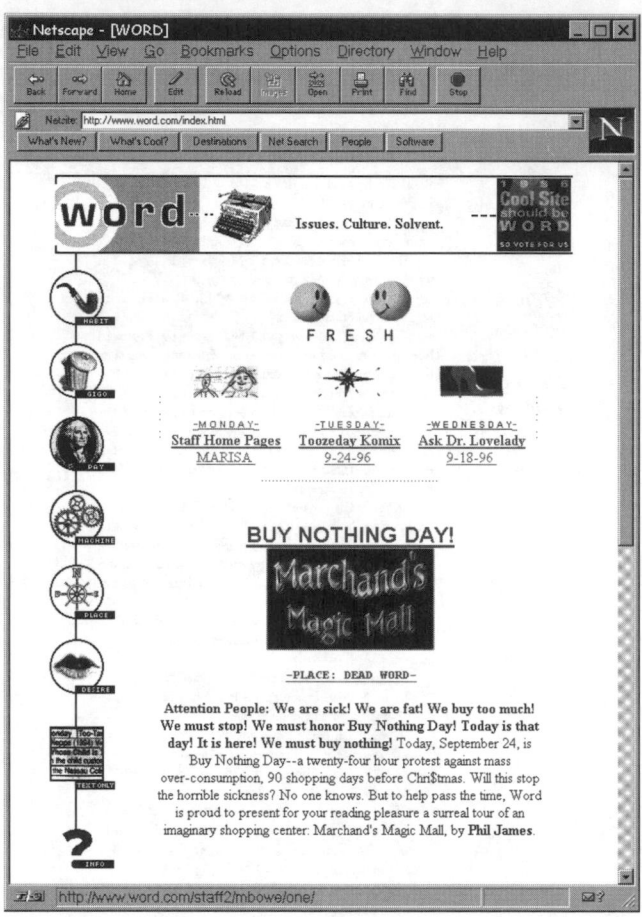

Figure 9.10   White space used effectively (www.word.com).

effective use of white space enables readers to scan the page quickly and pick out what's available and what's important.

Professionals use white space to accomplish a number of objectives:

- **Making text more readable**   From the standpoint of text readability, one of the least appealing characteristics of Web browsers is that they dynamically size lines of text: The wider the screen, the longer the line. You can defeat dynamic resizing by creating a single-column table with a fixed pixel width (see Chapter 18). The column should be narrow enough to leave white space on either side, creating a clean, sophisticated look.

• **Emphasizing text or graphics** White space can be used for emphasis: Something with more space has greater importance than something with less space. For example, a major heading needs more space above and below it than a minor heading.

• **Establishing balance** You can use white space to create a sense of balance and harmony on a page, offsetting (for example) large graphics with white space and smaller, separated units of text.

• **Controlling the overall color of the page** In typography, "color" refers to the overall tonal balance of a page—whether it's light (full of white space) or dark (loaded with graphics and text). Strive for balance (an overall "gray"), but it's better to err on the light side— it's easier to absorb information from a lighter page. Note that this point applies even if you're using a dark background and light type, but it's just the reverse: A "dark" page will have an airy, open feel, while a "light" one will have too much text.

 Considering Screen Width
Your Web page will be viewed by people using a wide variety of monitors and screen resolutions—and that's too bad. All the effort you're putting into your page design could very well be wasted if your page won't fit within the screen widths most people are using. Screen widths are measured in *pixels* (short for "picture elements")—basically, the dots that make up the screen. Just how many pixels a monitor can display depends on the monitor's capabilities and those of the video card the system is using. To make sure everyone can view your page, keep the maximum width to 640 pixels.

Navigability

Once you've established consistency, predictability, and accessibility, put the final touches on your design by ensuring navigability. This makes your web into a supple, usable resource that readers will appreciate.

Including Functional Navigation Aids

As you're planning your site's navigation aids, bear in mind an important distinction between functional navigation aids and content navigation aids.

- **Functional Navigation Aids** These aids help users deal with the hypertext functions of your site, such as returning to the welcome page (home). In addition, you should provide links to other functional pages, such as your What's New page, your Info page, and so forth (see Chapter 8 for a list of possible functional pages to include in your site).

- **Content Navigation Aids** These aids help users locate content within your site.

 A key question you'll need to consider is, Should you group the functional and content aids together? If you plan to include many functional aids, you may prefer to keep them separate. If you organize your document using frames or tables, you can separate the functional and content aids by placing them in separate panels.

Choosing the Appropriate Type of Navigation Aid

To provide navigation aids, you can choose from a variety of options, as the following list indicates. Choose the navigation option that's right for your site and technical abilities.

Row of Navigation Icons (Figure 9.11)
Advantages: Prominent and easy to use. Disadvantage: Requires original artwork or the use of overworked public domain icons.

Figure 9.11   Navigation icons: Planet Lunch.

Table Layout with Column of Navigation Links (Figure 9.12)
Advantages: Easy to implement, downloads quickly, and works with any table-capable browser. Disadvantage: Links scroll out of view when you scroll the page down.

Simple Text Links Separated by Bars or Brackets (Figure 9.13)
Advantages: Very easy to implement, downloads quickly, and works with any browser (including text-only browsers). Disadvantage: Looks low-tech.

Figure 9.12 Navigation links in vertical table: clnet.

SERVICES ONLINE | FREE SOFTWARE | INFO CENTRAL | WHAT'S NEW | HELP/SEARCH
TRACKING | DELIVERY OPTIONS | SHIPPING | DROPOFF LOCATOR

Figure 9.13 Simple text links separated by bars: FedEx.

Navigation Aids Displayed in Horizontal or Vertical Frames (Figure 9.14)

Advantages: Visible even if user scrolls other panels. A frame containing navigation aids can be made to stay in place while the user accesses additional pages at your site. Disadvantages: Requires a browser capable of displaying frames, requires complex frames tags, and downloads more slowly.

Clickable Imagemaps (Figure 9.15)

Advantages: Opens up a world of design possibilities. Disadvantages: Requires server-side programming. If the imagemap isn't designed with clear boundaries separating the embedded links, the user might not know where to click.

Navigation Metaphor (Figure 9.16)

By use of a navigation metaphor, you organize your site as if it were something else (such as an automobile, a house, or a garden). In Figure 9.16 you see one of the pages of the Internet Public Library, which presents a virtual library using imagemaps.

To maximize your site's navigability, consider blending two or more of the above methods. In Home Arts' professionally designed welcome page (Figure 9.17), you see a variety of methods: links in tables, navigation buttons in a vertically aligned frame, and scattershot links.

Planning a complex site? Consider adding a roadmap. A *roadmap* (also called an *index, table of contents,* or a *directory*) provides a list of all the pages in your web. If your web contains more than a half dozen pages, you may wish to add a roadmap page that lists all your pages and briefly describes their purpose.

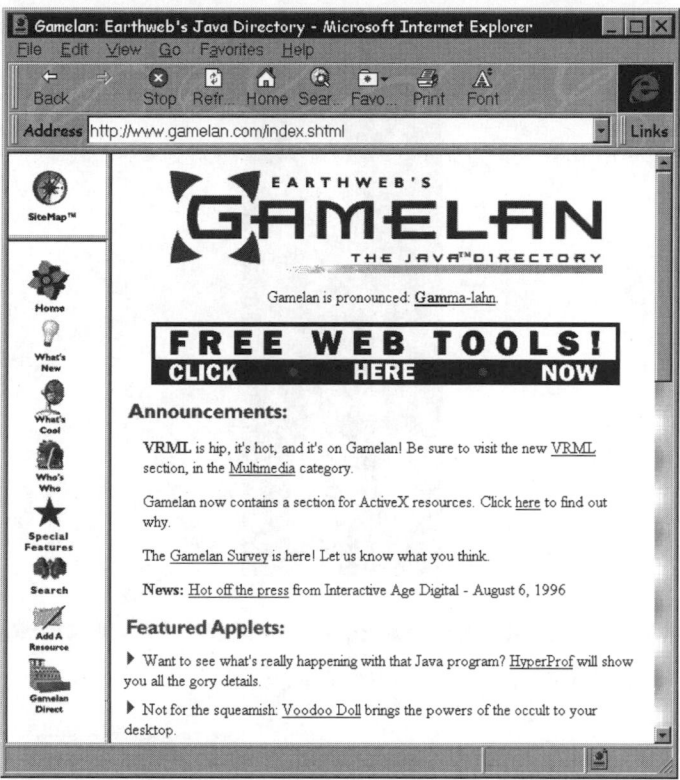

Figure 9.14 Navigation icons in vertical frame: Gamelan.

Enabling User Searches

Providing keyword searching for a large web requires special software, programming ability, and a powerful computer. But there are alternatives. The easiest way to add search capabilities is to create an alphabetical index page, such as the one shown in Figure 9.18. Each character in the alphabet is linked (by means of internal targets) to specific locations in the list.

 If you decide that you must include keyword search capabilities, you'll need to find a search engine that works with the server you're using. This topic is beyond the scope of this

Figure 9.15   Clickable imagemap: Peeps Republic.

book, but check out Excite for Web Servers (EWS) at

http://www.excite.com/navigate/home.html

At the time this book was written, Excite was giving away this search engine, which runs on UNIX and Windows NT. It gives your site the same intelligent search capabilities that you find on Excite's Web search service (http://www.excite.com). Excite hopes to make money by selling maintenance contracts to high-volume users.

Making Each Page Stand Alone

When people access your web, they'll do so through your welcome page—or so you hope. But the Web's search spiders are hard at work cataloging every page you put up, and it's very likely that somebody will learn of your web—and gain entrance to it—through a search engine. When they do, they'll probably find themselves on one of the secondary pages of your web (one could term this *lateral access*). Will they have any way of knowing

Figure 9.16 Navigation metaphor: Internet Public Library.

where they are, what your web's purpose is, and how they can access your welcome page?

To make sure your pages stand alone, do the following:

- **Clearly indicate the title of your web on every page.** You can do this by means of a logo or a title visible on the page. Don't rely on the <TITLE> tag, which displays an oft-ignored title on the browser's title bar.

- **Provide links to your welcome page.** You should place this link at the bottom as well as the top of the page. The more accessible your welcome page is, the better.

- **Provide links to an information page.** The information page should clearly and succinctly explain the purpose of your web, your intended audience, and the type of content you're offering.

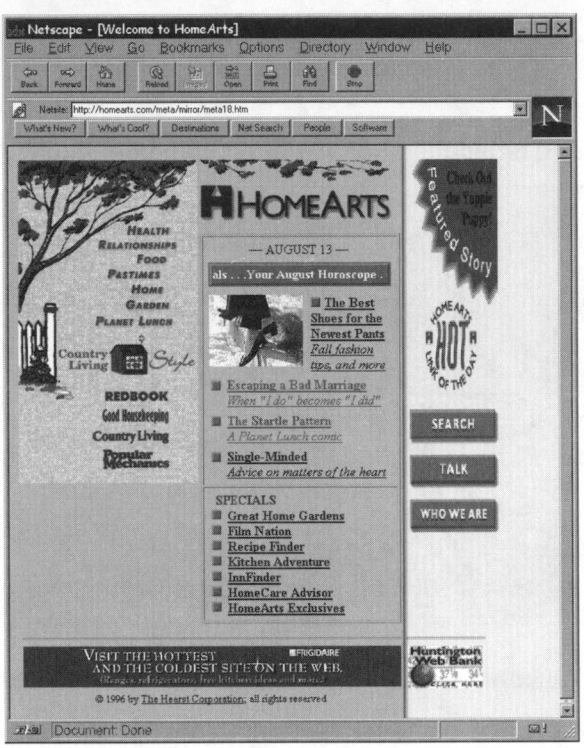

Figure 9.17   Home Arts' welcome page with three types of navigation aids.

Provide Alternatives to Graphical Navigation Aids

Although graphical navigation aids (such as icons) are attractive and useful, they pose problems for users who either cannot display graphics or choose not to do so. Your site may not be navigable if you do not provide alternatives to graphical navigation aids.

You can provide these alternatives in the following ways:

- **Create an alternative version of your page that contains text-based navigation aids**   In Figure 9.19, you see a version of ESPNet's graphics-intensive home page that offers text-based navigation aids rather than graphical icons. This page downloads much faster and can be read with non-graphical browsers.

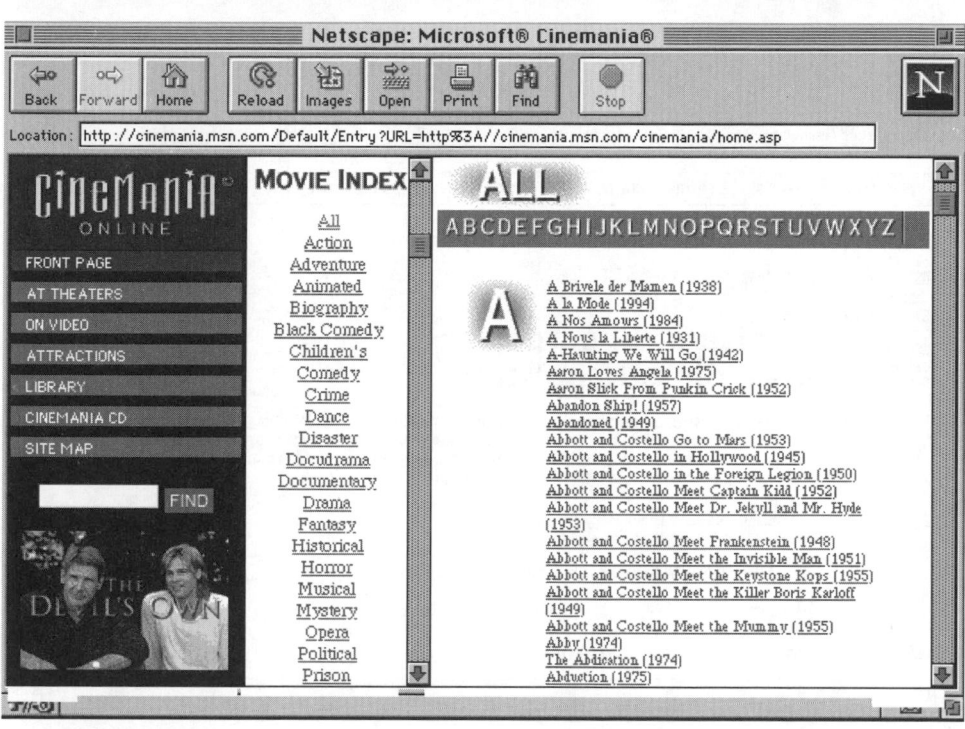

Figure 9.18 Alphabetical guide to movie reviews: Microsoft Cinemania.

- **Include an additional panel containing text-based navigation aids** In Figure 9.20, you see AvWeb's welcome page. Note the text-based navigation aids at the top of the page, which offer an alternative to the graphical aids below.

Provide Textual Descriptions of Graphic Navigation Aids

Many users switch off graphics in order to speed up downloads over slow modem lines. Consider what your site might look like if the graphics are turned off! In Figure 9.21, you see a page that has been stripped of *all* information by turning off graphics. You can prevent information loss by including text descriptions of a graphic's content. Figure 9.22 shows a page with embedded text descriptions; it's not very attractive, but it does provide

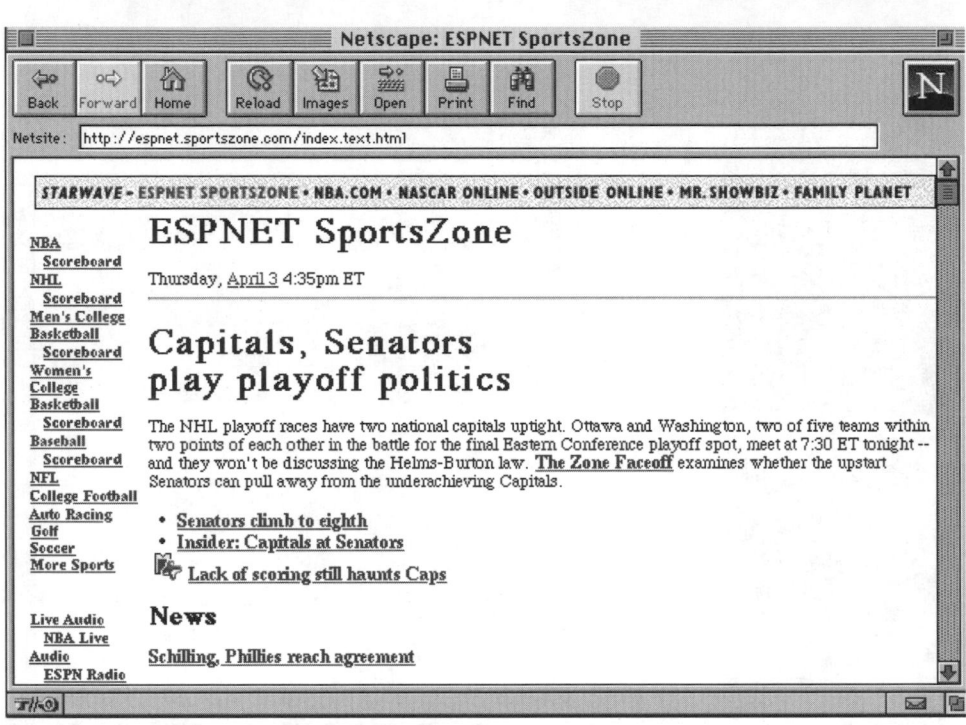

Figure 9.19   Text-only version of ESPNnet home page.

enough information for navigation purposes. Each image can be displayed selectively if the user wishes to see the graphics.

CREATING AN EFFECTIVE WELCOME PAGE

Your site's welcome page provides the face that you show to the world. If you want users to get interested in your site (and what you have to say), you'd be wise to ancipate users' questions, highlight what's important, and keep your page fresh.

In most cases, you shouldn't use your design grid for your welcome page—it makes your site too monotonous if *every* page looks exactly the same. In addition, your welcome page

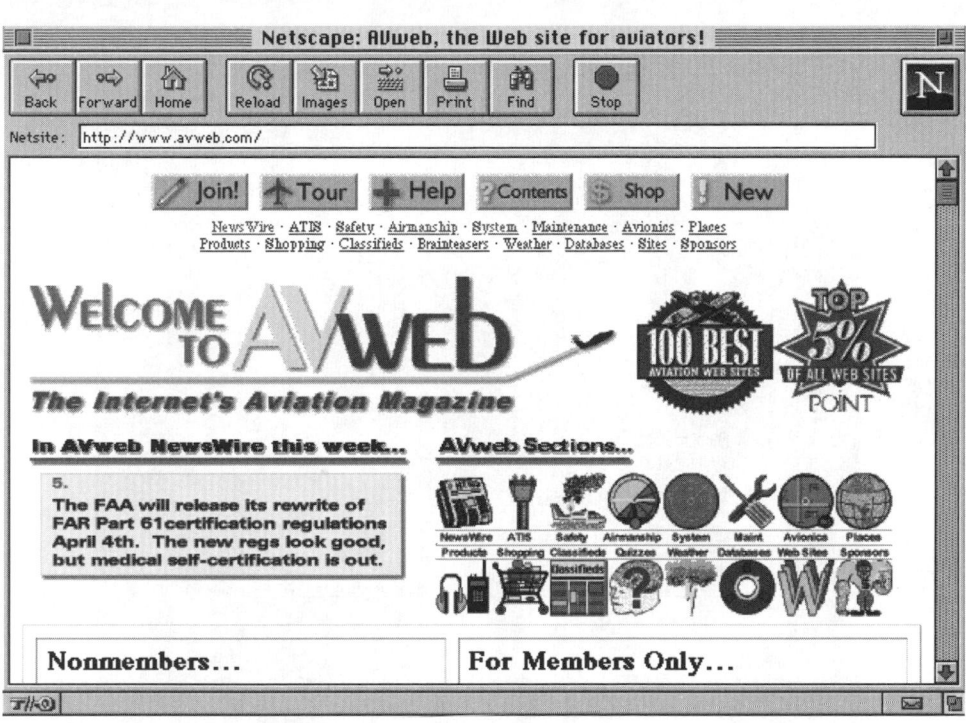

Figure 9.20 AvWeb welcome page with text-based navigation aids.

probably has a different task to perform than your content pages, as explained in this section. For this reason, a different layout will probably be needed. However, you *should* employ the same overall color scheme, navigation aids, and other consistency features.

Anticipating Users' Questions

As you browse the Web, you'll find that the typical page leaves many questions unanswered. Not all of these questions need to be dealt with on the welcome page itself, but there should be links that deal with all or most of them.

- **Who created this site?**   A Web site shouldn't appear out of the blue. Identify the organization or company that's responsible for placing this material on the Web.

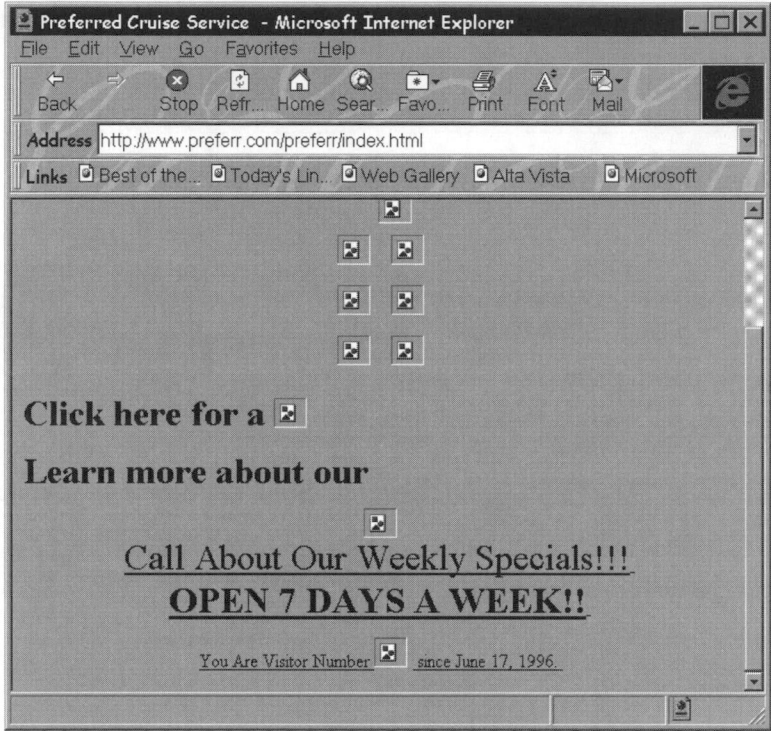

Figure 9.21   Information loss due to switching off graphics.

- **What's your purpose?**   What is the purpose of placing this material on the Web—to inform, to persuade, to sell? This should be obvious immediately, if you've chosen an effective design.

- **What are your credentials?**   What expertise do you possess in this area? What is your background or experience that makes you such an authority in this area?

- **What led you to place this page on the Web?**   What's the history here? Is this a new venture for you and your organization? Does it duplicate something you're doing outside of cyberspace?

- **How up-to-date is this site?**   Prominently date every page with a "Last updated" note.

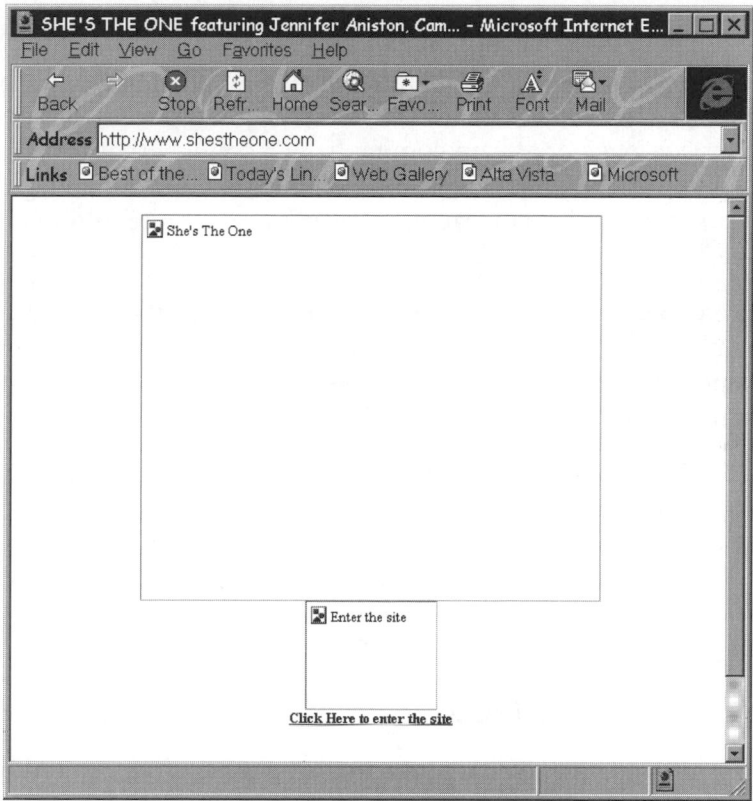

Figure 9.22   Text appearing when graphics are switched off.

- **How frequently is this site updated?**   Daily? Weekly? Monthly? When should I check back?

- **What are the limitations of this site's coverage?**   Do you emphasize one aspect of the subject more than others?

- **Where should I go to find more information?**   Provide a Links page that tells people where to find material that you don't cover.

- **How can I contact someone connected with this page?**   Provide e-mail addresses for contacts.

- **What's your address and phone number?**   Often omitted, this information may provide additional leads and sales, assuming you have the resources to field the letters and calls.

- **Where are you located, geographically?**   Cyberspace can be disorienting, and there's always the threat that one is looking at an imposter page or a scam coming from a country that lacks consumer regulation. An organization or firm takes on additional legitimacy in users' eyes when they can see that it has a definite, physical location somewhere respectable.

- **What can I copy and how can I use it?**   Merely placing a copyright symbol on your page isn't sufficient to prevent users from copying your graphics and text. What uses do you permit, and what uses do you forbid?

- **What's your policy on privacy?**   Internet users are getting increasingly annoyed with organizations and vendors who collect information without asking for consent or divulging the purpose of collecting the information. If you want people to visit your site, you'd better be forthcoming about this.

Keeping Your Pages Fresh

How many pages have you run into that obviously aren't maintained? To attract visitors to your site, you should constantly update it. Each time you do, you should highlight new material. In addition, date your page. Even better, provide a log of updates, in reverse chronological order.

Consider running a Java applet or CGI script that automatically inserts today's date on your page. For making your page appear fresh, this can't be beat.

Remember, you can't count on people seeing your static site and returning, even if they like what they see. That's like turning on the television and seeing the same show all the time: Even if it's a great show, you'll quickly tire of it and stop turning on the TV. All the hottest Web sites, including Yahoo, Word, StockMaster, and others, have content that changes constantly—from one hour to the next, even.

To make your site successful, ensure that all these points apply to your pages:

- You update your pages regularly and religiously at least once per week.

- Your pages have some sort of connection to what's going on in the world—news, quotes, whatever.

- Your pages are useful every day, and not just in the sense that they're pretty to look at, either.

 Please don't use "Under Construction" messages or graphics. If your page isn't ready to publish, don't publish it. Even if you're planning to add more material, you still shouldn't state that your page is "under construction." *Every* Web page should be under *constant* construction. If it's not, it's not worth visiting.

FROM HERE

- By now, you've made important decisions about your Web's building blocks (the chunked pages), its architecture (expressed in your storyboard), and its design (embodied in your page grid). You're ready to start translating your ideas by means of HTML. In the next chapter, you'll learn what types of programs are available for creating Web pages.

Chapter
10

Choosing Software for Creating Your Pages

Y ou've developed a plan for your web, and you're ready to start coding your pages. The question is, what type of program should you use? This chapter surveys your available software choices. There's a wide variety of programs you can use to create a Web page, ranging from simple text editors all the way to expensive Web site maintenance packages, such as NetObjects Fusion. Just which one you'll prefer depends on your Web publishing needs, the number of pages you plan to place on your site, and your knowledge of HTML. This chapter surveys your options, beginning with an introduction to the types of Web-creation programs available and the features you'll find in each.

For the Time-Challenged

♦ HTML translators (also called HTML converters) enable you to transform documents created with proprietary programs (such as word processors or desktop publishing programs) into HTML automatically. This is a good choice if you want to publish many existing documents on the Web.

♦ Text editors enable HTML experts to create pages quickly, but they're not a good choice for beginners.

♦ HTML editors are text editors that include convenience features, such as automatic entry of HTML tags and spell-checking. The better ones include wizards for creating tables and frames.

♦ WYSIWYG editors enable you to work with your document while viewing the way it will look in a browser. You don't need to know HTML to use one of these programs, such as Netscape Gold. The advanced ones include site-management capabilities.

UNDERSTANDING YOUR SOFTWARE OPTIONS

HTML editors fall into the following categories:

• **HTML Translators**   These programs take a file created in a word processing program, such as Microsoft Word, and transform the file into HTML. Depending on which translator you're using, the effect could be very basic—just text with formatted headings—or quite impressive.

• **Text Editors**   A text editor is a simple word processing program that saves text to an ASCII file. Many accomplished HTML coders prefer using text editors because they can write code quickly. However, you need to know HTML very well, and you can't see how your page will look while you're working on it.

• **HTML Editors**   An HTML editor resembles a text editor in that you see the HTML tags on-screen, and you don't see what your page looks like until you switch to your browser. But HTML editors make it easier for beginners to enter tags: You can choose them from menus or toolbars. Some include automated features for inserting tables, frames, and forms.

- **WYSIWYG Editors** A what-you-see-is-what-you-get (WYSIWYG) editor enables you to create your Web page without knowing any HTML. You work in a graphic environment that displays your page just the way it appears in your browser. You enter formats using commands closely resembling a word processing program's formatting commands. Some programs in this category include tools for organizing and maintaining entire Web sites with dozens or even hundreds of documents.

HTML TRANSLATORS

Would you like to avoid learning HTML altogether? Do you have dozens or even hundreds of word processor documents that need to be made available on the Web? An HTML translator or converter might be the way to go. These programs take a formatted document and automatically transform it into HTML.

Microsoft Office 97 applications feature HTML converters: You can save files in HTML format from any Office 97 program, including Publisher, Excel, Word, Access, and PowerPoint. Using the Publish to the Web wizard that appears when you save an Office 97 document in HTML, you can publish presentations, spreadsheets, Word documents, Access query results, Excel charts, and Publisher page designs. This is a very powerful method of creating Web pages.

 Although the Office 97 converters can create Web pages automatically, you will still want to learn a little HTML. The pages you create with a converter won't have internal navigation aids or hyperlinks; you'll need to insert these manually.

The Cadillac of HTML converters is HTML Transit, a pricey ($495) but comprehensive converter. Capable of working with most popular word processing and desktop publishing programs, HTML Transit enables you to customize the relationship between a word processing program's named styles (such as Heading 1 or Body Text) and the corresponding HTML tag. Also included is a gallery of more than 1000 graphics, such as bullets and rules, and even some Java-based animations. Unlike most converters, HTML Transit can split lengthy documents into a series of hyperlinked pages that include navigation buttons, a table of contents, and an index. For a busy company that needs to put a lot of documents on the Web, HTML Transit is well worth considering. For more information on HTML Transit, access www.infoaccess.com.

TEXT EDITORS

A *text editor* is a very simple word processing program with minimal formatting capabilities. Programmers use text editors to write and edit computer programs. Many HTML authors use them, too.

Here's why text editors are so popular with programmers and HTML authors: By default, text editors save your work to a plain ASCII (text) file, with no proprietary formatting commands. In addition, text editors are quick and supple.

Provided with Microsoft Windows is Notepad, a classic text editor (Figure 10.1). It's probably the most widely used program among HTML authors today!

The downside of using a text editor is that you have to know HTML perfectly. The program gives you no assistance with coding HTML tags: There's no means of checking for errors, including spelling errors. Worse, you'll have to enter table and frame tags manually (a tedious process).

For beginners, a text editor is a poor choice. You're much better off with an HTML editor, which gives you help with the HTML tags, or with a WYSIWYG editor, which enables you to avoid learning HTML if you just want to create simple pages.

If you like the idea of using a text editor to create your Web pages, consider trying TextPad (www.textpad.com), shown in Figure 10.2. This is a full-featured text editor that's won rave reviews from programmers and Web authors. You can open multiple files, check spelling, and much more that Notepad can't do. Great program! To download a copy, visit www.textpad.com. Registration is $29. If you plan to compose HTML with a text editor, this is the way to go.

```
welcome.htm - Notepad                                           _ □ X
File   Edit   Search   Help
<!DOCTYPE HTML PUBLIC "-//W3C//DTD HTML 3.2//EN">
<HTML>
<HEAD>
    <TITLE>A Parent's Guide to Anime</TITLE>
    <META NAME="GENERATOR" CONTENT="Mozilla/3.0Gold (Win95; I) [Netscape]">
    <META NAME="Author" CONTENT="Julia Pfaffenberger">
    <META NAME="Description" CONTENT="I was forced to do this! There are la
</HEAD>
<BODY TEXT="#D8D8BF" BGCOLOR="#666666" LINK="#CFB53B" VLINK="#B78A04" ALIN



<script Language="JavaScript">function goback(){        alert("Good Bye!")
ld replace the above with this         // and have a clock on the status ba

<TABLE>
<TR>
<TD VALIGN=MIDDLE ALIGN=RIGHT WIDTH=156><IMG SRC="GIGA0152.jpg" HSPACE=5 V
<TD VALIGN=MIDDLE ALIGN=left WIDTH=410 CELLPADDING=4><TT><FONT COLOR="#CFB
Parent's Guide<BR>
To Anime</FONT></FONT></TT></TD>
</TR>
</TABLE>
```

Figure 10.1 Notepad, a text editor included with Windows, is probably the most popular HTML editor in use today, but it's the ultimate no-frills approach.

HTML EDITORS

HTML editors are basically text editors in that you work with tags and text in an ASCII text environment. But they include tools that simplify the process of entering HTML tags. To use an HTML editor, you'll need to know HTML pretty well, but you don't have to memorize all the HTML tags. That's a plus, and many Webmasters use HTML editors to simplify the process of creating Web pages.

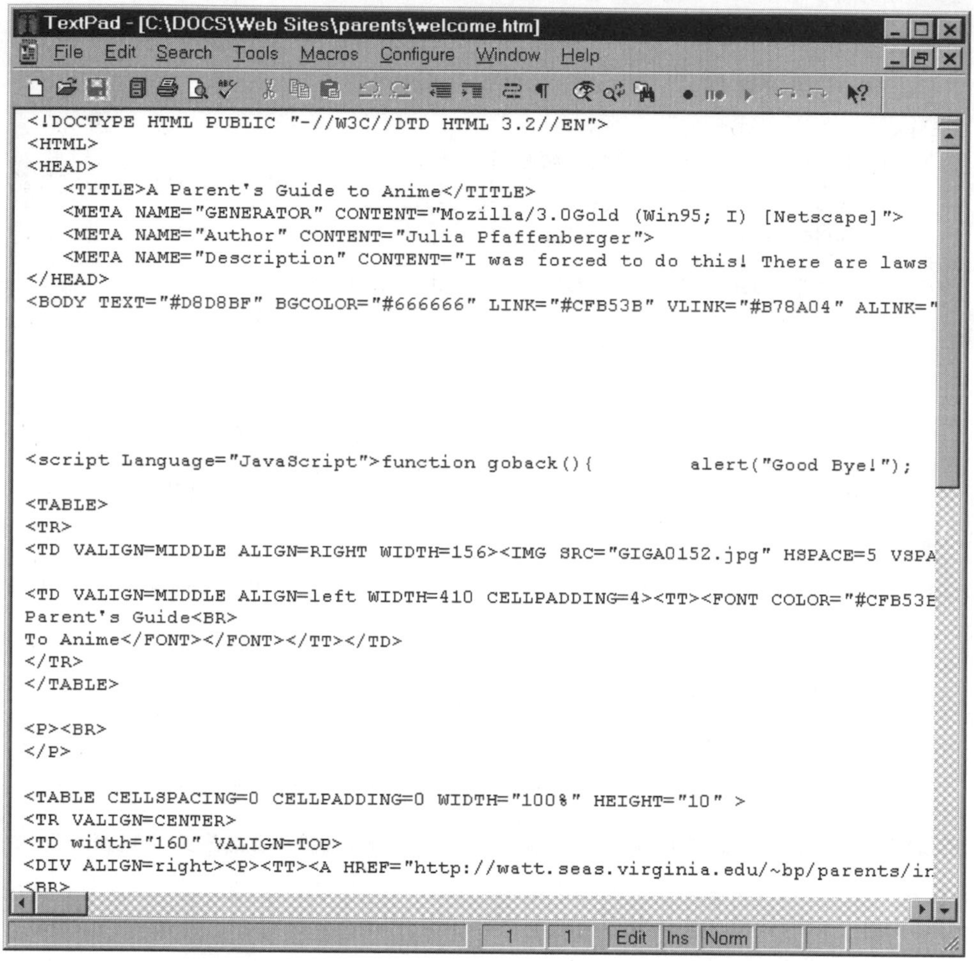

```
TextPad - [C:\DOCS\Web Sites\parents\welcome.htm]              _ □ ×
 File   Edit   Search   Tools   Macros   Configure   Window   Help      _ 司 ×

 □ ☞ ⊟   ⊟ 凸 ₪ ✔   ✗ ⓔ ⓔ   ⊐ ⊐   ←⊐ ⊐→   ⊇ ¶   ℚ ℚᵗ ⓐ   ● ▮▮ ▶   ⊓ ⊓   ⃗?

<!DOCTYPE HTML PUBLIC "-//W3C//DTD HTML 3.2//EN">
<HTML>
<HEAD>
    <TITLE>A Parent's Guide to Anime</TITLE>
    <META NAME="GENERATOR" CONTENT="Mozilla/3.0Gold (Win95; I) [Netscape]">
    <META NAME="Author" CONTENT="Julia Pfaffenberger">
    <META NAME="Description" CONTENT="I was forced to do this! There are laws
</HEAD>
<BODY TEXT="#D8D8BF" BGCOLOR="#666666" LINK="#CFB53B" VLINK="#B78A04" ALINK="




<script Language="JavaScript">function goback(){        alert("Good Bye!");

<TABLE>
<TR>
<TD VALIGN=MIDDLE ALIGN=RIGHT WIDTH=156><IMG SRC="GIGA0152.jpg" HSPACE=5 VSPA

<TD VALIGN=MIDDLE ALIGN=left WIDTH=410 CELLPADDING=4><TT><FONT COLOR="#CFB53E
Parent's Guide<BR>
To Anime</FONT></FONT></TT></TD>
</TR>
</TABLE>

<P><BR>
</P>

<TABLE CELLSPACING=0 CELLPADDING=0 WIDTH="100%" HEIGHT="10" >
<TR VALIGN=CENTER>
<TD width="160" VALIGN=TOP>
<DIV ALIGN=right><P><TT><A HREF="http://watt.seas.virginia.edu/~bp/parents/in
<BR>
                                    1    1    Edit  Ins  Norm
```

Figure 10.2   TextPad is the best text editor for Windows 95 systems; included
are spell checking, search-and-replace, and many other features you'll like.

Features To Look For

In addition to automating the entry of HTML tags, some HTML editors
include features that make them all but indispensable, including spell check-

ers that focus on the text and don't report HTML tags as misspellings. Another very nice feature of the better editors is the ability to publish your finished page to an FTP site. Here's an overview of HTML editor features that you'll find in the best programs:

Font Control/ Style Sheets	New HTML 3.2 specifications enable you to assign fonts and other formats to your Web pages. You'll definitely want to take advantage of this.
Forms	Most HTML editors enable you to create forms using the forms tags, but this information isn't processed unless the server has the appropriate forms-processing scripts. A few new programs include *client-side forms processing*, which doesn't require server programming.
Frame Editor	This feature enables you to create frames (with a specified number of windows) without having to write frame tags.
Image Library	Some programs come with a library of graphics (possibly including animated GIFs) that you can use without worrying about copyright hassles.
Imagemaps	This feature enables you to create *imagemaps*, graphics that contain mouse-sensitive areas. When you click one of these areas, you see a different page. There are two kinds of imagemaps: *server-side* and *client-side*. Server-side imagemaps require a CGI program running on the server. Client-side imagemaps use Java or JavaScript programs and thus do not require server programming.
Java Applets and JavaScript	Increasingly, HTML editors come with Java applets and/or JavaScript scripts that you can plug into your pages to perform a variety of tasks.
Macros	This feature enables you to save and retrieve a series of commands—a very useful feature for automating repeated tasks.
Publish to Web Site	If you're uploading your page to an ISP, this feature virtually automates the procedure of sending your page and all associated graphic images. This is a great time-saver.

Search and Replace	Enables you to search through your pages globally, replacing one tag or one text string with another. A tremendous time-saver!
Spell Checker	Virtually indispensable for serious Web publishing. Too many Web pages contain spelling mistakes because text editors and word processors can't ignore the HTML tags and, in consequence, HTML authors don't bother checking their spelling.
Table Editor	This feature enables you to create tables with a specified number of rows and columns without having to write table tags.
Templates	Some programs come with a variety of customizable Web page templates, complete with graphics and animations.

Overview of HTML Editors

Here's a quick overview of the features of the leading HTML editors.

- **Aardvark Pro** (www.tmgnet.com/aardvark/) Easy to use, but imperfectly implemented for the Windows 95 environment (long file names don't work). Features include a project manager, templates, a URL library, image conversion, plug-in support, built-in preview, spell checker, macros, wizards for entering difficult formats (tables, URLs, images, Java applets, and more), publish via FTP (file uploading), and drag-and-drop insertion of multimedia files.

- **Coffee Cup** (www.coffeecup.com) Easy to use, this program includes lots of goodies that can help you create eye-catching pages (such as animated GIFs). However, the program is short on features (there are no wizards for entering tables and frames, for example). Features include drag-and-drop insertion of multimedia files, 50 animated GIFs, 10 JavaScripts, and a color wizard.

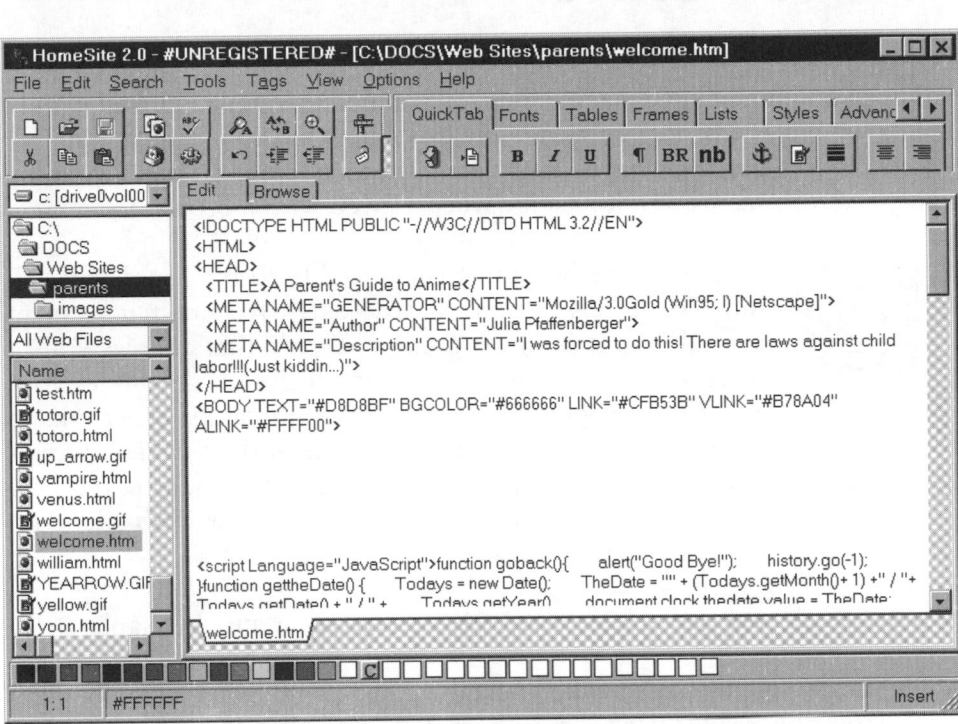

Figure 10.3 Homesite is the best of the current crop of HTML editors, but it's a complex program and requires knowledge of HTML to use its advanced features.

- **Homesite** (www.desnet.com/homesite.html)   Homesite is the most full-featured of the editors, but requires knowledge of HTML to make full use of the many advanced features (see Figure 10.3). Features include automatic, customizable color-coding of HTML tags; a built-in HTML browser for viewing the Web appearance of your documents; a spell checker; publish to Web site (file uploading); open documents directly from the Web; a built-in image and thumbnail viewer; templates; frames; multiple undo; search and replace; auto-detection of image sizes; and the ability to work with multiple pages.

WYSIWYG Editors

A what-you-see-is-what-you-get editor enables you to design a Web page without knowing HTML. You work in a graphical environment that closely resembles a word processor or a simple desktop publishing program. To enter HTML features, you choose items from menus. As you're creating your page, you see what it looks like when viewed with a browser.

 Some of these programs (such as Microsoft Front Page 97 and NetObjects Fusion) include extensive site-management capabilities, including a graphic display that enables you to visualize the relationships among all the documents in your site. These programs also search for and check hyperlinks to make sure they're accurate, and some of them even automatically change hyperlinks if you drag a document into a new directory. If you have to manage a complex Web site, consider buying one of these programs.

Here's a quick overview of the WYSIWYG editors currently available.

- **Backstage Internet Studio** (Macromedia, $299)   If you're planning to publish your pages on a server that runs Microsoft Windows NT and you need to include database searching, this is the way to go. Backstage Internet Studio provides excellent WYSIWYG tools for creating great-looking pages. Where the program really shines, however, is database access: Built-in routines enable you to create forms for querying Paradox, FoxPro, dBASE, Excel, and Microsoft Access databases. These tools only work on Windows NT systems, though.

- **Claris Home Page** (Claris, $99)   This is the easiest WYSIWYG program: In just a few minutes, anyone can create great-looking Web pages, complete with tables and frames, just by choosing options from menus.

- **Microsoft Front Page 97** (Microsoft Corporation, $149)   If your Web server supports Microsoft's WebBots server extensions, this program enables you to easily create Web pages with advanced features (including password authentication, discussion forums, site searching, and much more). Excellent site-management features enable you to manage a complex Web site with ease. You can still use the program if your server doesn't support the WebBot extensions, but you can't take advantage of the advanced features.

- **NetObjects Fusion** (NetObjects, Inc., $495) This is an advanced program that incorporates the latest philosophy of Web page design: using Java and JavaScript objects in place of server extensions. Unlike Microsoft Front Page, NetObjects Fusion does not require special server extensions or CGI programs to enable advanced features such as forms processing, database searching, and password authentication. Advanced site management features automatically alter links when you drag a document from one directory to another.

- **Netscape Gold 3.0** (Netscape, $79) The editor portion of Netscape Gold doesn't include many features: notably absent is support for frames, which Netscape pioneered. However, if you would like to create pages that consist of little more than text and graphics, perhaps with a table layout (see Figure 10.4), Gold is very easy to use and produces good results. A page publishing feature enables you to publish your pages via FTP with a click of a button on the toolbar.

- **Netscape Composer** (Netscape, price not determined at time of publication) Part of Netscape's sweeping revision of Netscape Navigator, called Netscape Communicator, Composer is a simplified version of Netscape Gold's editor. Cool new features include a spell checker and a new <LAYER> tag, which enables interleaving of text and graphics on a single page.

FROM HERE

- Give it a try! In Chapter 11, you create your first HTML document. It's easy!

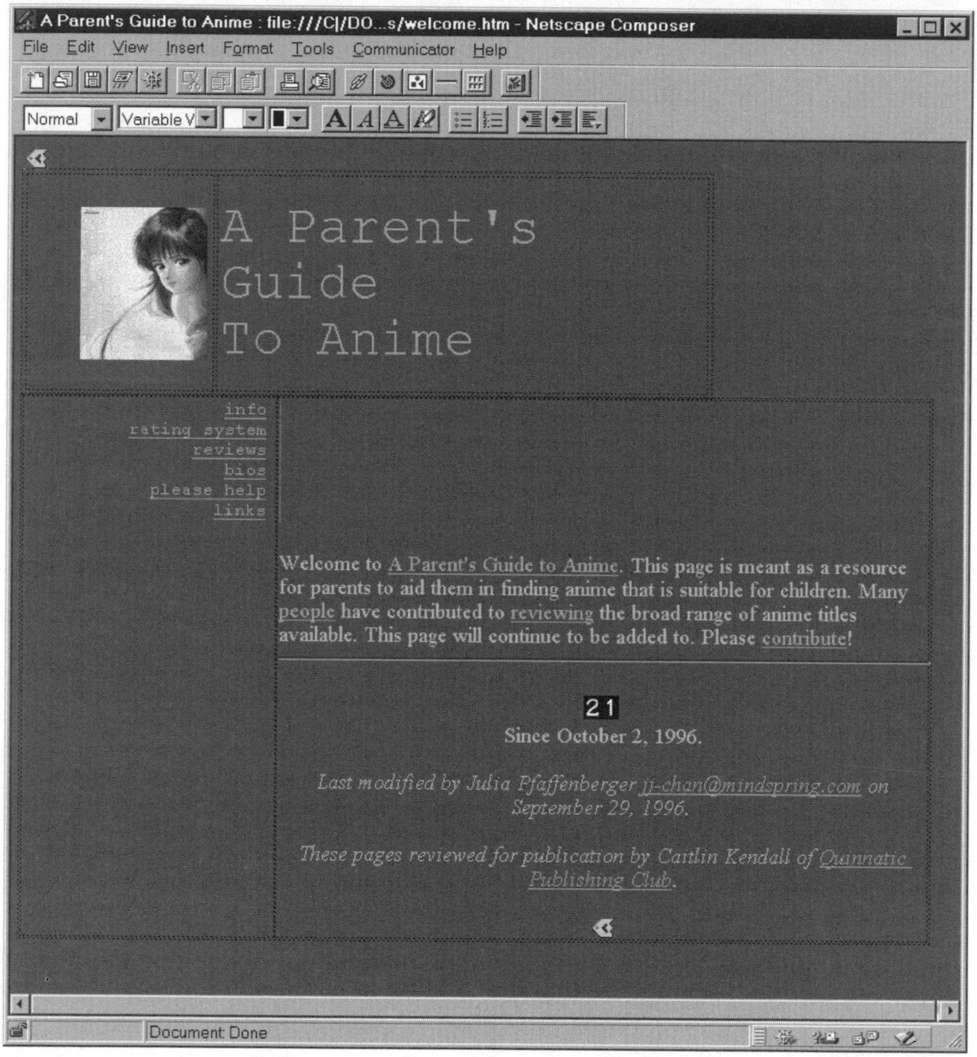

A Parent's Guide to Anime : file:///C|/DO...s/welcome.htm - Netscape Composer

File   Edit   View   Insert   Format   Tools   Communicator   Help

Normal   Variable V

A Parent's Guide To Anime

info
rating system
reviews
bios
please help
links

Welcome to A Parent's Guide to Anime. This page is meant as a resource for parents to aid them in finding anime that is suitable for children. Many people have contributed to reviewing the broad range of anime titles available. This page will continue to be added to. Please contribute!

21

Since October 2, 1996.

Last modified by Julia Pfaffenberger jj-chan@mindspring.com on September 29, 1996.

These pages reviewed for publication by Caitlin Kendall of Quannatic Publishing Club.

Document: Done

Figure 10.4   If you want to create relatively simple pages that include text, graphics, and a table layout, Netscape Page Composer (part of the Communicator package) provides a quick way to create good-looking Web pages with a minimum of fuss.

File Edit View Favorites Help

Address: http//www

Part III

CREATING

YOUR WEB

WITH HTML

Chapter
11

Your First HTML Document

The easiest way to get started with publishing your information on the Web isn't by getting bogged down in the rules of HyperText Markup Language (HTML). You'll learn the details of HTML in the following chapters. Instead, the best way to learn HTML is the same as the best way to learn to dance: Just try it, and know that you can't mess up too badly. In this chapter, we'll build a home page—one of the simplest and most frequently encountered type of document on the Web. You can make this page the default home page for your browser, and there it will be every time you start the program.

This chapter presents a tutorial that you can adapt to your own purposes—put in your own name, for instance, and add hyperlinks to your own favorite sites. It would be nice if you could get a friendly soul to scan a small photograph of yourself into a JPEG or GIF file (no more than 20 KB or 25 KB in size, please), although this isn't necessary to complete the tutorial.

Here's a sweetener: After reading this chapter, you'll know a great deal of the HTML that's actually used to put pages on the Web!

A Few Basics

As with dancing, there are certain ground rules in HTML. Chapter 12 delves into these rules in more detail; this is just a quick introduction.

A few basic points to remember:

- HTML isn't a formatting language. Rather, it defines the *parts* of a document, such as titles, heading, body text, and block quotations. These parts are called *elements*.

- To define an element, you use *tags*.

- Tags take the form of angle brackets surrounding letters, numbers and other information, such as <B> or <H2>.

- Tags usually come in pairs, with one tag at the beginning of text to be formatted a particular way and another at the end. For example, the expression "<B>Hey, You</B>" would make the words "Hey, You" appear in boldface type in a Web browser.

- Tags that come in pairs have a start tag (such as <H1>) and an end tag (such as </H1>). The slash mark is used to denote the end tag. All the text within the start and end tag is to be considered part of the element that the tag defines.

That's it! Remember that all HTML is ASCII text with special tags embedded in it, and you have a conceptual framework on which to hang details about specific tags and fancy formatting techniques. Let's get started on your first HTML document, your home page.

For the Time-Challenged

◆ An HTML document is simply ASCII text, which you can create with a word processing program. Web browsers read HTML and transform the codes into a richly formatted document.

◆ Every HTML document should begin with an <HTML> tag and end with an </HTML> tag.

◆ The heading tags (<H1> through <H6>) enable you to establish a logical structure of headings for your document. Remember, though, that most people will feel that your <H1> tag is your document's title.

◆ Web browsers don't read your word processor's hard returns. To break paragraphs, you must surround the paragraph text with <P> and </P> tags.

◆ To center text, use the ALIGN=CENTER attribute of the <P> tag (as in <P ALIGN=CENTER>Here is the centered text</P>).

◆ To see how your HTML code looks, save your document and open it with a Web browser. You'll surely find mistakes—fix them, save the changes, and click the Reload or Refresh button in your browser.

◆ Use the <BR> tag to force a line break.

◆ There are two kinds of hyperlinks, one that links to an external document (<A HREF>) and one that links to a location within the same document (<A NAME>). To link to an external document, you must precisely specify the URL, as in the following example: <A HREF="http://watt.seas.virginia.edu/ ~bp/parents.html"> Parent's Guide to Anime </A>. It's easy to make typing mistakes when typing links, so check your work carefully.

◆ Use the <UL> and <LI> tags to make a bulleted (unordered) list.

◆ Add inline images with the <IMG> tag, but be sure to specify the location of the graphic correctly (<IMG SRC="portrait.jpg">) and enclose the file name in quotation marks. You can use the ALIGN and WIDTH attributes to control the graphic's appearance.

◆ To add a rule (a line spanning the screen), use the <HR> tag—but don't overdo it.

◆ Always sign your document with the <ADDRESS> tag. Include your e-mail address and the date of last modification.

◆ To enable people to reply to your page by e-mail, use the following tag: <A HREF = "mailto:*e-mail address*">*e-mail address*</A>.

Starting Your Home Page

To create your HTML file, just use your word processing program. But be sure to save the file as plain text. Most word processors save documents to a proprietary file format, which uses lots of formatting codes that will show up as garbage in a Web browser.

 Consider using the Notepad utility that comes with Windows to create your HTML file. It isn't fancy, granted, but you don't need fancy word processing capabilities to create an HTML file. And Notepad has one huge advantage: It automatically saves files as plain text, with no formatting codes.

You can call your HTML document by any legal filename you want, but in order for Web browsers to recognize the file as one containing HTML text, you must give it a special extension. In most operating systems, the extension is .html. Microsoft Windows3.x systems, however, allow extensions of only three characters, so on those systems the proper extension for HTML documents is .htm.

Before adding any other text or tags to your document, type

```
<HTML>
```

Then press Enter, and type

```
<HEAD>
```

Press Enter again, and type

```
</HEAD>
```

Continue by typing the following, each on its own line followed by a hard return (Enter):

```
<BODY>
</BODY>
</HTML>
```

In this and subsequent chapters, you'll see boxes such as the following whenever a new HTML element is introduced. The box sums up important information about the element. Don't worry if you don't understand all the contents of these boxes right now; you'll learn later, for example, what attributes are and how to use them. You'll also find a review of HTML in Appendix A.

HTML

Purpose:	Tells Web browsers that your document is in HTML.
Usage:	<HTML>. . .</HTML>
Example:	<HTML>Rest of document text here.</HTML>
Don't Forget:	Within this tag you must include the <HEAD>. . .</HEAD> and <BODY>. . .</BODY> tags.
Hot Tip:	Although most browsers will figure out that an HTML document is in HTML even without these tags, it's a good idea to include them anyway for the benefit of those with less-sophisticated browsers.

BODY

Purpose:	Defines the body of the HTML document (the portion that's seen in the browser's display window).
Usage:	<BODY>. . .</BODY>
Example:	<BODY><P>This is the text of the document.</P></BODY>
Don't Forget:	Elements that can go into the BODY element can't go in the HEAD element, and vice versa.
Hot Tip:	Although most browsers will figure out that an HTML document is in HTML even without these tags, it's a good idea to include them anyway for the benefit of those with less-sophisticated browsers.

HEAD

Purpose:	Defines the head of the HTML document. The head contains the document title and certain other elements.
Usage:	<HEAD>. . .</HEAD>
Example:	<HEAD><TITLE>This is the document's title</TITLE></HEAD>
Don't Forget:	The document's title will appear on the title bar of most browsers, and may not be noticed; be sure to reiterate the document's title in an H1 element.
Hot Tip:	Virtually the only HEAD element in common use is TITLE.

WHAT DID YOU JUST DO?

You just set up the basic structure that every HTML document should have. It looks like this:

```
<HTML>
<HEAD>
</HEAD>
<BODY>
</BODY>
</HTML>
```

Note the following about this basic structure. First, every HTML document has two overarching sections:

- **The Head** Within the head, demarcated by <HEAD>. . .</HEAD> tags, you position the document's title and certain other information. This information does not appear within the browser's document display area. The head contains information *about* the document.

- **The Body** Within the body, you create the document. The body will be displayed within the browser's document display area. The body contains the *content* of the document.

Note also that HTML tags can be *nested* (positioned within each other). This is a little easier to see if you use tabs to indent the nested codes, as in the following example:

```
<HTML>
  <HEAD>
  </HEAD>
  <BODY>
  </BODY>
</HTML>
```

As you can see, the <HEAD>. . .</HEAD> tags and the <BODY>. . . </BODY> tags are contained (nested) within the <HTML>. . .</HTML> codes. Or to put it another way, every HTML document consists of a head and a body.

GIVING YOUR HOME PAGE A TITLE

The title of an HTML document appears only in the browser's title bar—not anywhere in the document's body. A document's title should be both descriptive of the document's contents and short enough to fit on small monitors.

<TITLE> and </TITLE> tags surround the title of an HTML document. On the line right after the one containing <HEAD>, type the following, except substitute your own name for the one given in the example:

```
<TITLE>Sue Thompson's Hotlist</TITLE>
```

The line you just entered into your document will make a Web browser show the words "Sue Thompson's Hotlist" in its title bar when it displays your page.

At this point, your file should look like this:

```
<HTML>
<HEAD>
<TITLE>Sue Thompson's Hotlist</TITLE>
</HEAD>
<BODY>
</BODY>
</HTML>
```

If the TITLE element only appears in the title bar, why bother creating it?

It's required, for one thing, and really persnickity HTML editors will balk at reading your document unless it's included. Most browsers won't panic if a TITLE element isn't included, though. Still, it's best to use it. Web spiders look for titles and attach a great deal of weight to the words contained therein. In addition, most browsers use your document's title in history lists. So be sure to use a title that really describes what's in your document. Don't say "My First Try"; say "Arizona Iguana Habitat Hotline."

TITLE

Purpose:	Displays the document's title on the browser's title bar.
Usage:	<TITLE>. . .</TITLE>
Example:	<TITLE>Arizona Iguana Habitat Hotline</TITLE>
Don't Forget:	Please don't omit the TITLE element—and be sure to make your title as descriptive as possible.
Hot Tip:	Make your title as descriptive as possible, but make it short enough so that it fits within a browser's history list window. For best results, stick to 60 characters or fewer.

ADDING HEADINGS

Documents are much easier to read when they're broken into sections. HTML is designed to accommodate as many as six different sizes of headings, which can be used to organize your document into paragraphs of decreasing importance or increasing specificity. There are six heading tags: <H1>, < H2>, < H3>, < H4>, < H5>, and <H6>. Just how these headings appear depends on which browser you're using; Figure 11.1 shows how Netscape renders the six levels of document headings.

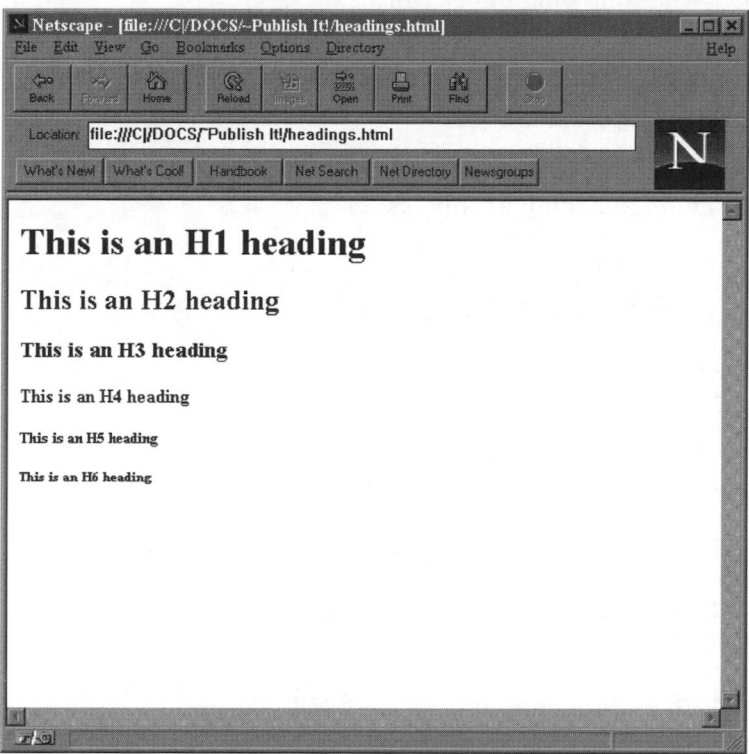

Figure 11.1   Headings rendered by Netscape Navigator.

The title of your document usually appears as an H1 heading at the top of the body text. Right below the <BODY> tag, echo your document's title surrounded by <H1> tags:

```
<H1>Sue Thompson's Hotlist</H1>
```

You can use other heading tags to establish a logical order of headings and subheadings in your document. Try entering an H2 subheading now. Type:

```
<H2>Music Sites</H2>
```

The H2 heading is less dramatic than the H1 heading, and attracts less attention. You can use the various heading tags together to create an outline of information. But please don't use them out of sequence: You shouldn't stick an <H6> tag into a document that only has <H1> and <H2> tags.

Using the heading tags, you can define your document's logical structure. Try entering the following under Music Sites:

```
<H3>Grunge</H3>
<H3>Industrial</H3>
<H3>Techno-Rave</H3>
<H3>Trance</H3>
```

Start a new H2 heading as follows:

```
<H2>Movies</H2>
```

Add some H3 headings under this:

```
<H3>Classics</H3>
<H3>Horror</H3>
<H3>Science Fiction</H3>
```

At this point, your file should look like this:

```
<HTML>
<HEAD>
<TITLE>Sue Thompson's Hotlist</TITLE>
</HEAD>
<BODY>
<H1>Sue Thompson's Hotlist</H1>
<H2>Music Sites</H2>
<H3>Grunge</H3>
<H3>Industrial</H3>
<H3>Techno-Rave</H3>
<H3>Trance</H3>
<H2>Movies</H2>
<H3>Classics</H3>
<H3>Horror</H3>
<H3>Science Fiction</H3>
</BODY>
</HTML>
```

 You don't have to make your document's title the same as the first heading; in fact, doing so is somewhat inefficient since you're displaying the same information twice. It may also be a good idea to use H2 or H3 as the largest heading in your document, since most browsers display H1 in very large type that takes up valuable screen real estate.

What's the difference between a title and a first-level heading (H1)?

It's where the title appears. Bear in mind that your document's title will only appear on the title bar of the browser—and it might not be very noticeable. So you'll need to use the <H1> tag, discussed below, to make your title more visible. But please, don't skip the title—Web spiders and search engines consult the title in order to build searchable databases of Web documents.

H1, H2, H3, H4, H5, H6

Purpose:	Define headings and subheadings within the document body.
Usage:	<H1>. . .</H1>
Example:	<H1>This is the "real" document title, as browsers display it</H1>
Don't Forget:	The heading tags should be used in a logical sequence; in other words, don't use <H5> if you haven't used <H4>.

ADDING BODY TEXT

Most of the information included in your Web documents will be in the form of body text. Body text is the kind of text you use for paragraphs that require no special formatting. In your home page file, below the <H1> line, type something about yourself, such as the following:

```
<P>I'm a communications consultant at Tao Enterprises,
located in Eugene, Oregon. Here are some of my favor-
ite sites. </P>

<P>Please let me know if you have any cool additions
to the sites I've listed. My email address is
suet@fictitious.com</P>
```

The above lines, when read by a Web browser, will yield two distinct paragraphs. Though the details of formatting the paragraphs (size, typeface,

Solutions

Making Your HTML Easier to Read

Since browsers ignore the extra spaces, tabs, and hard returns you insert into your HTML documents, you might as well use these to clarify your code's structure. Here's the document we're working on right now, after inserting tabs and blank lines to clarify its structure:

```
<HTML>
  <HEAD>
    <TITLE>Sue Thompson's Hotlist</TITLE>
  </HEAD>

<BODY>
    <H1>Sue Thompson's Hotlist</H1>
      <H2>Music Sites</H2>
        <H3>Grunge</H3>
        <H3>Industrial</H3>
        <H3>Techno-Rave</H3>
        <H3>Trance</H3>
      <H2>Movies</H2>
        <H3>Classics</H3>
        <H3>Horrow</H3>
        <H3>Science Fiction</H3>
  </BODY>
</HTML>
```

color, etc.) are left up to individual browsers, it is safe to assume that text formatted as body text will have less emphasis than text formatted as any sort of header.

Note: In previous versions of HTML, you could use the <P> tag to separate paragraphs; it was not necessary to begin a paragraph with <P> and end with </P>. Most browsers will read paragraphs formatted in this (incorrect) way. There's still considerable controversy over this point, but to be on the safe side, you should use the <P>. . .</P> tags in pairs rather than breaking paragraphs with <P>.

 **I separated my paragraphs with a hard return, but the Web browser won't pick up the paragraph breaks!**

That's right. As far as your Web browser is concerned, a hard return is the same as a space. If you want to set off a paragraph, you must use the <P>. . .</P> tags. Even if you press Enter to start a new word processing program's paragraph within these tags, your browser will still read all the enclosed text as a single paragraph. Try it!

The <P>. . .</P> tags are useful because HTML does not understand the significance of the ASCII carriage return character (the character generated when you press the Enter or Return key). If you don't use <P>...</P> tags, all your body text paragraphs will merge into one giant, unreadable glob of text. The <P>. . .</P> tags ensure that each paragraph of body text is neatly separated from the others.

At this point, your file should look like this (except that you're substituting your own name and areas of interest):

```
<HTML>
  <HEAD>
    <TITLE>Sue Thompson's Hotlist</TITLE>
  </HEAD>

<BODY>
  <H1>Sue Thompson's Hotlist</H1>
    <P>I'm a communications consultant at Tao
    Enterprises, located in Eugene, Oregon. Here
    are some of my favorite sites. </P>

    <P>Please let me know if you have any cool
    additions to the sites I've listed. My email
    address is suet@fictitious.com</P>

    <H2>Music Sites</H2>
      <H3>Grunge</H3>
      <H3>Industrial</H3>
      <H3>Techno-Rave</H3>
      <H3>Trance</H3>
    <H2>Movies</H2>
    <H3>Classics</H3>
```

```
        <H3>Horror</H3>
        <H3>Science Fiction</H3>
   </BODY>
</HTML>
```

- -

P

Purpose:	Defines a unit of text as a single paragraph.
Usage:	<P>. . . </P>
Don't Forget:	Web browsers will ignore tabs, spaces, and hard returns entered by your word processing program.
Hot Tip:	To center text, use the <P> tag with the ALIGN attribute, as in the following example: <P ALIGN = CENTER>This is the centered text </P>.

- -

HEY! WHAT DOES IT LOOK LIKE SO FAR?

Why not find out? Save the HTML file to disk, fire up your browser, and use the Open File command in the File menu to open the document you're creating. It should look like the one in Figure 11.2.

The browser just ignored some of my tags!
That's what happens if they're not correctly written. Check the following:

- Did you enclose each tag with angle brackets?

- Does each start tag have a matching end tag? You can't start with <H3> and end with </H4>.

- Did you type the tags correctly?

Keep looking—you'll find the error. Correct the error, and resave the document. In your browser, click the Refresh button to load the corrected version of the file.

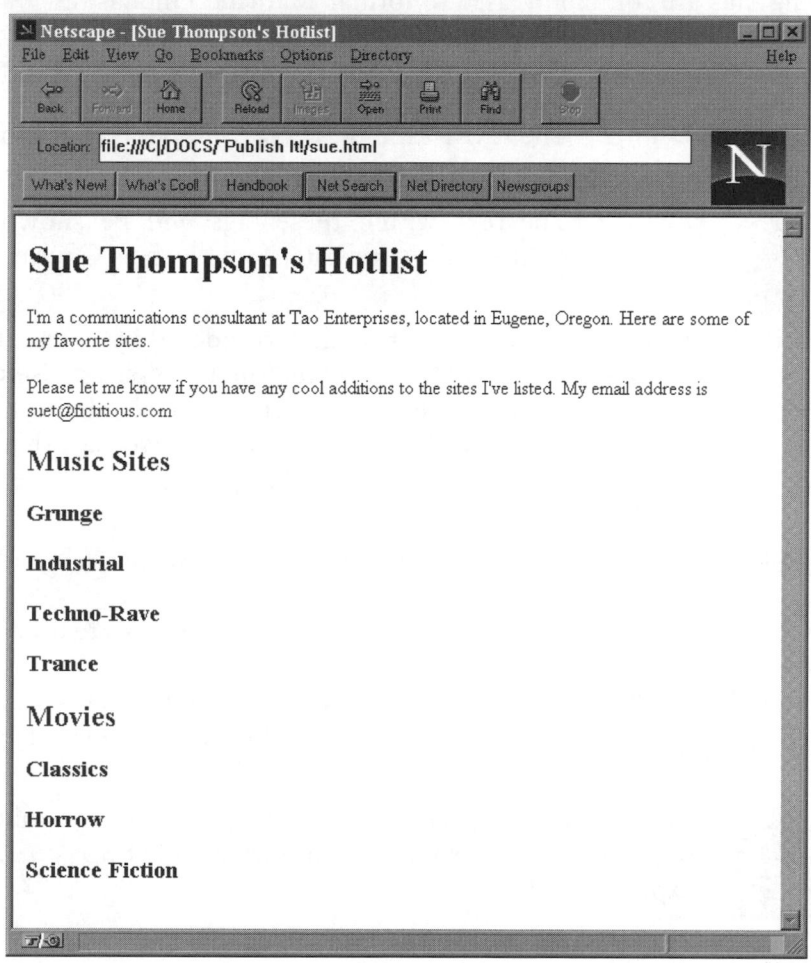

Figure 11.2 The file thus far (as displayed by Netscape Navigator).

CHARACTER FORMATTING (ITALICS, BOLDFACE, AND UNDERLINING)

HTML is designed to identify document elements, and it leaves the formatting up to the browser. However, some latitude is given to document designers in the area of emphases, such as italics, boldface, and underlining. The following tags are commonly used to format character emphases:

<I>. . .</I>	The text within these tags will be italicized.
<B>. . .</B>	The text within these tags will be shown in bold-face type.
<TT>. . .</TT>	The text within these tags will be shown in a mono-space typewriter font, such as Courier.

Note that the <I>, <B>, and <TT> tags are considered by some HTML purists to violate the spirit of HTML—they tell the browser precisely how to format the text. However, that doesn't stop very many people from using them! If you'd like to be an HTML purist, you can use two tags that leave the formatting up to the browser:

<STRONG>. . .</STRONG>	Most browsers show this text in bold.
<EM>. . .</EM>	Most browsers show this text in italics.
<CODE>. . .</CODE>	Most browsers show this text using a monospaced font of some kind.

 You can nest character formats. For example, the following tags are used to produce these formats: *I'm not an HTML expert . . . YET!*

<I>I'm not an HTML expert...<B>YET!</B></I>

Note that you must include stop tags for both of the emphases.

· ·

B

Purpose:	Boldfaces the marked text.
Usage:	<B>. . .</B>
Example:	<B>Text to be boldfaced.</B>

Don't Forget: Not all browsers can display boldface. A text-only browser such as Lynx will display this format with underlining.

Hot Tip: Use character emphases sparingly.

- -

- -

CODE

Purpose: Marks text for display in a monospace font.

Usage: <CODE>. . .</CODE>

Example: <CODE>Text to be shown in monospace</CODE>

Don't Forget: This format is a good choice if you want to display a single line of computer code, but you should use it in combination with the <PRE> tag for multiline examples.

Hot Tip: Use character emphases sparingly.

- -

- -

EM

Purpose: Emphasizes the marked text; most browsers display italics.

Usage: <EM>. . .</EM>

Example: <EM>Text to be emphasized.</EM>

Don't Forget: Not all browsers can display boldface. A text-only browser such as Lynx will display this format with underlining.

Hot Tip: Use character emphases sparingly.

- -

- -

I

Purpose: Displays text in italics.

Usage: <I>. . .</I>

Example:	<I>Italicized text</I>
Don't Forget:	Not all browsers can display italics. A text-only browser such as Lynx will display this format with underlining.
Hot Tip:	Use character emphases sparingly.

STRONG

Purpose:	Emphasizes the marked text; most browsers display bold.
Usage:	<STRONG>. . .</STRONG>
Example:	<STRONG>Text to be emphasized.</STRONG>
Don't Forget:	This format is a good choice if you want to display a single line of computer code, but you should use it in combination with the <PRE> tag for multiline examples.
Hot Tip:	Use character emphases sparingly.

TT

Purpose:	Displays text in a monospace typewriter font.
Usage:	<TT>. . .</TT>
Example:	<TT>Text to be shown in monospace</TT>
Don't Forget:	Not all browsers can display italics. A text-only browser such as Lynx will display this format with underlining.
Hot Tip:	Use character emphases sparingly.

BREAKING LINES

When you're working with body text, you'll find it helpful occasionally to be able to determine precisely where a line breaks. Suppose you're working with an address, such as the following:

```
        If you'd like more information on Tao Enterprises,
        please contact:

        Tao Enterprises
        11219 19th Street NW
        Eugene, OR
```

Unfortunately, your browser will format this text as follows:

```
        If you'd like more information on Tao Enterprises,
        please contact:Tao Enterprises 11219 19th Street NW
        Eugene, OR
```

To force the browser to start a new line just where you want it, you can use the <BR> tag, as follows:

```
        If you'd like more information on Tao Enterprises,
        please contact:<BR>
        <BR>
        Tao Enterprises<BR>
        11219 19th Street NW<BR>
        Eugene, OR <BR>
```

Note that the <BR> tags should come at the *end* of the line, not at the beginning—unless you deliberately want to insert a blank line *before* the line that contains the tag.

- -

BR

Purpose:	Forces a line break.
Usage:	 (no stop tag)
Example:	This item should end with a line break.
Don't Forget:	Browsers ignore the hard returns you enter with your word processor.
Hot Tip:	Need a blank line? Just enter on a line by itself.

- -

ADDING HYPERLINKS

One of the Web's strongest appeals is its ability to handle hyperlinks, which enable people viewing your document to jump to other Web resources. Like all other special features, hyperlinks are encoded into HTML documents with tags.

The Two Types of Hyperlinks (<A HREF> and <A NAME>)

To add a hyperlink, you use the <A> tag. You can hyperlink in two ways:

1. **To another document**   To create a hyperlink to another document, you use the <A HREF> form of the <A> tag.

2. **To another place in the same document**   To create a hyperlink to another place within the same document, you use the <A NAME> form of the <A> tag. You'll learn more about <A NAME> in Chapter 14.

The form of an <A HREF> tag looks like this:

```
<A HREF="the URL of the site you're linking to">The
hyperlink text</A>
```

Things to Remember When Typing Hyperlinks

To type a <A HREF> tag, you need the exact URL of the document to which you are linking. Be sure to test the URL with your browser before attempting to write a hyperlink. Note that URLs are case-sensitive: you must follow the exact pattern of uppercase and lowercase letters.

Here's an example of a properly written <A HREF> tag:

```
<A HREF="http://watt.seas.virginia.edu/~bp/par-
ents.html">Parent's Guide to Anime</A>
```

It's easy to make a mistake when you're typing hyperlinks—and you'll know if you made one of the more serious ones, because you'll see the hyperlink code rather than the hyperlink text itself. Be sure to check the following:

- Did you enclose the entire URL within quotation marks?

- Did you forget the equals sign?

- Did you omit the stop tag (</A>)?

- Did you omit the slash mark in the stop tag?

- Is the URL correct?

- Did you leave a space between A and HREF?
- Did you place any extraneous spaces at the beginning or end of the hyperlink text (the text that will appear in the browser)? Don't place any spaces after the start tag's trailing bracket (>) or before the end tag's beginning bracket (<). Such spaces will produce unwanted spacing errors in your document.

Adding Hyperlinks to Your Document

Let's add some sites about grunge music to the home page you're creating. Under <H3>Grunge</H3>, type the following:

```
<A HREF="http://www.vtek.chalmers.se/
~v94zinn/">The Grunge Page</A>

<A HREF="http://www.vtek.chalmers.se/~v94zinn/
Grunge.html">Some of the best GRUNGE Links</A>

<A HREF="http://www.engin.umich.edu/~galvin/pearl-
jam.html">The Pearl Jam Page</A>

<A HREF="http://geffen.com/hole.html">The Hole
Page</A>

<A HREF="http://www.ncsa.uiuc.edu/SDG/Software/
Mosaic/Docs/whats-new.html">New Web Sites</A>
```

Save your document and use your browser to take a look at the links you've created. It won't look very nice—you'll find out why in a moment—but for now test the hyperlinks to see that they're working. Note that some of the above sites may have folded or moved since this book was written; that is the Way of the Web.

Hey, the hyperlinks all run together!
They sure do. Unlike the heading and subheading tags you've added to your document, the <A> tags don't imply any formatting. To make your hyperlinks look nice, you'll need to include them within some text or add them to a list. In the following section, you'll learn how to add them to a list.

A HREF

Purpose:	Defines a unit of text as a hyperlink to another Web document.
Usage:	<A HREF=*"Universal Resource Locator"*>Text to appear in browser</A>
Example:	<A HREF="http://geffen.com/hole.html">The Hole Page</A>
Don't Forget:	You must enclose the URL within quotation marks.
Hot Tip:	Be sure to check for errors—angle brackets, extraneous spaces, mistakes in typing the URL, lack of a trailing stop tag.

MAKING A LIST

Among body elements, one of the most frequently used is the list. With HTML, you can create two kinds of lists:

Ordered Lists	An ordered list is a numbered list. The browser will number the items automatically.
Unordered Lists	An unordered list is a bulleted list. The browser will insert the bullets automatically.

In this section, you'll transform the poorly organized series of hyperlinks you just added into a nicely formatted bulleted list.

Tags Needed for an Unordered (Bulleted) List

To create an unordered (bulleted) list, you need to add two HTML tags:

1. **<UL> . . . </UL>**   Place the <UL> tag at the beginning of the list, and the </UL> tag at the end.

2. **<LI> . . . </LI>**   Place the <LI> tag at the beginning of each item you want preceded by a bullet, and close the item with </LI>.

Here's an example of a properly formatted unordered list:

```
<UL>
<LI>This is item Number 1.</LI>
```

```
<LI>This is item Number 2.</LI>
<LI>This is item Number 3.</LI>
</UL>
```

Figure 11.3 shows how the list looks when formatted by a browser.

Adding the Tags to the Hyperlink List

Here's what the hyperlink list looks like with the added tags, shown in bold. Try adding these to your home page document:

```
<UL>
<LI><A HREF="http://www.vtek.chalmers.se/~v94zinn/
">The Grunge Page</A></LI>
<LI><A HREF="http://www.vtek.chalmers.se/~v94zinn/
Grunge.html">Some of the best GRUNGE Links</A></LI>
<LI><A HREF="http://www.engin.umich.edu/~galvin/
pearljam.html">The Pearl Jam Page</A></LI>
<LI><A HREF="http://geffen.com/hole.html">The Hole
Page</A></LI>
</UL>
```

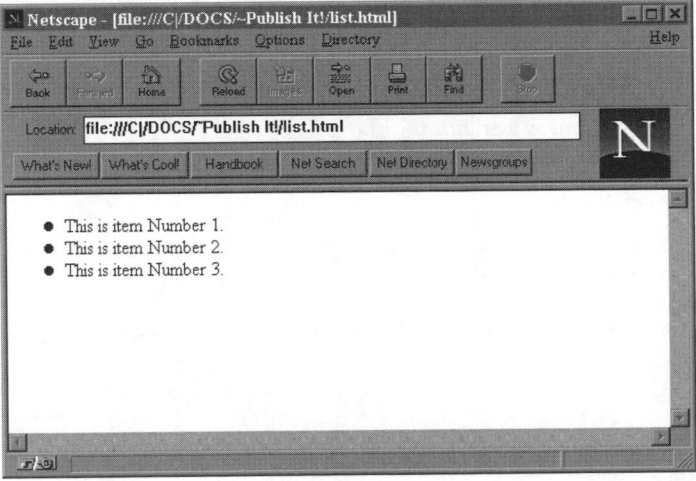

Figure 11.3 Unordered list.

It's a huge drag to type these tags!
Yup. Confusing, isn't it? That's why HTML editors have been created. For more information on editors, see Chapter 10.

For now, do everything you can to make your HTML document as readable as possible. For example, separate each of the list items with blank lines (they won't show up in the document as viewed by the browser).

UL

Purpose:	Creates an unordered (bulleted) list.
Usage:	<UL>...</UL>
Example:	<UL><LI>This is item no. 1</LI><LI>This is item no. 2</LI></UL>
Don't Forget:	Within the list, you need to demarcate each item with <LI>...</LI>.

LI

Purpose:	Demarcates an item in an unordered (bulleted) or ordered (numbered) list.
Usage:	<LI>...</LI>
Example:	<LI>This is item no. 1.</LI>
Don't Forget:	The list must begin with the <UL> or <OL> tags, and must end with the </UL> or </OL> tags.
Hot Tip:	Most browsers will format the list correctly if you omit the stop tag (</LI>), but it's still good form to use it.

Use your word processor's copy and repeat commands to make HTML coding easier!
One way you can reduce the tedium of writing HTML is to make full use of your word processing program's copy and

repeat functions. If you must enter several <LI> tags, for example, you can copy this tag to the Clipboard and insert it repeatedly. Microsoft Word users, note that you can use the Repeat command (Edit menu) to repeat the last editing action. Try typing <LI>, and then position the cursor where the next instance of <LI> should occur; choose Repeat, or use the Control-Y keyboard shortcut.

ADDING INLINE IMAGES

Another appealing capability of the Web is that of embedding graphics and other multimedia objects in your document. The <IMG> tag makes it easy to include inline images in your document.

Do you have a scanned photograph of yourself? If so, you can follow this tutorial. If not, use your browser to capture an inline graphic from a Web page, just for purposes of experimentation. (To capture an inline graphic with Netscape, point to the graphic and click the right mouse button. When the pop-up menu appears, choose Save This Image As from the pop-up menu and choose a name for the graphic. Be sure to store the graphic in the same folder as your test document.)

About Inline Images

You'll learn more about inline images in Chapter 15, but here's a quick overview. Most browsers can handle GIF images directly—and increasingly, they can also handle JPEG. JPEG graphics have many advantages: The JPEG compression format results in files that are considerably smaller than GIF graphics, by a factor of up to 4:1.

Whatever else you do with inline graphics, keep them small. Millions of people are browsing the Web using slow, dialup connections. It's very irritating to sit there while your browser downloads a huge graphic. Try to keep inline images as small as possible, with a maximum of roughly 25 KB.

The <IMG> Tag

To add an inline graphic to your document, you use the <IMG> tag. If your graphic is named "PORTRAIT.JPG," here's what the <IMG> tag looks like:

```
<IMG SRC="portrait.jpg">
```

In the above tag, SRC is an *attribute*, which you'll learn more about in the coming chapters. It identifies the location of the graphic. As this tag is written, the browser will assume that the graphic is located in the same directory as the document—and if it isn't, the browser will insert a placeholder instead of your graphic.

Please note the following:

- There's no stop tag.

- There's a space between "IMG" and "SRC".

- You must enclose the graphic's filename within quotes.

- Don't forget the equals sign!

Embedding the Inline Graphic within the <H1> Tag

You've probably seen lots of Web pages that show an inline image positioned flush left against the document's H1 heading, as in Figure 11.4. You can produce the same effect by positioning the <IMG> tag within the <H1> tag, as follows:

```
<H1><IMG SRC="portrait.jpg">Sue Thompson's
Hotlist</H1>
```

By default, the <IMG> tag aligns the text at the bottom of the graphic. You can change this by adding an ALIGN attribute within the <IMG> tag, as follows:

```
<H1><IMG ALIGN=MIDDLE SRC="portrait.jpg">Sue Thomp-
son's Hotlist</H1>
```

• •

IMG

Purpose:	Inserts an inline image into the document.
Usage:	<IMG SRC="*location of graphic file*">
Example:	<IMG SRC="portrait.jpg">
Don't Forget:	Unless you specify another location, the browser will assume that the graphic is located in the same directory as the HTML document containing this tag.
Hot Tip:	Use the ALIGN attribute to control the position of the graphic when embedded within headings. For example, <IMG SRC ALIGN=MIDDLE SRC="portrait.jpg"> aligns

the text at the middle of the graphic, which is positioned flush left. Use the WIDTH attribute to control the size of the graphic. WIDTH="3%" limits the width to 3% of the available window width.

This graphic's too big!

You can limit the size by using the WIDTH attribute, which specifies the percentage of the available window space that the graphic occupies. For example, the following <IMG> tag inserts a graphic but limits the size of the graphic to 1/3 the available window size:

<IMG SRC="portrait.gif" WIDTH="33%">.

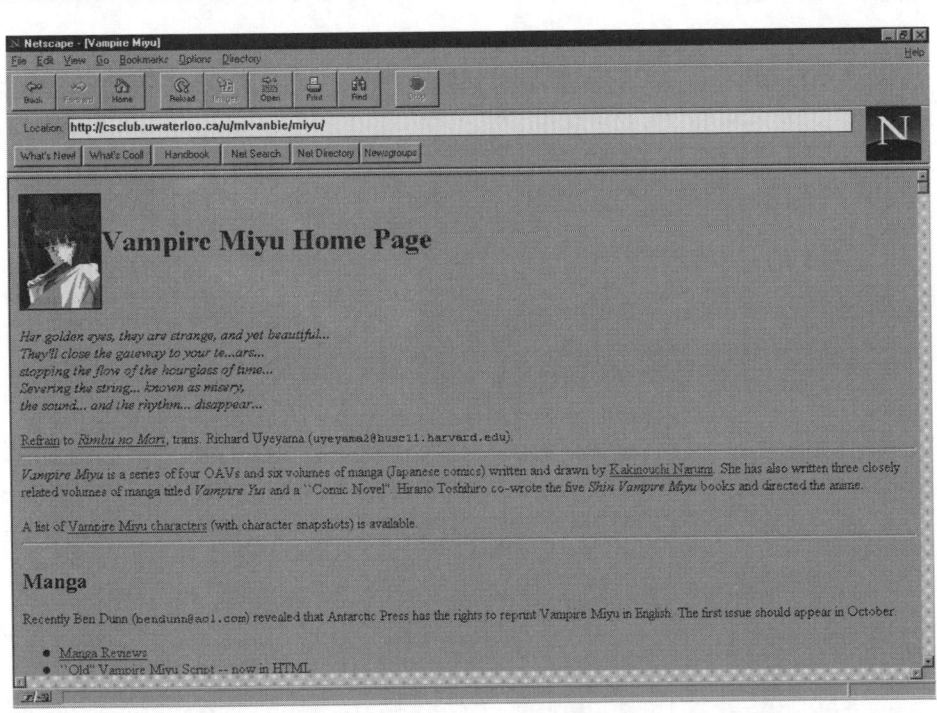

Figure 11.4 Web page with inline graphic positioned flush left against Heading 1 (H1).

ADDING RULES (LINES)

It's very easy to add horizontal rules (lines) to a hypertext document. Rules serve to divide a document into sections even more clearly than headings, so be sure to use rules to organize your information.

To create a rule, just insert the <HR> tag where you want it to appear.

HR

Purpose:	Inserts a rule that spans the active browser window.
Usage:	<HR> (no stop tag)
Example:	<HR>
Don't Forget:	Use rules to demarcate the logical sections of your document.
Hot Tip:	To make sure that the rule stands alone on a line, surround the rule with <P> tags, as in the following: <P> </P>

ADDING YOUR ADDRESS

On the Web, it's customary to add a note at the end of the document indicating who's responsible for it and when it was last updated. You can do this with the <ADDRESS> tag, which displays the information in a distinctive format.

To add an address tag at the bottom of your home page, type the following just before the </BODY> tag (but substitute your own name and e-mail address):

```
<ADDRESS>This document created by Sue Thompson
(suet@fictitious.com). Last modified 21/14/97.
</ADDRESS>
```

ADDRESS

Purpose:	Shows the document's author and e-mail address in a distinctive format.
Usage:	<ADDRESS> . . . </ADDRESS>
Example:	<ADDRESS>This document created by Sue Thompson (suet@fictitious.com). Last modified 21/14/97.</ADDRESS>
Don't Forget:	Include your e-mail address and the date of last modification.
Hot Tip:	Enable e-mail replies using MAILTO.

ENABLING E-MAIL REPLIES

Without any programming, you can enable a simple but very useful form of reader feedback: automatic e-mail replies. When the reader clicks your e-mail address, the browser—if it's capable of doing so—displays an e-mail reply box that is automatically addressed to you.

To enable e-mail replies, you use an <A> tag written as follows:

```
<A HREF = "mailto:e-mail address">e-mail address</A>
```

Here's an example:

```
<A HREF="mailto:suet@fictitious.com">suet@ficti-
tious.com</A>
```

Note that the e-mail address is given twice. The first one doesn't appear; it's a hyperlink. The second instance appears in the document and is rendered with the usual hypertext formatting (with most browsers, blue color and underlining). You could just as well include the text "Click here to send me e-mail," but some people would prefer to send you e-mail using their e-mail packages rather than the somewhat primitive e-mail capabilities of most browsers.

FROM HERE

- Learn more about the HEAD of your document in Chapter 12.

- Learn all the BODY elements—plus all the cool attributes you can use—in Chapter 13.

- Delve into hyperlinks in Chapter 14.

- Learn more about graphics, and learn how to add movies, sounds, and animations to your documents, in Chapter 15.

- For advanced HTML, check out Chapter 16 on enabling user feedback with forms, Chapter 24 on clickable imagemaps, and Chapter 18 on tables and frames.

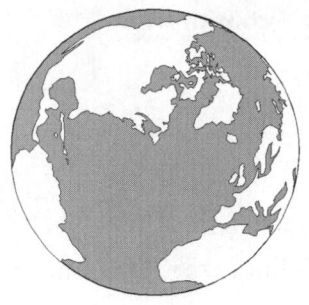

Chapter
12

HTML
Fundamentals

What's that you're saying? Enough already with this hands-on stuff? You want some theory and structure? Well, okay. You're like lots of Web publishers—willing to blindly follow recipes only so long. When it comes time to design your own Web publication, you want to understand the thinking behind the method. This chapter's for you.

Here, you'll learn the reasons why you did what you did in the last chapter, and prepare to learn more advanced HTML in Chapters 13–18. After reading this chapter, you'll understand the differences among the various versions of HTML, the ways you can use attributes to control how tags alter text, and the various tools you can use to generate HTML source code. You'll also be prepared to write HTML code that looks good on text-only Web browsers as well as graphical ones, and to use nested HTML tags to format text and graphics the way you want.

For the Time-Challenged

♦ HTML is a declarative markup language. It's based on defining the function or appearance of text with tags.

♦ HTML versions are really Document Type Definitions (DTDs) in Standard Generalized Markup Language (SGML). DTDs define the tags publishers can use to describe the text in their documents.

♦ Two major versions of HTML exist: version 2.0 and version 3.2. Almost all Web browsers support HTML 2.0, but HTML 2.0 doesn't support tables and other fancy formatting like HTML 3.2 does.

♦ On top of HTML 2.0 and HTML 3.2, there are the Netscape extensions to HTML 2.0. Only Netscape Navigator supports the Netscape extensions, a set of tags that complement those included in HTML 2.0.

♦ Elements define the function of text and other media in HTML documents. Elements take the form of <ELEMENT> . . . </ELEMENT>.

♦ Attributes modify the function of elements. For example, the SRC attribute in <IMG SRC="boat.gif"> defines the graphic that an IMG element inserts in a document.

♦ You can nest many elements together to get special effects.

♦ HTML documents have a head section, which contains general information about the document and is of great interest to the spiders that feed search engines, and a body section, which contains the information you see displayed by a Web browser.

♦ There's a serious debate in the Web community about logical formatting as opposed to physical formatting. The <STRONG> tag is an example of logical formatting—it says "emphasize this text somehow." The <B> tag says "make this text bold."

♦ You can insert all the returns and spaces you want in your source code. This helps make your source code easy to read without altering your document's appearance to Web browser users.

♦ You can make HTML documents with an ASCII text editor or word processor. However, special HTML editors make coding HTML much easier. Converters exist for translating documents in various formats into HTML.

♦ Several types of Web browser exist. Graphical web browsers are the most common, and allow visitors to view graphical images and fonts of different sizes. The latest graphical Web browsers support HTML 3.2, which allows tables, among other things. Some Web users have text-only browsers, though, so you have to keep them in mind when designing your site.

♦ Entry-level Web sites use the codes you learned in Chapter 11 (basic text and image formatting). More advanced sites use the material in Chapter 13 (more elaborate formatting). Really cool sites use the codes you'll learn about in Chapters 16–18, including clickable imagemaps, tables, frames, and forms.

HTML: A MARKUP LANGUAGE

You're probably used to thinking of computer programming languages as ways of encoding instructions for a computer to follow. Languages like C++, BASIC, FORTRAN, and Pascal are based on the model of a computer starting at the beginning of programs and moving line by line through the program, doing whatever each line tells them to do. These languages, called *procedural languages,* rest on the idea of executing instructions in series over a span of time.

Other languages, including HTML, aren't based on the sequential execution of instructions. Instead, they rely on declared data and so are called *declarative languages*. COBOL is a good example of a declarative language, as is the database query language SQL. These languages require someone to define the state of certain things—the serial numbers of all the Bravo Units a company has sold or the way a Web browser should format a particular passage of text, for example. The programs then analyze this declared information and derive something useful from it. In the case of HTML, Web browsers process tagged text and yield attractively formatted Web documents.

An apt comparison may be made between PostScript and HTML. Post-Script, a page-description language most frequently used to communicate page layouts to laser printers, is a procedural language. Though most PostScript code comes from programs (page layout and desktop publishing programs, typically), you can (if you're *really* hard up for something to do) sit down with a PostScript compiler and write a program in PostScript. Your code would, in English translation, say things like "Place the text contained in variable BODY_TEXT in two columns, spaced one quarter of an inch apart and never approaching the page edges closer than an inch, and set the text in 23-point Regular Blathering Fool. Put a 10-percent gray screen over the entire page." In other words, you'd be laying out a procedure for the computer (or printer, which is really a specialized computer) to follow.

When coding in HTML, you're not telling the computer what to do, you're telling it how things *are*. HTML code says, "This passage is a Level 1 heading, this passage is a Level 2 heading, this passage is an Abstract, and this big passage is Body Text. A picture belongs over here." HTML code consists of a series of statements, not a series of commands—at least in the minds of purists. Lately, with the commercialization of the Web, HTML has become significantly more instructional. Is the <B> tag (which makes text bold, and which you learned about in the last chapter) a declaration—"This passage is bold"—or a command—"Format this passage in bold type"? You'll learn more about this debate later in this chapter and in Chapter 30.

HTML Versions

Like anything worth learning about, HTML is always changing. In the Web community, several factions argue about what they want HTML to do, and the various standard-making bodies have to make decisions about which new tags to include and which to leave out. As of this writing, HTML exists in at least three variations. Some sites embrace the older standards and guarantee themselves the largest possible audience, while other sites use the advanced features of the newer standard, but risk losing the patronage of those with browsers older than a few months. Is there an "official" version of HTML? Yes, and it's set by the World Wide Web Consortium (W3C). The current proposed standard is HTML 3.2.

This section discusses the differences among the various flavors of HTML, and the advantages and disadvantages of using each of them. First, though, you'll learn the real significance of a "version" of HTML.

Document Type Definitions

This stuff falls into the category of things you should know if you want to have a complete understanding of the topic, but which otherwise aren't much use. Read on in this subsection if you want to temporarily abandon practical applications of HTML and delve into the intricacies of the language's origins and defining characteristics.

HTML is a special kind of Standard Generalized Markup Language (SGML), a language used mainly in colleges and universities to facilitate the exchange of papers and other documents among researchers. SGML consists of a set of very broad protocols for marking up different types of documents with logical labels—things like "Here's my document's title" and "Here's a footnote." The rule sets that govern the marking up of each type of document are called Document Type Definitions (DTDs). HTML has several DTDs for hypertext documents, each of which represents a "version" of HTML. When someone "knows HTML," they really know one or two of the DTDs of SGML.

You can think of DTDs as lists of the tags with which you can mark up a particular kind of document. HTML DTDs tell what the <A> tag means, for instance, and explain what to do with the URL that follows the HREF attribute. But the <A> tag isn't a great example, because it's constant among all the various implementations of HTML. What are the differences among the versions? Read on and learn.

HTML Versions 2 and 3.2

The two HTML versions in widespread use currently are 2.0 and 3.2. There was a version called 3.0, but it has been dropped in favor of 3.2. For this reason, "standardization" of HTML versions lags far behind the state of the art in HTML—even further than standardization in other areas of personal computing, such as modem protocols.

HTML 2.0, for which a formal written standard exists, is old hat. Its main selling point is that nearly every Web browser supports it, and Web publishers can be sure that visitors to their documents will see a document formatted in some kind of coordinated fashion. The problem with HTML 2.0 is that its capabilities are so pedestrian. Serious HTML developers want to use slicker features supported only by the proposed HTML 3.2 standard.

What's special about HTML 3.2, then? Lots of stuff that doesn't sound significant in print, but that makes the difference between a merely serviceable site and a really cool one (see "Levels of HTML Sophistication," later in this chapter). Some of the features supported by HTML include tables, colored and patterned backgrounds, multicolored text, a CENTER attribute for several text-formatting tags, fonts, and style sheets.

Proprietary Extensions

Standards bodies have no power to enforce the standards they create. Companies with financial interests in the Web may try to take advantage of this to introduce new tags unilaterally. These tags are called *extensions*. What's the goal here? If you can get everyone to use your tag, you've made your browser indispensable. The down side of this strategy, though, is that you've made yourself out to be an enemy of the standardization process—and without standards, the Internet loses the technical lingua franca that's made it such an enormous success. Some of the extensions eventually find their way into HTML standards; in fact, HTML 3.2 incorporates quite a few of Netscape's extensions to HTML 2.0, and other browsers will eventually incorporate them. For you, the dilemma posed by extensions is this: They give you cool new ways to design your page, but using them may mean that the feature you're tagging won't be visible unless people are using a browser that recognizes the tag.

What happens when a browser sees a tag it doesn't support? In a nutshell, it ignores the tag. Here's some HTML code for creating a table—something that's supported by HTML 3.0-compliant browsers but not HTML 2.0-compliant browsers.

```
<TABLE COLSPEC="C20 C20 C20 C20" CELLPADDING=5>
<CAPTION ALIGN=top>An Example Table</CAPTION>
<TR><TH></TH><TH>Cars
</TH><TH>Trucks</TH><TH>Buses</TH></TR>
<TR><TH>May</TH><TD>17</TD><TD>23</TD>
<TD>23</TD></TR>
<TR><TH>June</TH><TD>15</TD><TD>14</TD>
<TD>13</TD></TR>
</TABLE>
```

Take a look at Figure 12.1, which shows the table displayed by Netscape Navigator, which supports tables. Now look at Figure 12.2, which shows the same code as interpreted by an old version of Microsoft Internet Explorer. Quite a difference, huh? That's why many people forego fancy formatting for the benefit of those with older browsers.

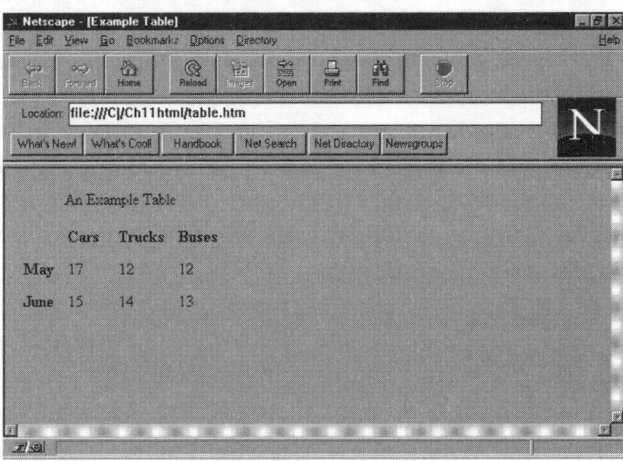

Figure 12.1 A table in Netscape Navigator.

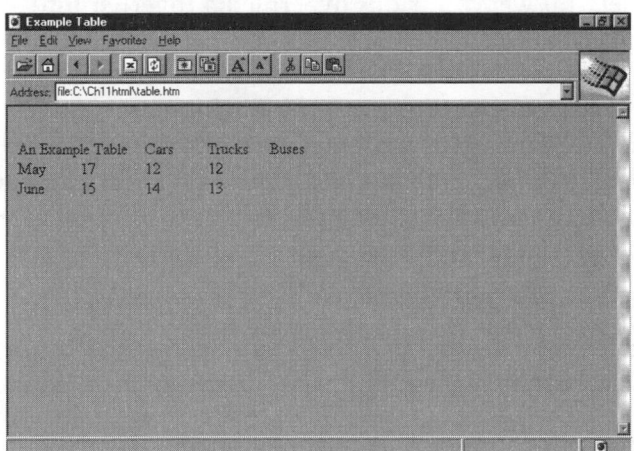

Figure 12.2 Table code as interpreted by an old version of Microsoft Internet Explorer. (The current version reads tables correctly.)

THE NAMING OF PARTS

The English poet Henry Reed, writing in 1945 about his army training, wrote "And today we will have the naming of parts." Reed's poem, part of *Lessons of the War,* depicts a training officer lecturing a group of recruits about the components of their rifles. This section doesn't purport to embody the irony or wit of Reed's poetry, but it's meant to do the same job as the officer Reed wrote about: to instruct the uninitiated about the tool of a trade.

Here, you'll learn the difference between an *element* and an *attribute,* learn what characters you can use in HTML source code and which characters you can't use, and learn how to combine elements to achieve special effects. You'll understand how logical formatting contrasts with physical formatting, and how you can use white space to make your code more readable.

As Reed wrote, today we have the naming of parts.

Elements (Tags)

In high school chemistry, you learned that elements compose all matter. The same holds true, more or less, in HTML. Without elements, you'd have nothing but a disorganized collection of text, graphics, video, and sound files. Elements let you weave various hypermedia together into Web publications and link Web documents to one another.

In all cases, elements are the first set of characters to appear after the < character (later sets of characters may be attributes or values assigned to attributes. You'll learn about attributes later in this section). HEAD, U, BLOCKQUOTE, and CITE all are elements. They declare the nature or function of the text to which they're attached.

Usually, elements take this form:

```
<ELEMENT>...</ELEMENT>
```

In this arrangement, the <ELEMENT> tag defines the beginning of text defined by the element, and the </ELEMENT> tag defines the end. Here's an example:

```
<BLOCKQUOTE>A wide plain, where the widening Floss
hurries on between green banks to the sea, and the
loving tide, rushing to meet it, checks its passage
with an impetuous embrace.</BLOCKQUOTE>
```

Note that BLOCKQUOTE elements surround the passage (the first sentence of George Eliot's *The Mill on the Floss*). When a Web browser looks at the code above, it will treat the text as defined by the BLOCKQUOTE element. Usually, that means it will indent the text from both margins and separate it from other text above and below.

Not all elements follow the <ELEMENT> . . . </ELEMENT> model, though. Many elements, particularly those found in document heads, are said to be *empty*; that is, they contain no text. The IMG element is an empty element. There is no </IMG> tag. The same holds true for the HR and META elements. These elements, along with several others, are inserted in text. They represent something that fits within the text (such as a graphic), but does not alter the text itself.

A few elements are not empty, but don't strictly require the </ELEMENT> portion of their syntax. For example, in a series of body-text paragraphs, you can get away with just putting <P> tags at the beginning of each paragraph, without worrying about putting </P> tags at the end of each paragraph. The <P> tag at the start of one paragraph implies the </P> tag at the end of the previous paragraph. Lists work the same way—you don't have to use the </LI> tag if you don't want to.

Element Nesting

You're not limited to tagging text with only one element. Often, you'll want to tag text with more than one element to achieve special effects. Taken literally, nearly all tags in HTML documents nest inside other tags, since the HTML, HEAD, and BODY elements surround large portions of documents and the tags those portions contain.

Here's an example of nested elements:

```
<ABSTRACT>In this article, the author explodes the
widely held conception that the character Stella in
Tennessee Williams' <CITE>A Streetcar Named Desire</
CITE> is a parallel to the declining culture of the
Old South and instead argues that she represents the
results of a conflict between post-World War II con-
sumerism and Depression-era austerity.</ABSTRACT>
```

Figure 12.3 shows how a browser renders this code. Note that the entire passage is formatted as an abstract, but only "A Streetcar Named Desire" appears formatted as a citation.

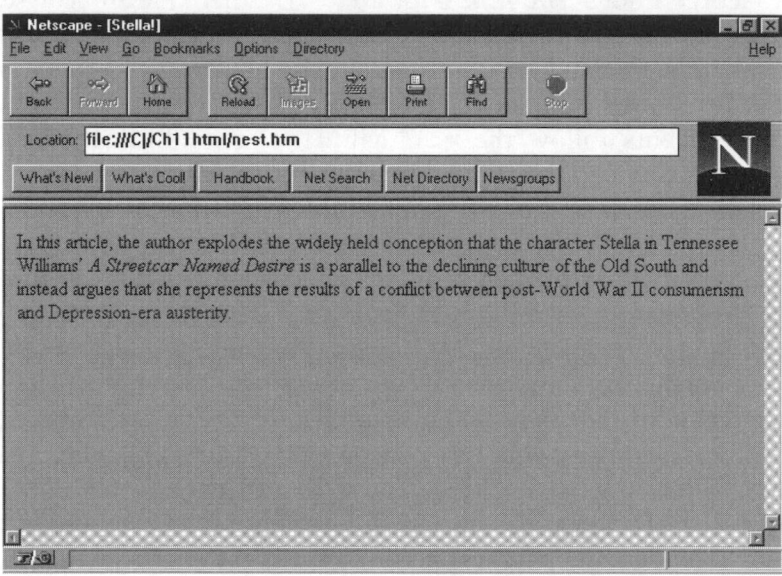

Figure 12.3   The results of nesting elements.

Attributes

Elements aren't the whole story, though. You use *attributes* to modify the basic function of elements. Take the IMG element, for example. It inserts a graphic into an HTML document, but how does it insert that graphic? Is the top of the graphic flush with the top of the line of text, or is the bottom of the graphic level with the bottom of the text characters? Or should the center of the image align with the center of the line of text? You have to use attributes to specify how a Web browser should display the graphic. In the case of IMG and some other elements, you also have to specify the source of the graphic—a path to a graphics file.

In the IMG example, the ALIGN attribute is the attribute that determines the alignment of the graphic, and the SRC attribute specifies the source of the graphics file. The SRC attribute, in fact, is mandatory—you can't insert a graphic without telling the computer where to find the desired image file. The syntax looks like this:

```
<IMG SRC="glider.gif" ALIGN=MIDDLE>
```

In this example, the SRC attribute specifies that the inline image comes from the image file called glider.gif and that the center of the image should align with the center of the text in the line. MIDDLE in this example is a value assigned to ALIGN—the other two options are TOP and BOTTOM. Many attributes take numerical values, such as the thickness of table grid elements in pixels or the amount of white space that should surround graphics.

Entities

In an HTML document, you can use any of the characters in the International Standards Organization (ISO) Latin-1 character set, which is also known as the ISO 8859/1 character set. Within this character set, you find the following:

- The first 238 characters of the 7-bit United States ASCII character set.

- An additional 238 characters that contain most of the accented and other characters needed to type words in European languages.

There's no problem with the first 238 characters, the ones included in the ASCII character set: You can type them on any computer keyboard, they'll appear on the screen, and they'll look fine when your HTML document is viewed by a Web browser. The problem lies with the next 238 characters. These characters, commonly called *extended characters*, are coded differently by different computer manufacturers. If you use the Macintosh codes to insert an accented character in an HTML document, for instance, it won't be displayed correctly when your document is accessed by a program running on a Windows or UNIX system.

To deal with these discrepancies in extended character coding, you don't type the extended characters directly, the way you would if you were preparing a document with a word processing program. Instead, you use *entities* (also called *entity references*), which enable you to type the extended characters using a special code that all HTML browsers recognize. For example, to include an "e" with an acute accent, you type the following code:

é

Note that you must begin the code with an ampersand (&) and end it with a semicolon. For a full list of the entity codes you can use, see Appendix B.

I typed an ampersand in my document but my browser ignores it!
HTML uses several ASCII characters for special purposes, such as the ampersand. If you use one of these characters in ordinary text, the browser will try to interpret the character as an expression (such as an entity code), and it may simply ignore the character if it can't make sense out of what follows.

To include a special character in ordinary text, type the following codes:

Character	Code
Ampersand (&)	&amp;
Double quotation (")	&quot;
Left angle bracket (<)	&lt;
Right angle bracket (>)	&rt;

Overall Structure

In Chapter 11, you created a well-structured HTML document without really understanding what you were doing. Here, you'll learn what those <HTML>, <HEAD>, and <BODY> tags meant.

The HTML element is a holdover from the era of SGML, when it was important to specify which Document Type Definition a document employed. In good HTML style, you put an <HTML> tag at the beginning, an </HTML> tag at the end, and nest all other elements inside the <HTML>. . .</HTML> pair. In practice, you don't have to include the HTML element—just like you don't *have* to wear pants and shirts that match. Using the tags is part of good style, though, so bracket your documents with <HTML>. . .</HTML> tags.

Aside from the overall <HTML> tag bracketing, HTML documents have two distinct components: the document head, designated with the <HEAD>. . .</HEAD> tags, and the document body, defined by the <BODY>. . .</BODY> tags. The head contains information *about* the document, including the document's title and details about its creator. The body contains the stuff you see when you view the HTML code with a Web browser—the text and its attached formatting tags, and the images and rules that appear in the text.

Don't neglect your documents' heads just because visitors to your Web site can't see them. Web spiders—which feed data into search engines—pay special attention to the head section. With a carefully designed head, you can generate more search-engine hits on your site and thereby draw more members of your target audience.

Logical Formatting vs. Physical Formatting

Debates about programming styles parallel debates about religion and politics—everyone has ideas, and it's nearly impossible to convince people that their ideas are wrong. In HTML, a debate rages about the extent to which tags should be logical (that is, the extent to which they should state the function of the text they define, and leave formatting to the browser) and the extent to which they should be physical (the extent to which they should say exactly how the browser should format text). Proponents of logical formatting say the true flexibility of markup languages lies in the ability of the Web browser—and the person who configures it—to make formatting decisions. Those who favor absolute formatting—and the ranks of this faction are swelling as the Web gets more commercial—say publishers should have control over the appearance of their publications.

Here's an example of logical and physical formatting tags that, in most browsers, yield the same results.

```
<P>The party was, like, a total
<STRONG>blast!</STRONG> There was this guy there who
ate, no joke, <B>fifteen</B> goldfish!</P>
```

Figure 12.4 shows the code above as interpreted by a browser. Note that "blast!", tagged with the logical tag <STRONG>, is rendered the same as "fifteen," tagged with the physical tag <B>.

This book, lest it be featured at burnings sponsored by one faction or the other, doesn't endorse either position. Both sides' arguments make sense, and though it seems that the physical-formatting proponents have the upper hand now, things may change in a matter of months. Time will tell whether HTML remains a classic markup language or a quasi-procedural language almost like PostScript.

Readability

As long as they're outside tags that protect preformatting (such as the <PRE> and <LIT> tags), you can insert all the spaces and returns you want into your HTML documents. Look at this example:

```
<P>Perhaps it was          the middle of
January of the

present year that
I looked up and saw the mark on the wall.</P>
```

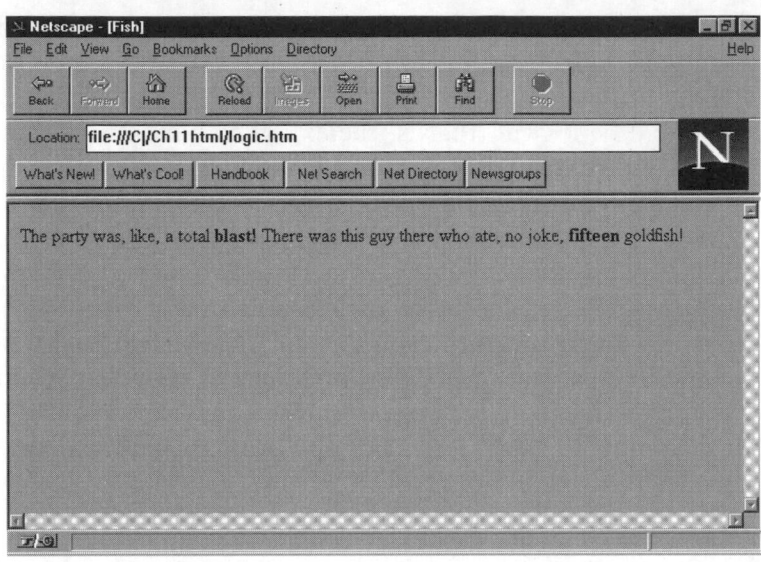

Figure 12.4   The identical results of logical and physical formatting tags.

Now look at Figure 12.5. Virginia Woolf's prose appears as if the extra spaces and returns weren't there. Why is this an advantage? Because it enables you to make your source code easier to read. By inserting spaces and returns—white space—you can separate logical portions of your source code and thereby make it easier to understand. Don't hesitate to take advantage of this feature of HTML—you'll thank yourself later, when you have to modify old, complex HTML documents.

How to Create an HTML Document

Okay, all that's great, you say, but you want to know how to code HTML. What programs do you need—is there an HTML compiler or assembler? Should you look into buying HTML code libraries? No. There's no such thing as an HTML compiler, and HTML code libraries don't exist, though they probably soon will. All you really need to write HTML code on the

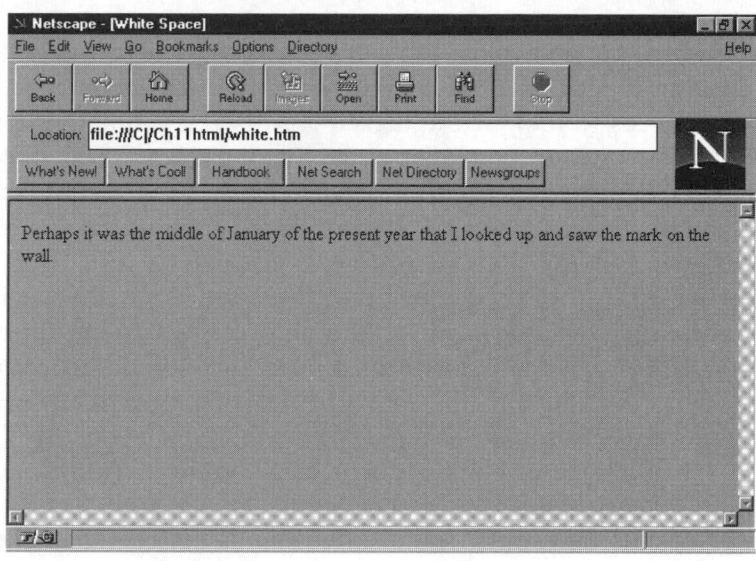

Figure 12.5   Space- and return-ridden code, interpreted by a browser.

cheap is a text editor. If you want, you can find a fancy HTML editor to absolve you of the need to type all those tedious tags. Or, if you already have a document in one format and want to convert it to HTML, you can use a converter. This section explains the advantages and disadvantages of these programs for writing HTML code.

Word Processing Programs and Text Editors

You learned in Chapter 11 that HTML code is nothing more than ASCII text with some special character sequences thrown in among the normal text. Therefore, you can use an ASCII text editor to write and edit HTML source code. You probably have at least one text editor on your machine (if you don't, several good ones are available for free on the Web), so using a text editor is the most economical way to get into Web publishing. By using your word processing program (as long as it saves in ASCII format), you gain a few features on top of those offered by text editors—the ability to insert boilerplate text, for instance, and to use macros.

HTML AND WEB BROWSERS

HTML code by itself isn't much fun—it's plain ASCII text, made less readable by the insertion of bracketed tags. For HTML to serve its purpose, a Web browser needs to look at the tagged ASCII text, evaluate the position and significance of the tags, and display an interpretation of the tagged text. Technically, a Web browser is called a *parser*, because it parses (sorts) out the tags from the text and uses the tags to decide how to display each passage of text.

The section earlier in this chapter that discussed the controversy about physical formatting versus logical formatting described an argument about the function of Web browsers. How much flexibility should browsers—and the people who configure them—have in deciding how to display text? HTML purists say they should have lots of flexibility, while many Web publishers say that the tags in HTML documents should leave little room for creative (and potentially ugly) interpretation.

This section describes some of the several kinds of browsers on the Web today and tells you how to code for each of them.

Text-Only Web Browsers

They're in the minority, but they're still out there—people who use text-only browsers, that is. The introduction of the Web marked the establishment of a distinction among Internet users. Prior to the Web's advent, pretty much everyone with a modem and a computer that could emulate a VT-100 terminal had access to the same information. Now, if you don't have a computer that can handle the latest Web browsers and a fast modem or a network connection, you're at a serious disadvantage in terms of getting access to information. Lots of Web surfers in schools and libraries and in the Third World still use text-only (also called character-based) browsers.

As a Web publisher, you can make life easier for users of text-only browsers by attaching descriptive captions to your images, or by using the ALT attribute of the IMG element, which defines the text that appears in place of a graphic on a text-only browser. You may also want to have a text-only version of your document, both for users of character-based browsers and users of graphical browsers who don't want to wait for graphics to download.

Graphical Web Browsers

Most Web surfers use graphical browsers, such as Netscape Navigator or Microsoft Internet Explorer. Graphical Web browsers have the ability to display different-sized typefaces and different fonts, as well as rules, icons, colored text, and graphics. Historians of the Internet likely will remember graphical Web browsers, along with the Web pages they traverse, as the Net's "killer app"—the application that brought the Internet out of academia and into the mainstream.

Most of this book deals with publishing for graphical Web browsers. Though you have to be mindful of those stuck using text-based Web browsers, assume that most of your audience will be able to look at fancy formatting and images. The extent to which a Web browser understands fancy formatting depends on which version of HTML it's designed for. Today, the most advanced Web browsers interpret HTML version 3.0.

HTML 3.2-Compliant Browsers

The latest Web browsers support HTML version 3.2—the version of HTML that allows tables and other fancy formatting tricks. If you want to code for the cutting-edge portion of the Web community, you'll want to use the semi-standard HTML 3.2 specification.

LEVELS OF HTML SOPHISTICATION

In any area of expertise, someone with a little knowledge of the subject can differentiate those without a clue from those with average knowledge, and those with average knowledge from the experts. In personal computing generally, you know that people who have no interest in the Internet and have little desire to squeeze every ounce of power from their computers aren't at the cutting edge of the field. Real computing experts want to publish on the Web, of course!

This section teaches you how to distinguish the amateur sites from the merely average sites and the fantastically cool sites. After reading this, you'll know what to look for before declaring a site the cat's pajamas.

Entry-Level HTML

This is what you learned in Chapter 11. Entry-level sites distinguish themselves from more advanced sites with their heavy reliance on single-column text layout and minimal use of graphics and other multimedia. Not only will you never see a table in beginners' sites; you'll never see text formatted with much other than the header tags and the body text tag. Clickable imagemaps and forms fall far outside the realm of comprehension of these sites' owners.

Pretty Cool HTML

Entry-level sites don't fool anyone using a graphical Web browser. They're minimalist, and they look the part. Once people have seen a lavishly illustrated site, with careful formatting and hierarchical organization, they'll turn up their noses at plain-vanilla text-oriented sites.

In Chapter 13, you'll learn to code enough HTML to impress most people, if for no other reason than that most Web users don't understand the HTML discussed in Chapters 16–18. This code will earn you entree into the Web-publishing mainstream. Your site will fall somewhere on the coolness continuum between functional and nifty, but it won't achieve the upper echelons of Web-surfer esteem.

Totally Boffo, Webmaster-Class HTML

This kind of HTML is what makes surfing fun. If you can achieve this level of coolness in your site, people who aren't even interested in your topic will check out your site just to see what you've done there. Some of the hallmarks of wondrous HTML:

- Forms
- Clickable imagemaps
- Tables
- Frames
- Java and JavaScript

Even these things, with HTML editors easing their creation, have started to become vaguely déclassé, and by the time you read this you may have to stretch even further to achieve coolness.

Don't forget, though, that just having "cool" features on your documents doesn't make them hot stuff. You can put tables together sloppily, or have slow, counterintuitive CGI scripts backing up your imagemaps. You have to have the content to back up the flash.

FROM HERE

- Okay, class dismissed. Get back to the practical applications of HTML. In the next chapter, you'll learn HTML tricks slicker than those you saw in Chapter 11 and move into the Web-publishing mainstream.

Chapter

13

Building Your Document

Now that you understand the fundamentals behind HTML, you're ready to move beyond the basic stuff you did in Chapter 11 and do some niftier stuff with HTML. Granted, the material here won't win you any raves, but this material will take you beyond the realm of the HTML novice. When you master these tags, you can say you've achieved HTML fluency for all practical purposes.

MAKING YOUR HTML EASIER TO UNDERSTAND

You can get by with plain HTML code if your documents are simple, you are the only one who will modify them in the future, *and* you have a flawless memory. If, on the other hand, your documents employ complex tags and features and other people will have to work with your code without your help, you should document the code in your HTML publications. This section is a guide to ways in which you can make your code easier to read, modify, and expand.

When typing HTML source code, do whatever you can to make it easier to read. You've already seen that Web browsers ignore extra spaces and line breaks in the source code—you have to use the <BR> tag to insert a line break in a line of text instead of just pressing Return, for example—but you can use this to your advantage. Insert lots of extra line breaks in your code to make it easier to read, breaking your code into logical units with white space.

You can also use the space key—which Web browsers ignore when it's outside text that appears in the document—to indent subsidiary document elements relative to higher-order ones. For example, you might indent all the items in a list three spaces, while leaving the <OL>, <UL>, or other list-definition tags on their own lines and flush with the left margin. You can also use the Tab key for this purpose.

Using Comment Tags

On top of its ability to handle source code loaded with returns and spaces, HTML (like most advanced programming languages) has a procedure for encoding English-language comments in source code, and before you learn more advanced HTML tags and techniques, you should learn it. Web browsers ignore any text inside comment tags (which take the form <!-- ... ->), so you can surround helpful hints with comment tags to make the hints visible to human beings studying your HTML code but invisible to Web browsers. Remember that some browsers don't recognize comments that span more than one line, so surround each line of comments with its own set of comment tags.

Here's an example of HTML code with a comment buried inside it.

```
<P>Here's a list of the steps you need to follow in
order to play water polo. </P>
<!-- The following code creates an ordered list, which
the browser numbers automatically ->
<OL>
<LI> Find a ball.
<LI> Find a large body of water.
```

For the Time-Challenged

♦ Don't forget: You can insert returns and spaces in many places in your HTML source code without affecting the appearance of your document when a Web browser interprets it. Take advantage of this capability to make your documents easier to read.

♦ Use <!-- . . . -> tags to surround comments. Comments make it easier for others to understand your HTML code and modify it in your absence.

♦ Use the <BLOCKQUOTE> tag to distinguish a long text excerpt from the rest of the paper in which it appears.

♦ Use the <CITE> tag to highlight the title of a book or article.

♦ Use <DL>, <DT>, and <DD> tags to format text for use in a glossary or dictionary.

♦ Use the <OL> tag, in conjunction with the <LI> tag, to create a list of items that Web browsers number in sequence automatically.

♦ Use the <DIR> and <MENU> tags like <UL> tags. Many browsers format the three tags the same way.

♦ The <PRE> tag protects the spacing and returns in an imported passage of text. Use the <PRE> tag whenever you want to incorporate previously formatted text in your document.

♦ Use the <KBD> tag to distinguish text that you want someone to type on a keyboard.

♦ Use the <STRIKE> tag in editorial and legal applications to show text that will be removed.

♦ The <ABSTRACT> tag distinguishes a document's abstract—its summary—from its body.

♦ The <BLINK> tag makes text flash on and off, but it can easily get annoying if overused.

```
<LI> Find a horse that can swim.
</OL>
```

Look at Figure 13.1 and note that the comment doesn't display when a Web browser interprets the code.

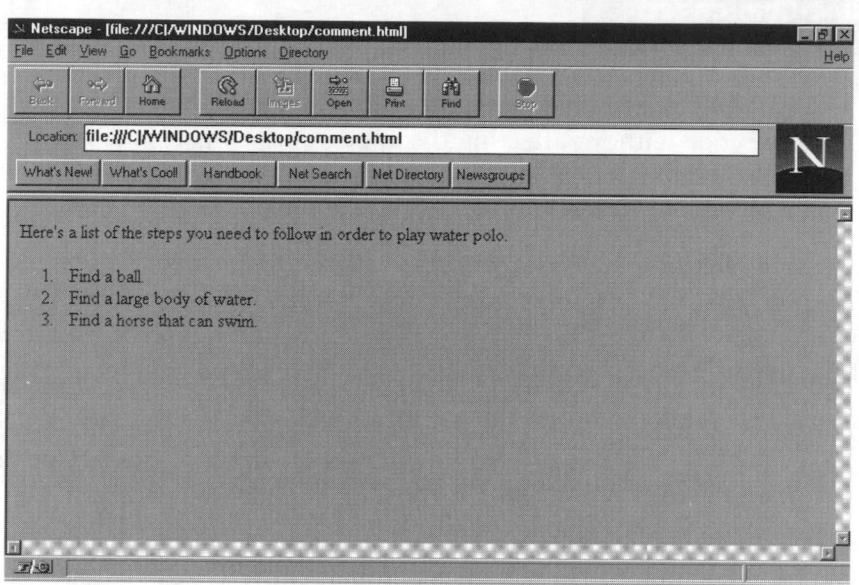

Figure 13.1   Comment hidden when document is displayed.

<!--...->

Purpose:	To allow HTML programmers to insert comments in their code, thereby making it easier for people to study and debug.
Usage:	<!--...->
Example:	<!--The tags in the next line create a form that prompts the user for a password.->
Don't Forget:	Not all Web browsers support multiple-line comments. Break your comments into chunks of less than line length, and enclose each chunk in <!--...-> characters.
Hot Tip:	Use comments liberally, especially if other people will need to modify your code.

REFERRING TO OTHER WORKS: THE \<BLOCKQUOTE> AND \<CITE> TAGS

Since it's based on the academically oriented Standard Generalized Markup Language (SGML), HTML has lots of features that derive from the traditional organization of academic articles. Since one of the defining characteristics of academic writing is reference to past works, HTML has a couple of tags for distinguishing someone else's work from your own.

Imagine you're writing a paper about Jonathan Swift for publication on the Web. You want to include an excerpt from his satirical classic, *A Modest Proposal*. If you were writing for publication on paper, you'd single space the excerpt and indent it from both margins, and underline the name of the essay or put it in italics. When coding in HTML, however, you'd write the following code:

```
<P>Swift's biting, irreverent wit is nowhere more evi-
dent than in his <CITE>A Modest Proposal</CITE>,
in which he writes, </P><BLOCKQUOTE>I have been
assured by a very knowing American of my acquaintance
in London, that a young healthy child well nursed is
at a year old, a most delicious, nourishing, and
wholesome food, whether stewed, roasted, baked, or
boiled; and I make no doubt that it will equally serve
in a fricasse or a ragout.</BLOCKQUOTE> <P>Swift's
willingness to poke fun at "serious" topics also
emerges in his <CITE>Gulliver's Travels</CITE></P>...
```

The results of this code appear in Figure 13.2.

BLOCKQUOTE

Purpose: To set text off from other text as a quote excerpted from another source.

Usage: \<BLOCKQUOTE>. . .\</BLOCKQUOTE>

Example: \<BLOCKQUOTE> \<P> When in the course of human events it becomes necessary to dissolve the political bands. . .\</P> \</BLOCKQUOTE>

Don't Forget: To add more white space around the quote, surround the text with \<P>...\</P> tags or other paragraph-separation tags, as in the example above.

Hot Tip: Always use \<BLOCKQUOTE>, not other formatting tags, to distinguish excerpted material.

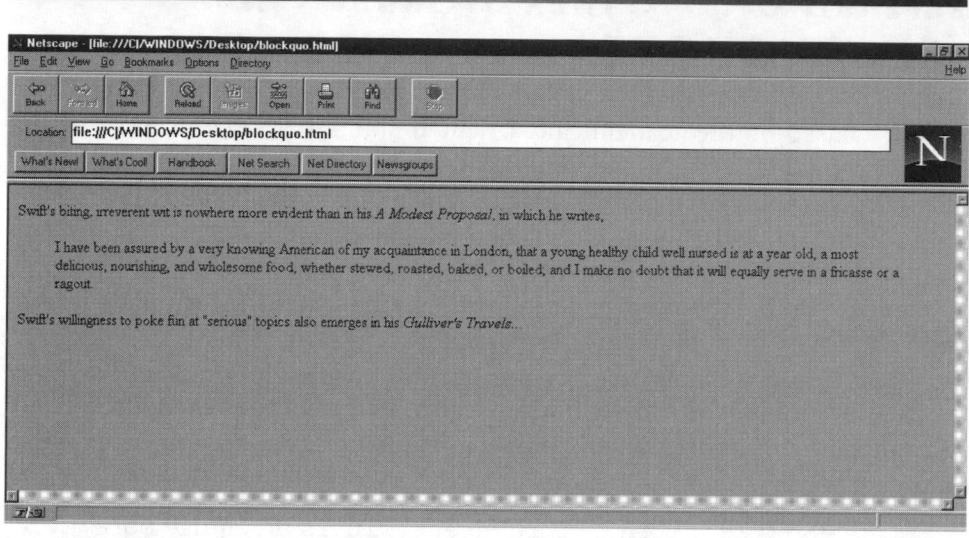

Figure 13.2   <BLOCKQUOTE>

- -

CITE

Purpose:	To define a short reference to another work, usually in a bibliography.
Usage:	<CITE>. . .</CITE>
Example:	<CITE>Terkel, Studs. <I>Working.</I> New York: Ballantine, 1972.</CITE>
Don't Forget:	Use the <CITE> tag for bibliographic references; use the <BLOCKQUOTE> tag for excerpted passages.

- -

CREATING A DICTIONARY OR GLOSSARY

You learned in Chapter 5 that one of the main Web publishing genres is documentation—text that explains a concept or a procedure. Often, documentation requires explanations of jargon or other specialized vocabulary, and that requires a dictionary or glossary. Use the three tags described below to organize a list of terms and their definitions.

To create a dictionary or glossary, you'll use three tags: the <DL> tag, the <DT> tag, and the <DD> tag. The <DL> tag identifies a dictionary-style list; the <DT> tag tells the Web browser to format the text it surrounds as a term in the dictionary; and the <DD> tag tells the browser to format the text it surrounds as a definition in the dictionary.

Here's an example of how to use the three dictionary tags:

```
<DL>
<DT>Onomatopoeia</DT>
<DD>Words that, when pronounced, sound like that which
they represent. Examples of onomatopoeia include
"splat," "bang," and "crackle."</DD>
<DT>Scansion</DT>
<DD>The arrangement of words in a poem on a printed
page. Loose scansion can give a poem an airy feeling,
while tight scansion can convey a feeling of ten-
sion.</DD>
</DL>
```

Figure 13.3 shows how this code appears when interpreted by a Web browser.

- -

DL

Purpose:	To identify a list of items as entries in a dictionary or glossary.
Usage:	<DL>...</DL>
Example:	<DL> <DT>Acoustic coupler</DT> <DD>An especially vocal lover.</DD> </DL>
Don't Forget:	Organize the text inside <DL>...</DL> tags logically, with <DT>...</DT> and <DD>...</DD> tags, as in the example above.
Hot Tip:	You can use the COMPACT attribute (written <DL COMPACT>...</DL>) to reduce the amount of space a dictionary list occupies.

- -

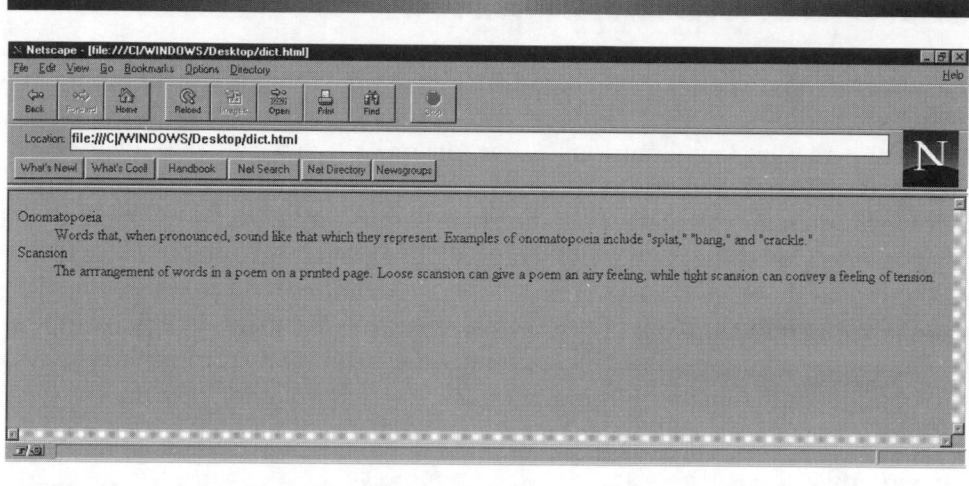

Figure 13.3   The dictionary tags in action.

DT

Purpose:	To format text as a term in a dictionary or glossary.
Usage:	<DT>. . .</DT>
Example:	<DT>Acoustic coupler</DT>
Don't Forget:	Web browsers usually format <DT>-tagged text as flush left and bold or italic.

DD

Purpose:	To format text as a definition in a dictionary or glossary.
Usage:	<DD>. . .</DD>
Example:	<DD>An especially vocal lover.</DD>

OTHER LISTS

Not all the lists you'll want to include in your Web documents will take the form of dictionary entries and definitions. You may want to include a list of steps in a procedure, or a roster of people in an organization. You might also want to publish a list of the contents of a disk directory, or a price list. The tags in this section may come in handy for you.

Remember, you already learned about the unordered list (<UL>) tag in Chapter 11. It's similar to the <MENU> tag described in this section—try both (and view the results on various Web browsers) to see which better serves your needs.

Ordered Lists

Lots of good Web publications offer documentation for software and hardware products, and that means many Web publications have lists of procedural steps. How do Web publishers code ordered lists? With the <OL> tag, as in the following example:

```
<OL>
<LI>Open the drain valve.
<LI>Allow all the coolant to drain.
<LI>Loosen the fill cap slightly.
<LI>Allow pressure to fall.
</OL>
```

Figure 13.4 shows how a Web browser interprets this code.

OL

Purpose:	To identify an ordered list, in which the browser numbers list items sequentially.
Usage:	<OL>...<OL>
Example:	<OL><LI>Loosen wing nut. <LI>Clip red wire. </OL>
Hot Tip:	The COMPACT attribute reduces the space occupied by an ordered list.

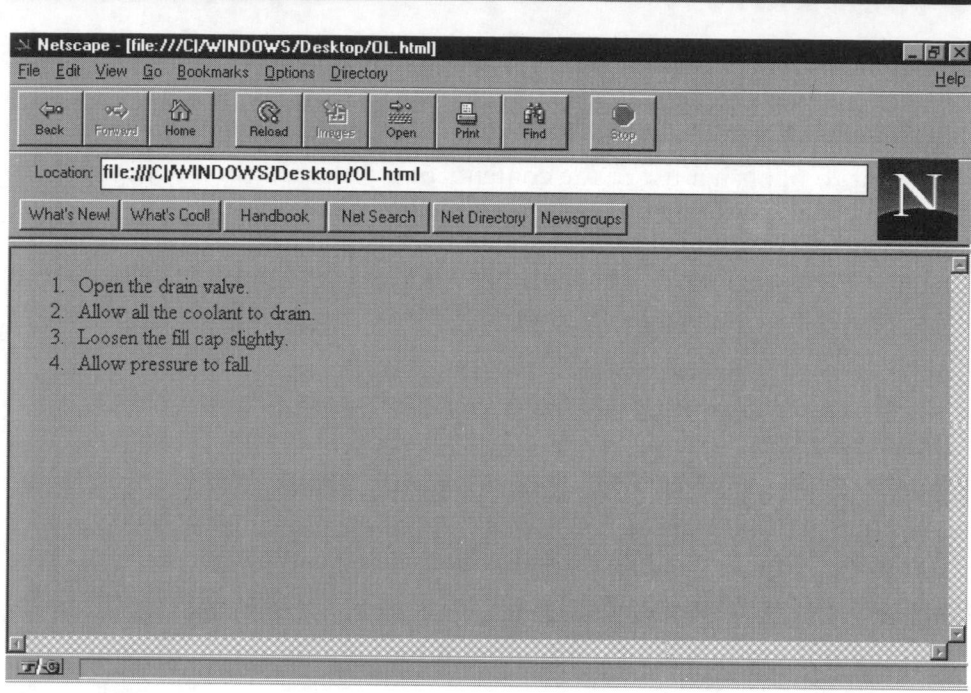

Figure 13.4   Ordered list.

Unordered Lists

Not happy with the way <UL> formats your data? Try the <DIR> or <MENU> tags. Some browsers try to arrange text tagged with <DIR> in columns, if space allows, with the first list item in the first column, the second item in the second column, and so on, wrapping around to a new row when space is exhausted. Other browsers, including Netscape Navigator, treat <DIR> tags just like <UL> tags. <MENU> tags yield results very similar to <UL> tags, too. In Netscape Navigator, in fact, the two tags are treated the same.

Here's an example of <DIR> tags in action:

```
<DIR>
<LI>Apples
<LI>Bananas
<LI>Oranges
```

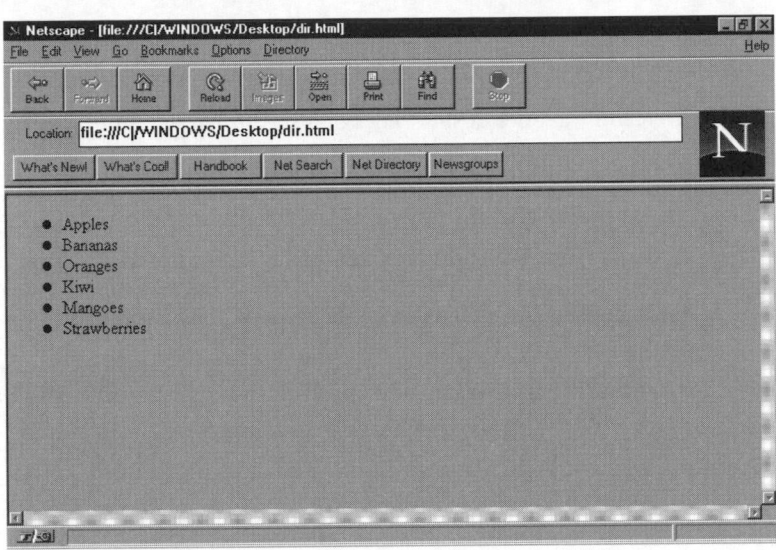

Figure 13.5   Unordered list (<DIR>) displayed by Netscape.

```
<LI>Kiwi
<LI>Mangoes
<LI>Strawberries
</DIR>
```

This code, interpreted by a Web browser, appears in Figure 13.5.

If <DIR> tags don't do what you want, try <MENU> tags. Here's the same list formatted with <MENU> tags:

```
<MENU>
<LI>Apples
<LI>Bananas
<LI>Oranges
<LI>Kiwi
<LI>Mangoes
<LI>Strawberries
</MENU>
```

DIR

Purpose:	To identify a series of short lines of text (20 characters or fewer).
Usage:	<DIR>. . .</DIR>
Example:	<DIR> <LI>Hamburger: $0.89 <LI>Fries: $0.65 </DIR>
Don't Forget:	If there's room, Web browsers will display items in a <DIR> list in columns across the screen. The first item in the list will appear in the first column, the second item in the second column, and so on, until the browser runs out of screen real estate and must start a second row.
Hot Tip:	To reduce the space occupied by a <DIR> list, use the COMPACT attribute (written <DIR COMPACT>. . .</DIR>).

This code, interpreted by a Web browser, appears in Figure 13.6. Note that in this browser, Netscape Navigator, <MENU> and <DIR> appear the same way. Other browsers try to display the list more compactly than a <UL> list.

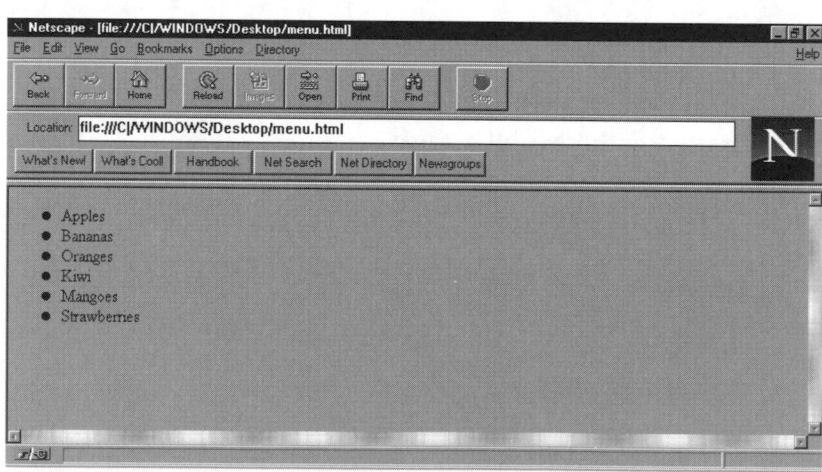

Figure 13.6   Menu list.

 If you'd like to specify how the bullet appears, try using the HTML 3.2 TYPE attribute (for example, <UL TYPE=square>). With HTML 3.2-compliant browsers, this produces a square bullet. You can also choose *disc* or *circle*.

MENU

Purpose:	To define a list of short text items.
Usage:	<MENU>. . .</MENU>
Example:	<MENU> <LI> Music URLs <LI> Dance URLs </MENU>
Don't Forget:	<MENU> acts very much like <UL COMPACT>. Try both list syntaxes on your data to see which makes it look better in various browsers.
Hot Tip:	Unless it helps you understand the logical function of a passage of text in a document, use less obscure tags, such as <UL>, for formatting lists.

PREFORMATTED TEXT

Usually, surrounding excerpted text with <BLOCKQUOTE> tags solves the problem of formatting it as something taken from another work. Sometimes, however, the formatting of excerpted text is just as important as the words. In these cases—poetry, computer source code, and computer output, for example—use one of the preformatted text tags. You already learned about the <CODE> tag—used to identify computer source code—in Chapter 11.

If you want to encode text in which the placement of line breaks and spaces is important, and you don't want to insert a million <BR> tags or risk trusting the placement of those characters to Web browsers, use the <PRE> tag. Browsers usually render text surrounded by <PRE> tags in a monospace font, such as Courier, and they respect line breaks created with the Return key—there's no need for the <BR> tag within <PRE>-tagged text. Here's an example:

```
<P>Here's some text that the browser will format in
whatever way it wishes. Note that this line wraps much
further along than the lines below. That's because I
inserted line breaks—with the Return key, not the BR
tag—in the lines below.</P>

<PRE>Scientist fears worst;
predicts sky will fall soon

By George Arbogust
Baltimore Sun Staff Writer

According to University of Virginia
physicist Davis Bonner, Chicken
Little was right.
The world-renowned atmospheric dynamics
expert announced today that because of
a rare climatological phenomenon called
the "Spiral of Death," the altitude of
the uppermost reaches of the atmosphere
is decreasing. </PRE>
```

Figure 13.7 shows how a Web browser interprets this code.

PRE

Purpose:	To preserve the line breaks and spaces in an excerpted passage of text.
Usage:	<PRE>. . .</PRE>
Example:	<PRE>By Jeffrey M. Leeds Staff Reporter of the Los Angeles Times</PRE>
Don't Forget:	Text formatted with the <PRE> tag usually appears in a monospace font like Courier. Also, <PRE> doesn't preserve spacing at the beginning of lines—to do that, consider using the little-supported <LIT> tag.
Hot Tip:	<PRE> has an attribute—WIDTH, used <PRE WIDTH=X>. . .</PRE>—that lets you specify how many characters the Web browser should allow in each line (X, in the example above, represents the number of characters). Most browsers ignore this attribute, as it defeats the purpose of the <PRE> tag.

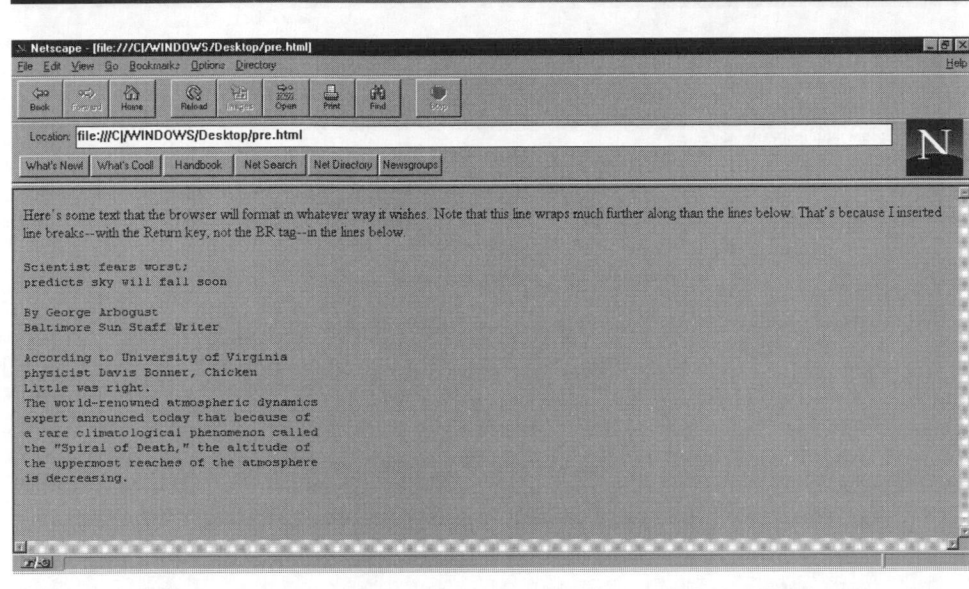

Figure 13.7 Preformatted text.

More Text-Formatting Tags

By now, you're familiar with several absolute text-formatting commands, including the <B> tag for boldface text and the <I> tag for italic text. Here are a few more absolute and logical formatting tags.

Representing Keyboard Input

Before long, you'll probably want to tell the reader of your Web publication to type something on a keyboard. How, in an HTML document, should you tag the text the reader is supposed to type? With the <KBD> tag, naturally. Here's how you use it:

```
<P>When you reach the BLORP! prompt, type: <KBD>Self-
destruct sequence one, one-a.</KBD> and take off for
the door.</P>
```

Figure 13.8 shows this code interpreted by a Web browser.

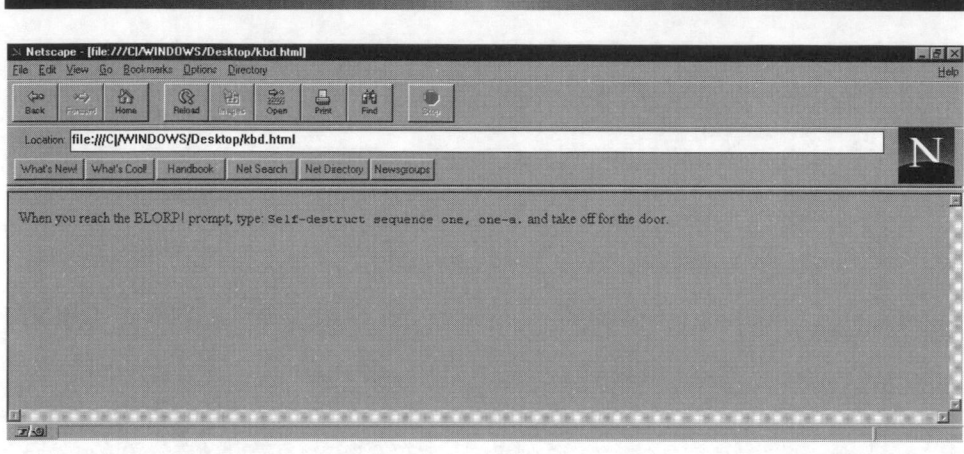

Figure 13.8 Keyboard input.

KBD

Purpose:	To identify text as text that would be entered into a computer via the keyboard.
Usage:	<KBD>. . .</KBD>
Example:	<P>Type <KBD>rlogin foo.foo.com</KBD> at the UNIX prompt.</P>
Don't Forget:	Web browsers usually render <KBD>-tagged text in monospace fonts, typically Courier.
Hot Tip:	Try putting <KBD>-tagged text on its own line to further distinguish it from other text in your document.

Typing Variables

Reflecting HTML's origins in a scientific community, the <VAR> tag enables Web authors to represent math variables (generally, in italics).

VAR

Purpose:	To indicate a variable.
Usage:	<VAR>...</VAR>
Example:	<VAR>x<\VAR>
Hot Tip:	You can achieve the same results by using the <I> tag—and you'll know for sure that all browsers will display the variable in italics.

Representing Editorial Strikeouts

Sometimes, just deleting text isn't enough. When collaborating on a writing project or editing legal material, you'll want to cross words out, but keep them legible until all parties involved in the project can agree on what should be deleted permanently and what should not. In HTML, use the <STRIKE> tag to format text as stricken (usually with a horizontal line running through the center of the characters). Here's an example:

```
<P>It was a dark and stormy night. Suddenly, a
<STRIKE>bone-jarring series of revolver
shots</STRIKE>kiss rang out.</P>
<P>
<P>Author: I think the market's ready for a mushy
book. I altered your opening sentence accordingly. THE
EDITOR.(Apologies to Charles Schulz.)</P>
```

Figure 13.9 shows this code rendered by a Web browser.

STRIKE

Purpose:	To show characters as stricken, that is, deleted from a document but still visible for reference purposes.
Usage:	<STRIKE>. . .</STRIKE>
Example:	<P><STRIKE>We the men and women</STRIKE> We the People</P>
Don't Forget:	Don't use <STRIKE> unless someone else needs to approve deletions you've made. <STRIKE> tends to make your document look cluttered and muddy.
Hot Tip:	Don't embed hyperlinks in <STRIKE>-tagged text. With the strikethrough line and the underscore most Web browsers attach to hyperlinks, the combination looks terrible and is logically confusing—does the link work, or not?

Identifying a Paper's Abstract

With its strong ties to academia, HTML has tags for identifying the parts of an academic paper. One of the tags that's useful in both academic and non-academic publishing is the <ABSTRACT> tag, which formats a summary of

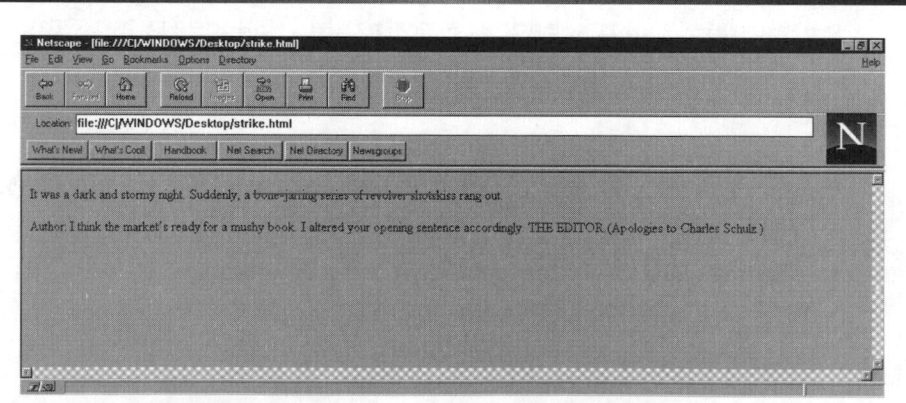

Figure 13.9   Editorial strikeout.

a document's contents differently from the body text itself, or at least separates the two. You can use the <ABSTRACT> tag to create an "executive summary" in nonacademic papers. Here's an example:

```
<ABSTRACT>In this paper, the author examines the
implications of multitasking operating systems on the
perceived stress levels of their users. Anecdotal evi-
dence is presented that supports the idea that human
beings are capable of doing only so much work each
day, and that advances in technology can only boost
that workload a little bit. The author argues that
further advances in computing technology will only
serve to annoy human users and make them feel inade-
quate.</ABSTRACT>

<P>It's a well-known fact that the advent of personal
computers hasn't brought the productivity increases
their marketers promised. Why is this? The solution to
the productivity enigma may lie in the nature of human
beings' relationship to work, and about how much work
is enough for one workday.</P>
```

Figure 13.10 shows how a browser interprets this code.

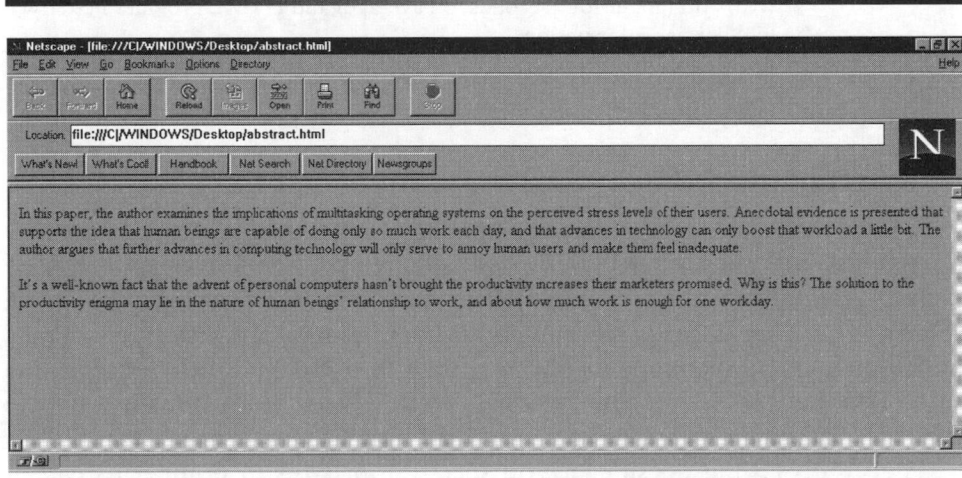

Figure 13.10 Abstract.

Blinking Text!

Yes, you can make text in your documents flash on and off, too, thanks to one of the least-appreciated Netscape extensions. Some Web users find this effect pretty nifty; many others find it seriously annoying and consider it show-offish. Sometimes flashing text is nice for highlighting a link to something new or the most important aspect of your site. Evaluate the pros and cons on your own, and make your own decision. <BLINK> code looks like this:

```
<P>Check out the new <BLINK><A HREF="http://
foo.foo.com/~bill/html/gerbil.html>Gerbil Page!
</A></BLINK>
```

BLINK

Purpose:	To make text flash on and off.
Usage:	<BLINK>. . .</BLINK>
Example:	<P><BLINK>Today Only!</BLINK></P>
Don't Forget:	Lots of browsers—including nearly all text-only browsers—don't support the <BLINK> tag.
Hot Tip:	Use the <BLINK> tag sparingly. It's annoying after the initial "oh, cool!" effect wears off (about four seconds, on average) and HTML provides better ways of highlighting information.

Choosing Font Sizes

HTML is supposed to be a markup language—you identify the parts of the document, but the formatting choices are left up to the browser. As more people create Web pages for marketing and business purposes, however, there's been a push to increase Web authors' control over the document's appearance—and Netscape has been willing to oblige (all too willing, some say). Among the more controversial of the Netscape extensions is the <FONT> tag, which enables you to specify font size.

The <FONT> tag doesn't let you specify font sizes in points; instead, it uses SIZE attribute values ranging from 1 (the smallest) to 7 (the largest). Size 3 is the default font size for a document (if a document doesn't use a <FONT> tag, that's the size that Netscape uses to display the body text).

You can use the <FONT> tag in two ways:

- **By specifying the font size in absolute terms** (<FONT SIZE=5>. . . </FONT>). All the text within the tags is displayed in the size you've chosen.

- **By specifying the font size in relative terms** (<FONT SIZE=+2>. . . </FONT>. Within the tags, the font size is increased by two font sizes. To increase the font size, type a number from 1 to 7 with a plus sign; use a minus sign to decrease the font size.

 **I used the <FONT> tag to create headings, but they show up as ordinary text in Mosaic!**
That's right. Not all broswers support the <FONT> tag. To create headings, use the headings tags (<H1>, <H2>, <H3>, and so forth).

- -

FONT

Purpose:	Spccify the font size.
Usage:	<FONT>. . .</FONT>
Example:	<FONT SIZE=5>This will be shown in Font Size 5</FONT>
Don't Forget:	You can specify the size in absolute terms (<FONT SIZE=3>) or in relative terms, increasing or decreasing the size from the base font size (default = 3): <FONT SIZE=+2>.
Hot Tip:	To change the base font setting from the default size 3, begin your document's body with the <BASEFONT> tag (for example, <BASEFONT SIZE=4>).

- -

FROM HERE

- Between what you learned from this chapter and what you learned in Chapter 11, you know much more HTML than the average Web publisher. You can make cool-looking pages with graphics, fairly fancy formatting, and hyperlinks. But what if you want forms, or clickable imagemaps, or tables, or embedded multimedia? Read on.

Chapter
14

Adding Hyperlinks

The truly revolutionary capability of the Web is the ability to handle hyperlinks and thereby support the creation of hypertext documents. Hyperlinks give power back to the reader of a document, 600 years after it was taken away by the static printed word, and give them the ability to view the contents of one or several documents in whatever sequence they wish.

How can you incorporate hyperlinks in your document? It's really not hard: there's just one tag involved (you already learned a little about the <A> tag in Chapter 11) and a couple of important attributes. Before long, your Web publications will feature links within themselves and to other documents, both in your directory and elsewhere on the Web. You'll have links attached to inline graphics, including small ones that look like icons, so you'll be able to simulate the appearance of a graphical user interface if you want.

For the Time-Challenged

♦ With the <A NAME="*keyword*"> . . . </A> tag and attribute combination, you can define a place in your document to which others can link instead of having to link to the top of your document.

♦ With the <A HREF="#*keyword*"> . . . </A> tag and attribute combination, you can jump to a defined location in the same document.

♦ You can follow the HREF attribute with the filename of the target document (if the target document is in the same directory as the document in which the hyperlink is embedded), a directory and filename of the target document (if the target document is on the same machine but in a different directory), or a complete URL.

♦ With the <A HREF="*URL#keyword*"> . . . </A> tag and attribute combination, you can establish a hyperlink to a location defined with the NAME attribute in another document.

♦ You can embed an <IMG> tag in an <A>. . .</A> tag to hyperlink an inline image to another document.

♦ Be sure to describe, in text, what will happen if a user clicks a hyperlinked graphic. This is especially important for site viewers with character-based browsers, but it helps those with graphical browsers too.

INTERNAL HYPERLINKS

If you have a long Web document (one that takes up more than three screens when viewed on a Web browser), you'll want to use internal hyperlinks in it to help readers navigate. Often, section headings are copied to the top of a document, where they're hyperlinked to the start of the sections they describe. In this way, the copied, hyperlinked headings serve as a sort of table of contents. Often, when documents that were written for plain paper printing are converted to HTML, the person doing the conversion will insert some kind of internal navigation scheme to aid the reader and conceal the fact that the document was written before the author was Web-aware.

Internal hyperlinks also are useful for reference information. If the readers of your document will have to refer to an item of information, such as a mathematical equation or a passage of text, as they read a document, be sure to use internal hyperlinks to prevent the need for scrolling. Every paragraph or so, have a link that leads to the reference information, then have links near the reference passage that lead back to the various links in the text.

This section explains the technicalities of internal hyperlinks. Don't forget, you can combine the information here with the information in the section entitled "Attaching Hyperlinks to Graphics" if you want to create an icon-based internal navigation scheme.

Defining Targets to Which Hyperlinks Lead

In order to use internal hyperlinks, you must define the points (called *targets*) to which links will lead. You do this with the <A> tag—the same tag used to create a hyperlink—but with a special attribute, the NAME attribute. The NAME attribute allows you to assign a plain English (or French, or German) name, such as "Procedure" or "Conclusion" or "Shakespeare_Allusions," to a point in a document and make links lead to that particular point. If you want to name a point in a document, follow this example:

```
<A NAME="keyword">. . .</A>
```

"*Keyword*" is the word you want to use to represent that point in the document. Your keyword should be descriptive, since a word like "Third_Point" doesn't describe the function of the material around the named point very well. Something like "Reduced_Taxes" or "Health" is better.

The closing </A> tag isn't as important in this case as it is when you're defining a hyperlink with the HREF attribute. You should put the </A> tag immediately after the > character in the opening tag so you know precisely where the internal links will lead and you don't have bits of HTML code scattered around your document, making it hard to study and modify.

Linking to Other Points in the Same Document

Now that you've established targets to which hyperlinks can lead, you'll want to build hyperlinks that lead to them. Creating internal hyperlinks is just like building external ones, without the complete URL. You include only the # character and the keyword (which you learned how to define in the previous section) in an internal hyperlink. Internal hyperlinks should look like this:

```
<A HREF="#keyword">. . .</A>
```

When making a hyperlink to a point in the same document, as with all other hyperlinks, you need to be careful of where you place the </A> closing tag. Make sure you place the <A> tag before the text you want to link, and the </A> tag after it. Carefully placing your tags ensures that only words that accurately describe the linked material are treated as links.

The use of # and the keyword isn't limited to internal hyperlinks. If you want (and if your document is long enough to merit use of the NAME attribute, you probably should) you can include *#keyword* at the end of a complete URL. The next section discusses linking among different documents.

EXTERNAL HYPERLINKS

One of the real beauties of the Web is the ability to link documents on widely separated servers. This section teaches you how to enable the people who visit your site to jump from one of your documents to another, or from one of your documents to a document maintained by someone else, who may be physically far away from you. This section also incorporates some of the lessons of the previous section, in that this section teaches you to link to points in a target document defined with the <A NAME="*keyword*">. . . </A> tag.

Linking to Documents on Another Server

You already learned how to do this in Chapter 11. To link a word or series of words to a document (usually, but not necessarily, on another server), use the following form:

```
<A HREF="http://www.donut.com/jones/
glazed.html">This text is linked to Marvin Jones'
Glazed Donut Page.</A>
```

That code will create a link in your document that leads to the URL http://www.donut.com/jones/glazed.html, the fictitious Glazed Donut Page, maintained by Marvin Jones. Since you already read about creating hyperlinks in Chapter 11, there's no need to elaborate on the basic concept here. You can learn about special applications of interdocument hyperlinks in the following sections.

Link to a Specific Point in Another Document

It won't do you much good to establish a hyperlink to a giant document if the information you want is buried deep in the document's text. For this reason, you can establish a link to a point established with the NAME attribute of the <A> tag in the other document.

The problem is, you can't insert named points in someone else's document. You have to count on them to organize their documents well by inserting named points to which you can link. If they didn't include such points when they created their document, you can ask them to insert the needed tags, but you can't do it for them (unless you can get permission to copy the document and reformat it properly as part of your site). If they don't put the tags in, all you can do is link to the top of their document and tell the reader of your document where he or she should look in the linked document for the needed information.

The HTML code for linking to a specific point in another document looks like this:

```
<A HREF="URL#keyword">. . .</A>
```

In the above example, "*URL*" is the URL of the document to which you're establishing a hyperlink, and "*keyword*" is the keyword established by a NAME attribute in an <A> tag in the target document.

If you need to do so, you can combine the NAME attribute with the HREF attribute to simultaneously establish a hyperlink and designate a point to which other hyperlinks can lead. A combination of the HREF attribute and the NAME attribute would look like this:

```
<A NAME="Kangaroo" HREF="http://www.koala.org/
documents/html/eucalyptus.html"> This point in
the document is both a point to which other
hypertext links can lead, and a hyperlink to a
document at koala.org.</A>
```

With the above code in your document, others would be able to refer to the #Kangaroo location in your document, and your site visitors could click the words "This point. . ." to jump to the document eucalyptus.html at koala.org.

Linking to Documents in the Same Directory (Relative URLs)

If you have a series of HTML documents in a single directory and you need to have many hyperlinks among them, it's cumbersome to type the complete

URL (machine name, domain name, directory, and filename) every time you want to make a hyperlink. Fortunately, you don't have to do that. HTML provides for *relative URLs*, which enable you to specify just part of the URL in order to save coding time. Relative URLs usually refer to documents in the same directory as the document in which the relative URL is embedded, as in the following example:

```
<A HREF="sting.html">This is a relative link to
sting.html.</A>
```

This relative URL would tell the browser to look in the current directory for a file called sting.html. There was no need to type the machine name, domain name, or directory path—they're all understood to be the same as the current document unless otherwise specified.

What if the document you want to link to is on the same machine, but in a different directory? No problem. To have the browser look in the directory www/music/spanish_language for sting.html, you'd use the following code:

```
<A HREF="/www/music/spanish_language/sting.html">
This is a relative link to sting.html, which is
in a different directory.</A>
```

Note that the forward slashes are UNIX symbols. That's what you use, even if you're going to put the document on a PC or Macintosh server. Remember that these lines "speak" to the browser, not directly to the operating system.

This relative link doesn't work!
Not surprising—they *are* pesky critters. Bear in mind that the frame of reference for writing relative URLs is the directory or folder in which the current document is stored. Suppose the current document is stored in

/htdocs/manual/chapters

A link to another document in the same directory need only include the filename:

"chapter1.html"

Suppose, though, that the /chapters folder contains the following folders: part1, part2, and part3. To link to a chapter in the part2 folder, you must include the folder name:

"part1/chapter2.html"

What if you want to link to a document that's *above* the current folder? You must use the UNIX parent directory symbol—two dots (..). To link to a document in the /htdocs/ manual directory, which is one level up, you use this URL:

"../contents.html"

To link to a document *two* levels up, you use two parent directory symbols:

"../../intro.html"

To link to a document that's in an adjacent directory tree, you must use the parent directory symbols to go up—and then you can go over:

"../../moredocs/newstuff/hot.html"

Fun, huh? It's much easier to link to documents *below* the current document, but sometimes this isn't possible.

ATTACHING HYPERLINKS TO GRAPHICS

You can combine two of the Web's coolest features by nesting an inline graphic in a hyperlink tag. By doing this, you can create a graphical user interface that approximates that of the Macintosh or Microsoft Windows 95. You can also, if your site is some kind of image archive, provide a small rendition of each image in your collection to help people decide if they want to commit to downloading the large version or not.

Coding Hyperlinked Graphics

To treat an image as a hyperlink to another document, put an <IMG> tag inside an <A> tag with an HREF attribute. In the following example, the picture called sting.jpg is linked (via a relative URL—see the previous section) to a document called sting.html:

```
<A HREF="/www/music/spanish_language/sting.html">
<IMG SRC="sting.jpg"></A>
```

When a browser interprets this code, the browser will display sting.jpg (usually surrounded by a colored border) and will retrieve sting.html when the viewer of your document clicks the image. Don't assume that images are self-explanatory, though—include some text to explain where the graphics' links lead.

You'll learn about creating imagemaps—fancy graphics that have different hyperlinks in different portions of themselves—in Chapter 24.

Being Considerate of Those with Text-Only Browsers

Though their ranks are thinning, there is still a significant number of Web surfers whose browsers can't display graphics. Graphical browsers require computers of significant power—computers that are beyond the means of lots of people. Browsers like Lynx show a characters-only rendition of Web pages, which is fine, except when a graphic represents a hyperlink. Then, character-based browsers display "[image]" or something equally cryptic, and users are left to guess what happens if they follow hyperlinks attached to inline graphics.

HTML, fortunately, offers a solution to this problem: the ALT attribute. Use the ALT attribute inside the <IMG> tag to explain what a graphic depicts. In the following example, the ALT attribute is used to explain sting.jpg:

```
<A HREF="/www/music/spanish_language/sting.html">
<IMG SRC="sting.jpg" ALT="A picture of Sting per-
forming at a concert."></A>
```

The ALT attribute, as used above, explains what the picture shows—but doesn't say what the hyperlink does. Users of both graphical and text-based browsers will need explanatory text before they can decide whether to follow a link.

FROM HERE

- Hyperlinks are probably the biggest single appeal of publishing on the Web, but the ability to include multimedia in presentations is a big draw, too. In the next chapter, you'll learn how to incorporate still graphics, sounds, and video into your Web publication.

Chapter 15

Adding Graphics, Sounds, and Movies

L ike the days of black-and-white television, the era of text-only Web pages is past. Though a small minority of people still browse the Web with character-based browsers such as Lynx (just as some people still watch black-and-white television), most of your audience will have a multimedia-capable browser. To keep the attention of your audience, you'll have to take advantage of multimedia and engage as many of your viewers' senses as possible.

It may be true that the only reason text predominates on the Web is its past dominance of communication. People have been communicating at a distance with written words for thousands of years; long-distance audio and video communications are a phenomenon unique to this century. Lots of tools exist for writing text, while relatively few exist that a lay person can use to generate sound and video communications. Perhaps someday audio or video will rule the Web, and text will be an anomaly.

For the Time-Challenged

♦ Embedded multimedia, when used correctly, can communicate your message faster than text. Though it's kind of special now, sound, video, and graphics may represent the bulk of the information on the Web someday.

♦ Embed still graphics with HTML code such as the following: <IMG SRC="smiley.gif" ALIGN=middle ALT="Smiley face">.

♦ Embedding sound, video, and animation files is just like creating hyperlinks to other HTML documents.

♦ The HTML code for embedding a sound looks like this: <A HREF="toodle.wav"> <IMG SRC="wavicon.gif" ALIGN=middle ALT=".wav sound file"></A>Click here to hear my kazoo skills (a 150K .wav file).

♦ The HTML code for embedding a video or animation clip looks like this: <A HREF="Patti_on_bike.mpg"> <IMG SRC= "mpegicon.gif" ALIGN=middle ALT=".mpeg video file"></A>Click here to see my kid ride her bike (a 500K .mpeg file).

♦ You should always attach an icon to linked multimedia files and indicate how large a file is before your reader commits to downloading it.

This chapter doesn't address producing multimedia files—that's dealt with in Chapters 22 through 26. This chapter discusses the advisability of including multimedia features in your Web site, and explains the HTML required to embed multimedia in your documents. This chapter also shows how you can use small inline graphics as icons to keep links to your multimedia files visible, yet unobtrusive.

ADDING STILL GRAPHICS

Still graphics, large and small, are everywhere on the Web. This section explains how to embed still graphics (as opposed to moving graphics, which are covered in the "Adding Video and Animation" section) in your Web page.

Generally, when planning which graphics to include, think small. Smaller is better, since viewers don't have to wait a long time for small, icon-sized graphics to download but still benefit from the visual cues they provide.

Also, try to repeat small graphics, since that way Web browsers need only download a graphics file once, then pull it out of their cache for subsequent uses.

If you're interested in producing graphics to include in your Web site, take a look at Chapter 22.

Why Add Still Graphics?

It's a cliché, but it's generally true: A picture is worth a thousand words. On the Web, where communicating your message to a site visitor before he or she clicks away is key, graphics can send a signal that either satiates your visitors' needs right away or invites them to hang around. Graphics can also enhance the appeal of the other media on your pages. A good icon can induce visitors to play a sound or video file they otherwise might not play, or add a dimension of interpretation that text alone could not provide.

Also, graphics appeal to the members of an increasingly nonverbal society. Not only is a large portion of the population of Web users young, and therefore used to absorbing visual information from television and heavily illustrated magazines, but also many Web users don't speak the same language you speak. Simple icons that illustrate what a link does help those non-English speakers trying to navigate the Web. Additionally, a small but growing portion of the Web population is *very* young—children. If you have any interest in having early elementary-school-age children visit your site, make sure your graphics help compensate for their limited reading ability.

Introducing the <IMG> Tag

To add still graphics to your Web page, you use the <IMG> tag. This tag doesn't have a closing tag. You can add JPEG or GIF graphics to your Web page using this tag. (Actually, you can add other types of graphics as well, but most Web browsers can't display them without help.)

Referring to the Image's Source

Within the image tag, you'll place the URL of the image. You have the following options:

- **Relative URL** If you have included the graphic within the files in your Web publishing space (see Chapter 21), you can use a *relative URL*. A relative URL omits most of the file location information except for the file name (and the directory location, if it's beneath the directory in which your Web page will be located). The easiest way to deal with graphics is to simply place them in the same directory that contains your Web page; if you do so, the URL is simply the name of the file, surrounded by quotation marks ("picture.jpg"). If you have many pages and many graphics, though, you may wish to place the graphics in a directory called /images, which you should place within the directory that holds your Web page. If you place the image in a subdirectory, the URL should contain the path information showing where it's located vis-à-vis the Web page that contains the <IMG> tag ("/images/picture.jpg"). Note: There's a major drawback to using a relative URL. If you move the Web page containing the <IMG> tag to a new location, the link to the graphic won't work unless you also move the graphic.

- **Absolute URL**   If you think that you might move your Web pages around on your server, it's a good idea to use *absolute URLs*. An absolute URL specifies the file's location precisely. If you use an absolute URL ("http://watt.seas.virginia.edu/~bp/c34/c34markIIsailplan.jpg"), you can move your page anywhere and the image link will still work.

I'm confused! Where should I keep my graphics?
Do things the simple way: Keep graphics in the same directory that contains your Web page. If you later move the page, just remember to move the graphics too, keeping them in the same directory that contains the page. Just follow these rules and you'll never have problems with "not found" graphics.

As you've just learned, you can use an absolute URL in an <IMG> tag. Does this mean you can include a link to a graphic that's on another server? Technically, yes. In terms of etiquette, though, it's a bad idea—especially if you're doing so to avoid having to ask permission to use a graphic. Also your inclusion of the graphic places additional strain on the server where the graphic is stored, since everyone accessing your page is also simultaneously accessing the graphic's server.

Using the Source Attribute

So how do you refer to the image's source once you've decided whether to use relative or absolute URLs? You use the SRC attribute. Here's an example, with a relative URL (the graphics file is in the same directory as the page that contains this tag):

```
<IMG SRC="picture.jpg">
```

Simple, huh? Try it. Don't forget the quote marks around the URL!

What about an absolute reference? Here's an example:

```
<IMG SRC="http://www.bogus.arf/images/
copyrighted_picture.html">
```

IMG

Purpose:	Adds an inline graphic to your page. The graphic appears where you place the <IMG> tag.
Usage:	<IMG ALIGN="alignment" ALT="alternative text" BORDER="pixels" HEIGHT="pixels" HSPACE="pixels" SRC="URL" VSPACE="pixels" WIDTH="pixels">
Example:	<IMG ALIGN="middle" ALT="Catalina 34 Mark II" SRC="c34.jpg" WIDTH="100">
Don't Forget:	Include alternative text for people using text-only browsers (ALT="Catalina 34 Mark II").
Hot Tip:	Control the graphic size by using only the WIDTH attribute; the browser will automatically calculate the correct aspect ratio for HEIGHT.

Adding Alternate Text

Lots of people browse with graphics switched off, and some people are still using text-only browsers. Don't leave them out in the cold. You can include *alternate text,* which the browser automatically displays in place of the graphic. For an example, see Figure 15.1.

To add alternate text, use the ALT attribute and add the text that you want to include. (Don't forget the quotation marks!) Here's an example:

```
ALT="Lake Champlain"
```

Don't forget alternate text. A *lot* of people browse with graphics switched off.

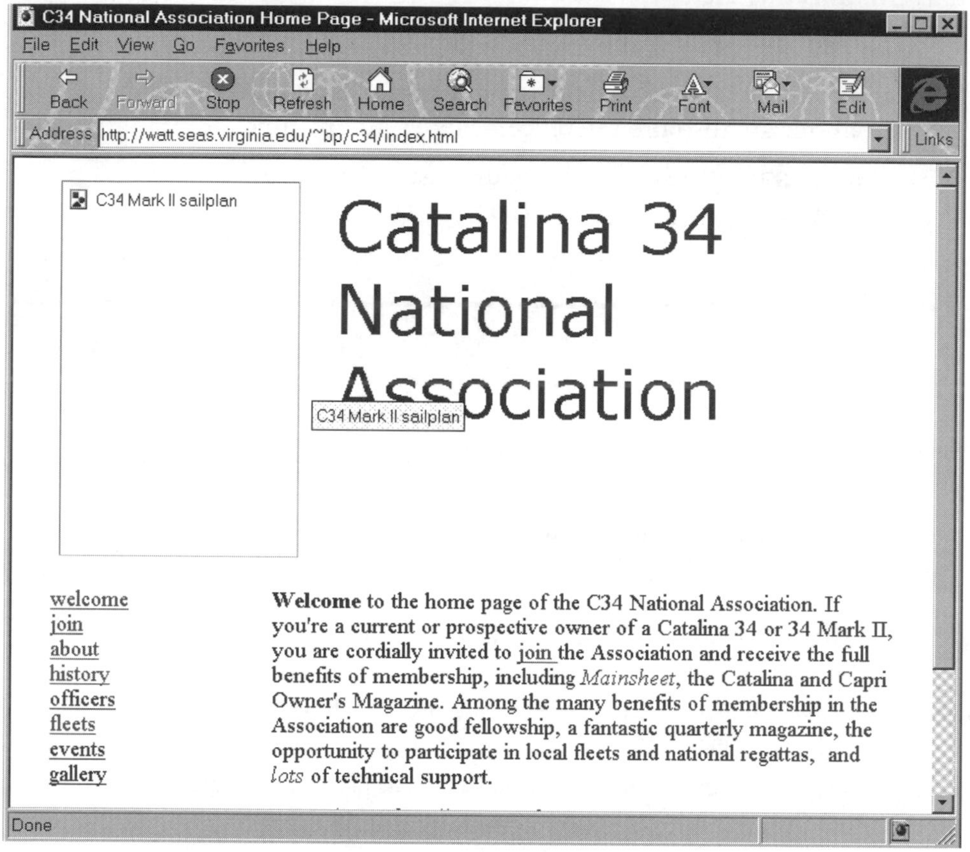

C34 National Association Home Page – Microsoft Internet Explorer

File Edit View Go Favorites Help

Back Forward Stop Refresh Home Search Favorites Print Font Mail Edit

Address http://watt.seas.virginia.edu/~bp/c34/index.html   Links

C34 Mark II sailplan

Catalina 34
National
Association

C34 Mark II sailplan

welcome
join
about
history
officers
fleets
events
gallery

Welcome to the home page of the C34 National Association. If you're a current or prospective owner of a Catalina 34 or 34 Mark II, you are cordially invited to join the Association and receive the full benefits of membership, including *Mainsheet*, the Catalina and Capri Owner's Magazine. Among the many benefits of membership in the Association are good fellowship, a fantastic quarterly magazine, the opportunity to participate in local fleets and national regattas, and *lots* of technical support.

Done

Figure 15.1   Alternate text shows up when users switch off graphics.

Controlling Image Size

By using the HEIGHT and WIDTH attributes, you can control image size. Be aware, though, that some browsers can't handle these attributes. If you use these attributes to shrink a big picture, the picture might still look big to some people. It's better to use a graphics program to resize the picture physically.

If you'd like to control image size using these attributes, watch out for *aliasing* distortions. These occur if you reduce or enlarge the picture in a way that disturbs the proportion between the height and the width (called the *aspect ratio*).

 To avoid aliasing, control image size by specifying only a WIDTH attribute, in pixels (such as WIDTH="100"). Most browsers size the image in a way that preserves aspect ratio if only one of the WIDTH or HEIGHT attributes is included.

Adding Space around the Image

To keep text from getting too close to the image, you may wish to add a few pixels of white space around it. You can do so using the VSPACE and HSPACE attributes (for example, HSPACE="5" VSPACE="5").

Making an Image into a Link

An image can serve as a hyperlink. Just embed the <IMG> tag within an <A HREF> tag, as follows:

```
<A HREF="yakyak.html"><IMG SRC="yakking.gif"></A>
```

This tag displays the image yakking.gif. When you click it, you see the document yakyak.html.

Displaying a Thumbnail

Don't place really huge pictures on your site. Instead, display a small version of a large picture, called a *thumbnail*. Make this a link to the larger picture, as follows:

```
<A HREF="c34.gif"><IMG SRC="thumb1.gif"></A>
```

This tag displays the image thumb1.gif. When you click it, you see the larger image, c34.gif. For an example of a thumbnail in action, see Figure 15.2.

To make a thumbnail, use a graphics program such as Paint Shop Pro to resize the image. Decide on a standard width (such as 100 pixels) for all the thumbnails you use.

 To suppress the border around a graphic when it functions as a hyperlink, add the attribute BORDER=0.

 As you can see from Figure 15.2, tables provide a great way to organize and display thumbnails. Use a two-column table, and limit the first column's size to the width of the graphic.

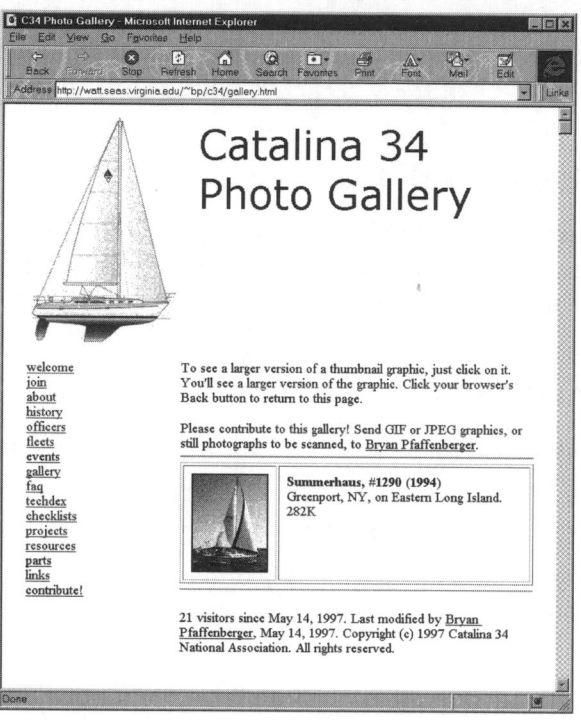

Figure 15.2   Use thumbnails to provide access to large pictures.

Aligning Graphics

By default, browsers align text at the bottom of the graphic. However, you can use the values middle and left to control the position of text next to the graphic (see Figure 15.3). You can also use the attributes left and right to control the position of the graphic relative to the edge of the browser window.

ADDING SOUND

This section teaches how to attach sounds to your Web document. The process isn't complex—it's the same as establishing a hyperlink to another Web page—but when it's done correctly, sound adds a lot to a site's overall

Solutions

Paint Shop Pro: Inexpensive and Capable

One of the best shareware programs available is Paint Shop Pro, a Windows graphics program created by Jasc, Inc. Paint Shop Pro enables you to resize graphics, to change their file format, to adjust color and brightness, and to perform many additional image modification tasks, and all without spending days learning how to master a more complex graphics application. Among people who publish frequently on the Web, it's a mainstay.

You can order from Jasc, Inc. by payment with check or credit card (Master-Card and Visa). The numbers for ordering are 1-800-622-2793 or Voice (612) 930-9800 or Fax (612) 930-9172, or place your order on Jasc's secured web server, http://www.jasc.com.

appeal. Don't forget to add icons to your links to embedded sounds, since icons will tip off visitors to your site about what's at the other end of a link.

If you're interested in producing sounds to include in your Web site, take a look at Chapter 23.

Why Add Sound?

Viewers' eyes get a workout when browsing the Web. Viewers read text, look at icons, and absorb large graphics. Video, however cool it is, still engages the viewer's vision. Adding sound files to your site engages another of your visitors' five senses, and thereby draws them further into the total multimedia experience your site represents. Current technology limits Web publishers to engaging two of the five senses (maybe later editions of this book will have sections on "Adding Smells," "Adding Tastes," and "Adding Tactile Feedback"), so it's critical that you pay attention to them both.

Certain kinds of information can only be communicated fully in sound format. Though you can display music graphically (through musical notation), reading music isn't the same as hearing it performed. A large portion of the Web population can't read music, so displaying music solely in written

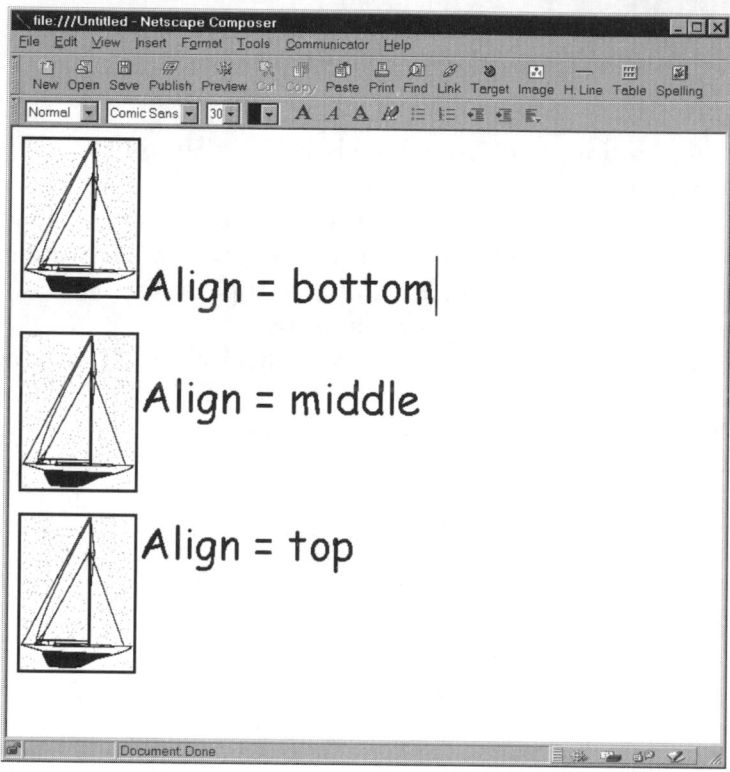

Figure 15.3   Image alignment options.

form cuts them out from experiencing it. You'll need to learn how to embed sound files in your pages if communicating naturally audible information is a goal of your site.

HTML for Sound

Construction of a hyperlink to a sound file mimics construction of a hyperlink to a video file or another HTML document. The code looks like this:

```
<A HREF="toodle.wav">Click here to hear my kazoo
skills.</A>
```

This code, when viewed in a browser, will yield the words "Click here to hear my kazoo skills." The words will be hyperlinked to the file "toodle.wav," which will download and be played by the application that the browser associates with the .WAV extension.

Good Web page design, however, dictates that you provide a visual clue as to what's at the other end of a link—an icon that shows that a link connects to a sound file. You should also give information about the size of the file, so viewers of your site can anticipate how long they will have to wait for the file to download. With RealAudio, a visitor to your site doesn't have to download the whole file before it starts to play, but it's still a good idea to say how big a file is. The following is a more proper way of embedding a sound file:

```
<A HREF="toodle.wav"> <IMG SRC= "wavicon.gif"
ALIGN=middle ALT=".wav sound file"></A>Click here to
hear my kazoo skills (a 150K .wav file).
```

This code yields an active icon—an icon you can click to follow a hyperlink—and a detailed explanation of the linked file and its size. There's no ambiguity about what the link does.

Playing a Sound Automatically When Your Page Opens

Microsoft Internet Explorer (MSIE) introduced a tag that enables you to play a sound when a page opens. However, I don't advise you to employ this tag, since nobody but MSIE users will hear it. It's much better to use the <EMBED> tag, which was introduced by Netscape and is now (partially) supported by Internet Explorer. You're still taking a chance, though. This won't work with anyone using early versions (prior to 3.0) of MSIE.

The <EMBED> tag tells the browser to start a plug-in. When we talk about sounds, that means, essentially, all the popular sound file formats, since MSIE and Netscape both support a good range of them (at least, in the most recent versions of these programs). You'll learn more about file formats in Chapter 20, but for now, you should know that this technique will work for *.wav (Windows), *.au (Sun/NeXT), and *.mid (MIDI) files.

The <EMBED> tag works like the <IMG> tag. The main attribute is SRC, which enables you to name the file. You can also use the following attributes:

- **AUTOSTART** (example: AUTOSTART=true) This causes the browser's sound plug-in to start playing automatically, without the user having to click the Play button.

- **HIDDEN** (example: HIDDEN=true)   This hides the sound player, which makes the sound appear to play in the background. This attribute isn't of much use, though, if you're not using AUTOSTART=true!

- **LOOP** (example: LOOP=true)   The LOOP attribute causes the sound file to be played in a continuous loop.

In Chapter 19, you'll learn another way to play a sound automatically when a page opens: by means of a Java applet.

EMBED

Purpose:	Inserts a file that is designed to be played by a plug-in program.
Usage:	<EMBED SRC="URL">
Example:	<EMBED SRC="interview.au"
Don't Forget:	This tag is very useful for embedding sounds and movies as well as plug-ins.
Hot Tip:	To play a sound automatically when a page opens, and to keep playing it continuously, use <EMBED SRC="URL" AUTOSTART=true HIDDEN=true LOOP=true>.

ADDING VIDEO AND ANIMATION

Adding video and animation to your site adds a lot to its appeal, mainly since so few sites feature moving graphics. This section teaches how to embed video and animation files in your HTML documents—a process that's identical to embedding sounds. It's important with video, as with sounds, to label links with icons and to give some indication of how long a file will take to download.

If you're interested in producing videos and animations to include in your Web site, take a look at Chapter 24.

Why Add Video and Animation?

Video and animation are the fine wine grapes of Web publishing: they're rare, and when you can pull them off successfully, they're delicious. It's unusual to find video on the Web that simultaneously entertains, communicates a message, and doesn't clog communications channels. When a video or animation clip succeeds in all three criteria, it dramatically improves the quality of the site on which it appears.

Also, video and animation approximate television, a medium from which many Web users are used to absorbing information. For this reason, messages you communicate in the form of video files may be better absorbed. Visitors to your site may pay extra attention to video and animation clips, both because they're novelties and because the visitors had to wait a while for the clips to download and don't want their time investment to go to waste.

HTML for Video and Animation

Happily, both Netscape and MSIE include plug-ins for playing the more popular types of movies, including MPEG and AVI (Windows) movies. The best way to include movies in your document is to use the <EMBED> tag, as explained in the section on adding sounds to your document.

If you're including an animation, chances are that you're using an animation that's designed to be played back by a plug-in program, such as Macromedia's Shockwave. Use the <EMBED> tag to include your animation, as explained in the next section.

EMBEDDING PLUG-IN DATA

If you've created multimedia files that are designed to start a plug-in program, use the <EMBED> tag to include these files on your page. For example, you may wish your VRML (three-dimensional) worlds to be displayed with a 3D plug-in, which both Netscape and MSIE include. If you add these files using the <EMBED> tag, they'll start the plug-in.

You can use the following attributes with EMBED:

- **HEIGHT** (example: HEIGHT="100") specifies the height of the object in pixels.

- **SRC** (example: SRC="interview.ra") locates the data to be played by the plug-in.

- **WIDTH** (example: WIDTH="187") specifies the width in pixels of the space created for the object.

Other attributes are supported by specific plug-ins.

 Netscape and MSIE can handle most of the common sound and movie file formats (see Chapters 23, 24, and 25 for an explanation of these formats). If you include data that requires a plug-in that doesn't come with these browsers, you should include a link to the plug-in's home page, so that users can learn more about the program and download it independently, if they wish.

FROM HERE

- Multimedia gets raves, but it's the status quo on the Web. To make your site stand out, you need forms, imagemaps, and tables—HTML programming tricks discussed in the next three chapters.

- Learn how to add fonts to your document in Chapter 17.

Chapter 16

Enabling User Feedback

To create a top-flight Web site, you need to provide ways for your readers to interact with your site—and with you. In this chapter, you'll learn how to use HTML tags that enable user feedback. Although most of them require server-side scripts to process the data originated by users, you'll be happy to learn that one of them—the MAILTO URL—can be implemented without any scripts or programming.

Please bear in mind that not all browsers are capable of dealing with forms. However, most are—and the trend is in the direction of forms capabilities for all browsers. The other thing you'll need to consider is that the form tags discussed in this chapter can produce HTML documents with interactive features such as list boxes and radio buttons, but these features won't do anything unless there's a script to handle them. And with most servers, you'll be in for a bout of programming—or a time-clocked session with a CGI programmer. If you're using Win-HTTPD, WebSite, or ZBServer, you're in luck—you can take advantage of user-friendly utilities that enable you to process forms without doing any programming whatsoever.

This chapter fully introduces all the tags you'll need to understand in order to create an interactive Web document.

HTML ATTRIBUTES AND TAGS FOR ENABLING USER FEEDBACK

This chapter discusses the following HTML attributes and tags. Here's a quick overview:

MAILTO URL | When used with the <A> tag, this attribute opens an e-mail dialog box enabling the user to send e-mail to you. The MAILTO URL does not require a script, but not all browsers are equipped to display an e-mail dialog box when this URL is clicked.

<ISINDEX> | The <ISINDEX> tag opens a simple text search box, which enables the user to type keywords for searches. This tag won't do anything unless there's a script to process the search box's output.

<FORM> | The <FORM> tag creates an environment within which you can use the <INPUT>, <SELECT>, and <TEXTAREA> tags to create user-friendly input fields.

<INPUT> | With its various attributes, the <INPUT> tag provides many of the tools you need to create highly interactive Web documents, replete with check boxes, radio buttons, fill-in text boxes, and more. Included are two essential buttons, Submit and Reset. Submit sends the filled-out form data to a script, while Reset clears all the user's choices.

<SELECT> | This tag enables you to create drop-down list boxes with as many predetermined options as you wish.

For the Time-Challenged

♦ You can use several HTML tags to create interactive elements in your Web presentations, but most of them won't do anything unless you can provide a server-side script.

♦ The exception to this rule is the MAILTO URL, which enables your readers to send you e-mail.

♦ Within the environment set up by a <FORM> tag, the user makes choices and enters text. When the user clicks the Submit button, the browser sends this information to a script in the form of name + value pairs. The script then decodes the incoming information and does something—at the minimum, writing the incoming information to a document and sending a confirmation. Some scripts do much fancier things, but they require equally fancy programming.

♦ Use the <INPUT> tag within the <FORM> container to create single-line text boxes, check boxes, radio buttons, and the Submit and Reset buttons.

♦ Use the <SELECT> and <OPTION> tags to create drop-down list boxes.

♦ Use the <TEXTAREA> tag to create a scrollable text box for lengthy user feedback.

<TEXTAREA>   This tag creates a large, scrollable text box, within which your readers can wax prolific in providing feedback to you.

The following sections discuss these attributes and tags in more detail.

I created these tags, and the check boxes and stuff appear in my document, but they don't *do* anything!
That's right. The <FORM> tag creates an environment in which you can add interactive features to your documents. When you click the Submit button, the browser originates a

message—but it must be pointed to a specific script, which in turn must be designed to handle the information it's getting. If there's no script, your form won't do anything. Note, though, that there's one very important exception to this rule: If you create your forms with WebForm, you'll be able to process forms without doing any programming. For more information, skip to "Introducing WebForms," later in this chapter.

Enabling User Feedback the Easy Way: Using the MAILTO URL

By far the easiest way to enable user feedback is to use the MAILTO URL, which looks like an ordinary hyperlink on-screen but performs a very different function. When you click a MAILTO URL, your browser opens an e-mail dialog box, which is (usually) preconfigured with the appropriate e-mail address. The user can then type a message and click the OK or Send buttons to send feedback.

Please note that not all browsers support the MAILTO URL. If somebody accessing your site is using a browser that doesn't support MAILTO, an error message will appear when the MAILTO URL is accessed. Happily, almost all of today's popular browsers (including Mosaic 2.0 and Netscape) support MAILTO. Still, it's considered good Web manners to include a note such as this one: "If your browser doesn't support e-mail, use your e-mail program to send a message to [your e-mail address]."

To create a MAILTO URL for the e-mail address "webmaster@homely_house.rivendell.edu," you type the following:

```
<A HREF="mailto: webmaster@homely_house.riven-
dell.edu"></A>
```

Any text enclosed within the beginning and closing <A> tags is rendered as a hyperlink.

Solutions

Signing Your Page

You can use the MAILTO URL with the <ADDRESS> tag to create a nice-looking signature to your Web pages. For a reply to "webmaster@homely_house.rivendell.com," you'd code the tag as follows:

```
<ADDRESS> Please send comments or suggestions to <A
HREF="mailto: webmaster@homely_house.rivendell.edu">
webmaster@homely_house.rivendell.edu </A> </ADDRESS>
```

Note that the e-mail address appears twice in the code; that's intentional. One of them is the MAILTO URL; the other appears as the text of the hyperlink, so that someone who prefers to use an e-mail program (rather than a browser's built-in e-mail capabilities) can do so by copying the e-mail address to the Clipboard and pasting it in the To field of the e-mail program. On-screen, this code looks like this:

Please send comments or suggestions to <u>webmaster@homely_ house.rivendell.edu</u>

How Forms and Scripts Work

Unless you use the WebForms application discussed later in this chapter, there's no convenient way to enable user feedback without employing *scripts*. A script is a brief program that provides a Web server with the ability to deal with user feedback.

In very general terms, here's how a script works:

1. **A Web user accesses a Web document that contains a <FORM> tag.** Within the <FORM> tag are one or more <INPUT> tags, which create input areas on the screen. Each of these input areas has a unique identifying name.

2. **The user fills out information on the screen and clicks the Submit button.** If a mistake is made, the user can correct the mistake before clicking Submit. To clear all the input, the user can click Reset.

3. **The browser originates a message and sends it to the server.** For each input field, the browser sends the name of the input field plus the value chosen by the user (such as the text that was entered in a text box).

4. **The server passes the message to the script.** The script is designed to *parse*, or make sense out of, the name + value pairs submitted by the browser.

5. **The script interprets the message and performs the requested action.** This may involve performing a search, recording the user's input, or generating a list. Lots of scripts don't do much more than parse (decode) the incoming name + value pairs, write them to a file in a nice, bulleted list, and send the user a confirmation message stating that the data has been received. Some scripts do much fancier stuff.

6. **Optionally, the script prepares an HTML page reporting on the results of its action.** For example, the page may show the results of a search.

7. **The server sends the new page, or at least a confirmation message, to the browser.**

Here's an example of how <FORM> tags and scripts work in tandem. Figure 16.1 shows a very nice mortgage calculator, offered by HSH Associates (http://www.hsh.com/mort_calc.html). When you fill in the various boxes and options and click Calculate Mortgage, your browser sends a message to the script that's identified in the <FORM> tag (www.hsh.com/cgi-bin/calc). This script parses and processes the data, and generates a new HTML page (Figure 16.2) on the fly.

ENABLING SEARCHES WITH <ISINDEX>

The <ISINDEX> tag requires a server-side script, as do all the rest of the tags discussed in this chapter. Please note, though, that this tag is infrequently used these days, since it's much easier to create a useful search entry form with the <FORM> tag.

<ISINDEX> tells the browser to display a search text box, such as the one shown in Figure 16.3. The user can then type in one or more search words and press Enter to initiate the search—but please remember, this tag doesn't do anything unless there's a script to field the output of this tag.

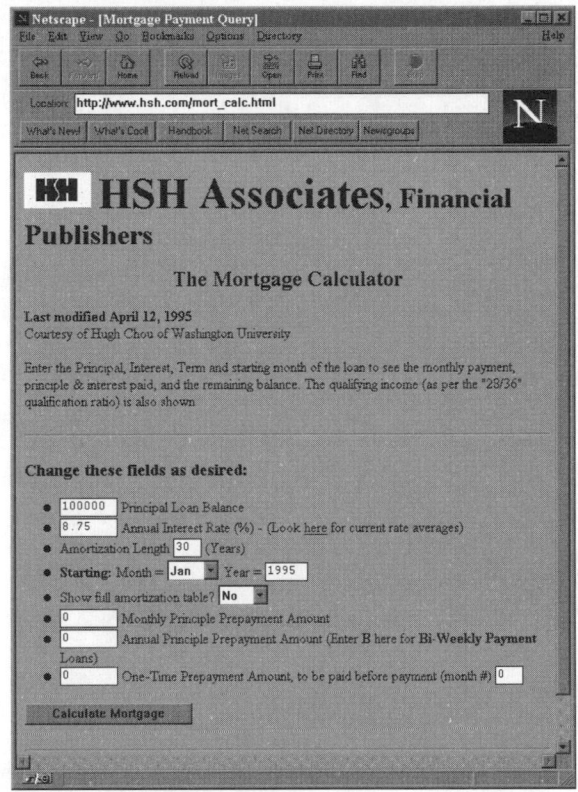

Figure 16.1 Mortgage interest calculator created with <FORM> tags.

<ISINDEX> isn't very difficult to code; you just place the <ISINDEX> tag within the <HEAD> element, as follows:

```
<HEAD>
<TITLE>A Searchable Document</TITLE>
<ISINDEX>
<P>Please type your search terms.</P>
</HEAD>
```

After the user presses Enter, the browser creates a new URL, which it sends to the server for processing. For example, suppose the user types "California," "Chardonnay," and "Reviews" in the text box. The browser adds the following to the current document's URL:

```
California+Chardonnay+Review
```

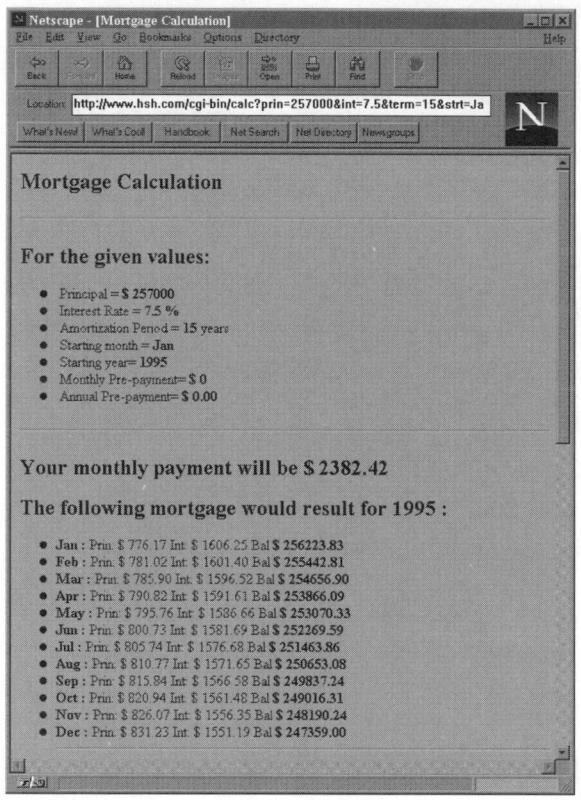

Figure 16.2   Page generated by script.

When this URL is sent to the server, the server looks for the appropriate script, which must be prepared in advance and in anticipation of the types of searches users want to make. The server then prepares a list of items or documents that correspond to the search words, if any, and sends this list back to the browser in the form of a new HTML document.

USING THE <FORM> TAG

To create a Web document with interactive capabilities, you begin by adding the <FORM> tag to your document. The beginning and end <FORM> tags

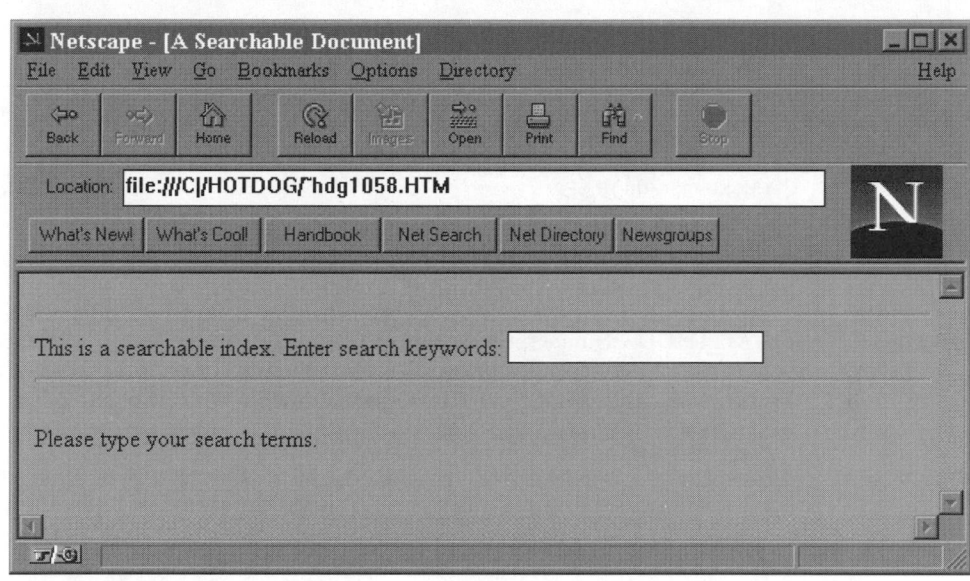

Figure 16.3 <ISINDEX> search field.

(<FORM>...</FORM>) enclose all the HTML that displays elements such as radio buttons, check boxes, and text entry areas.

The <FORM> tag has two required attributes:

METHOD: This attribute has two possible settings, METHOD=GET and METHOD=POST. The POST method is the best one for most servers, but check your server's documentation. In the POST method, the form's output is sent as a separate message. The GET option appends the form's output to a URL, very much like the <ISINDEX> output does.

ACTION: Here, you name the script that is designed to receive the form data.

A completed <FORM> tag looks like this:

```
<FORM METHOD="post" ACTION="cgi-win/polyform.exe">
</FORM>
```

FORM

Purpose:	Creates the environment within which <INPUT> tags can be used to add interactive features to your Web documents.
Usage:	<FORM>. . .</FORM>
Example:	<FORM METHOD="post" ACTION="cgi-win/polyform.exe"> <P>Please type your name:<INPUT TYPE="text" NAME="username"> </FORM>
Don't Forget:.	The METHOD attribute specifies how the data is sent to the server. With the GET option, the data is appended to the URL. With the POST option, the data is sent as a separate message. Most servers are designed to work with the POST option. The ACTION attribute is required. It names the script that handles the form's output.
Hot Tip:	Although it's possible to create more than one form in a single Web document, it doesn't make sense to do so—when the user clicks the Submit button for the first button, the browser displays the response page, so the user would have to use the Back button to redisplay the second form. One page, one form.

If you're planning to create your forms with WebForms, the forms application discussed later in this chapter, you do not need to learn how to create the forms tags yourself. In fact, you shouldn't attempt to directly edit a WebForms form; doing so could destroy the program's ability to collect form responses and enter them into the WebForms database. If you're not planning to link your forms with CGI scripts, you can skip directly to the section titled "Introducing Web-Forms," later in this chapter.

USING THE <INPUT> TAG

By itself, the <FORM> tag doesn't do anything. To make interactive input areas appear on-screen, you must use the <INPUT> tag. Here are some important facts about the <INPUT> tag:

- You can add two or more <INPUT> tags to your document, but you must place them all within the <FORM> tag.

- The most important <INPUT> attribute is NAME. This attribute assigns a name to the values the user chooses. For example, suppose you name a text box "username," and the user types "bp." When the user clicks the Submit button, the browser sends the name + value pair "username = bp" to the script.

- Another important <INPUT> attribute is TYPE. This attribute enables you to select the type of input area you want (such as text area, check box, radio button, and more).

Here's a quick overview of the TYPE options currently available (later sections of this chapter go into most of these in greater detail):

Text	This option creates a text box in which the user can type information.
Password	Like the text option, this one creates a text box, but the text the user types is obscured by asterisks.
Checkbox	This option creates a check box; each check box has a unique name, and it can have only two values: checked and unchecked.
Radio	In a group of radio buttons that all have the same name, only one can be chosen. You can have more than one group of buttons in a form.
Image	This option displays a graphic, the location of which must be identified in the same way you do using the IMG SRC attribute. Clicking the image submits the form, and what's more, the coordinates of the mouse click. A really clever script programmer could use this capability to advantage, but some fancy programming would be required.
Hidden	This option is used in advanced scriptwriting. It enables programmers to write a script that constructs a new document on the fly, drawing on portions of two other ones.
Submit	This option creates a Submit button that, when clicked, submits the form data to the server.
Reset	This option creates a Reset button that, when clicked, clears all the user's data and restores the default settings in the form.

The TYPE options don't include all the possible input areas you can define, as you'll see in the next two sections.

- -

INPUT

Purpose: Creates a text box, radio button, check box, clickable image, hidden message, Submit button, or Reset button.

Usage: <INPUT> (no end tag needed)

Example: <INPUT NAME="Your_Name" TYPE="text" VALUE="Type your name here" SIZE="40" ALIGN=left>

Don't Forget: To determine the input field type, you use the TYPE attribute. The NAME attribute is required. The <INPUT> tag must be enclosed within beginning and ending <FORM> tags.

Hot Tip: Use the VALUE attribute (for example, VALUE="Type your name here") to define a default entry, which the user can change. In a radio button or check box, use VALUE="Checked" to show a dot or check mark.

- -

Adding a Text Box

To add a single-line text box to your document, you can use the <INPUT> tag with the TYPE="text" attribute, as in the following example. Note the explanatory text that's added to the <INPUT> tag. And remember, this tag must be positioned within <FORM>...</FORM> tags, or it won't show up in your browser.

```
<P>Please type your name here: <INPUT TYPE="text"
NAME="User_Name" SIZE="50" MAXLENGTH="100"></P>
```

Figure 16.4 shows what this code looks like on-screen.

I just tried this but I can't get the text box to display!
Did you enclose the <INPUT> tags within the <FORM> tags (<FORM>. . .</FORM>)? Also, check for mistakes—did you leave off the trailing angle bracket? If there are any errors, your browser will ignore the tag.

If you create an <INPUT TYPE="text"> tag, you can use the following attributes:

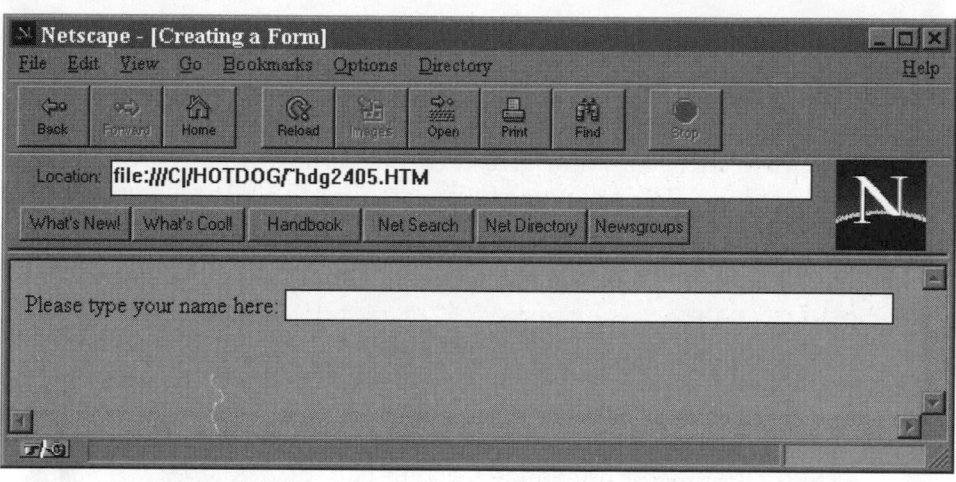

Figure 16.4 Text box created with <INPUT TYPE="text"> tag.

- **NAME** (required)   Here, you give a name to the data the user will type. For example, suppose you are creating a form that asks people to type their favorite color. You could name this text box "color" (NAME="color").

- **ALIGN** (optional)   By default, text is aligned flush left. You can change the alignment to centered or flush right, if you wish.

- **VALUE** (optional)   If you would like the text box to contain some default text, which the user can leave or change as desired, you can use this attribute. For example, you could show a default value of "blue" in the Color box (VALUE="Blue").

- **SIZE** (optional)   Specifies the visible length of the text box, in characters. The attribute SIZE=50 specifies a text box 50 characters in length. *Note:* The user can enter a longer entry, up to the maximum permitted by the MAXLENGTH attribute.

- **MAXLENGTH** (optional)   Specifies the maximum number of characters the user can type in a text box. The attribute MAXLENGTH=120 limits total text input to 120 characters.

Adding Radio Buttons

When you add two or more radio buttons in a group, the user expects to be able to click just one of them (and have the other ones blanked automatically)—and that's just what the TYPE="radio" attribute does. To create a bank of radio buttons, you assign all the buttons to the same name, using the NAME attribute, and give each button a distinctive value using the VALUE attribute. The following illustrates the HTML needed to set up a bank of radio buttons:

```
<P>Indicate your level of experience with wine:</P>
<INPUT NAME="Experience" TYPE="radio" VALUE="Begin-
ner">
Beginner <BR>
<INPUT NAME="Experience" TYPE="radio" VALUE="Novice">
Novice <BR>
<INPUT NAME="Experience" TYPE=radio" VALUE=
"Experienced"> Experienced <BR>
<INPUT NAME="Experience" TYPE="radio" VALUE=
"Connoisseur"> Connoisseur <BR>
```

Figure 16.5 shows how these radio buttons appear in Netscape.

The following attributes are used with radio buttons:

- **NAME** (required) To create a bank of radio buttons in which the user can only choose one of them, you use the same NAME for all (for example, NAME="Experience")

- **VALUE** (required) In radio buttons, the VALUE attribute is required because it identifies the value that will be sent by the browser in the name + value pair. In a bank of radio buttons that share the same NAME, each button should have a unique VALUE (for example, VALUE="Novice").

- **CHECKED** (optional) If you add this attribute to one of the radio buttons in a bank of buttons, the option will appear with a dot within the circle. The user can change this, but the setting reverts to this option if the user clicks the Reset button.

 To mark one of the radio buttons in a bank of buttons as the default (marked) value, use the CHECKED attribute, as in this example:

```
<INPUT NAME="Experience" CHECKED TYPE="radio"
VALUE="Novice" > Novice <BR>
```

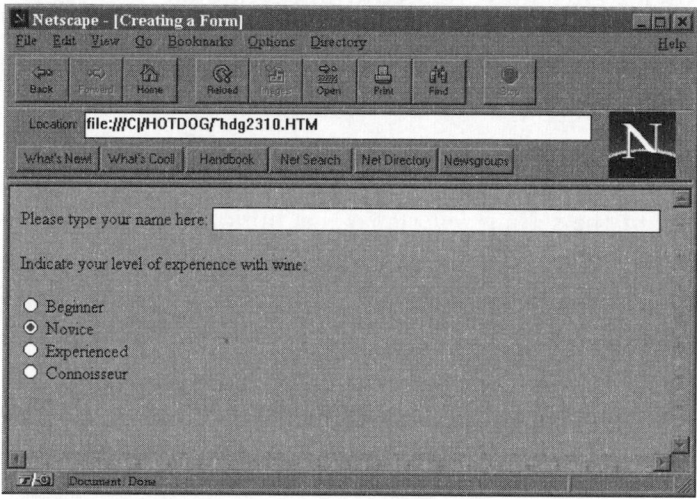

Figure 16.5 Radio buttons.

Adding a Check Box

Check boxes are like radio buttons in that the user can choose an option by clicking the option on or off. However, the user can choose more than one check box. Each check box has its own name (such as NAME="Sweet"). By default, the VALUE of each check box is "off", so an unchecked box isn't included when the browser sends the name + value pairs. If the check box is checked, then the VALUE changes to "checked," and the name + value is included in the messsage. Here's an example of a bank of check boxes:

```
<P> Take a sip of Pinot Noir.<BR>
How would you best describe the taste you just experi-
enced?<BR>
<INPUT NAME="Strawberry" TYPE="checkbox">
Strawberry<BR>
<INPUT NAME="Cedar" TYPE="checkbox" > Cedar <BR>
<INPUT NAME="Blackberry" TYPE="checkbox" >
Blackberry<BR>
<INPUT NAME="Raspberry" TYPE="checkbox" >
Raspberry<BR>
<INPUT NAME="Tobacco" TYPE="checkbox" > Tobacco <BR>
```

Figure 16.6 shows how these check boxes appear in Netscape.
The following attributes are used with check boxes:

- **NAME** (required)   In a group of check boxes, each check box should have its own NAME (as in NAME="Strawberry").

- **CHECKED** (optional)   If you add this attribute to a check box, the box will appear with an "X" within the circle. The user can change this, but the setting reverts to this option if the user clicks the reset button.

To turn on check boxes by default, use the CHECKED attribute, as in this example:

```
<INPUT NAME="Blackberry" TYPE="checkbox" CHECKED>
```

Adding the Submit and Reset Buttons

These buttons are very easy to add. Here's the HTML:

```
<INPUT TYPE="Submit"><BR>
<INPUT TYPE="Reset">
```

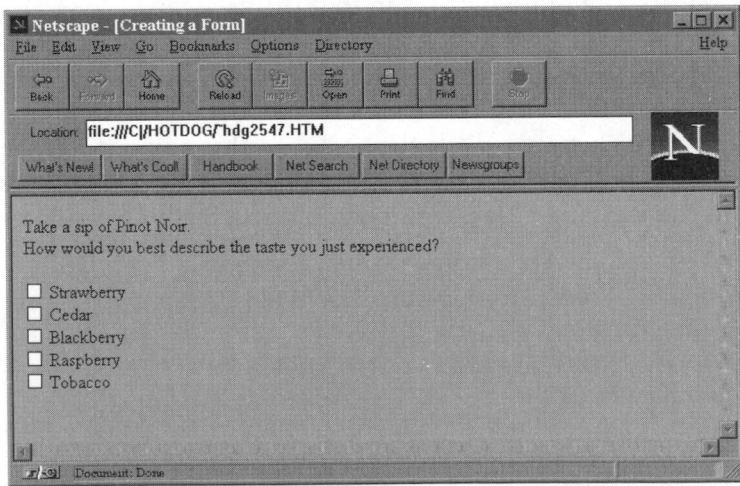

Figure 16.6   Check boxes.

Figure 16.7 shows the Submit and Reset buttons, as displayed by Netscape.

 By default, the Submit button displays the text "Submit" on the button, while the Reset button displays—you guessed it—"Reset." You can change these defaults by using the VALUE attribute, as in the following example:

```
<INPUT TYPE="Submit" VALUE="Submit Comments"> or
<INPUT TYPE="Reset" VALUE="Clear Form">
```

ADDING A DROP-DOWN LIST BOX

In a drop-down list box, the user can select from a list of predefined options. In many cases, list boxes are a better choice than text fields in that a list box enables you to group responses together because they are all spelled in exactly the same way. Suppose, for example, you ask your readers to identify

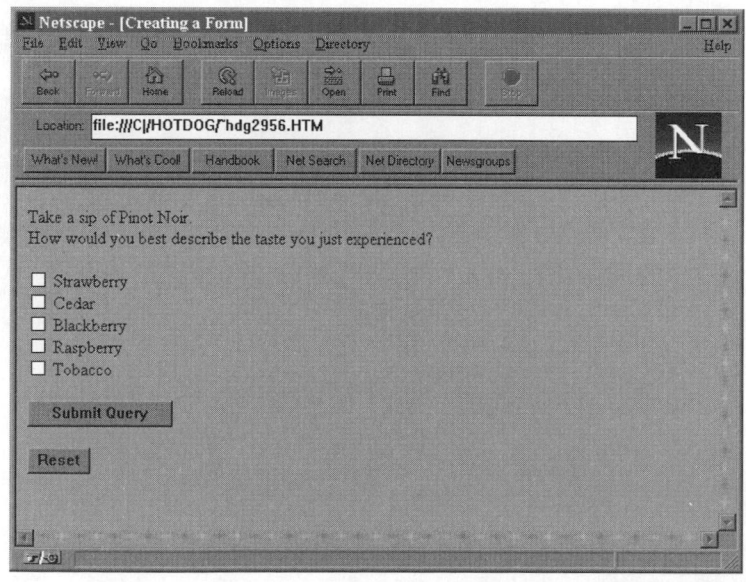

Figure 16.7 Submit and Reset buttons.

the wine they're tasting; in a text box, some might type "Chardonnay," while others type "Chard," "Chartoney," or maybe just "White wine."

To create a drop-down list box, you use the <SELECT> and <OPTION> tags:

```
<P>What is the red wine varietal you are tasting?</P>
<SELECT NAME="Varietal">
<OPTION>Cabernet Sauvignon
<OPTION SELECTED>Pinot Noir
<OPTION>Merlot
<OPTION>Zinfandel
<OPTION>Cabernet Franc
<OPTION>Syrah
<OPTION>Blend or not sure
</SELECT></P>
```

Figure 16.8 shows the list box before it's clicked, while Figure 16.9 shows the entire list.

To define one of the options in the list as the default value, so that it appears in the text box, use the SELECTED attribute (<OPTION SELECTED>).

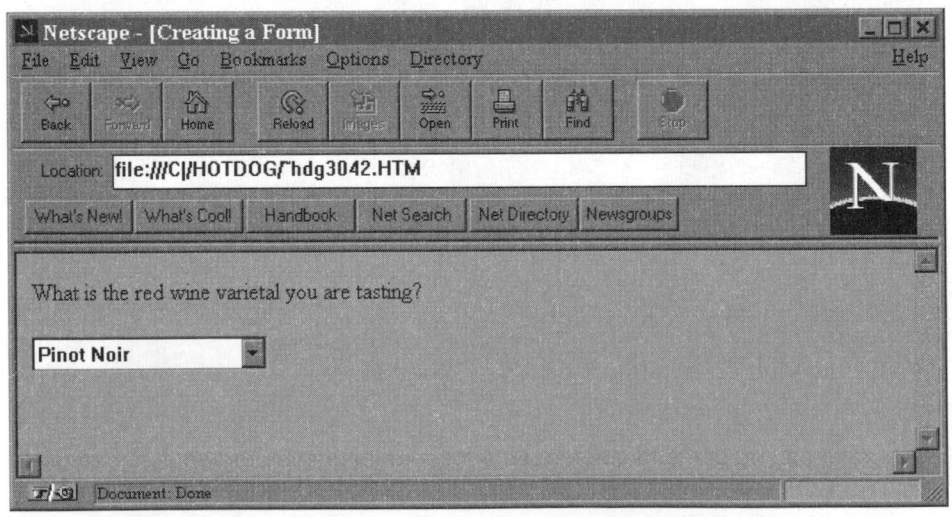

Figure 16.8 Drop-down list box (before clicking the down arrow).

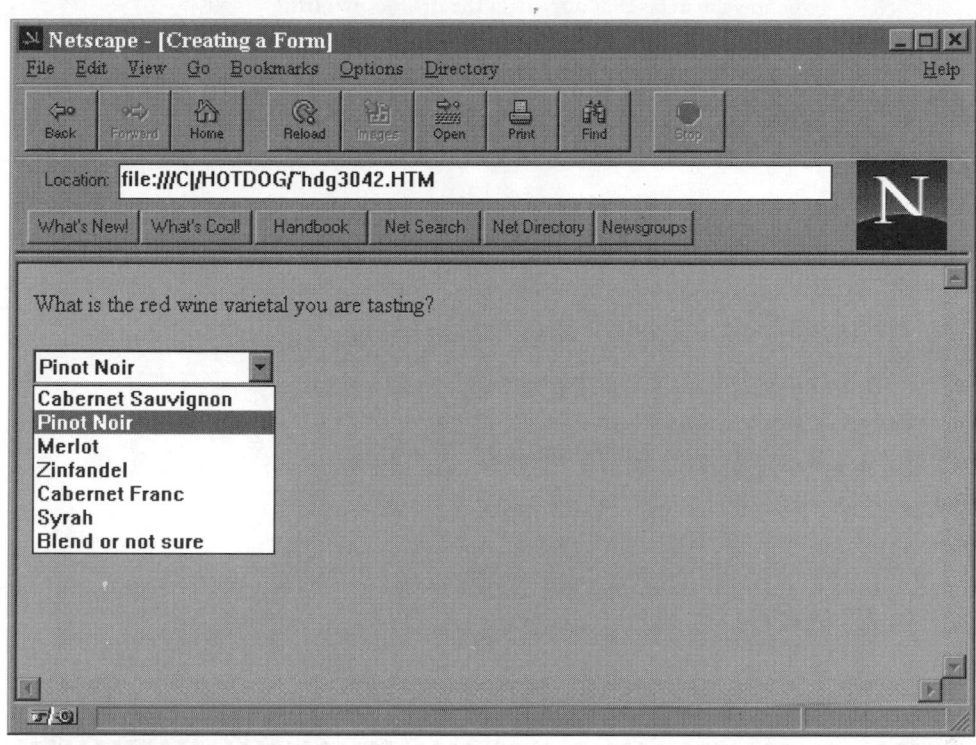

Figure 16.9 Drop-down list (the whole list displayed).

SELECT

Purpose:	Creates an environment for the <OPTION> tag, which you can use to create a drop-down list box within a <FORM> environment.
Usage:	<SELECT>. . .</SELECT>
Example:	

```
<SELECT>
  <OPTION>Red
  <OPTION>White
  <OPTION>Rose
</SELECT>
```

Don't Forget: By itself, the <SELECT> tag doesn't create a list; you must use the <OPTION> tag to define the items that appear in the drop-down list.

Hot Tip: You can use the SIZE attribute to determine the number of choices that appear on-screen, within the text box. The default is one. If you use the attribute <SELECT SIZE=5>, five of the options appear within an enlarged text box.

OPTION

Purpose: Creates an item in a drop-down list box.

Usage: <OPTION> (no end tag)

Example: <OPTION>Rhode Island

Don't Forget: To create the drop-down list, you must surround the <OPTION> tags with <SELECT> tags.

Hot Tip: To mark one of the options as the one that appears by default in the list box, use the SELECTED attribute (<OPTION SELECTED>).

ADDING A TEXT ENTRY AREA

If you would like to provide your readers with the ability to enter more than a single line of text, the <TEXTAREA> tag is just the ticket. Here's the HTML that creates a scrollable text box:

```
<P>Please type any additional comments you might
have:</P>
<TEXTAREA NAME="Verbiage" ROWS="10" COLS="50">
</TEXTAREA>
```

Note that an end tag is required (</TEXTAREA>). Figure 16.10 shows the results of this tag.

You must use the following attributes with the <TEXTAREA> tag:

- **NAME**   This attribute specifies the variable name so that the text will be associated with a name + value pair.

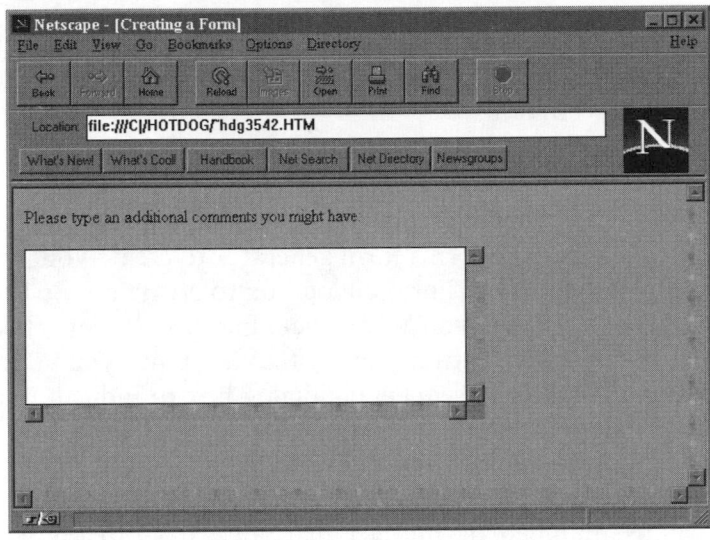

Figure 16.10   <TEXTAREA> for unlimited text entry.

- **ROWS**   This attribute specifies the default number of rows that are visible on-screen.
- **COLS**   This attribute specifies the width of the text entry window, in characters.

TEXTAREA

Purpose:	Creates a text box for text entries of more than one line.
Usage:	<TEXTAREA></TEXTAREA>
Example:	<TEXTAREA NAME="Verbiage" ROWS="10" COLS="50"></TEXTAREA>
Don't Forget:	To create a single-line text entry area, use the <INPUT TYPE="text"> tag.
Hot Tip:	If you include any text within the beginning <TEXTAREA> and ending </TEXTAREA> tags, this text is displayed as the default text, which the user can modify or erase. Don't use any HTML tags in this text.

INTRODUCING WEBFORMS

If you don't want to get into CGI scripts, you can still create a Web page with forms, and receive the responses via e-mail. The key is a very clever application called WebForms.

Creating the Form

You begin by using the WebForms form generator to create your form. Basically, you use the Create New Form dialog box to create all the text entries, titles, and form objects that you want, including text boxes, check boxes, extended text boxes, radio buttons, and list boxes. Once you've created the controls you want, you use a sequencing dialog box to indicate the order in which you want these controls to appear. This is a bit confusing until you get the hang of it, but eventually you will.

If you've gone to great lengths to create a "look" for your site, you may be somewhat disappointed by the fact that you can't directly edit a Web-Forms form. However, you can choose a background color, a text color, and a background graphic, and you can include graphics on your page. Even though you won't be able to replicate a fancy table layout, you can still retain enough of your design themes so that the form doesn't seem out of place. A cool feature: You can include a scrolling banner (text that scrolls on the browser's status bar).

Uploading the Form and Adding Links

Once you've created your form, upload it to your Web site, and modify your existing pages to link to the form you've created.

Reading Responses

When people respond to the form, the response is mailed to you. In your mailbox, it looks like so much gibberish. But WebForms contains another utility that automatically scans your mailbox to look for incoming forms. When it detects a response, the program automatically downloads the response, decodes it, and inserts it into a very nice-looking database. The database window organizes the messages according to a number of sorting options, including date, whether you've read the response, the sender, and the subject. You can selectively print the responses, choosing just the records and the fields you want to print.

FROM HERE

- The latest wrinkle in Web publishing takes HTML closer to desktop publishing: fonts. Learn how to incorporate them into your Web page in the next chapter.

- Organize your page layout with tables and frames, as discussed in Chapter 18.

Chapter
17

Adding Fonts and Style Sheets

I t's the final frontier, some Web designers would say: being able to include fonts in Web documents. And it's about to happen. Right now, you can include HTML tags that display fonts. But there's one little drawback. If these fonts aren't available on the user's system, the browser defaults to the plain, old, ugly default fonts—probably Times and Courier.

But take heart. Soon, the World Wide Web Consortium will rule on a new Dynamic HTML standard, which will enable Web designers to embed font outlines in their documents. These fonts will download with the document. This doesn't take as much time as you'd think, because you're not really downloading a whole font, but rather just a font definition, which takes up much less space. Most of the fonts you can use with Dynamic HTML take up about as much downloading time as the average small GIF graphic on a Web page.

For the Time-Challenged

♦ You can add fonts to your document with the <FONT> tag, but they won't
  show up on viewers' screens unless users have the font installed on their systems.

♦ The <FONT> tag is also useful for adding color and font sizes to your text.

♦ Style sheets enable you to define a collection of formats for any HTML tag.
  Whenever you use that tag in your document, these formats automatically
  apply.

♦ You can create a master style sheet that affects the style of all the HTML documents linked to it.

♦ With Dynamic HTML, users can download the fonts needed to see your font
  choices—but there are two competing standards at present.

For now, you can learn how to take advantage of the existing <FONT>
tags, which both Netscape and Internet Explorer recognize. You can also take
advantage of *cascading style sheets*, which enable you to define fonts (and
other style parameters) for any instance of a given HTML tag that you use in
your document. And you can play around with Netscape's Dynamic HTML
standard, which stands a good chance of becoming the official standard.

ADDING FONTS TO YOUR
DOCUMENT WITH THE <FONT> TAG

Realizing that Web designers want to include fonts in their documents,
Netscape added the <FONT> tag unilaterally in version 2.0 of Netscape.
Not to be outdone, Microsoft decided to support the tag in version 3.0 of
Microsoft Internet Explorer. Seeing such unusual signs of unanimity in the
industry, the World Wide Web Consortium decided to ratify the tag in
HTML 3.2. Thanks to this tag, you can include an instruction in your docu-
ment that tells the browser, in effect, to display the tagged text in Times
Roman—or heck, why not something wilder, like Microsoft Comic Sans or
Black Letter Gothic?

That's good news, right? Not so fast. The fonts don't show up on-screen unless they're installed on the user's system. And precious few fonts are installed on everyone's system. In practice, you're talking about Times Roman, Courier, Helvetica (or its Windows analogue, Arial), and perhaps a few others. So, in reality, the <FONT> tag just takes us back to where we were before all this started, namely, relying on the default font definitions in the users' browsers (probably Times Roman and Courier).

If you'd like to add font definitions to your document, by all means go ahead—the worst that will happen is that your document will look like it would have looked without them. Should you by chance manage to hit a font that's on the user's system, bingo! Your page will look really nice.

Perhaps this sounds a bit too pessimistic. If so, bear in mind that you can name a whole series of alternative fonts. Here's how it works. If the browser doesn't find font 1, it looks for font 2. If it doesn't find font 2, it looks for font 3, and so on. Eventually, if you're lucky, you'll hit a font that the user actually has. What's more, the <FONT> tag does more than just choose the typeface, as you'll see: You can also choose the font color and size. That's enough to ensure that you'll want to make use of this tag in your documents.

Adding the <FONT> Tag to Your Document

To affect the typeface, color, or font size of text in your document, surround the text with the <FONT> tag.

FONT

Purpose:	Define the typeface, color, or size of text enclosed within the tags.
Usage:	<FONT>...</FONT>
Purpose:	<FONT FACE="Times Roman, Times, New York Times">....</FONT>
Don't Forget:	You can list several alternative fonts. Who knows? You might get lucky.
Hot Tip:	This tag is best used to define font colors. You can really jazz up your document by adding some color to your fonts.

When you're listing fonts, be sure to include (last in the list) a generic font that sums up the basic font style that you're trying to achieve. Netscape is distributing freebie system fonts with generic names (serif, sans serif, cursive, mono-space, and fantasy) with Windows, Macintosh, and UNIX versions of Netscape Communicator. There's a good chance that one of these fonts will be picked up, even if none of the other ones you've listed is present on the user's system.

Defining the Typeface

To change the typeface of text surrounded with the <FONT> tag, use the FACE attribute. You can list several alternative fonts. If the first font isn't installed on the user's system, the browser attempts to use the second, and so on. Be sure to enclose the font names—the whole list, with items separated by commas—within quotation marks, as in the following example:

```
<FONT FACE ="Times Roman, Caesar, Claudius">I am still
Emperor!</FONT>
```

If none of these fonts is present on the user's system, the browser defaults to the standard font used to display proportional fonts.

To make fonts more widely available for use on the Web, Microsoft designed and is giving away two very beautiful fonts, Verdana and Georgia. You can download them from www.microsoft.com/truetype/.

Defining the Font Color

To define font colors, use the COLOR attribute, as well as an RGB code for the color (see Appendix C). Here's an example of a <FONT> tag that displays red text:

```
<FONT COLOR=#FF0000">This is HOT!</FONT>
```

Defining the Font Size

To define font size, use the SIZE attribute. This attribute takes absolute sizes, in the range of 1 to 7, or you can use relative size markers, which increase or decrease the current font size by the amount you've specified. For example, if you use the tag <FONT SIZE=+1>, the browser increases the current font size by one size. Here's an example of a <FONT> tag that's correctly set up to define font size:

```
<FONT SIZE=5>Hey! Pay attention to this!</A>
```

USING CASCADING STYLE SHEETS

Style sheets are a concept with which you're probably already familiar. In Microsoft Word, for example, you can define a style for normal text paragraphs, so that every time you enter a paragraph, it takes on the style you've defined: a one-half inch indentation, Garamond font so that it looks like you're writing an Apple press release, double line spacing, the whole nine yards.

The advantage of a style sheet is that you create a style definition just once. After you create it, everything you format with that style automatically takes on the formatting options you've chosen. What's more, if you put the style sheet in a separate file, you can use it for a whole series of documents. To change all of the formatting in those documents in one fell swoop, you just make the change to the underlying style sheet and—voila!—all the files linked to the sheet are changed, too.

If you've already spent long hours formatting the text in a Web site, I'm sure you'll appreciate style sheets. They're a tremendous innovation, and it's easy to learn how to use them. Best of all, both Netscape Navigator and Microsoft Internet Explorer support the current (HTML 3.2) definition of style sheets, although, in their own inimitable ways, they're trying to push the standard this way and that. Let's ignore such machinations for the moment and concentrate on the fundamentals of cascading style sheets, as defined in the HTML 3.2 spec. The style sheets we're talking about here are Level 1, which means that they're thinking of changing this as soon as the dust settles in the marketplace.

Cascading Style Sheet Concepts (You've Got Class, Baby)

The basic idea here is that you can redefine existing HTML tags with a style sheet so that they take on the formats you specify. These formats are listed within a <STYLE> tag, which you position at the beginning of the body of your document. (Alternatively, you can place a link to the style sheet, but we'll get to that later.)

For example, suppose you define the <H1> tag with the following formats: Helvetica, 24pt, and 1 additional space between characters. After you've defined <H1> this way, all the text you tag with <H1> looks like this. Easy!

You've got the basic idea. But here's the kicker—you can do things with style sheets that you can't do any other way. Figure 17.1 is an example of a format that couldn't be entered any other way: double-spaced paragraphs with an indentation on the first line. Now, let's look at the formats that you can define this way.

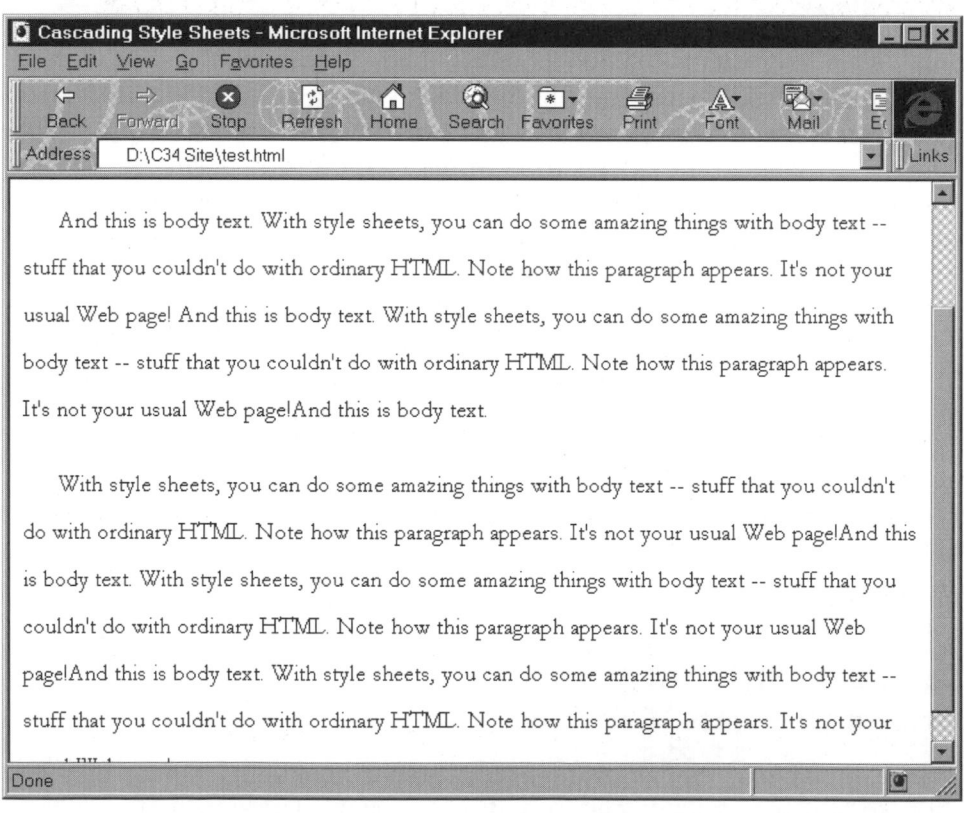

Figure 17.1   Style sheets enable you to create formats that you can't enter any other way.

Formats You Can Assign Using Style Sheets

You can define any of the formats shown in Table 17.1 with style sheets. If you spend a few minutes looking over this table, you'll be amazed at what you can do with cascading style sheets. For example, you can define separate background graphics for each element. Amateur Web designers already have enough rope to hang themselves as it is, as you'll doubtless conclude after browsing the Web and seeing unreadable text against impossibly busy backgrounds; cascading style sheets will only amplify this unfortunate trend. Still, there's plenty of flexibility here, and I'll bet you'll want to give it a try.

Table 17.1 Formats Available with <STYLE> Tags

Property	Options	Example
font-family (defines the font)	State a font name (place in quotes if white space occurs within the font name)	H1 {font-family: Helvetica, "sans serif"}
font-style (defines the font style, such as normal or italic)	Choose normal, italic, oblique	BLOCKQUOTE {Italic}
font-weight (defines the heaviness of the font, from light to bold)	Choose bold, bolder, lighter, 100, 200, 300, 400, 500, 600, 700, 800, 900	H1 {font-weight 800}
font-size (defines the size of the font)	Specify an absolute size in points (pt) or a relative size	P (font-size 12pt}
font (enables you to enter several font choices at once)	Specify all your choices for the above	P {font: Helvetica, normal, 400, 10pt}
color (defines the foreground color of an element)	Type a color name in natural language (red), an RGB code (255, 0, 0) or a color code (#00FFFF)	H2 {color: red}
background-color (defines the background color of an element)	Type a color name in natural language (red), an RGB code (255, 0, 0) or a color code (#00FFFF)	H4 {background-color: white}
background (defines the background graphic of an element)	Supply a file name	P {background="parchment.gif"}

Table 17.1 *Continued*

Property	Options	Example
word-spacing (specifies how much space is inserted between words in an element)	Add space by typing a measurement in points or an absolute measurement (in inches, ems, or cm)	OL {word-spacing: 2pt}
letter-spacing (specifies how much space is inserted between characters in an element)	Add space by typing a measurement in points or an absolute measurement (in inches, ems, or cm)	H1 {letter-spacing: 2pt}
text-decoration (enables you to choose various text decorations)	Choose underline, overline, line-through, blink	H3 {text-decoration: blink}
vertical-align (specifies the vertical alignment of an element)	Choose baseline, sub, super, top, text-top, middle, bottom, text-bottom, or a percentage	H1 {vertical-align: top}
text-transform (specifies how text should be capitalized)	Choose capitalize, uppercase, lowercase, none	H1 {text-transform: capitalize}
text-align (specifies how text should be aligned horizontally)	Choose from right, center, left, justify	P {text-align: justify}
text-indent (specifies how the first line should be indented)	Type a fixed measurement or a percentage of line width	P {text-indent: 12pt}
line-height (specifies the line height)	Type a number by which the current font height should be multiplied, or a percentage	P {line-height: 2}

Adding a Style Sheet to Your Document

Now that you've got the basics down, you can try adding a style sheet to your document. Here are some rules:

- Style sheets go in the HEAD, not the BODY. If you put a style sheet in the body of your document, it won't work.

- Surround your style sheet definitions with <STYLE> and </STYLE> tags. Within these tags, define the styles for each of the tags that you want to affect.

- Since there are different types of style sheets around, you need to tell the browser which type you're using. Here, you're using CSS Level 1 style sheets. You indicate this in the <STYLE> tag with the attribute TYPE="text/css".

Simple enough. Here's what a style sheet looks like:

```
<HTML>

<HEAD>

<STYLE TYPE="text/css">

H1 {font-family: "Wide Latin"; font-size: 24pt}

P {font-family: Garamond; text-indent: 17pt; line-
height: 2}

</STYLE>
```

Note a couple of things. For a font that has white space in its name, you need to surround the font name in quotes. Also, there's no space between the number and the pt abbreviation when you're specifying point sizes.

Try this in your browser. Internet Explorer does a pretty good job with cascading style sheets; Netscape Communicator less so, but then again, I'm using a beta copy (the final version isn't out yet).

- -

STYLE

Purpose:	Creates a style sheet.
Usage:	<STYLE>...</STYLE>
Example:	<STYLE TYPE="text/css"> P {font-family: Helvetica; font-size: 12pt} BLOCKQUOTE {font-family: Helvetica; font-size; 10pt} </STYLE>
Don't Forget:	Place the style sheet in your document's head, not the body.
Hot Tip:	Remember that many browsers do not support CSS Level 1 style sheets yet, and some do only partially.

- -

LINKING TO A MASTER STYLE SHEET

Style sheets are cool. So do you have to put one in all of your documents? Nope. You can create a master document and then use the <LINK> tag to reference it. What's so great about this is that you can make just one little change to the master document, and the change is made automatically to all the documents that have linked to the master style sheet. This is a real time-saver if you're creating a big site with many separate pages.

What does your master style sheet look like? It could be an HTML document with other content—perhaps the welcome page of your site (called index.html). Or it could be a standalone document, with nothing else in it but the <STYLE> tag. It's up to you.

To link an HTML document to a master style sheet, insert the <LINK> tag in the head of the document, with the following attributes:

REL	Use the value *stylesheet*.
HREF	Indicate the URL of the master style sheet.

Here's an example:

```
<LINK REL=stylesheet HREF="http://www.server.com/
myfolder/home.html">
```

THE DIVISION TAG

There's one other thing to mention while we're talking about style sheets. As part of the HTML 3.2 style sheet definition, the HTML committee formalized the DIV tag, which Netscape had introduced a while back. Basically, the DIV tag lets you set aside a whole portion of a document to which you can assign an alignment (the options are left, right, and center). Consider this example:

```
<DIV ALIGN = CENTER>

<P>A paragraph of text</P>

<OL>
<LI>First item.
<LI>Second item.
<LI>Third item.
</OL>

<P>Another paragraph of text</P)
```

```
</DIV>
```

Within the <DIV> tags, everything is centered. Of course, you could do the same thing with Netscape's unorthodox (and nonstandard) <CENTER> tag, but this is cleaner. Nicer. More logical. So use it!

DIV

Purpose:	Enables you to set aside a section of your document, within which all the text has the same alignment.
Usage:	<DIV>...</DIV>
Example:	<DIV ALIGN = RIGHT> <P>A paragraph of text</P> <BLOCKQUOTE>A quote.</BLOCKQUOTE> <P>A concluding, summarizing paragraph of text.</P> </DIV>
Don't Forget:	This a more logical, more Vulcan way of centering a whole bunch of stuff than the <CENTER> tag.

IT'S DYNAMIC!

The latest wrinkle in the font sweepstakes is Dynamic HTML, which will dynamically download the fonts needed to display Web documents. It sounds great, right? The problem is, there are two different versions, Netscape's and Microsoft's. Microsoft's version wasn't available at this writing, but the word on the street is that it contains, as usual, a not-so-subtle compulsion to make sure you're using Microsoft Windows. Netscape's solution is genuinely cross-platform, and I really like it—at least, based on the very preliminary stuff that's available at this writing.

Netscape's Dynamic HTML Fonts

Netscape's version of Dynamic HTML uses Bitstream's TrueDoc technology to download fonts to the user's system. The result is really nice-looking and downloads very quickly (see Figures 17.2 and 17.3).

Be aware that you're not really downloading a whole font when you access a page that has dynamic fonts—all you're downloading is just enough to display the font, not to capture it for your own use on your system. TrueDoc "captures" the outlines of a font and then compresses the description for fast, on-the-fly transmission. What gets downloaded isn't a font that you can steal and use on your system. So don't look in your fonts list for the fonts that you've seen on Bitstream's demo pages.

Here's how Netscape's dynamic font solution works. On your server, you need to keep a font definition file (which may contain one or more fonts).

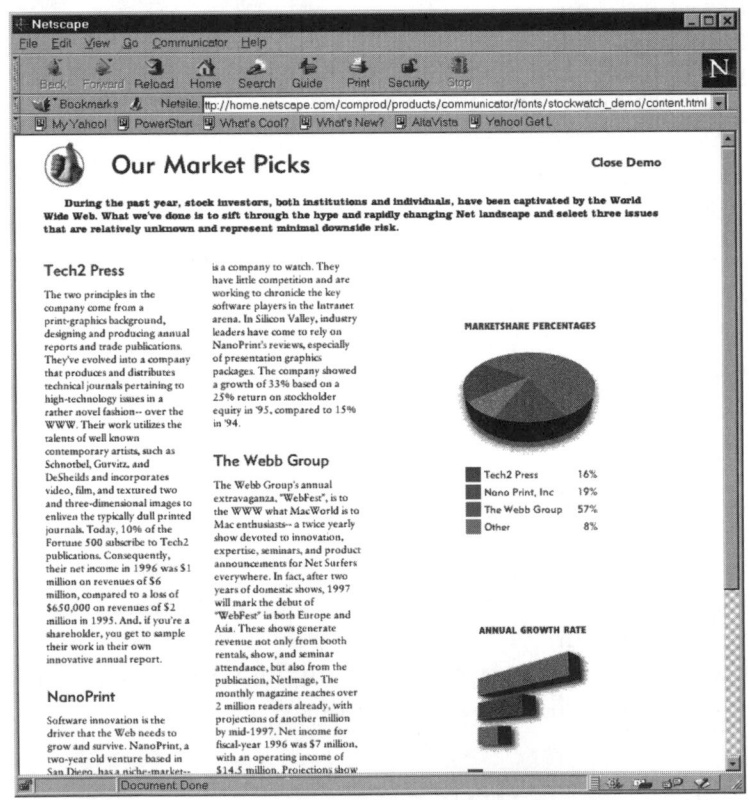

Figure 17.2   Netscape's dynamic font solution uses Bitstream's TrueDoc technology.

This is a Bitstream file with the extension *.pfr. To include the fonts in your document, you reference the PFR file in a <STYLE> definition, or in a <LINK> tag.

To include the fonts using a <STYLE> definition, use the following syntax:

```
<STYLE TYPE="text/css">

<!--@fontdef url(http://home.netscape.com/fonts/
sample.pfr);-->

</STYLE>
```

Figure 17.3 Bitstream's site (www.bitstream.com) shows off TrueDoc font technology.

To include the fonts using a <LINK> tag, use the following syntax:

```
<LINK REL=fontdef SRC="http://home.netscape.com/fonts/
sample.pfr">
```

It's a bit simpler to include the fonts with a <LINK> tag, as you can see, and there are fewer chances for a typo.

Once you've linked your document to a PFR file, you can use the <FONT FACE> tag to define any of the fonts included in the PFR file. You can also use style sheets to define fonts for your document. And the user sees them, no matter what!

Where can you get PFR files containing Bitstream fonts? Netscape plans to distribute four of them with Communicator.

Microsoft's OpenType

I haven't seen Microsoft's answer to TrueDoc, but it's more of the same: A very clear message that you ought to be using Windows (or maybe the Mac). Unlike TrueDoc, which downloads a bitmapped approximation of the original font, Microsoft wants you to download the real font, packaged in a secure container to keep it from being stolen. The task of displaying the font shouldn't be handled by the browser, Microsoft believes, but rather by the operating system—ahem, Windows. Chances are the technology will work fine and look great, but it's going to shut out all the UNIX users out there, and of course the Mac will play Johnny-come-lately. I'd prefer a genuinely cross-platform solution, and it looks like TrueDoc is much closer to that ideal.

FROM HERE

- In the next chapter, learn how to add tables and frames to your document.

- Fed up with typing all those HTML tags? Now that you have HTML down and learned the concepts, consider using an HTML editor. This has a number of advantages, including making it much easier to publish and maintain your documents Get the lowdown in Chapter 20.

• Learn how to publish and publicize your Web site in Chapter 21.

Chapter

18

Creating Tables and Frames

One of the newest and most useful features of HTML 3.2 is the <TABLE> tag, which enables you to create nicely formatted tables (see Figure 18.1). HTML 3.2's table capabilities can be used for multiple-column layouts, too, such as the *Wall Street Journal* daily investment newsletter shown in Figure 18.2. You can also create pages using frames, which are independently scrollable panels (see Figure 18.3). This chapter covers the HTML that goes into making tables and frames.

Before adding tables or frames to the documents in your Web site, consider that someone accessing your site with a browser that isn't capable of formatting tables is going to see a jumble of unformatted text. Do you want a site with pages that look extra nice—or would you rather make sure that

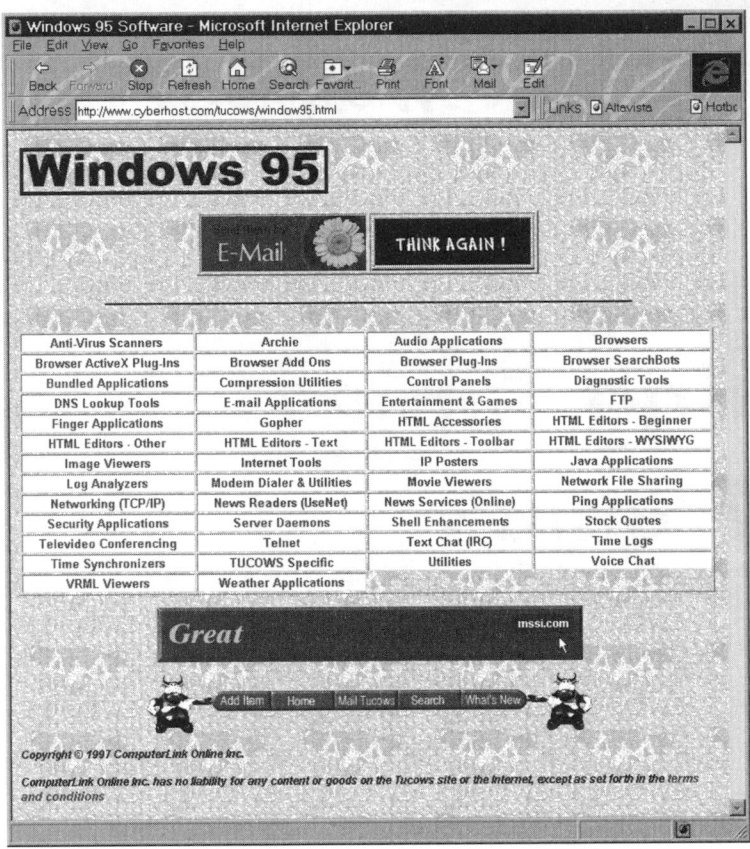

Figure 18.1   Tables can be used to organize data.

everyone can read the content you have to offer? It's your call. To be sure, most browsers now support tables—reportedly, there's a version of the text-only browser Lynx in the works that supports tables (but not frames).

As you work through this chapter, you will surely agree that the HTML table and frame tags are difficult to work with. But there's a reason—they weren't *meant* to be worked with. The design of these tags is optimized so that editor programs can automate the table-creation process. Although this chapter discusses manual table formatting, you would be well advised to forget the manual formatting and create tables with a WYSIWYG editor.

For the Time-Challenged

♦ If you're planning to use the HotDog Web Editor that's discussed in Chapter 20, don't bother learning the <TABLE> tags—it's much easier to create your tables with HotDog's WYSIWYG ("what you see is what you get") table editor.

♦ In HTML 3.2, a table begins with the <TABLE> tag, and ends with </TABLE>.

♦ A table consists of rows and columns, which together form table cells.

♦ You define the table row by row, using the <TR> tag.

♦ To create headings within cells, you use the <TH> tag. The heading will be shown in emphasized type (bold). By default, headings are centered.

♦ To create a data cell, you use the <TD> tag. By default, data is aligned flush left.

♦ You can control the horizontal and vertical alignment of table data using the ALIGN and VALIGN attributes of the <TH> and <TD> tags.

♦ To create frames, you use the <FRAMESET> and <FRAME> tags. The best way to learn frames is to work through the tutorial in this chapter.

♦ The Netscape extensions give you ways to increase your table's visual appeal, but the effects may not be seen by people using browsers other than Netscape.

 Before trying to code your table or frame layout, make a pencil sketch of what your table is supposed to look like. How many columns of data does it require? Do you have headings that span two or more columns? How would you like the data aligned? It's easier to code the table once you've made basic decisions such as these.

 Trying to choose between tables and frames? Bear in mind that tables are standard HTML—they're part of the 3.2 specification. Frames aren't, although frames are supported by the two leading browsers (Netscape Navigator and Microsoft Internet Explorer).

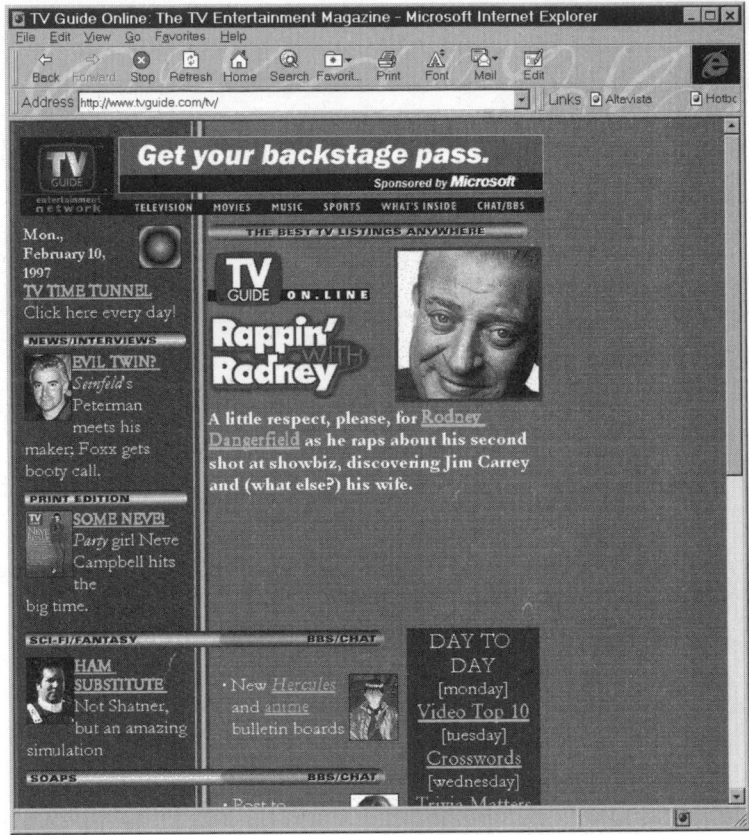

Figure 18.2   Tables can be used to create magazine-quality layouts.

THE BASICS: THE <TABLE> TAG

To create a table in your HTML document, you use the <TABLE> tag.
Here's the basic point about this tag: You create your table row by row,
showing the logical relationships among the parts of the table. The exact
details of the physical layout are handled by the browser. These details
include the width of individual cells. The width is adjusted depending on the
size of the current display font and the width of the current window.

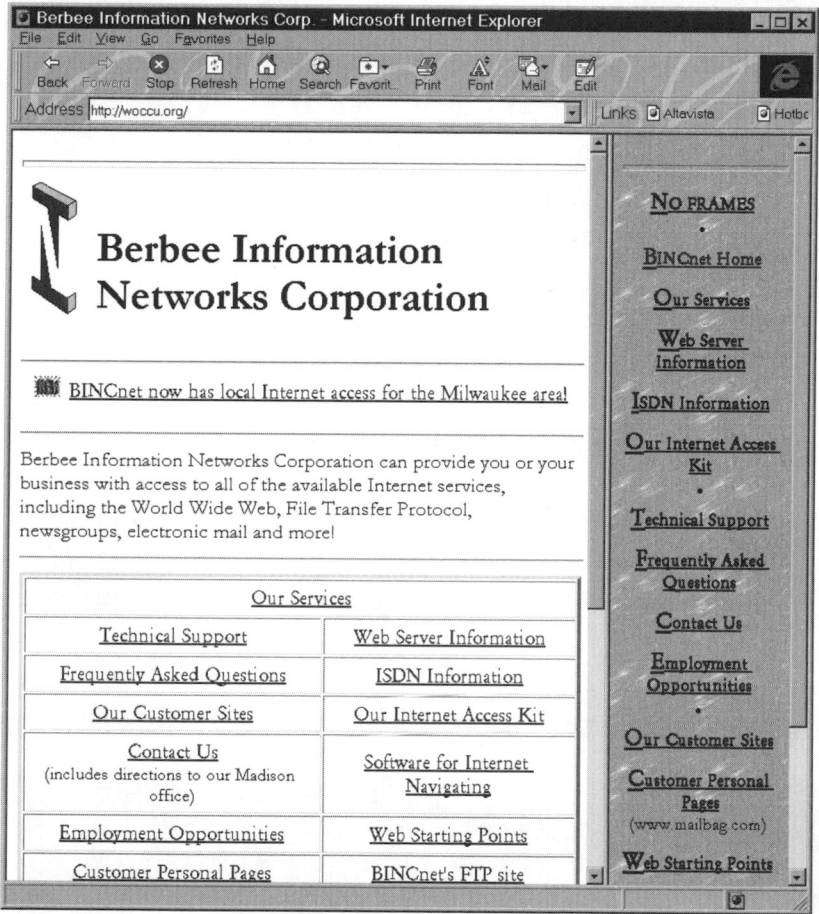

Figure 18.3 A Web page with two vertical frames.

When you create a table, you also use the following tags:

`<TR>...</TR>`	This tag defines a row of data in the table.
`<TH>...</TH>`	This tag defines a table heading, which is normally displayed with emphasis (bold).
`<TD>...</TD>`	This tag defines a table data item.

The following HTML code illustrates the fundamentals of creating a table with the <TABLE>, <TH>, and <TR> tags. Note that, within the <TABLE> environment, the <TR> tags are used to define individual rows of the table. Figure 18.4 shows what this table looks like.

```
<TABLE BORDER>
  <TR>
    <TH>Row 1
    <TD>Item 1</TD>
    <TD>Item 2</TD>
  </TR>
  <TR>
    <TH>Row 2
    <TD>Item 1</TD>
    <TD>Item 2</TD>
  </TR>
</TABLE>
```

 The <TABLE> tag's BORDER attribute (<TABLE BORDER>) automatically creates a border around the table and each cell. Just how the border appears depends on the browser you're using.

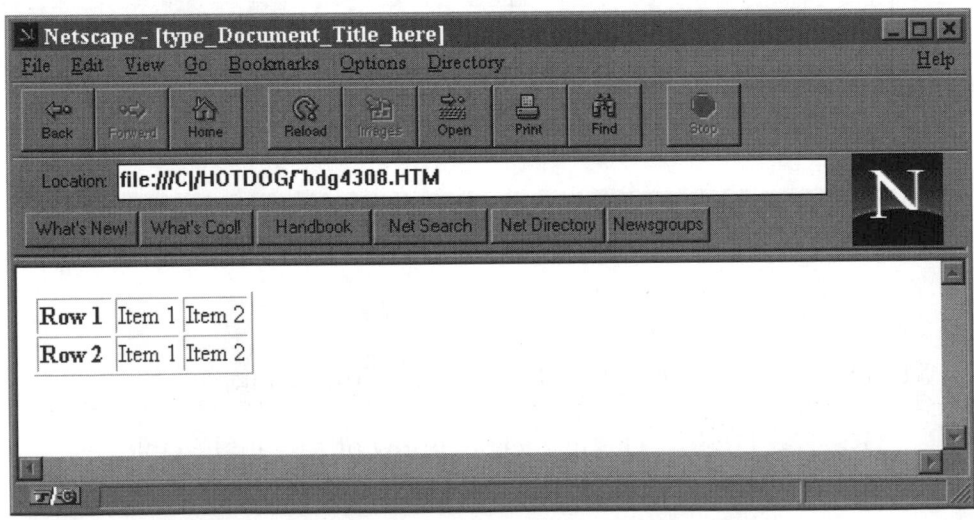

Figure 18.4   A simple table.

TABLE

Purpose:	Creates a table.
Usage:	<TABLE>. . .</TABLE>

Example:

```
<TABLE>
  <TR>
    <TH>Row 1</TH>
    <TD>Item 1</TD>
    <TD>Item 2</TD>
  </TR>
  <TR>
    <TH>Row 2</TH>
    <TD>Item 1</TD>
    <TD>Item 2</TD>
  </TR>
</TABLE>
```

Don't Forget: You set up your table by defining the table rows with <TR>.

Hot Tip: The BORDER attribute (<TABLE BORDER>) adds a border around the cells in your table.

TR

Purpose: Within a <TABLE> environment, creates a row of data cells.

Usage: <TR>. . .</TR>

Example:

```
<TABLE>
  <TR>
    <TH>Row 1</TH>
    <TD>Item 1</TD>
    <TD>Item 2</TD>
  </TR>
</TABLE>
```

Don't Forget: Within a <TR> environment, you can use the <TH> tag to create a header item, which is normally displayed in bold.

Hot Tip: By default, heading cells are centered horizontally and vertically within the cell space. When used with the <TR> tag, the ALIGN and VALIGN attributes allow you to define the default horizontal and vertical alignments for the entire row (<TR ALIGN=LEFT>, <TR ALIGN=CENTER>, <TR ALIGN=RIGHT>, <TR VALIGN=TOP>, <TR VALIGN=CENTER>, <TR VALIGN=BOTTOM>).

TH

Purpose:	Within a <TR> environment, creates a table heading (displayed in bold by most browsers). The heading is displayed in a cell like those created by <TD>.
Usage:	<TH>. . .</TH>
Example:	<TR> <TH>Row 1</TH> <TD>Item 1</TD> <TD>Item 2</TD> </TR>
Don't Forget:	By default, the table header is aligned at the center of the cell, both horizontally and vertically.
Hot Tip:	The ALIGN and VALIGN attributes allow you to define the horizontal and vertical alignments (<TH ALIGN=LEFT>, <TH ALIGN=CENTER>, <TH ALIGN=RIGHT>, <TH VALIGN=TOP>, <TH VALIGN=CENTER>, <TH VALIGN=BOTTOM>). To span columns, use the COLSPAN=*number* attribute; to span rows, use the ROWSPAN=*number* attribute (for example, <TH COLSPAN=2> spans two rows).

TD

Purpose: .	Adds a data cell to a table defined by the <TABLE> tag.
Usage:	<TD>. . .</TD>
Example:	<TR> <TH>Row 1</TH> <TD>Item 1</TD> <TD>Item 2</TD> </TR>
Don't Forget:	By default, the table data item is aligned at the center of the cell, both horizontally and vertically.
Hot Tip:	The ALIGN and VALIGN attributes allow you to define the horizontal and vertical alignments (<TH ALIGN=LEFT>, <TH ALIGN=CENTER>, <TH ALIGN=RIGHT>, <TH VALIGN=TOP>, <TH VALIGN=CENTER>, <TH VALIGN=BOTTOM>). To span columns, use the COLSPAN=*number* attribute; to span rows, use the ROWSPAN=*number* attribute (for example, <TD COLSPAN=2> spans two rows).

CREATING A HORIZONTAL HEADER

You've already learned how to create row headings using the <TH> tag. But how do you create a row of headings across the top of the table, as shown in Figure 18.5? There are a couple of tricks that you can use.

First, create the first row of your table using nothing but <TH> tags—don't use <TD>, as in the following example:

```
<TR>
  <TH></TH>
  <TH>Chardonnay</TH>
  <TH>Sauvignon Blanc</TH>
  <TH>Cabernet Sauvignon</TH>
  <TH>Merlot</TH>
  <TH>Pinot Noir</TH>
</TR>
```

In Figure 18.5, note that there's an empty cell. The first column doesn't require a heading, so this empty cell is needed to make the table look right. To create the empty cell, you can use <TH></TH> or <TD></TD>. Note that there's nothing between these tags, and the result is a blank space in the table.

Second, add rows with the same number of items, as in the following:

```
<TR>
  <TH></TH>
  <TH>Chardonnay</TH>
  <TH>Sauvignon Blanc</TH>
  <TH>Cabernet Sauvignon</TH>
  <TH>Merlot</TH>
  <TH>Pinot Noir</TH>
</TR>

<TR>
  <TH>Best with:</TH>
  <TD>Appetizers, cheese</TD>
  <TD>Seafood, pasta</TD>
  <TD>Red meat
  <TD>Pasta</TD>
  <TD>Lighter meats, pasta</TD>
</TR>
```

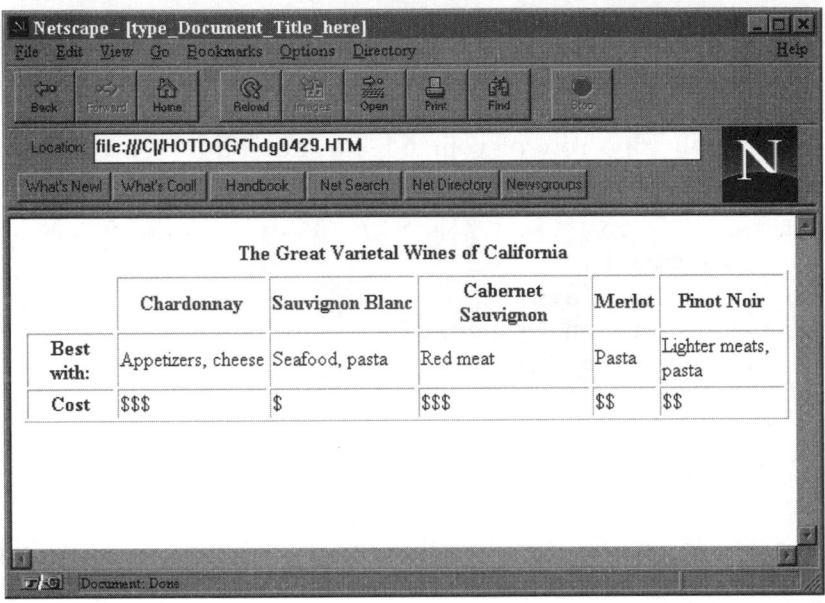

Figure 18.5   Table with horizontal row of headings.

```
<TR>
  <TH>Cost</TH>
  <TD>$$$</TD>
  <TD>$</TD>
  <TD>$$$</TD>
  <TD>$$</TD>
  <TD>$$</TD>
</TR>
```

ADDING A CAPTION

Tables don't have to have captions—they're optional. If you wish to add a caption, you can do so using an ordinary text paragraph (<P>. . .</P>), or you can use the <CAPTION> tag. The caption tag goes just after the <TABLE> tag. By default (with most browers), the caption is centered at the top of the table, as shown in Figure 18.5.

Here's the HTML that adds the caption shown in Figure 18.5:

```
<TABLE BORDER>
  <CAPTION><EM>The Great Varietal Wines of Califor-
nia</EM>
  <TR>
  [...]
</TABLE>
```

CAPTION

Purpose:	Adds a caption to a table or figure.
Usage:	<CAPTION>. . .</CAPTION>
Example:	<TABLE> <CAPTION>Caption Text</CAPTION> </TABLE>
Don't Forget:	The <CAPTION> tag must be placed within the <FIG> or <TABLE> tags.
Hot Tip:	To place the caption at the bottom of the table or figure, use the ALIGN=BOTTOM attribute (<CAPTION ALIGN=BOTTOM>).

ALIGNING TEXT WITHIN TABLE CELLS

By default, heading cells are centered horizontally and vertically within the cell, while data cells are centered only vertically; horizontally, they're aligned flush left. Take a look at Figure 18.6, and you'll see what I mean.

To modify the default alignments, you can use the following attributes of the <TH> and <TD> tags:

- **VALIGN (VALIGN=TOP, VALIGN=MIDDLE, VALIGN=BOTTOM)** Use these attributes to control the vertical alignment of the text within the data cell (for example, <TD VALIGN=TOP> positions the text at the top of the data cell).

- **ALIGN (ALIGN=LEFT, ALIGN=CENTER, ALIGN=RIGHT)** Use these attributes to control the horizontal alignment of the text within the data cell (for example, <TD ALIGN=RIGHT> positions the text flush right within the data cell).

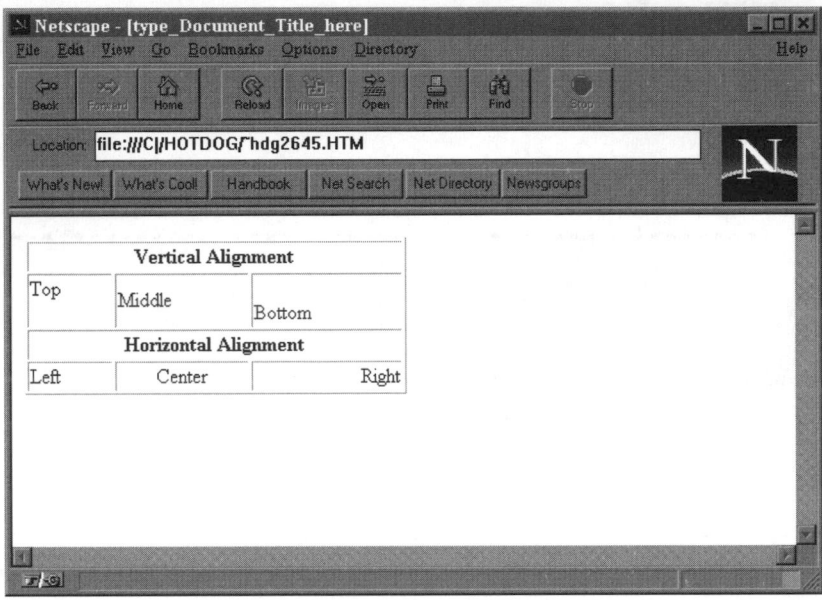

Figure 18.6　Horizontal and vertical alignments within data cells.

SPANNING ROWS AND COLUMNS

Sometimes you may wish to create a header cell that spans two or more columns, like the headers shown in Figure 18.7. In that figure, note the following:

- There is a large, blank area in the upper left of the table; this is a blank cell that spans two columns and two rows.

- The "Microprocessor" heading spans two columns.

- The "Amount of Installed RAM" heading spans two rows.

To span columns and rows, you use the COLSPAN and ROWSPAN attributes, which work with the <TH> and <TD> tags. For example, the tag <TH COLSPAN=3> spans three columns, while the tag <TH ROWSPAN=3> spans three rows.

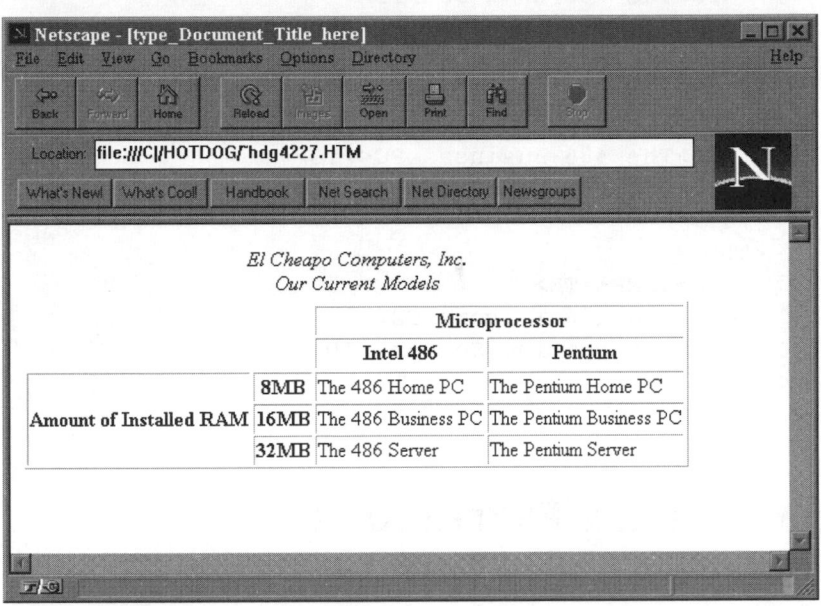

Figure 18.7 Spanning columns and rows.

Here's the HTML that produced the table shown in Figure 18.7:

```
<TABLE BORDER>
  <CAPTION>
    <EM>El Cheapo Computers, Inc.<BR>
    Our Current Models</EM>
  </CAPTION>
  <TR>
    <TH COLSPAN=2></TH>
    <TH COLSPAN=2>Microprocessor</TH>
  </TR>
  <TR>
    <TH COLSPAN=2></TH>
    <TH>Intel 486</TH>
    <TH>Pentium</TH>
  <TR>
  <TR>
    <TH ROWSPAN=3>Amount of Installed RAM</TH>
```

```
    <TH>8MB</TH>
    <TD>The 486 Home PC</TD>
    <TD>The Pentium Home PC</TD>
  </TR>
  <TR>
    <TH>16MB</TH>
    <TD>The 486 Business PC</TD>
    <TD>The Pentium Business PC</TD>
  </TR>
  <TR>
    <TH>32MB</TH>
    <TD>The 486 Server</TD>
    <TD>The Pentium Server</TD>
</TABLE>
```

THE NETSCAPE EXTENSIONS TO THE <TABLE> TAG

If you're willing to risk adding some features that non-Netscape browsers won't be able to format, you can add some visual spice to your tables by using the Netscape table extensions. Here's a quick overview of what you can do:

- **<TABLE WIDTH=*percent*>**   When used with the <TABLE> tag, the WIDTH attribute specifies how much horizontal space the whole table should occupy on the current display window. To make sure the table spans the whole display window, use <TABLE WIDTH=100%> (see Figure 18.8). If you prefer, you can type an exact pixel width.

- **<TH WIDTH=*percent*>, <TD WIDTH=*percent*>**   Here, the WIDTH attribute specifies how wide a particular column should be. To specify that a particular column should occupy 25% of the current window, use <TH WIDTH=*percent*>. See Figure 18.9 for an example of reducing a column's width with the WIDTH attribute. You can also type an exact pixel width, if you prefer.

- **<TABLE CELLSPACING=*number*>**   The CELLSPACING attribute controls the width of the borders separating cells. By default, the cells are separated by a border 2 pixels wide. See Figure 18.10 for an example of increasing the CELLSPACING attribute to 10.

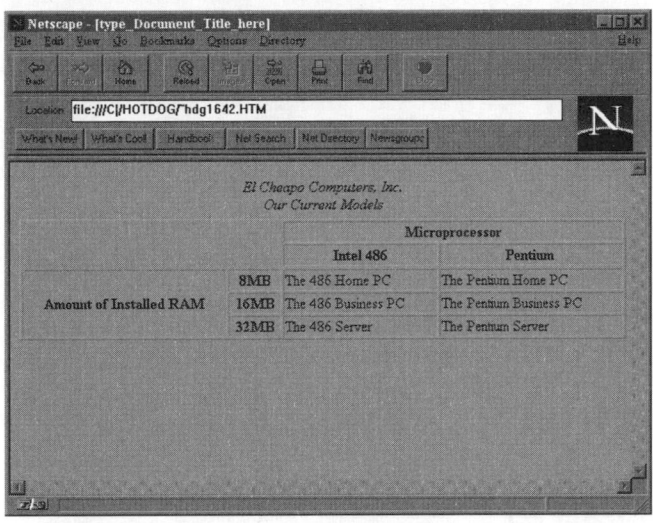

Figure 18.8 Table width set to 100% with WIDTH attribute.

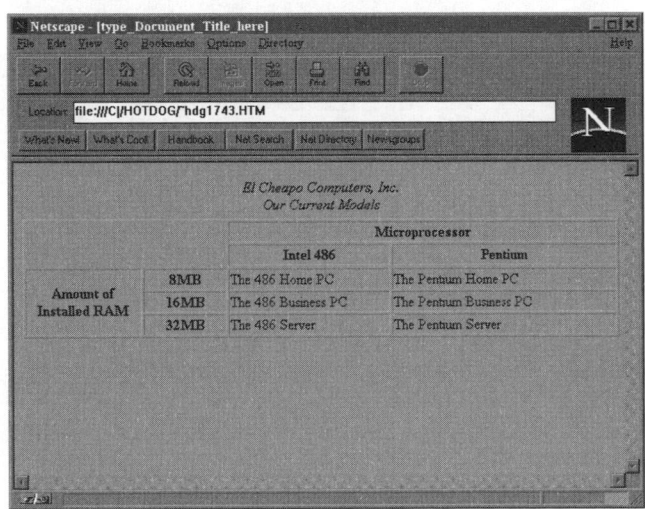

Figure 18.9 First column width set to 15% with WIDTH attribute.

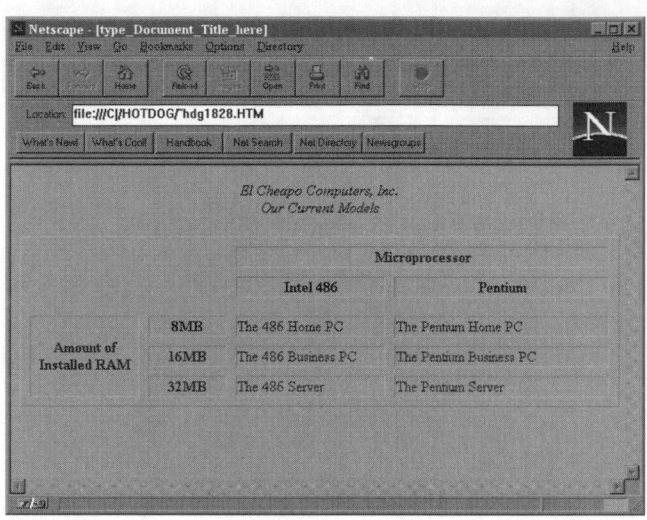

Figure 18.10   CELLSPACING attribute set to 10.

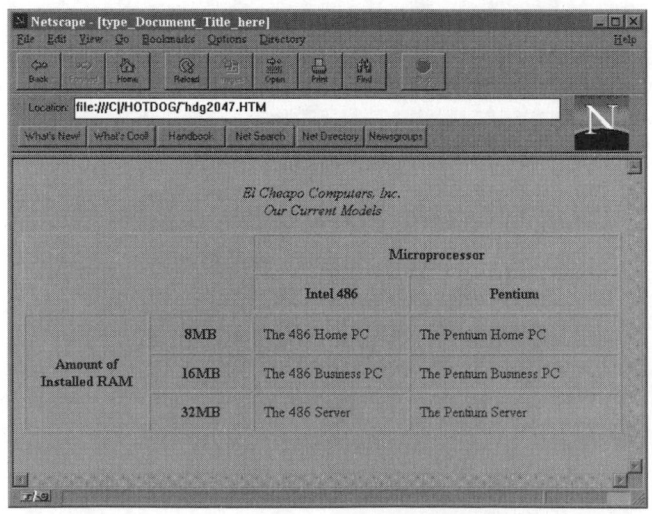

Figure 18.11   CELLPADDING attribute set to 10.

• **<TABLE CELLPADDING=*number*>** The CELLPADDING attribute controls the amount of blank space *within* the cell (the default is 1 pixel). Figure 18.11 shows the effect of changing the CELLPADDING to 10.

INTRODUCING FRAMES

Netscape's frame tags enable you to create a Web page that's divided into independently scrollable panels. Within each frame, you insert a separate HTML page.

Frames aren't popular with many Web authors because users find them difficult to use, and they're quite ugly on-screen (compared with a comparable table layout). Still, frames have advantages. For displaying a panel of navigation aids, frames can't be beat; the aids stay put, and remain visible, no matter how the user scrolls the other windows. The same can't be said of navigation aids placed in a narrow column with tables.

<FRAMESET> and <FRAME>: The Two Basic Building Blocks for Frames

Two nonstandard HTML tags, introduced by Netscape and emulated by any frame-capable browser, enable you to construct a framed page.

The first tag, <FRAMESET>, establishes the frame. Using this tag, you specify the number of rows or the number of columns using the ROWS or COLS attributes. (You can't specify both simultaneously.) If you want to begin your framed page with a cell that spans the top of the page, you begin by using the ROWS attribute. If you want to begin your page with a row containing more than one cell, you begin with the COLS attribute. To handle additional row or column layout changes, you nest <FRAMESET> tags. (Don't worry about this right now; I'll explain how this works in a moment.)

The other important tag is <FRAME>. This tag enables you to specify which HTML document appears in a cell. In addition, it enables you to use a number of attributes that control the cell's characteristics, including horizontal and vertical margins, whether the frame is scrollable, and whether the user can resize the frame.

A third tag, <NOFRAMES>, enables you to display a message if the user's browser can't handle frames.

I'm sure this is all clear as mud at this point, so let's try a tutorial.

FRAMESET

Purpose: Creates the frames, specifies the size of the frame, and lists the files to be displayed.

Usage: <FRAMESET>. . .</FRAMESET>

Example: <FRAMESET COLS="116, 26%, *">
                  <FRAME SRC="Document1.html">
                  <FRAME SRC="Document2.html">
                  <FRAME SRC="Document3.html">
                  </FRAMESET>

Don't Forget: You can also use the ROW attribute to divide cells vertically. Note that you can spec-
                  ify row height or column width using a fixed pixel setting (e.g., 116 in the above ex-
                  ample), a percentage of the screen (26%), or the remaining available space (*).

Hot Tip: If you place a number in front of the asterisk (for remaining available space), that
                  frame gets that many times as much available space. For example, COLS = "*, 2*"
                  gives one-third of the available space to the first cell, and two-thirds to the second
                  cell.

FRAME

Purpose: Specifies the document to be displayed within a frame cell.

Usage: <FRAME>. . .</FRAME>

Example: <FRAMESET COLS="116, 26%, *">
                  <FRAME SRC="Document3.html" NAME="menu" MARGINWIDTH="10"
                  MARGINHEIGHT="10" SCROLLING="yes" NORESIZE>
                  </FRAMESET>

Don't Forget: Note the many attributes. NAME gives the window a name, so that it can be made
                  a TARGET by other windows. MARGINWIDTH specifies a margin within the win-
                  dow, in pixels. MARGINHEIGHT specifies a vertical margin, again in pixels.
                  SCROLLING has three possible values: yes, no, and auto (auto scrolling kicks in if
                  the user resizes the panel so that it's smaller than the displayed text). NORESIZE
                  doesn't take a value; it prevents the user from resizing the frame.

Hot Tip: If you don't use the SCROLLING attribute, the page defaults to the auto setting—
                  which means that scroll bars appear if the cell is too small to display the data.

NOFRAMES

Purpose:	Specifies the document to be displayed if the browser cannot display frames.
Usage:	<NOFRAMES>. . .</NOFRAMES>
Example:	<NOFRAMES>
	<H1>You're using a browser that doesn't support frames</H1>
	<P>This document requires a browser capable of supporting frames. Please consider downloading <A HREF="http://home.netscape.com">Netscape Navigator </A> or <A HREF="http://www.microsoft.com">Microsoft Internet Explorer </A >, both of which support frames.</P>
	<P>If you prefer, you can view a <A HREF="nonframe.html">nonframed version of this site</A>.
	</NOFRAMES>
Don't Forget:	This is all the user will see.
Hot Tip:	Create a nonframed version of your site for people who prefer to use frameless browsers. It's a lot of work, but it's the only way you can be sure to reach the wide audience you're seeking.

A FRAMES TUTORIAL

To understand how the frame tags work, there's no substitute for a good, quick tutorial. Fire up your computer, and give this a try.

Creating the Documents

Use your HTML editor to create five HTML documents. In each, place nothing but a centered <H1> heading with the text "Document" followed by the number of the document (1 through 5). Save each document using the file names doc1.html, doc2.html, and so forth.

Creating the First Frame Document (Creating Columns)

The document containing the frame tags, which we'll call the *frame document*, references the pages you've just created. Open a new document, call it frame1.html, and type the following:

```
<HTML>
<HEAD>
<TITLE>Frame Experiment 1</TITLE>
</HEAD>
<FRAMESET COLS="180,15%,15%,*,2*">
<FRAME SRC="doc1.html">
<FRAME SRC="doc2.html">
<FRAME SRC="doc3.html">
<FRAME SRC="doc4.html">
<FRAME SRC="doc5.html">
</FRAMESET>
</HTML>
```

Open this document in your browser. You'll see the results shown in Figure 18.12. Note the following:

- Do not place the <FRAMESET> tags within the BODY element. If you do, your frames won't work.

- In the <FRAMESET> tag, you must specify column widths for all five of the documents referenced by <FRAME> tags. Since there are five documents listed, you need five values. Each value references one document, in the order you list them.

- The first value, 180, specifies a fixed length in pixels. This is a good approach for the first frame column, since that's the one you're likely to use for a column of navigation aids. You don't want the user to shrink this column so that the aids can't be seen. However, it's a poor choice for other columns, since you don't know how wide the user's screen will be.

- The second and third values, 15%, tell the browser to use 15% of the available screen width for these columns. Just how wide they are depends on how wide the user has sized the browser's window.

- The fourth value, *, tells the browser to use the remaining available space. If there is more than one column assigned the * value, the browser divides the space between them equally.

- The fifth value, 2*, overrides the equal division of remaining space among the columns marked with an asterisk. It tells the browser to give twice as much of the remaining space to this column as it gives to the others. Since there's only one other column marked with an asterisk, this value gives two-thirds of the remaining space to this

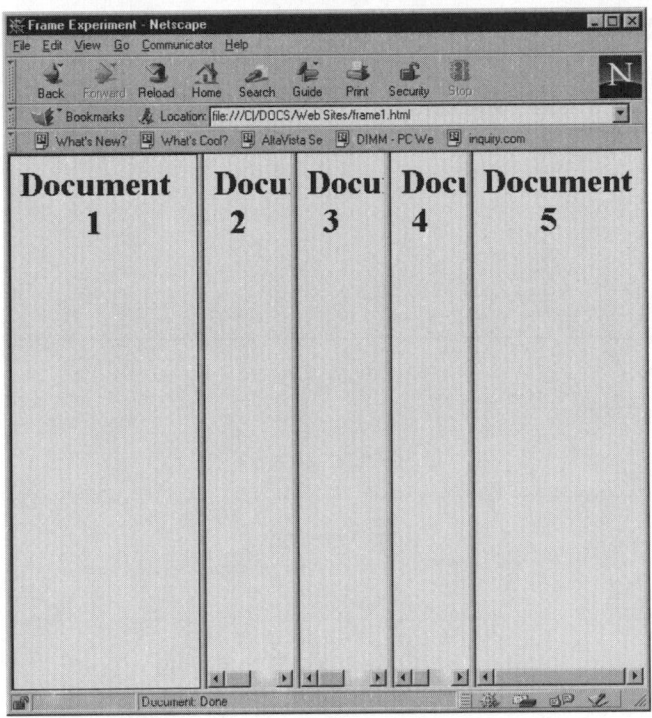

Figure 18.12 The COLS attributes determine how much space each frame takes up on-screen.

column, and one-third of the remaining space to the other column that's marked with an asterisk.

Creating the Second Frame Document (Displaying Rows)

Now open the first frame document, and make just one change: In the <FRAMESET> tag, change the COLS attribute to ROWS. Leave everything else unchanged, and save this document to a new filename (frame2.html). Open it with your browser; you'll see the results shown in Figure 18.13.

Notice that the frames appear in vertically stacked rows, but the ROWS values work the same way as the COLS values: You see the same division of space, except that the space is divided vertically rather than horizontally.

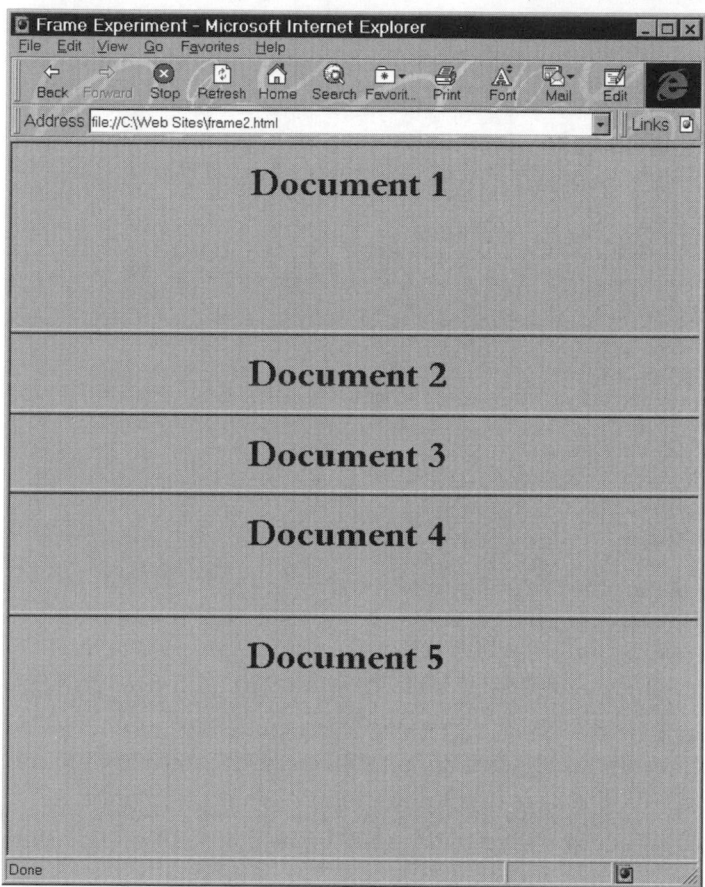

Figure 18.13   The ROWS attribute tells the browser to display the documents in vertically stacked rows.

The big question now, of course, is how to create a page that combines rows and columns!

Combining Rows and Columns by Nesting <FRAMESET> Tags

To combine rows and columns, you need to nest <FRAMESET> tags. Start with a plan. For example, suppose you want to display Document 1 in an unbroken row. In the second row, you want to divide the space equally between Documents 2, 3, and 4. Finally, you want Document 5 to appear at the bottom of the screen in a second unbroken row.

To create this document, type the following in your HTML editor:

```
<HTML>
<HEAD>
<TITLE>Frame Experiment 3</TITLE>
</HEAD>
<FRAMESET COLS="2*,*,2*">
<FRAME SRC="doc1.html">
<FRAMESET ROWS="33%,33%,33%">
<FRAME SRC="doc2.html">
<FRAME SRC="doc3.html">
<FRAME SRC="doc4.html">
</FRAMESET>
<FRAME SRC="doc5.html">
</FRAMESET>
</HTML>
```

The results are shown in Figure 18.14.

Note the following:

- The first <FRAMESET> tag establishes the overall row pattern. There are three rows. The first row takes up two-fifths of the space, the second row takes up one-fifth, and the third row takes up two-fifths. (See how the asterisks work?) These proportions remain the same even if the user resizes the window.

- The first <FRAME> tag places Document 1 in the top row.

- The second <FRAMESET> tag establishes columns for the second row. The space is divided into thirds. Following are the three <FRAME> tags that specify which documents appear in the frames. Note the ending </FRAMESET> tag.

- There's one row left over, so the last <FRAME> tag fills it.

 If you plan to use one of the rows for navigation aids, make sure to size it using a fixed pixel height. That way, it won't disappear or become unreadable if the user resizes the window.

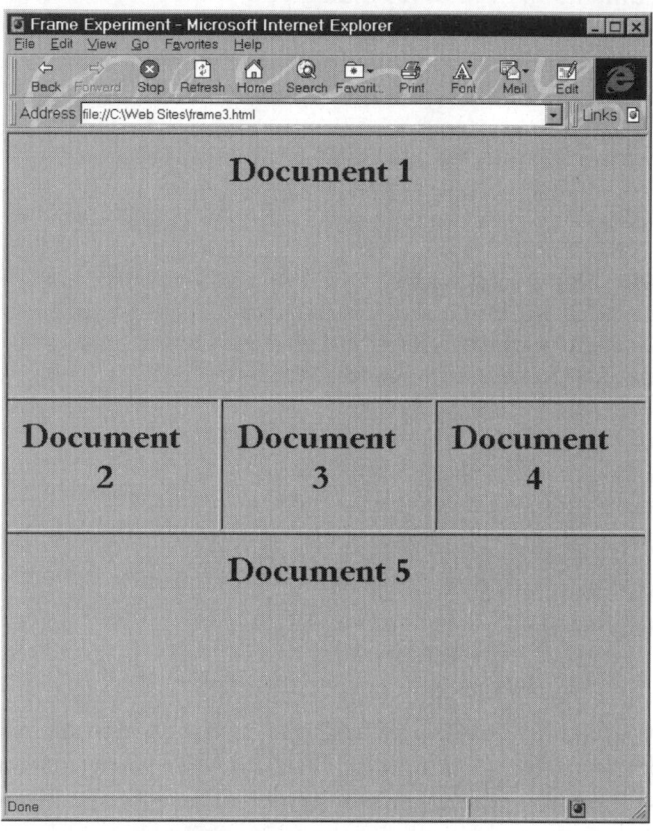

Figure 18.14 To create a page with rows and columns, you nest the <FRAMESET> tags.

Opening Documents in Frames

The previous examples display documents statically within their frames. A more common use of frames, however, is to display a panel of navigation aids; when you click one of these icons, documents appear dynamically in another frame on the same page. To do this, you must name the frames you create and create targeting references. Again, this won't become clear until you try it.

In your HTML editor, create the following document:

```
<HTML>
<HEAD>
<TITLE>Frame Experiment 4</TITLE>
</HEAD>
<FRAMESET ROWS "50%,50%">
<FRAME NAME="top" SRC="doc1.html">
<FRAME NAME="bottom" SRC="menu.html">
</FRAMESET>
</HTML>
```

Call this document frame4.html.

Now create a second document (menu.html) with the following code:

```
<TITLE>Menu</TITLE>
<HEAD>
<BODY>

<A TARGET="top" HREF="doc1.html">Document 1</A><BR>

<A TARGET="top" HREF="doc2.html">Document 2</A><BR>

<A TARGET="top" HREF="doc3.html">Document 3</A><BR>

<A TARGET="top" HREF="doc4.html">Document 4</A><BR>

<A TARGET="top" HREF="doc5.html">Document 5</A><BR>

</BODY>
</HTML>
```

When you open frame4.html, you see the results shown in Figure 18.15. Note the following:

- In the frame document code, note the NAME attribute in the <FRAME> tags. The two windows are named "top" and "bottom," respectively.

- In the menu document code, note the TARGET attribute for each of the referenced hyperlinks. This tells the browser to open the document in the named window.

CREATING A PAGE DESIGN WITH FRAMES

Here's a simple page design that you can use for your sites. There's a row at the top of the screen that displays your site's logo. The second row is

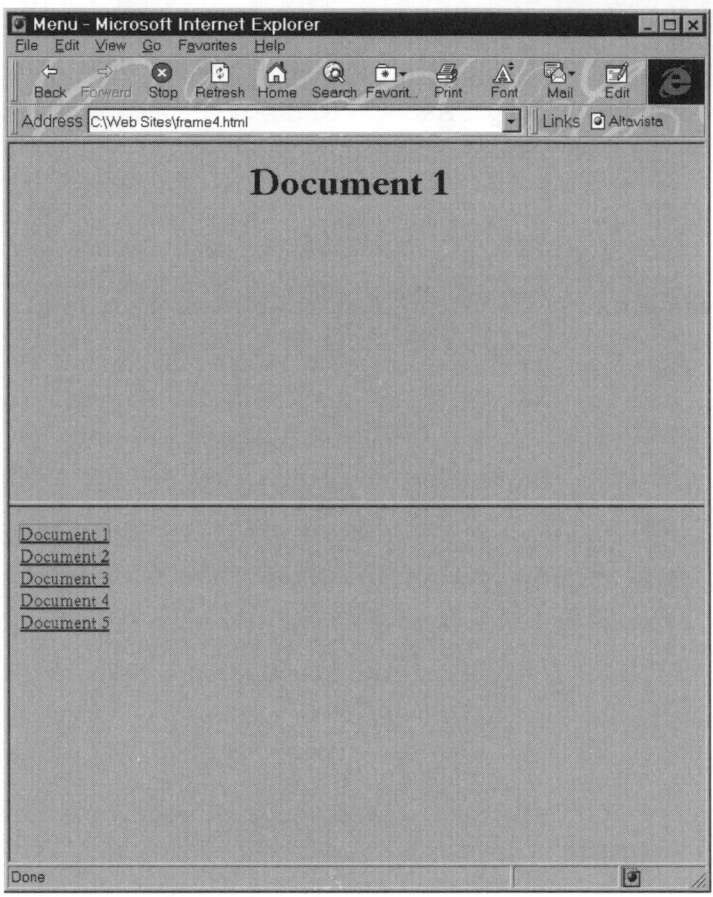

Figure 18.15   Navigation aids displayed within a frame.

divided into two columns: the first is a column of navigation buttons, while the second displays the documents you can choose from the navigation column. Take a look at Figure 18.16 to see how this looks.

To create this design, create a document called frame5.html, and type the following:

```
<HTML>
<HEAD>
<TITLE>Frame Experiment 5</TITLE>
</HEAD>
```

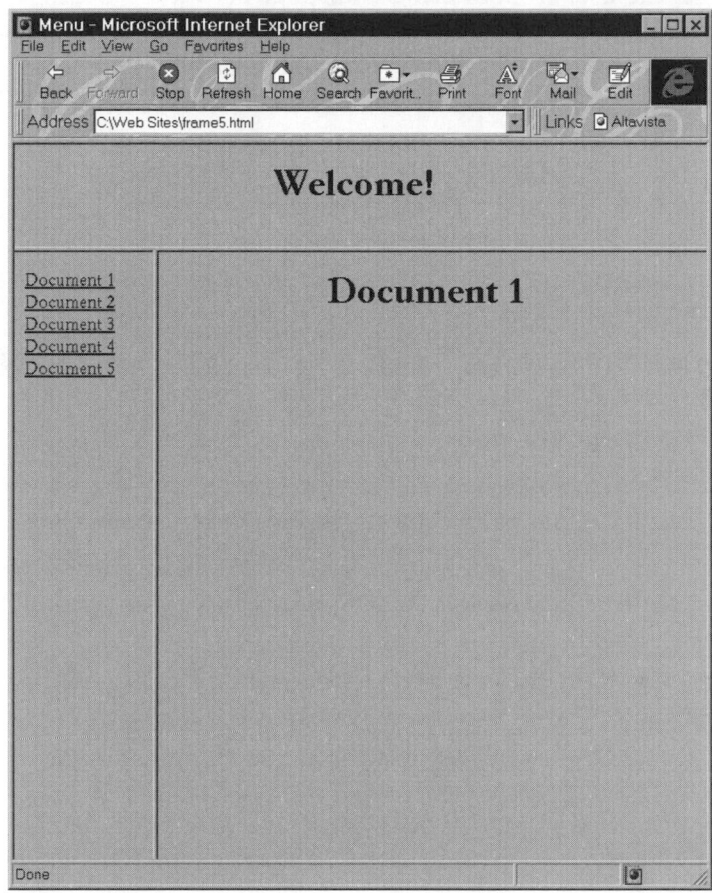

Figure 18.16 This simple document design is useful for many applications.

```
<FRAMESET ROWS "100,*">
<FRAME NAME="top" SRC="welcome.html" NORESIZE>
<FRAMESET COLS="135,*">
<FRAME NAME="navaids" SRC="menu.html" NORESIZE>
<FRAME NAME="display" SRC="doc1.html">
</FRAMESET>
</FRAMESET>
</HTML>
```

Note the NORESIZE attribute in the welcome and navigation aids frame. This prevents the user from altering your page layout.

Now create a document called welcome.html. This document should contain a brief welcoming message and your logo.

Finally, modify menu.html so that the referenced frame is "display" rather than "top," as follows:

```
<TITLE>Menu</TITLE>
<HEAD>
</BODY>
<A TARGET="display" HREF="doc1.html">Document 1</A>
<BR>

<A TARGET="display" HREF="doc2.html">Document 2</A>
<BR>

<A TARGET="display" HREF="doc3.html">Document 3</A>
<BR>

<A TARGET="display" HREF="doc4.html">Document 4</A>
<BR>

<A TARGET="display" HREF="doc5.html">Document 5</A>
<BR>

</BODY>
</HTML>
```

FROM HERE

- Learn how to add Java, JavaScript, and ActiveX controls to your pages—with no programming necessary. Find out how in the next chapter.

- Consider using an HTML editor to simplify tag insertion. See Chapter 20.

Chapter
19

Including Java, JavaScript, and ActiveX Controls

Y ou don't have to be a programmer to use Java, JavaScript, and ActiveX controls on your Web site. In this chapter, you'll learn the HTML that you need to incorporate these features into your pages.

FROM HELPER APPLICATIONS TO JAVA

There's a history to this. To best understand the significance of Java, JavaScript, and ActiveX controls, let's look at what preceded them.

Help Me, Helper Apps

The earliest browsers couldn't deal with any data other than HTML files and GIF graphics. (Netscape's was the first browser to deal natively with JPEG graphics.) To deal with other types of data, you had to equip your system with lots of *helper applications*, programs that dealt specifically with the type of data that's encountered in a file. For example, if you wanted to see MPEG videos, you had to configure your browser to start an MPEG player whenever an MPEG file was encountered. The configuration process was rather tedious, and you didn't see the data in the browser window—it was displayed in the helper application's window.

Plug In to This!

Recognizing the deficiencies of helper applications, Netscape developed a *plug-in architecture* for its browser. A plug-in is an accessory program that's designed to meld with a specific application, extending its capabilities. Many popular applications, such as Adobe Photoshop, offer a plug-in architecture that enables third-part developers to create accessory programs. These programs add functionality to the product, so everyone benefits. Plug-ins were designed to work only with Netscape. Happily, though, Microsoft decided to support Netscape's plug-in architecture with version 3.0 of Microsoft Internet Explorer. For this reason, there are lots of plug-ins in use, and some of them—notably Macromedia's Shockwave and RealAudio's sound player—have gotten pretty well established.

There's one big problem with plug-ins, though. They're a drag to download and install (see Figure 19.1). If you encounter data that requires a plug-in that you don't have, you're in for as much as ten or fifteen minutes of

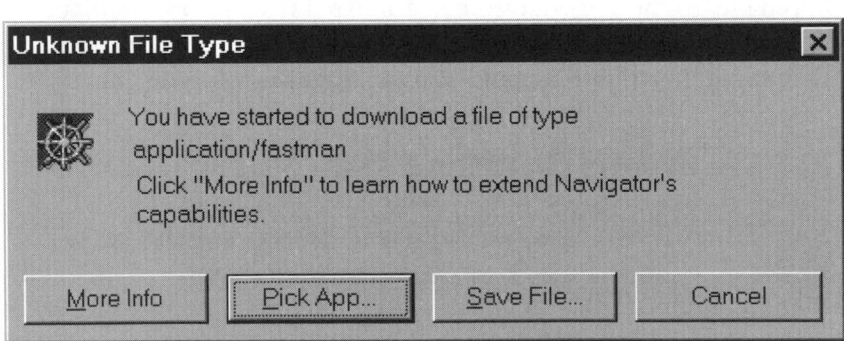

Figure 19.1   Plug-ins are cool, but if you don't have the right plug-in installed, you're in for a tedious download.

tedious downloading, followed by an installation routine and, probably, the need to restart your system. Bo-o-ring! For this reason, many people just skip plug-ins. Also, if you downloaded all the ones you run into, you'd quickly run out of space on your hard drive.

Plug-ins have other problems. They're tied to specific versions of your browser. They also might not be available for all computer formats (a given plug-in might be available for Windows 95, say, but not Windows 3.1 or the Macintosh, let alone UNIX).

Cross-Platform Programming Languages

So what's the solution to the plug-in dilemma? In a word: Java. Developed by Sun Microsystems, Java is a simplified version of the C++ programming language that has taken over professional software development labs worldwide. But that's not the most important thing. Java is the world's first cross-platform programming language.

What's the significance of this? Prior to Java, programs could not execute on a given computer unless they were specifically written for the computer's operating system and hardware. With Java, a software developer can create and distribute a program that will execute just fine on any computer that's capable of running a Java interpreter. And what's a Java interpreter? In its simplest form, it's a Java-capable browser, such as Netscape or Microsoft Internet Explorer (version 3.0 and higher).

You'll learn more about how Java works in a moment, but let's examine the plusses. When your browser encounters a page with a Java program (called an *applet*), the browser starts downloading the Java code, which starts executing immediately on reception. You don't have to do anything, such as approve the installation or restart your system. It's all automatic. As far as you know, the cool stuff you're seeing—like an interactive weather map (see Figure 19.2)—is part of the Web page itself.

Isn't this dangerous? What about security?
Java programs execute in a *virtual machine* (also called a *sandbox*), where they can't get direct access to your computer's file system. For this reason, they're considered pretty safe by most experts (although there are dissenters). The real problem with Java security is that the sandbox is too constraining. To do cool and useful things, Java programs do need access to your computer's file system. You'll learn later how this can be handled safely.

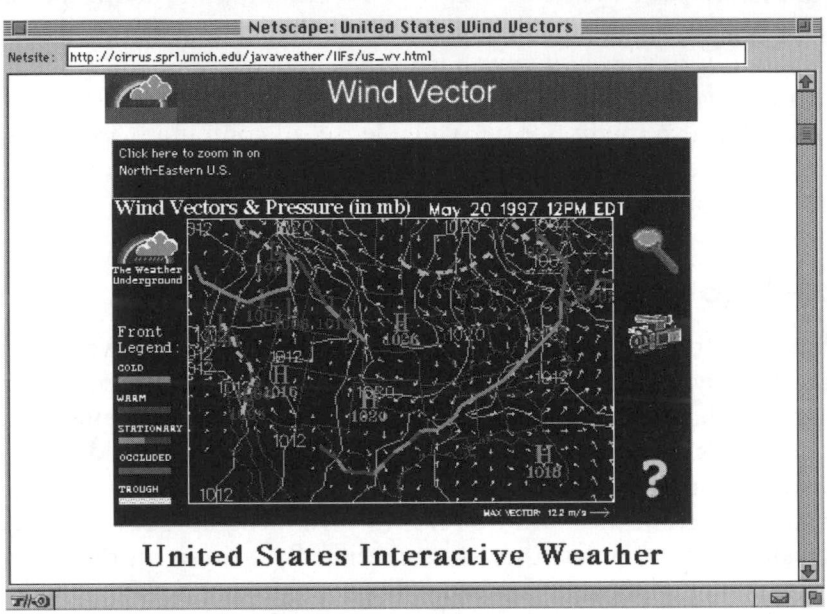

Figure 19.2   This Java applet downloads quickly and shows wind speed and direction in real time—the arrows move as the wind shifts!

The down side to Java is that Java executes more slowly than code written with your computer's specific hardware in mind. But Java's speed is improving. The day may come when most of the applications you run on your computer are centrally distributed on the Internet and will operate on any computer that's running a Java interpreter. Later in this chapter, you'll learn about net-casting ("push") technologies, which enable Web sites to transmit content to users. This is only one of the many wonderful things made possible by Java.

Java for Non-Programmers

So! You already know the basics about Java:

- It's a cross-platform programming language, the first of its kind.

- Java programs download and execute transparently.

- Your Java-capable browser functions as a Java interpreter.

Solutions
Java vs. CGI

As you've learned, the Common Gateway Interface (CGI) is one of several application programming interfaces (APIs) that enable a Web page to pass on data to an executable program. You can't get forms to work, for example, without some kind of API that passes the form data to a program, such as a CGI script. Script programming isn't for amateurs—it requires a lot of programming expertise.

Can Java get you out of this? It depends. Java applets are *client-side* programs; that means they execute on the user's system, not on the server. This means that some things just won't work with Java, or at least not very conveniently. For example, suppose you want to create an applet that searches an entire Web site for keywords that the user supplies. It's possible, but it works only by downloading the text of every darned page on the site—a very inefficient and time-consuming process. Since the applet can't communicate directly with the server or access the server's file system, that's the only way it can work.

What you probably don't know is how to program in Java. That's way beyond the scope of this book; indeed, it's a book in itself, or two or three. What you *can* do, however, is make use of freebie, shareware, and commercial Java applets on your Web pages. In this section, you'll learn how to incorporate Java applets on your pages. As you'll see, it's easy, and you do *not* have to be a programmer to do this. I promise!

INCORPORATING JAVA APPLETS ON YOUR PAGE

To incorporate Java applets on your page, you use the <APPLET> tag. This tag goes within the body of your document, right where you want the applet to appear and do its thing. Every Java applet runs in its own box, which is situated inline on the page. For this reason, you need to think about alignment; consider surrounding the <APPLET> tags with alignment tags (try <DIV ALIGN="center">...</DIV>).

<APPLET> Tag Attributes

The following attributes are used with the <APPLET> tag:

- **CODEBASE**   This tells your browser where the applet is located. You can use a relative link if the applet is in the same directory as your Web page, or in a directory beneath your Web page's directory. Otherwise, you have to describe the absolute directory path (on your server's system) leading to the applet. It's better to keep it in the same directory as your Web page. Note that Java applets always have the extension .class.

- **WIDTH**   This tells your browser how wide a box to make for the applet. You can find out which size to use by consulting the applet's documentation or by peeking at the source code of a page that uses the applet.

- **HEIGHT**   This tells your browser how tall a box to make for the applet.

- **PARAM NAME**   Most Java applets come with a number of user-definable *parameters* (options), such as text color. Just which parameters are available depends on the application. To find out, you need to read the applet's documentation or peek at the source code of a Web page that's included the application.

- **VALUE**   For each parameter, you have to specify a value. Again, the applet's documentation will tell you how to do this.

- -

APPLET

Purpose:	Inserts a Java applet at the tag's location.
Usage:	<APPLET>...</APPLET>
Example:	<APPLET CODEBASE="Javathing.class width=520 height=334> PARAM NAME=Hop VALUE="119" PARAM NAME=Skip VALUE="47" PARAM NAME=Jump VALUE="whee" </APPLET>
Don't Forget:	Each applet has its own *parameters* (definable characteristics), for which you can choose values. Use the PARAM NAME attribute to assign these values.

Hot Tip: You can display a message for non-Java browsers by inserting the following *within*
the <APPLET>...</APPLET> tags: <P>Sorry, you need a Java-capable browser to run
this applet.</P> (you can phrase this message any way you want). The reason this
works is that Java browsers ignore all the normal HTML within the <APPLET> tag,
while non-Java browsers don't.

Obtaining Applets

You can find lots of freebie applets on the Web. Some specify that they're
supposed to be used only for noncommercial or personal purposes. If you're
in doubt about whether your use of an applet is legit, write to the author
and request permission.

 The best place to hunt down cool applets on the Web is
Yahoo's Java applets page. Go to Yahoo at www.yahoo.com,
and type "Java applets" in the search box. You'll see a link
to the Java Applets page, shown in Figure 19.3.

Chances are that any applet you download will be compressed into an
archive that contains not only the compiled applet, but also documentation
and possibly the applet's source code. You may find that there are several
*.class files; all of these need to be uploaded to your server in order for the
program to work.

 Check out the applet's Web page to see whether the docu-
mentation is online (see Figure 19.4). Be sure to look for
information about how to configure the parameters. In Figure 19.5, you see the parameters for the Digital Clock
Applet. You click on these to find out how to configure the
Digital Clock for your Web site.

Reading the Documentation

Whether the documentation is found on the Web site or in a README file
(or some other file) that you download with the applet, you need to study it
carefully. As you'll see, each of the parameters gives you a set of options for
customizing the applet's appearance and performance. Note carefully which
values you can use.

Uploading Your Applet

When you've added the <APPLET> tag to your page and run some tests to make sure everything's working, you're ready to upload the page and the applet (and all of its associated *.class files) to your server. For more information, see Chapter 21.

INTRODUCING ACTIVEX

Microsoft has its own theory of how programs should be downloaded to users' systems by means of the browser. It's called ActiveX. Compared to Java,

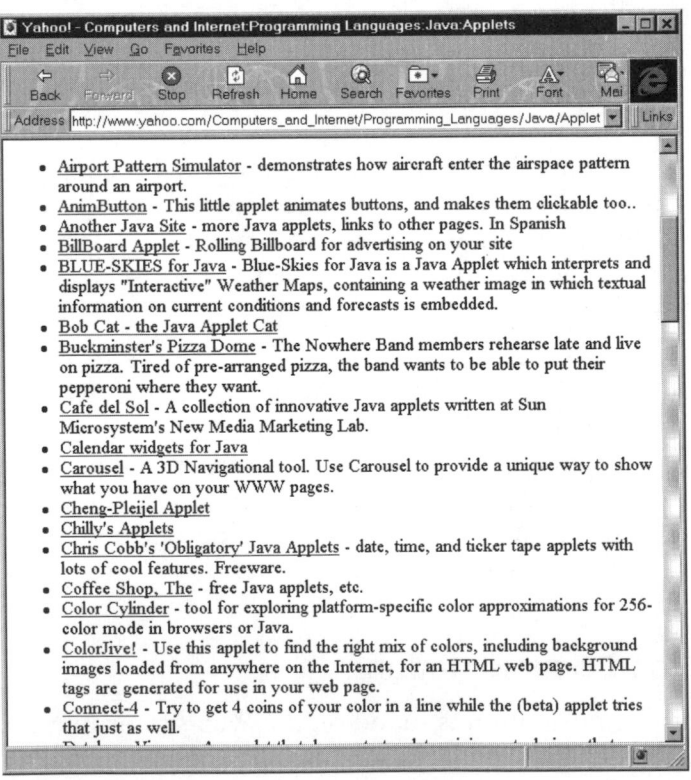

Figure 19.3   Yahoo offers lots of cool applets you can use.

it's not only a partial solution, but one that many suspect masks a not-too-subtle ploy on Microsoft's part to ensure the universality of Microsoft Windows.

From the user's perspective, ActiveX is a lot like Java: You go to a site with ActiveX programs (called *controls*), and things start to happen. But it isn't all automatic, like it is with Java. The reason is that ActiveX controls have full access to your computer's file system. It's pretty easy to write an ActiveX control that would essentially wipe out all the files on your hard disk. For this reason, ActiveX includes an authentication feature. When you start downloading an ActiveX control, you see a dialog box displaying a signed digital certificate that comes from the program's author. This certificate states that the program indeed comes from the author and that the author is indeed the person he or she claims to be. All this is attested to by a

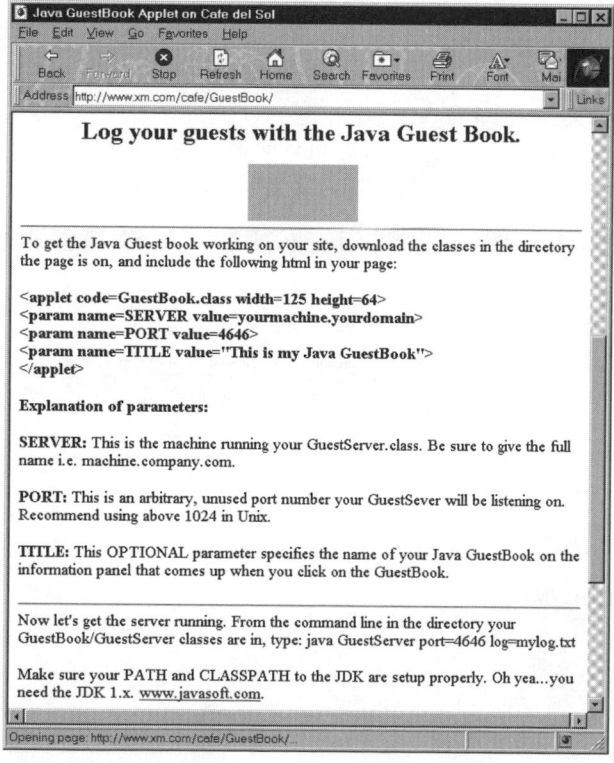

Figure 19.4   The applet's Web page offers important information.

signed digital certificate—which, incidentally, doesn't really assure you that the program is safe to use. It just says that the program comes from some software firm somewhere. Presumably, it's reliable, but one never knows, does one? Of course, we all download and run programs from trusted sites (such as www.download.com) and hardly stop to think twice about it, so I don't see why ActiveX controls should come under special criticism here. Parenthetically, Java's moving to a similar architecture, and for similar reasons—that sandbox is just too constraining. Applet authors also want access to your file system.

Although ActiveX resembles Java from the user's perspective, it's a different story under the hood. ActiveX isn't a programming language at all. It's more like a container for programs, and it enables them to talk to other

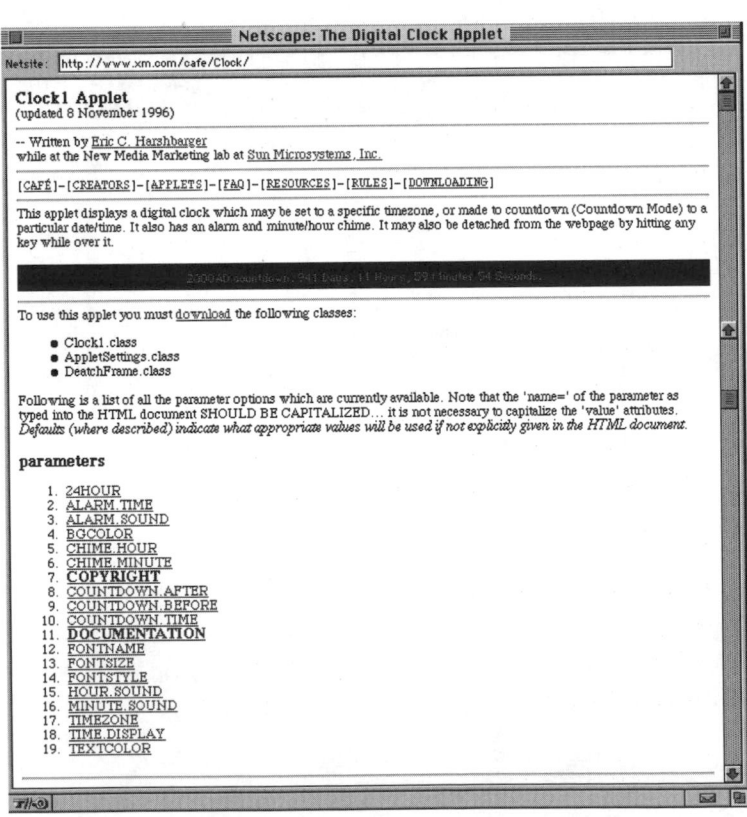

Figure 19.5 Look for information about how to configure the parameters.

applications by means of Object Linking and Embedding (OLE), a Microsoft technology that the firm has released to the public domain. That's all well and good, but in point of fact OLE is still 100% supported only by Microsoft Windows; there's a Mac implementation, but it's not quite as extensive, and UNIX versions are reportedly "in the works." For now, using ActiveX controls means restricting your audience mainly to Windows, and perhaps Macintosh users, so I don't recommend it. Use Java and JavaScript instead. (While we're on the subject, I should also point out that only Microsoft Internet Explorer fully supports ActiveX; Netscape reportedly plans to support it, but it does so right now only by means of a commercial and pricey plug-in. Using ActiveX means restricting your audience—and that's bad Web publishing.

Introducing JavaScript

Now that you've figured out what Java is, along comes another term: Java-Script. What's this? Let's start with the basics. Java is a full-fledged programming language, and Java applets are distributed in the form of compiled, executable (*.class) files. Java can do lots of neat things.

JavaScript resembles Java in some respects, but it's much simpler. Also, it's not a full-fledged programming language: It's a scripting language. What this means is that, instead of linking to an external program (a *.class file), JavaScript programmers write their code (called a *script*) right on the Web page. (This makes it pretty easy to "borrow" JavaScript code by copying and pasting, so "real" programmers prefer Java.)

Unlike Java applets, JavaScripts don't execute in their own window. Instead, JavaScripts are part of the underlying HTML code. You can do all kinds of cool, nutty, and useful things with JavaScript, including fading text color from one color to another, popping up a new window to display content, and enabling text scrolling areas within a page.

JavaScript isn't too difficult to learn, especially if you've done some programming before, but once again it's beyond the scope of this book. What you'll learn here is how to add existing JavaScripts to your page.

Obtaining JavaScripts

There are lots of freebie JavaScripts on the Web, many of them available with no restrictions whatsoever. If you're not sure, contact the author by e-mail and ask for permission.

 One place to hunt for JavaScripts is JavaScript Planet:

www.geocities.com/SiliconValley/7116/

It's pretty easy to obtain a JavaScript. Just display the Web page's source HTML and look for a bunch of incomprehensible stuff between the <SCRIPT> and </SCRIPT> tags (Figure 19.6). That's it! If you simply copy this to your page, you'll get the same results.

```
Document - WordPad
File  Edit  View  Insert  Format  Help

Trebuchet MS (Central European)          12      B / U

<SCRIPT LANGUAGE="JavaScript">
<!--
        Stamp = new Date();
        document.write('<font size="2" face="Arial"><B>' + (Stamp.getMonth() + 1)
+"/"+Stamp.getDate()+ "/"+Stamp.getYear() + '</B></font><BR>');
        var Hours;
        var Mins;
        var Time;
        Hours = Stamp.getHours();
        if (Hours >= 12) {
            Time = " P.M.";
        }
        else {
            Time = " A.M.";
        }

        if (Hours > 12) {
        Hours -= 12;
        }

        if (Hours == 0) {
        Hours = 12;
        }

        Mins = Stamp.getMinutes();

        if (Mins < 10) {
        Mins = "0" + Mins;
        }

        document.write('<font size="2" face="Arial"><B>' + Hours + ":" + Mins +
Time + '</B></font>');

//-->
</SCRIPT>
For Help, press F1
```

Figure 19.6   Here's what a JavaScript looks like (this one puts a date on your page).

SCRIPT

Purpose:	Demarcates an inline script.
Usage:	<SCRIPT>...</SCRIPT>
Example:	<SCRIPT LANGUAGE = "JavaScript">
	<!--
	Stamp = new Date():
	document.write('<B>' + (Stamp.getMonth() + 1)
	+ Stamp.getDate() + Stamp.getYear() + '</B>');
	//-->
	</SCRIPT>
Don't Forget:	The JavaScript is placed within comments (<!-- and -->), which hides the script from non-Java-capable browsers. Be sure to use the LANGUAGE="JavaScript" attribute to tell the browser that it's dealing with a JavaScript.
Hot Tip:	Place the script where you want the results to appear on your Web page.

Hiding the Script from Non-Java-Capable Browsers

To make sure that a non-Java-capable browser doesn't display your script as if it were text, be sure to place the entire script within HTML comment tags (<-- and -->). By the way, you may have noticed the two slash marks before the closing HTML comment tag (//-->). These tell JavaScript to ignore the HTML! Confusing, I know, but trust me—it works.

WHEN PUSH COMES TO SHOVE: NETCASTING TECHNOLOGIES

The latest wrinkle in the Web content delivery scene is the arrival of *push* technologies, which will be implemented in the forthcoming versions 4.0 of Netscape Navigator and Microsoft Internet Explorer (but in different ways, of course). To understand push media, it's best to think of an old-fashioned radio. Out there on the Web, there are *transmitters* that are capable of beaming out content. Users can "tune" their browsers to receive the content.

And what do you get? Automatically updated stuff, appearing in separate windows or even on the desktop itself. Right now, I've got my desktop tuned to clnet's news reports, MSNBC's news bulletins, and a whole bunch of other things, twinkling away at me (and keeping me from getting any work done, I might add). From the user's standpoint, the push media application—part of the browser, if he or she is using the 4.0s of the world—displays all the "channels" one can "tune" to. It's up to the user which (if any) of these is allowed to invade the desktop.

Push technologies can also be used to update Java applications. A *Java application* is more involved than an applet; it runs in its own window, and doesn't need any help from a browser. The most interesting and complex example I've seen yet is Corel's Java Suite, which is a Java version of the company's office applications suite. The Java version includes all-Java versions of WordPerfect and Quattro Pro (a spreadsheet program), among other things. Bug fixes, updates, and whatnot automatically download when necessary (as long as you're connected to the Internet, of course).

Can you get into push media yourself? Well, why not? You'll need to wait until the dust settles a bit, though. Right now, Microsoft and Netscape are pushing competing versions of push media standards, and it's going to take a while before it's clear which standard will prevail. The same is true for fonts and style sheets, as a previous chapter discussed.

One obstacle is cost. You need special server software to "transmit" your content, and it's pricey. In the future, you'll probably see Internet service providers selling premium Web publishing space that will include all the configuration necessary to broadcast your content via push media.

Frankly, push media amuse me. They've been developed out of concern that, with so many millions of Web sites out there, people won't access sites often enough to justify the huge investments that some companies are making. So they're developing push media, which they think will get their content in peoples' faces. So it will—for a while. And then there will be millions of push sites, and we'll be back to exactly the same situation!

FROM HERE

- Had it with typing those HTML tags? Try an HTML editor. You'll see how to use one in the next chapter.

- Finished your site? Cool! Test it like heck, upload it to your server, and publicize! Find out how in Chapter 21.

Chapter
20

Using an
HTML Editor

A n HTML editor can't write good HTML for you automatically, but a good editor is a genuine convenience. And right now, you'd have a tough time doing better than HotDog (Sausage Software). HotDog fully supports HTML 3.2 tags, including style sheets and fonts. Plus, there's a spelling checker. No more typos!

The best HTML editors provide (reasonably) user-friendly means of adding tags to your documents—for example, most permit you to add beginning and ending tags quickly by selecting a line or paragraph and then clicking a button (the beginning and ending tags appear automatically at the beginning and end of the selection). In addition, a good HTML editor should provide a quick and easy way to preview the results of your coding. HotDog's Rover panel displays the Web appearance of your document—you don't have to switch to a browser.

 For current information about HotDog, check out Sausage Software's Web site, at http://www.sausage.com. The version available at this writing was HotDog Professional 3.0.21.

GETTING STARTED WITH HOTDOG

HotDog version 3, the version discussed in this chapter, is a very cool version of the program if you like lots of sound, animation, and action. Turned on by default are a bunch of "HotDog" sounds, such as "Sit!" when you close a file. If this gets annoying, you can turn them off by choosing Options from the Tools menu and disabling the sounds.

Let's take a quick look at HotDog's window. Note that I'm not going to discuss all of HotDog's tools and capabilities—that would take a book in itself. In this chapter, I'll show you how to get started, and you can take it from there.

The HotDog Window

The HotDog window (Figure 20.1) is divided into two major panes. On the left is a pane called the Resource Manager that enables you to choose pages, files, favorites, and even Web sites. On the right is the document area, where you'll create and edit your HTML documents. The Rover page gives you tools for viewing the appearance of your page when it's published, and the Document Information tab enables you to set the page title and specify other background information.

The Toolbars

HotDog comes with five toolbars, which you select by clicking one of the tabs. Here's a quick look at what these toolbars do:

- **Elements**   This toolbar's buttons enable you to insert HTML tags into your document. Tags with start and stop tags are entered as pairs, with the cursor situated in the middle so you can start typing. If you select the text that you want to tag beforehand, clicking one of these buttons places the start tag at the beginning of the text and the end tag at the end of the text.

- **Insert** This toolbar's buttons enable you to insert images, objects, links, and targets in your page. It's so important that, when it's not selected, it runs down the middle between the two windows.

- **Format** On this toolbar, you can choose options that affect the appearance of characters in your document, such as bold and italic.

- **Tools** The Tools toolbar enables you to choose HotDog customization options, to check spelling, to verify the HTML syntax, and other neat things.

- **Styles** This toolbar enables you to define styles for your document according to the Cascading Style Sheet (CSS) Level 1 standard.

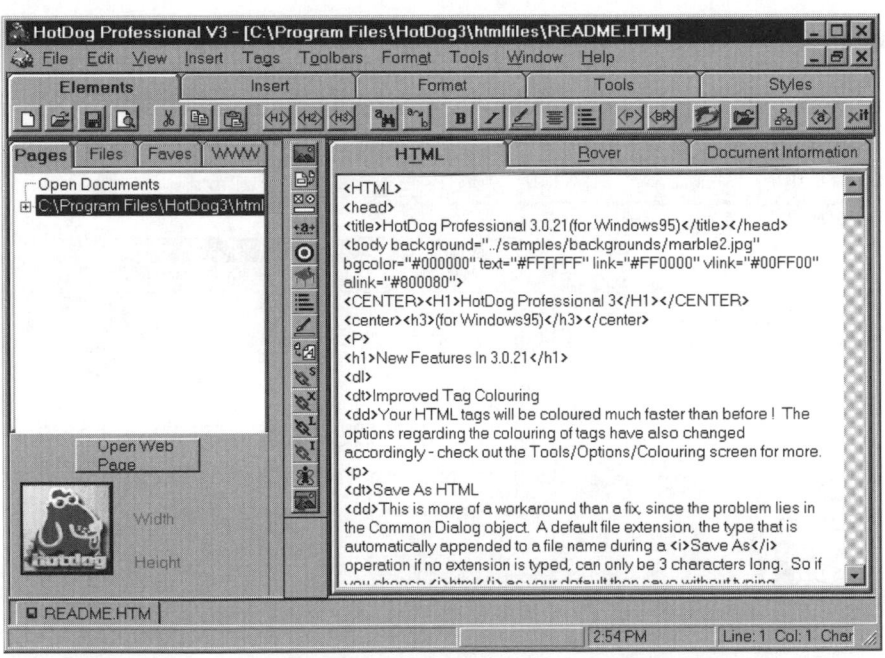

Figure 20.1 The HotDog Professional version 3.0.21 window.

More about the Resource Manager

Take a minute to look at the Resource Manager. If you click Pages, you'll see a list of all the documents that are referenced by hyperlinks in the current document (see Figure 20.2). If you would like to view any of these pages, just select it, click Open Web page, and use Rover to display the page.

If you click Files, you see a Windows-type file manager (see the Resource Manager panel in Figure 20.3) that enables you to locate and open files.

Click Faves to see the Faves panel. This is really a neat feature. You can place your favorite text, tags, and links here so that you can easily insert them in your documents. To add something to one of these boxes, select it in your document, hold down the Shift key, click the right mouse button, and drag the selected item to one of the panels. To insert something from a Faves panel, you just double-click it.

The WWW panel (Figure 20.4) enables you to connect with your ISP's FTP server, so that you can upload your files and graphics for publication on the Web. I'll tell you more about this cool feature in the next chapter.

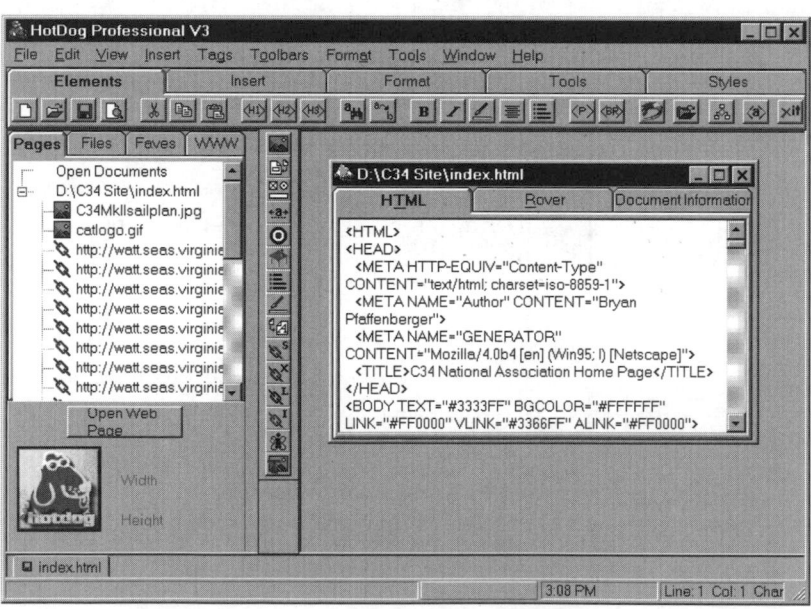

Figure 20.2   The Resource Manager's Pages option shows you all the pages to which you've linked.

CREATING AN HTML DOCUMENT WITH HOTDOG

When you create a new document with HotDog by choosing New from the File menu and selecting Normal from the template list, the program conveniently adds the basic HTML codes (Figure 20.5).

To add text and tags to your HTML document, you simply type the text and select it, as shown in Figure 20.6. You can then do one of the following:

- On the Elements toolbar, click the button for the tag you want to add.

- Open the Tags menu, and choose the tag you want from the submenus.

After you add a tag, you see the tags on-screen, as shown in Figure 20.7.

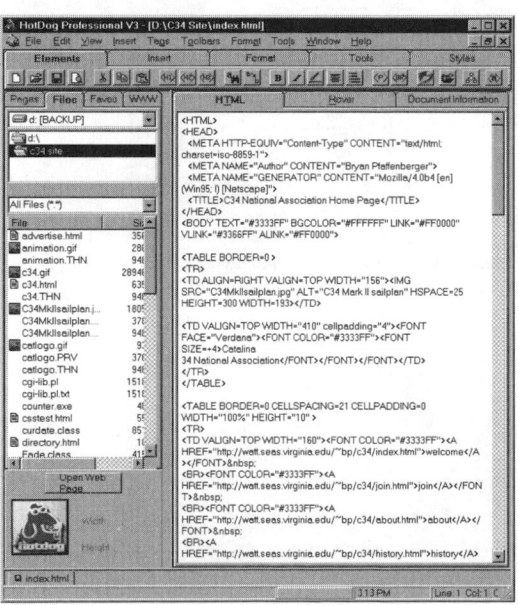

Figure 20.3 The Resource Manager's Files option gives you a Windows-type file management system.

There are *so* many buttons! What do they do?
Here's how to find out. Just move the pointer over the button and leave it there for a couple of seconds. You'll see a help box that explains what the button does. Take a few minutes to find out what's available. You'll like what you see.

As you experiment with HotDog, you'll quickly see how easy it is to build your document quickly. Try the following:

- Type a list and select it. Then click the ordered (numbered) or unordered (bulleted) list buttons. The program automatically adds the beginning and end tags—and what's more, it adds the pesky <LI> tag to the beginning of each line.

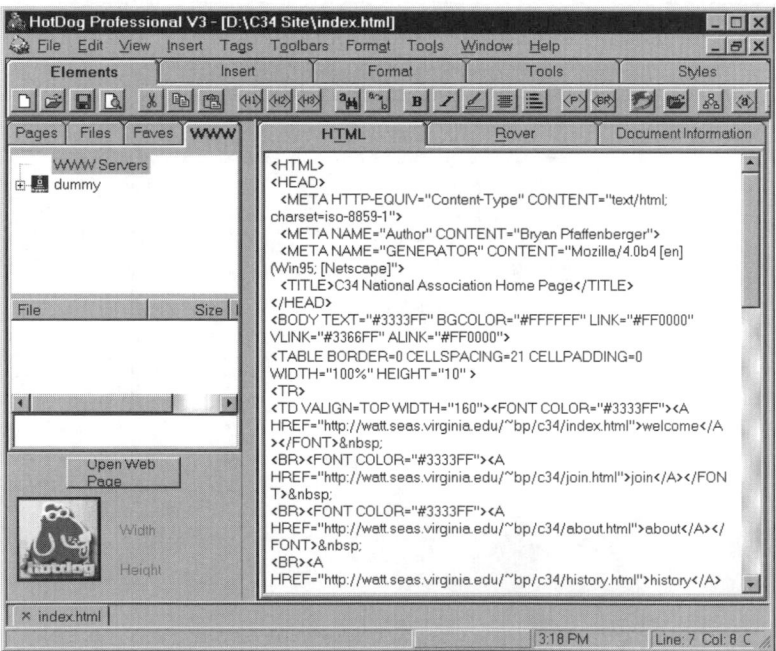

Figure 20.4 The Resource Manager's WWW tab enables you to upload files and graphics for Web publication.

- Select one or two words, and click one of the emphasis keys. Hot-Dog adds the appropriate emphasis tags at the beginning and end of the selection.

- To add paragraph breaks, you can click the Insert Paragraph button (to add a <P> tag) or the <BR> button. You'll find these on the Elements toolbar.

PREVIEWING YOUR DOCUMENT

To see the effects of your HTML tags, click the Rover tab. You'll see your document displayed. (It isn't necessary to log on to your service provider in order to use this feature.)

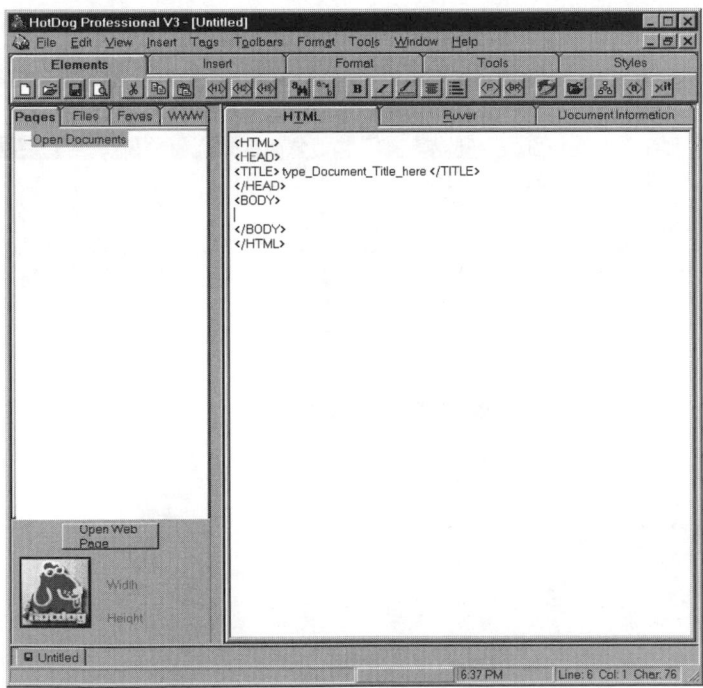

Figure 20.5 Basic document codes are added automatically.

DEFINING YOUR DOCUMENT

HotDog provides convenient tools that help you quickly construct a well-organized HTML document. To define the global structure of a document, including the base font size and background color, you should start by choosing the Document Information tab. You'll see the Document Information panel, shown in Figure 20.8.

The Document Information panel enables you to add the following:

- **Document Title** Type your document's title here. HotDog will automatically position your title between the <TITLE> tags.

- **Base HREF URL** Type your document's Web address here. This information could prove useful if somebody downloads your document and can't find out where it was obtained.

- **META Tag Information** Although the META tag isn't universally recognized by search engines, more of them are making use of it to figure out who created a document, what it contains, and what key-

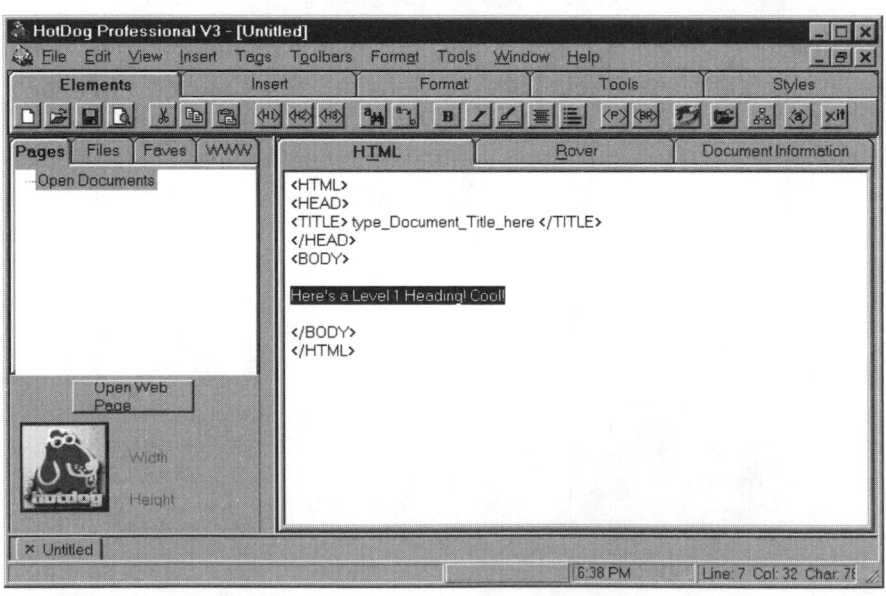

Figure 20.6   Selecting text before adding a tag.

words should retrieve the document. To maximize your document's retrievability with search engines, you should fill in the Document Author, Description, and Keywords fields.

Now click the Format Document Background button. You'll see the dialog box shown in Figure 20.9. Here, you can specify the following:

- **Background Graphic File**   Click the folder icon to add a local file, or click the hand icon to build a link to an external file.

- **Color of Document Text, Standard Text, Visited Links, and Active Links**   Just click one of these fields to bring up a Color dialog box, from which you can choose a default text color for these elements.

- **Background Color**   Click More to extend the dialog box, as shown in Figure 20.10. Here, you can choose a background color in a num-

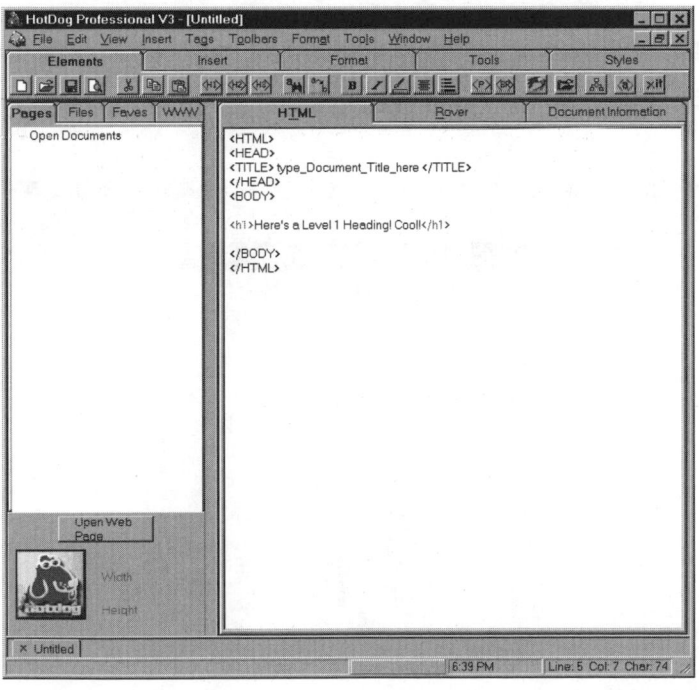

Figure 20.7   Beginning and end tags added to selection.

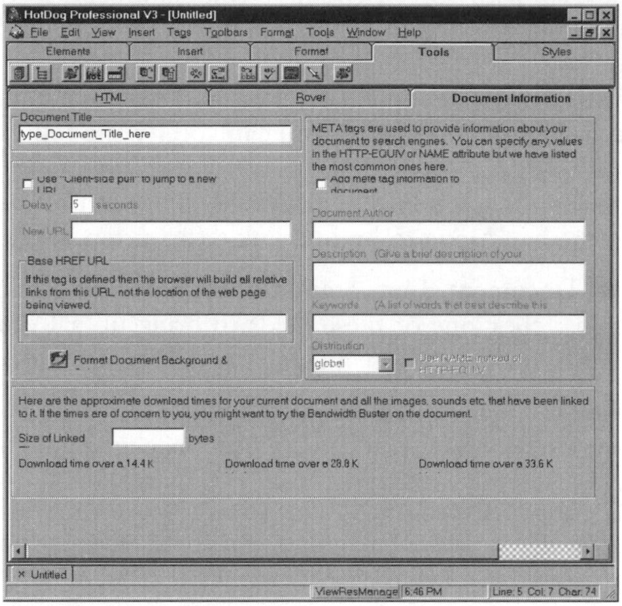

Here are the approximate download times for your current document and all the images, sounds etc. that have been linked to it. If the times are of concern to you, you might want to try the Bandwidth Buster on the document.

Figure 20.8   Document Information panel.

Figure 20.9   Color and background dialog box.

ber of ways, including typing the RGB code, choosing the color from a Color dialog box (click the color icon to do this), or dragging the Red, Green, and Blue sliders. Here's something cool: If you type an RGB code and click Decimal, HotDog automatically converts what you've typed to the corresponding hexadecimal code for that color. Neat!

 Have you moved a page and need to publish a page that guides your readers to the new location? You can make use of the Document Information page to create a page that will inform users of the new URL and then automatically take them to it using "client-side pull" techniques. To do this, click Use Client-Side Pull to Jump to a New URL. By default, the delay is 5 minutes; you can change this if you'd like. Also, indicate the new URL, that is, the page to which to jump. The jump will be automatic.

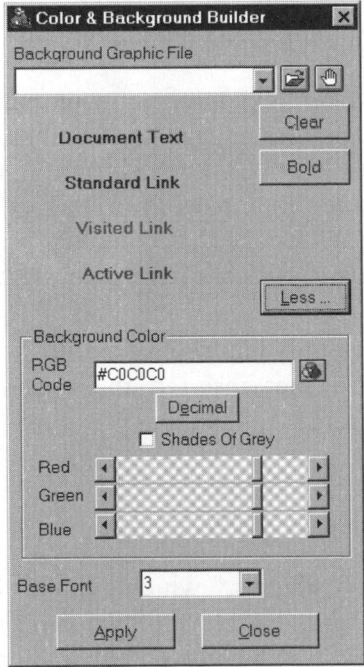

Figure 20.10 The extended Color & Background Builder, showing the options for choosing a background color.

When you're done choosing these document formats, click the HTML tab to return to your document.

BUILDING YOUR DOCUMENT

Once you've defined the page background, you're ready to start building your document. Here are some tips to help you take full advantage of Hot-Dog's convenient tools. You won't believe how many cool features are to be found in this program!

Instead of entering <P> and <BR> tags all the time, just press Alt + Enter for <P> or Shift + Enter for <BR>. To enter the <P> tag properly, with start and stop tags, select the paragraph text and press Alt + Enter.

Use the Resource Manager's Faves Page

Here, you can store favorite text (such as your mailto: address for e-mail replies, disclaimers, and other standard stuff that you enter into just about every page you write), frequently chosen tags, and frequently used Web links. In my opinion, this feature alone pays for HotDog, it's that useful. To add items to the panels, display a page that contains the item you want to add, hold down the Shift key, and click the item with the right mouse button.

To remove tags you've entered, just select the text and click the button that inserted the tags. Clicking it again will remove them.

Add Text Effects

This is one of HotDog's "Snaglets," which can best be described as utilities that add zing to your pages. The Text Effects Snaglet enables you to enter some heading text into the dialog box shown in Figure 20.11, and then choose from a variety of text effects such as Wavy, Spread, Scroller, Jump-Man, Mexican Wave, and Bounce. You can also choose fonts and font sizes. How is this done? This dialog box actually creates, compiles, and inserts a compiled Java applet on your page. Is this cool or what?

Use the List Tool

Need to enter a list? Position the cursor where you want the list to appear, and click the button entitled Create or Edit a List of Items, located on the floating toolbar between the two main panels. (It's also on the Elements toolbar.) You'll see the Create List Element dialog box (Figure 20.12). Identify the type of list that you want to create, and then click Add to add items. Click OK when you're done.

Color HTML Tags for Visibility

To make editing easier, you can add color to HTML tags. On the Elements toolbar, locate and click Color All HTML Tags Now. That's just what it does!

Check Your Spelling

One of the tremendous advantages of using an HTML editor (rather than a text editor) is that you can check your spelling. A text editor can't help you here because it doesn't know how to ignore the HTML tags, and you go nuts clicking the Ignore button. To check your spelling in HotDog, choose

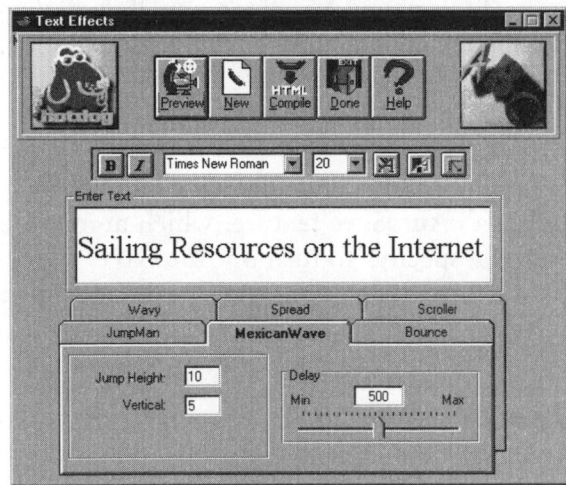

Figure 20.11 You can add jazzy text effects with this Snaglet.

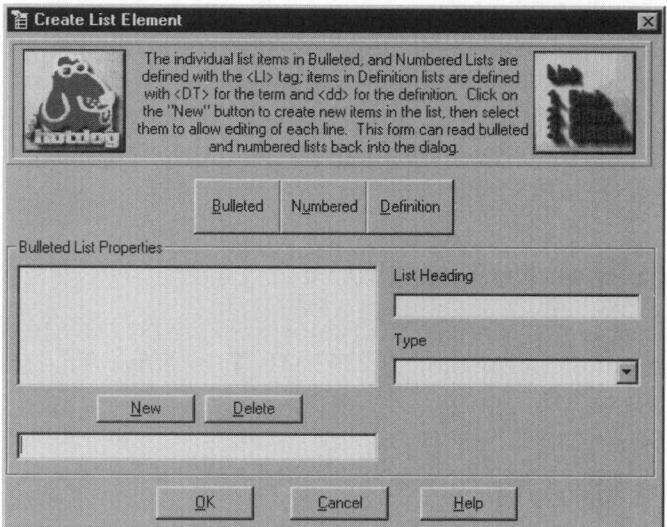

Figure 20.12 This dialog box enables you to create a bulleted, numbered, or definition list in short order.

Spell Check from the Tools menu. You'll see a spelling dialog box that's similar to a word processor's spelling checker (see Figure 20.13).

Use AutoSave

To protect yourself from losing work due to a power outage or computer crash, turn on HotDog's AutoSave feature, which automatically saves your file at intervals that you specify. To turn on AutoSave, choose Options from the Tools menu, click Save/Start, and type a save interval in the AutoSave text box.

View Color Choices

If you or HotDog has entered color codes in your document, you can see what the color looks like. Just double-click the color code to select it, click the right mouse button, and choose Edit Color from the pop-up menu. You can also use this to change a color.

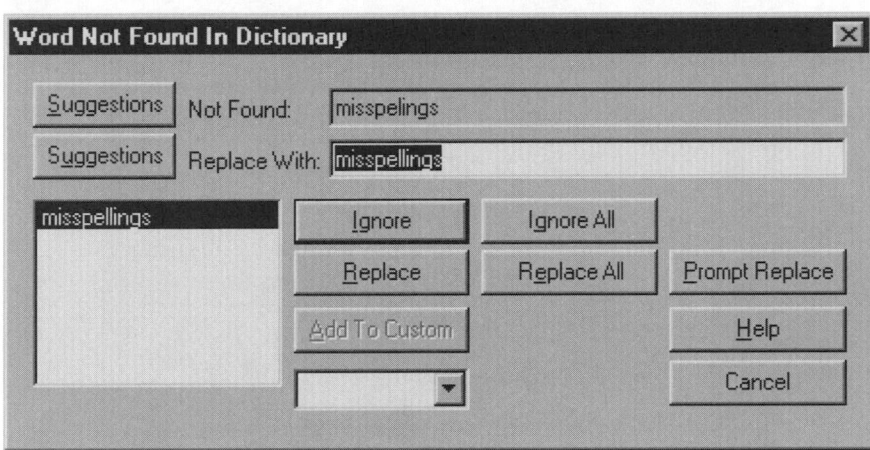

Figure 20.13 HotDog's spelling checker knows how to ignore the HTML tags.

Switch to Rover to See How Your Document Looks

While you're working, you should frequently switch to Rover to see how your document is coming along. This window enables you to see the way your page looks when viewed by a browser (see Figure 20.14). If you have more than one document open, you can use Rover's navigation tools to see how the other documents look.

By default, HotDog is configured to work with Microsoft Internet Explorer (MSIE), and Rover uses OLE (object linking and embedding) to bring MSIE's browser functions into the Rover window. If there's something wrong with your MSIE installation, however, HotDog may crash. If this happens, try configuring HotDog to work with a different browser. To change the default preview browser, choose Options from the Tools menu, click File Dirs, and choose a new browser in the Preview Browser field. On my system, HotDog works much better with Netscape.

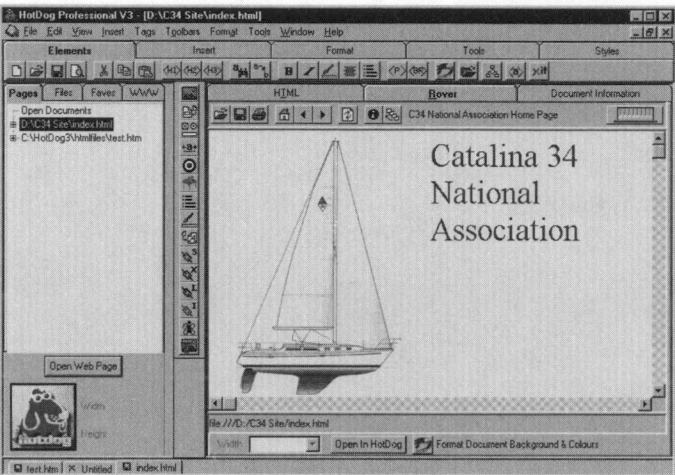

Figure 20.14   Rover displays your document as it appears in a browser.

Use the Documents Bar to Switch Documents

When you have more than one file open, you can quickly switch from one document to another by using the Documents bar, which is located at the bottom of the screen. Each opened document is represented by a tab. To see the document, just click the tab.

If a document has changed and you haven't saved the changes, the tab is colored red. Unchanged documents are shown with a floppy disk.

Use Special Characters

If you need to add special characters to your document, position the insertion point where you want the special character to appear, and choose Special Characters from the View menu or just press F7. You'll see a list of special characters. Double-click the one you want. HotDog adds the appropriate code to your document.

Time to Quit?

You're working on a big project, but hey, it's 3 A.M. The next time you start HotDog, you want to continue working where you left off. You can do precisely this by choosing the Restore Last Session option in HotDog's Option dialog box, accessible by choosing Options from the Tools menu. You'll find the Restore Last Session option on the Save/Start page.

WORKING WITH FONTS

HotDog takes full advantage of the new font-defining capabilities of HTML 3.2. You can choose a base font size for your whole document. You can also format selected text with a typeface, font size, text color, and a whole string of emphasis options.

Choosing a Base Font

To choose a base font for your document, click the Document Information tab, and click Format Document Background & Colors. Click More to bring more options into view. At the bottom of this dialog box, you'll find the Base Font Size box. Here, you can choose a default base font size using one of the relative font sizes (1 through 7). Click Close to confirm.

Choosing Font Attributes for Selected Text

To choose font attributes for selected text, do one of the following:

- Click the right mouse button. From the pop-up menu, you can choose Bold, italics, or a color.

  or

- Click the Format toolbar tab if necessary to bring it into view, and click the Bold or Italic button. You can also click the Instant Color Editor button to choose a color for your text.

  or

- Click Format on the menu bar. From the Format menu, you can choose Bold, Italics, Underline, Blinking, or Big First Letter.

or

- Choose Font from the Format menu, or just press F2. You'll see the Format Text dialog box, shown in Figure 20.15. Here, you can choose a font typeface, font size, color, and any of the available emphases.

 Thanks to HTML 3.2, you can change font sizes within a line. A cool use of this is the Big First Letter option, found in the Format menu. To use this feature, select a word and choose this option. HotDog adds the codes automatically.

ADDING HYPERLINKS

You can add hyperlinks to your HotDog document in any of the following ways:

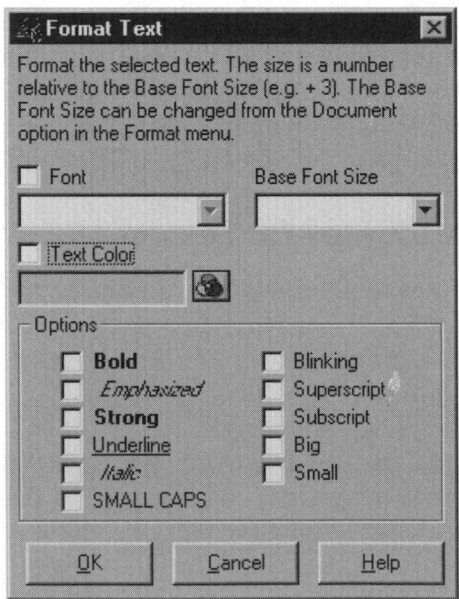

Figure 20.15   Press F2 to format selected text with any of these attributes.

- **Link to another local page** This command inserts a *relative URL* (such as <A HREF="readme.html">Read this now!</A>) into your document.

- **Link to a target** This command enables you to link to a target that you've previously defined. You must first define the target.

- **Link to an external page** This command displays the Build External Link dialog box, which gives you all the tools needed to build an external link.

- **Create a simple link** This command displays a simplified version of the Build External Link dialog box; it's useful when the link doesn't need any fancy extras. You also use this command to link to frames (more about that later).

Let's start with building an external link.

Creating an External Link

To create an external link, type the anchor text, select this text, and click Create a Link to Another Web Page (this button is on the Insert toolbar; it has a little X on it). Alternatively, after typing the anchor text and selecting it, you can choose Jump to a Document on Another System, or press Ctrl + H. You'll see the Build External Hypertext Link dialog box, shown in Figure 20.16.

To build the hyperlink, fill in the dialog box areas as follows:

Resource Type	From the drop-down list box, choose the appropriate resource type. For Web documents, the default choice—http—is correct.
Host	Type the host system's domain name here (such as hummer.cmsnet.org).
Port (optional)	If the URL you're typing has a port address, type it here. Skip this box for Web documents.
Path	Type the path name here.
Filename	Type the file name here.
Target	If you would like the browser to scroll to an internal link within this document, type the name of the link here.

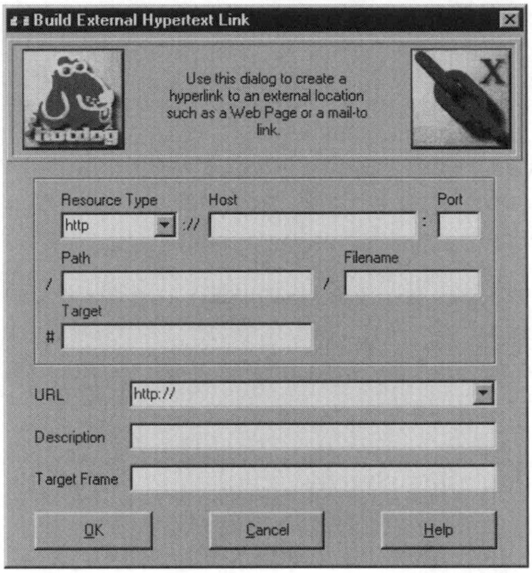

Figure 20.16   Build External Hypertext Link dialog box.

Description	In this box, type the text that you want to appear on-screen.
Target Frame	Type the name of the frame to which you want to link.

When you're done building the hyperlink, click OK. HotDog inserts the hyperlink in your document.

ADDING INTERNAL LINKS

An internal link consists of two components:

- **Internal Hyperlink**   An <A> tag that, when clicked, jumps to a specific location in the same document, called a *target*.

- **Target**   The place to which the link jumps. Each target has a name, defined by the <A NAME> tag.

Creating internal hyperlinks with HotDog couldn't be easier, thanks to an automatic feature that compiles a list of the targets you've created.

To add internal links to your document, follow these steps:

1. Select the text to which you want to jump.

2. Click the Target button. You'll see the Input dialog box.

3. Type the target name, and click OK. You'll see the <A NAME> tag in your document, with your target name inserted (for example, <A NAME = "Jump_Here">.

4. Repeat steps 1 through 4 to define additional targets, if desired.

5. Place the insertion point where you want the first internal hyperlink to appear.

6. Click Link to Another Position within this Document (on the Insert toolbar) or press Ctrl + K. You'll see the Select Hypertext Target dialog box. Note that HotDog has automatically listed all the targets you've defined.

7. Select a target. In the Description of Link box, type the text that you want to appear on-screen.

8. Click OK to create the internal hyperlink.

9. Repeat steps 5 through 9 to define additional internal hyperlinks, if you wish.

Creating a Simple Link

To create a hyperlink quickly, type the anchor text, select this text, and click Create a Simple Link to Another Web Page (on the Insert toolbar), or just press F4. You'll see the Insert URL dialog box. In the URL field, type the URL for the hyperlink and click OK.

HotDog remembers all the URLs you've added to your documents. To add a recently used URL, follow the above steps to open the Insert URL dialog box, and click the down arrow next to the URL list box. Choose a URL and click OK.

The Insert URL dialog box also enables you to create a local link; just click the open folder icon to choose a local file. If you feel you need the additional options in the Build External Link dialog box, click the hand icon to open this dialog box.

Creating Links using Drag and Drop

Absolutely the easiest and coolest way to create hyperlinks with HotDog is to drag them from the Resource Manager. Use the Resource Manager's Pages, Files, Faves, or WWW tabs to display a URL that you want to insert, and just drag it to your document. When you've positioned the pointer where you want the link to appear, release the mouse button. You can quickly build a huge list of links this way.

ADDING IMAGES

HotDog gives you two ways to add inline images to your document:

- **Insert Image dialog box**   This dialog box, shown in Figure 20.17, lets you add an image quickly. In the Image File box, type the graphic's location. Alternatively, you can use the folder icon to browse your local system, or the hand icon to build an external hyperlink. If you wish to link the graphic to a document, use the Document To Launch box. To access the Insert Image dialog box, click Put an Image in Your Document (on the Insert toolbar).

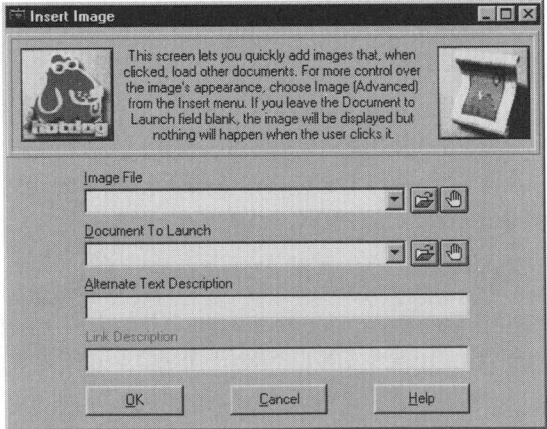

Figure 20.17   Insert Image dialog box.

- **Image Properties dialog box** This dialog box, shown in Figure 20.18, provides the full range of HTML 3.2 image attributes. To access the Image Properties dialog box, choose Set Advanced Options for Inline Images (on the Insert toolbar) or press Alt + M.

Inserting an Image

To insert an image without advanced options, do the following:

1. Position the cursor where you want the image to appear, and click Put an Image in Your Document (on the Insert toolbar).

2. In the Image File box, type the image file name or click the folder icon to browse for the file. You can also click the down arrow to choose the file name from a list of recently used images. If you'd like to link to an external image, click the hand icon and create the link using the Build External Hypertext Link dialog box.

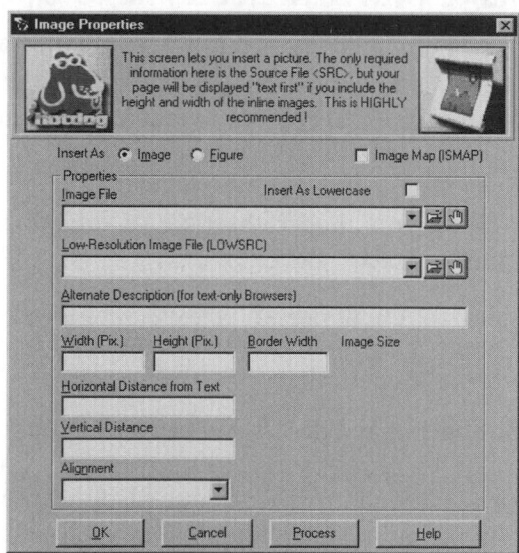

Figure 20.18 Image Properties dialog box.

3. If you'd like this image to function as a hyperlink, type the name of the document in the Document To Launch box (or click the folder icon to browse for a local file). If you'd like to link to an external document, click the hand icon and create the link using the Build External Hyperlink dialog box.

4. In the Alternate Text Description box, type alternate text to display for users who have text-only browsers (or people browsing with graphics switched off).

5. Click OK to confirm.

Inserting an Image with Drag and Drop

By far the easiest way to add images to your document is to drag them from the Resource Manager in just the same way that you drag hyperlinks into your document. Try it!

Inserting an Image with Advanced Image Options

If you would like to insert your image using advanced options, do so by clicking Set Advanced Options for Inline Images. You'll see the Image Properties dialog box, shown in Figure 20.18. Here's what you can do with this dialog box:

- **Insert As**   Here, you choose the type of image: an inline image, a figure, or an image map (ISMAP).

- **Image File**   Type the graphic's location. Alternatively, you can use the folder icon to browse your local system, or the hand icon to build an external hyperlink.

- **Low-Resolution Image File**   Some browsers support a quick download feature in which a low-resolution version of an image is downloaded first, followed by the higher-resolution version (which is "painted" on top of the lower-resolution version after the rest of the document is downloaded). If you've created a lower-resolution version of the image, type the graphic's location here. Alternatively, you can use the folder icon to browse your local system, or the hand icon to build an external hyperlink.

- **Alternate Description**   Type alternate text here to display if your page is accessed by somebody using a text-only browser or a browser with the graphics switched off.

- **Width**   To define the width of the graphic, type a number in pixels. Defining the size can increase downloading speed since the browser doesn't have to calculate the image size.

- **Height**   To define the height of the graphic, type a number in pixels. Defining the size can increase downloading speed since the browser doesn't have to calculate the image size.

- **Horizontal Distance from Text**   To control the space between the graphic and the nearest text horizontally, type a number (in pixels). You can use this to prevent text from appearing right next to a graphic.

- **Vertical Distance**   To control the space between the graphic and the nearest text vertically, type a number (in pixels). You can use this to prevent text from appearing right next to a graphic.

- **Border Width**   To specify a border size, type the border width here, in pixels. To suppress the border (especially valuable if you're making the image a hyperlink), type 0 (zero) here.

- **Alignment**   To align the image, choose one of the options in the drop-down list box.

To add the graphic to your document, just click OK.

 If you've added an image and want to change any of these attributes, select the entire <IMG> tag and choose Set Advanced Options for Inline Images. You'll see the current options. Make your changes and click OK.

Processing Images

A very cool feature of HotDog is the Process button in the Image Properties dialog box. If you've defined a graphic, press this button to see the Image Processing dialog box, shown in Figure 20.19.

A lot of the stuff in this box won't make sense to you until you've read Chapter 23, but do bear in mind that HotDog can perform a lot of the image-processing tasks that go into effective use of still graphics on the Web, including the following:

- Converting graphics from JPEG to GIF and vice versa, to capitalize on each file format's respective strengths.

- Defining one of the colors in the graphic as transparent, so that it blends with whatever background color you're using.

- Specifying the JPEG compression level.

After you've read Chapter 23, come back and try this dialog box with one of your graphics. It's a very nice feature.

While we're on the subject of graphics, note that HotDog can handle another of the advanced image applications discussed in Chapter 23, GIF animation. After you've read Chapter 23 and tried out GIF Construction Set or some other GIF animation tool, try HotDog's. To access HotDog's

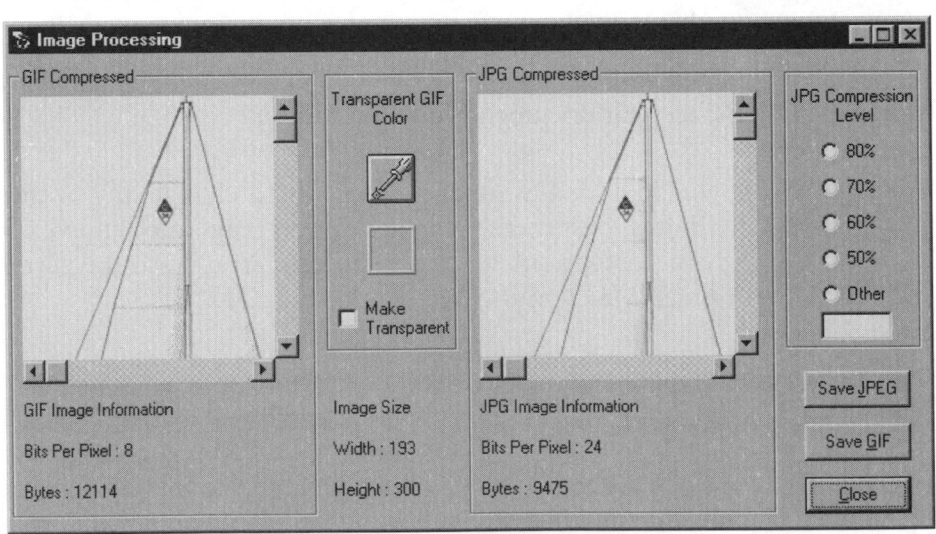

Figure 20.19   The Image Processing dialog box.

GIF animation tool, click Create Animations for Your Web Page (on the Insert toolbar). Yet another feature is client-side imagemaps, discussed in Chapter 24. Check out that chapter, and then try it with HotDog. To create a client-side imagemap with HotDog, click Create a Client-side Image Map (on the Insert toolbar).

CREATING TABLES

If you've fussed with the difficult table tags (see Chapter 18), you'll appreciate HotDog's WYSIWYG ("what you see is what you get") table editor.

To create a table, position the insertion point where you want the table to appear, and click Create a Table for Your Web Page (on the Insert toolbar); you'll see the Create Table dialog box, shown in Figure 20.20. The enormously cool thing about this dialog box is the Sample Table area, which

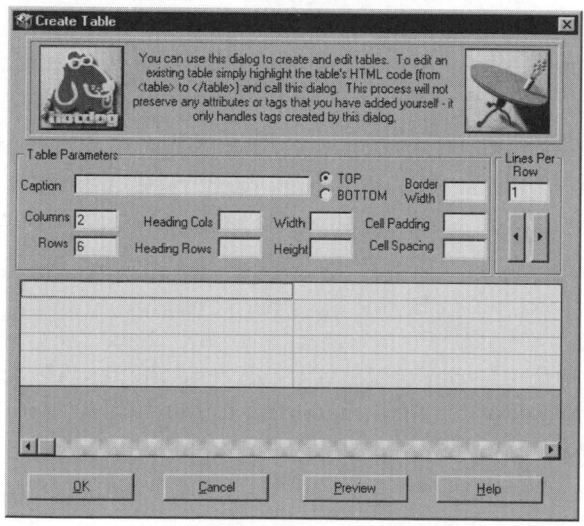

Figure 20.20   Create Table dialog box.

shows the effects of your choices on-screen. The dialog box has the following areas:

Caption	To add a caption to your table, type the caption here. Click TOP or BOTTOM to position the caption.
Border Width	Type a border width, in pixels. Type 0 (zero) to suppress borders.
Columns	Type the number of columns.
Rows	Type the number of rows.
Heading Cols	Type the number of heading columns.
Heading Rows	Type the number of heading rows.
Width	To define the default width of the columns, type a percentage of the screen width here. To change the width of an individual column, just drag the column border with the mouse.
Height	To define the default height of the rows, type a percentage of the screen width here.
Cell Padding	To add additional space within the table cells, type a number (in pixels) here. This isn't shown in the sample table.
Cell Spacing	To add additional space between cells, type a number (in pixels) here. This isn't shown in the sample table.
Border Width	To add a border, type a border width here. To make sure the table has no border, type 0 (zero).
Lines Per Row	Click the arrows to increase or decrease the number of lines per row.

Once you've defined your table, you can type the text directly in the sample table. Click Preview to see what your table looks like. Click OK when you're finished.

I can't span rows or columns!
That's right. HotDog doesn't have an equivalent of the ROWSPAN or COLSPAN attributes discussed in Chapter

18. You can add these manually after creating your table with the Create Table dialog box.

 To edit an existing table, just select all of the table tags that HotDog inserted, and choose Create or Edit a Table for Your Web Page.

CREATING FORMS

HotDog's forms tools are every bit as convenient as the table features—and if you're planning to add forms to your document (see Chapter 16), you'll appreciate using these tools. Remember, forms won't work unless they're directed to a script on your server. See Chapter 16 for details.

Here's a brief overview of the procedure you use to add a <FORM> section to your document:

1. Position the insertion point where you want the form to appear.

2. Click Build a Form for Your Document (on the Insert toolbar). You'll see the Define Form Elements dialog box, shown in Figure 20.21. In this dialog box, you choose the form element you want to create and then make choices in the panel at the bottom of the box.

3. Click a form element, and determine the attributes you want to use. Review Chapter 16 to find out what these attributes do.

4. When you're finished choosing the elements that you want to appear within your form, click OK. You'll see the Create Form dialog box, shown in Figure 20.22. Choose the <FORM> attributes you want for your form and click OK to create it.

The Create Form dialog box has the following areas:

- **Method** (required)   You can choose GET or POST. Note that most scripts require the POST method.

- **URL to Send Data to (ACTION)** (required)   Type the location of the script here. Alternatively, use the down arrow to select from the scripts that HotDog has found on your system or use the hand icon to link to a script on another system.

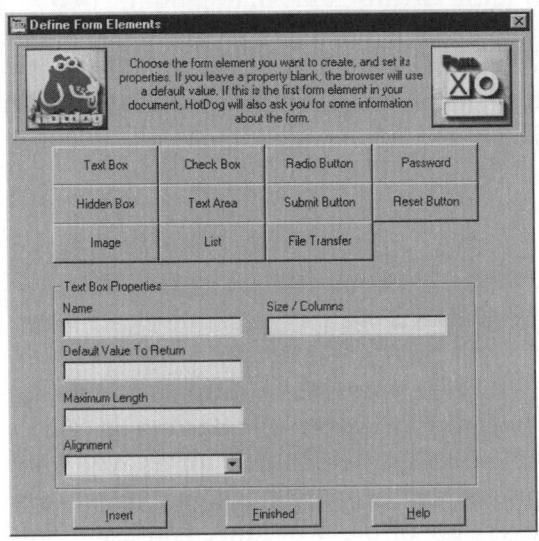

Figure 20.21   Define Form Elements dialog box.

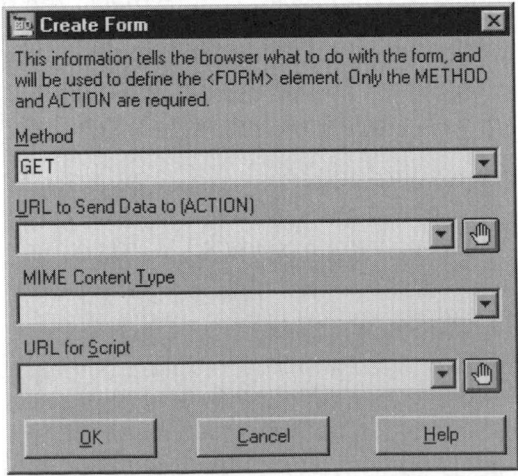

Figure 20.22   Create Form dialog box.

- **MIME Content Type** There's no need to change the default setting here.

- **URL for Script** HTML 3.2 provides the ability to download a script to the user's machine, which can then be processed locally. Skip this because it's not widely implemented.

CREATING FRAMES

One of the best features of HotDog is the program's Frames Snaglet, which enables you to create frames using a visual metaphor. If you tried creating frames with HTML (see Chapter 18), I'm sure you'll agree that it's tough to visualize what's going on. The Frames Snaglet makes frames easy by showing you a visual representation of your frames as you're creating them and then generating the necessary HTML code on the fly.

 If you haven't already done so, skim the basics of frames in Chapter 18. You don't really need to fully understand all the HTML code that goes into making frames, but a nodding acquaintance doesn't hurt.

Creating Documents to Include in Your Frames

Before you get started, plan how many total documents you are going to include in your framed document. (Each frame panel is actually a separate HTML document.) If you'd like to experiment with frames now, go ahead and create three simple documents called doc1.html, doc2.html, and doc3.html.

The first of these documents will serve as the master frame document. It's very important to delete the <BODY>...</BODY> tags from this document. The <FRAMESET>...</FRAMESET> tags take the place of these. If you leave the <BODY> tags in, your frames won't work.

In the second and third documents, place some identifying text. In the second document (doc2.html), type (within the <BODY> tags) "This is the first frame." In the third document (doc3.html), type "This is the second frame." It's OK for these documents to have <BODY> tags, but not the master frame document.

Adding Frames to Your Document

To add frames to your document, do the following:

1. Open the document that's going to serve as the master document for your frames. (If you're trying this as an experiment, open the first of the blank documents that you created above.)

2. Position the insertion point after the closing </HEAD> tag of the master frame document.

3. Click Add Frames to Your Document. You'll see the New Frames Setup window, shown in Figure 20.23. Here, you determine the overall frame structure. You can add additional subframes later, but first you must decide whether your overall frame layout will be based on columns (vertical partitions) or rows (horizontal partitions).

4. Click Columns to order your frames by column, or Row to order them by row. Indicate the number of total required columns or rows in the bottom part of the dialog box, and click OK. You'll see

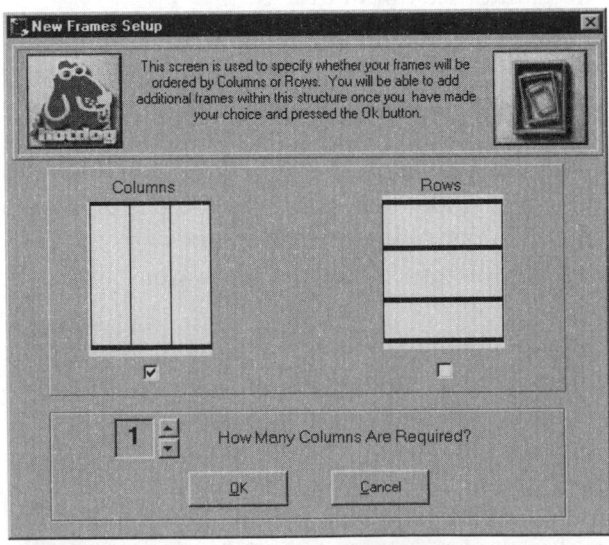

Figure 20.23   Begin by choosing to order your frames by columns or rows.

the Creating Frames dialog box, shown in Figure 20.24. Here, you specify the names and URLs of the documents to include in your overall layout. You can also add and size additional frames.

5. If you'd like to add additional frames within the basic structure, you can do so now. Select the frame that you want to divide, and click New. You can also size frames by dragging the borders.

6. Click Frame 1, and supply a name and URL. If you're trying the experiment recommended in the previous section, add doc2.html to Frame 1, and doc3.html to Frame 2. Repeat this until you've selected names and URLs for all the visible frames.

7. Click Compile HTML.

8. Click Done.

9. From the File menu, choose Preview Document (you can't use Rover to preview frames). You'll see your basic frame structure, like the one shown in Figure 20.25.

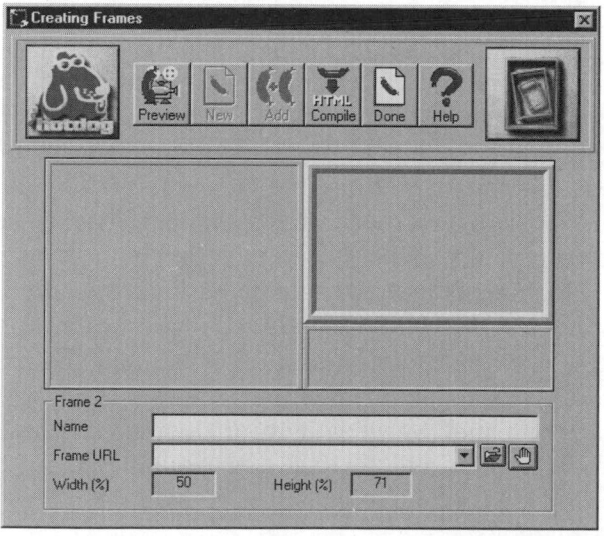

Figure 20.24 You can add frames, adjust frame size, and assign documents to each frame in the Creating Frames dialog box.

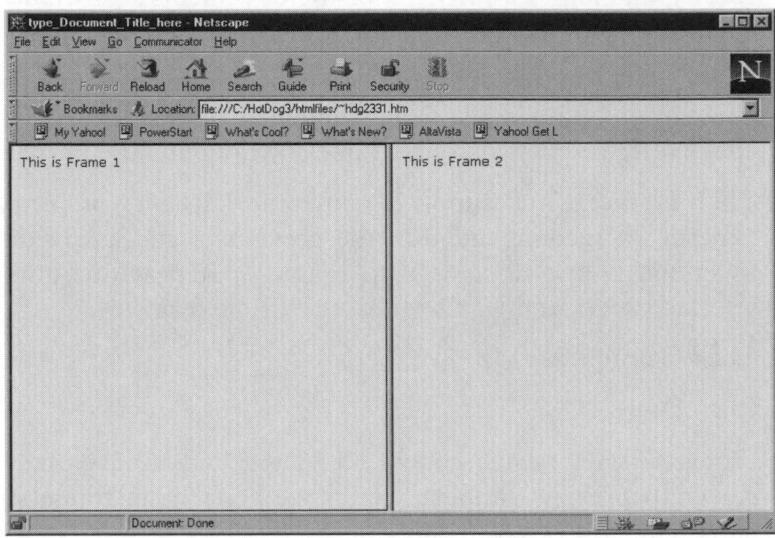

Figure 20.25   Here's what the basic structure looks like in a browser preview.

Adding Links to Frames

One of the most common uses for frames is to have one frame serve as a panel of navigation aids, while another panel is used to display targeted documents. To do this, decide which panel is going to serve as the panel that stays put; this is the panel you'll use for your navigation aids. Once you've decided which panel to use, open the document that's inserted into this panel and add hyperlinks to the documents that you want to display. For each of these documents, modify the hyperlink by adding a TARGET attribute that names the window in which you want the document to appear. (When you created your frames, you named the frame as well as supplied a default URL for that frame.)

Suppose that the panel where you want documents to appear is called "Display." Here's how to add TARGET attributes that make these hyperlinks show up in the Display frame:

```
<A HREF="fun.html" TARGET="Display">Fun things to do
</A>

<A HREF="about.html" TARGET="Display">About this
site</A>
```

 There's much more you can do with frames, but you'll need to tweak the existing HTML code within the HTML window to do so. Review Chapter 18 and tweak away!

FROM HERE

- When you're done with your page, it's time to publish it—and publicize it. Find out how in Chapter 21.

- Add exciting multimedia to your pages! Get started with Chapter 22.

Chapter

21

Testing, Publishing, and Publicizing Your Site

S o! You're done with your page! Now it's time for three important tasks: testing, publishing, and publicizing. All three are essential parts of Web publishing.

TESTING YOUR PAGE

How do you test your Web page? In every way possible. Begin by testing your pages on your local system. Use your browser's File Open command to open your files, and give them a real workout. Here's a list of hints:

- **Try every hyperlink.** If one of them doesn't work now, it's not going to work after you've uploaded your pages to your Web server.

♦   Test, test, and test before you upload. Test with lots of different browsers and on different platforms.

♦   Uploading your files with an FTP client is a lot easier than learning UNIX.

♦   In order for your site to serve its purpose, you have to advertise.

♦   If you can, send e-mail directly to people you know will be interested in your site. Direct electronic mail gets a great response rate.

♦   Post announcements where you know people interested in your site's topic will see them. Mailing lists are best; Usenet newsgroups are good, too.

♦   Make sure you fill out the URL-addition forms at any search engines, including Lycos, that accept site submissions.

♦   Submit your site's information to the maintainers of the various What's New sites on the Web, including those run by Netscape and NCSA Mosaic.

♦   Post a notice to comp.infosystems.www.announce.

- **Try different browsers.**   See what your pages look like on different browsers. If you don't have any other browsers, download them, install them, and try them out. Minimally, you should see what your page looks like with Netscape Navigator and Microsoft Internet Explorer. You'll be surprised to find that, even with these two relatively well-standardized browsers, there are differences!

- **Try browsing your pages with graphics turned off.** Did you remember to put alternate text in place of graphics?

- **Try viewing your pages on a Macintosh.**   Copy your Web pages to a floppy disk and find a friendly Macintosh owner who's willing to examine them using the Macintosh version of popular browsers. You may be surprised to find that graphics that you thought fit the page don't quite fit on a Mac screen, which offers only 72 dpi (contrasted with the standard PC resolution of 96 dpi). Consider shrinking your graphics to accommodate Mac users!

PUBLISHING YOUR PAGE

Unless you're running your own Web server, which is pretty unlikely, chances are you're planning to publish your page with the help of a friendly local Internet service provider (ISP). This section covers the general process of uploading your page (as well as all associated files, including graphics) to your ISP's server. To figure out how to do this exactly, though, you'll need to talk to your ISP and get specific instructions.

 Most ISPs give you some Web publishing space for free along with your Internet access. Be aware that this is limited, both in storage space allotted and bandwidth consumed. If your page starts getting so many hits that it's tying up your ISP's server, you'll hear from them! If you're publishing a Web site for a company or organization that's willing to devote some modest funding to Web publishing, you may wish to begin with an ISP that offers a decent amount of storage space and bandwidth for a reasonable, flat monthly fee. How much should you expect to pay? That depends, of course, on how much you're publishing and how many hits you expect to get, but figure on a minimum of around $50 per month.

To upload your files to your Internet service provider, you have several options. You can use an FTP program, such as Cute FTP or FTP Explorer. Alternatively, you can use HotDog or Netscape Page Composer, both of which enable you to upload your pages from within the program. Here, we'll take a look at uploading files with FTP Explorer, an FTP program for Windows 95/NT, and HotDog Professional, which is discussed in Chapter 20.

What You'll Need From Your Service Provider

In order to upload your Web page to your ISP, you'll need the following information:

- **Exact FTP address**   This isn't a URL, but rather a computer name, such as blowfish.cranberry.org.
- **Login name**   This may differ from the login name you use for Internet access.

- **Password**   Again, this may differ from the password you use for Internet access.

- **Path to your directory**   This will look something like the path names you see on your Windows system.

Be sure to obtain this information before you try uploading your files.

   On most servers, there's a default file name that's used for the welcome page of a site. Normally, this is index.html, but on some servers it's something else, such as default.html. Call your ISP to find out what the default welcome page file name should be, and rename your welcome page with this file name. After you upload your page with the default file name, people won't have to type the file name to access your site. For example, if your welcome page is http://www.blow-fish.org/~davis/welcome.html, they'll only have to type http://www.blowfish.org/~davis/.

Things to Remember about Relative URLs

If your Web publishing efforts include more than one HTML document, or any support files (such as sounds or graphics), make sure that you have referred to these files correctly. Ideally, you've used *relative URLs*, which don't specify an exact location for a file but rather specify the relative location within whatever computer's directory structure that the files happen to find themselves in.

Did you put all of your files—the HTML files, graphics, Java classes, the works—into one big directory, and used nothing but relative URLs to refer to them? No problemo. Just upload the whole collection to a single directory on your server. The problem with this is that it's hard to maintain a site where everything's thrown into one directory.

You may have decided to set up your site with separate directories for images, sounds, and the like. If so, you need to understand how relative URLs work in such a case. Suppose you created your Web pages in the following Windows directory:

    c:\docs\htmldocs

Within this directory, you created the following subdirectories:

```
c:\docs\htmldocs\sounds
c:\docs\htmldocs\graphics
c:\docs\htmldocs\Java_classes
```

Your site has several interlinked pages, and you keep all of them in c:\docs\htmldocs. Because you created the links using relative URLs, these pages work well when you test them locally with your browser. The links to the other pages look like this:

```
<A HREF="info.html">Information about this site</A>

<A HREF="welcome.html">Return to the Welcome Page</A>
```

What about the sounds, graphics and Java classes? With relative URLs, they're expressed like this:

```
<A HREF="/sounds/raspberry.wav">Welcome Sound</A>

<A HREF="/sounds/waringblender.wav">Peaceful Sound</A>
```

Note that the relative URLs express the sounds' location *relative* to the referring page, which is one directory above.

Now the trick here is that, if you've structured your relative URLs this way, you have to make sure that your pages are stored in the same directory structure on your server. In other words, within your home directory (the one in which you put your HTML pages), you'll need to create subdirectories, as follows:

```
/sounds
/graphics
/Java_classes
```

What's more, you'll need to make sure that each file gets uploaded to its correct directory.

 **I uploaded my files to the server, but none of the links work right!**
And now you know why. If you throw a bunch of files into one big directory when they're expecting to live in subdirectories, a lot of the links won't work. Another possibility: did you move any of the pages into different directories? If so, you may have murdered all or some of the relative link relationships.

 Due to the problems caused by relative URLs, I personally prefer to use absolute URLs. I plan out the directory structure I'm going to create on my server, and then create my hyperlinks with absolute URLs (in other words, "http://watt.seas.virginia.edu/~bp/c34/about.html" rather than "/c34/about.html"). That way, the link still works, even if I mindlessly move the referring page without thinking through the consequences.

Uploading Your Files with FTP Explorer

When you're uploading your Web page to an ISP, there's a pretty good chance that you'll be dealing with a UNIX computer on the other end. Unless you really want to take the time to learn how to deal with UNIX commands, it's wise to use an FTP client program such as FTP Explorer, one of my favorites. With an FTP client program, you don't have to use UNIX commands for such operations as changing directories, moving files, and deleting files.

FTP Explorer (www.ftpx.com) is especially appealing for Windows 95/NT users because it mimics the interface of Windows Explorer. In other words, you can use familiar skills to publish your Web files and maintain your site once you've uploaded your pages. The program is free for home or educational use; registration for other uses is only $30.

Creating Your Connection

To upload your Web pages and support files with FTP Explorer, begin by creating your connection. Here's how:

1. Start FTP Explorer. You'll see the main FTP Explorer window. The program automatically starts the Connect dialog box, shown in Figure 21.1. This dialog box will show information about one of the program's built-in FTP connections.

2. Click Add. This blanks most of the fields.

3. In the Profile Name box, type a name for the server to which you're uploading. You can use any name you wish—this is just for your convenience.

4. In the Host Address box, type the official Internet name (domain name) of the computer to which you're uploading. This will be a computer name with two, three, or more parts, separated by dots (such as www.isp.net).

5. In the Login box, type the login name that your ISP told you to use.

6. In the Password box, type the password that your ISP told you to use.

7. In the Initial Path box, type the path directory to your Web publishing space. You need to get this exact path name from your ISP.

8. Click Save to save this profile.

Uploading Your Web Page

Now you can upload your page and support files, following these directions:

1. In the Connect dialog box, choose the connection that you just created by highlighting its name in the connection list (left panel).

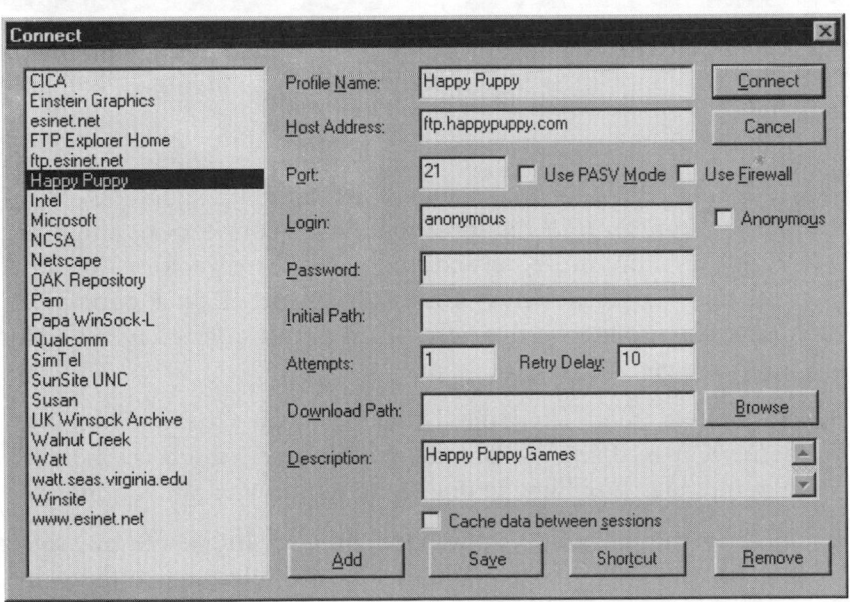

Figure 21.1 FTP Explorer's Connect dialog box enables you to specify uploading information.

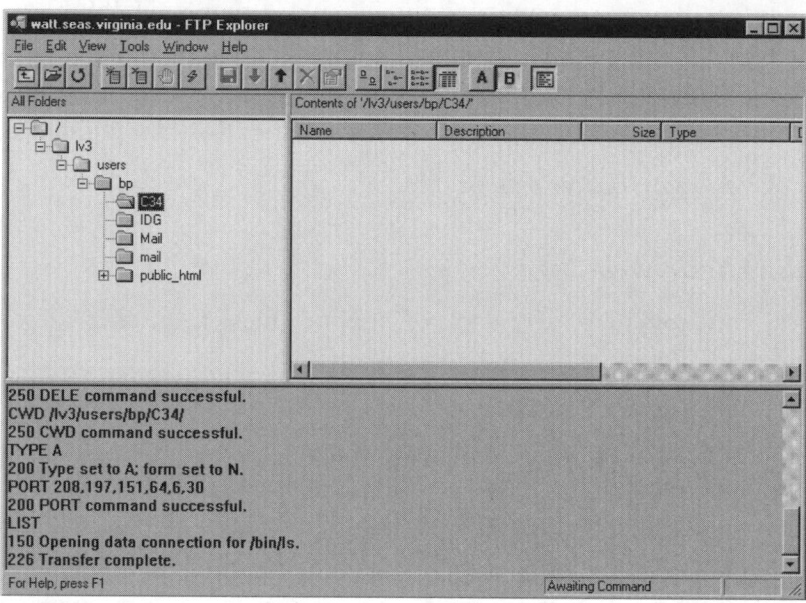

Figure 21.2 FTP Explorer makes your Web space look like a Windows disk.

2. Click Connect. FTP Explorer makes the connection, and you see a Windows Explorer-type window, with the directories on one side and the current directory's files on the other. In Figure 21.2, you don't see any files in the right panel because you haven't uploaded anything yet.

3. To upload files, click the Upload button (the one with the up arrow). You'll see the Upload dialog box, which is essentially an Open dialog box like the ones that Windows applications use.

4. Display the files that you want to upload. In the file list, select the file you want to upload. If you want to select more than one file, hold down the Ctrl key and click the files you want. To select all the files, press Ctrl + A. (Note that there's a limit to the number of files you can select this way; this is imposed by Windows, not FTP Explorer.)

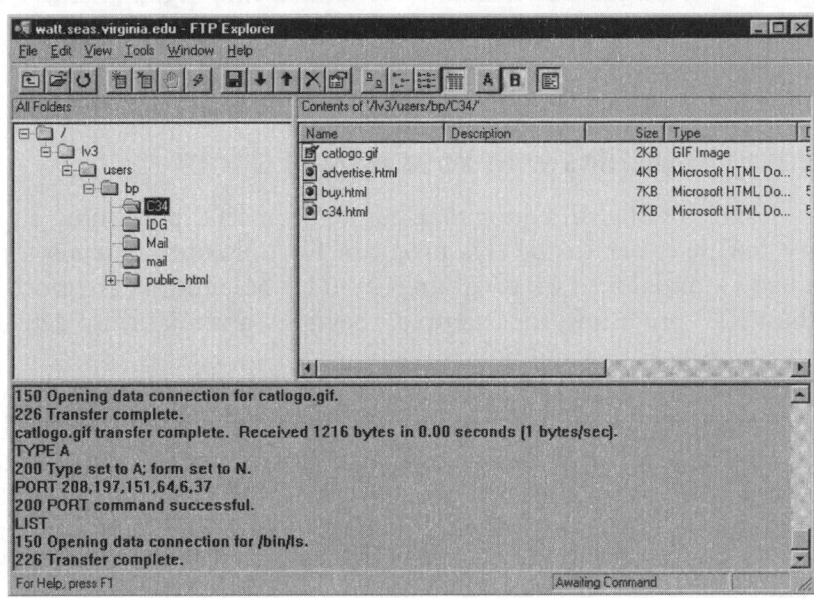

Figure 21.3 After you've uploaded your files, you see them in the right panel.

5. Click Open to begin uploading the files. In the bottom panel, you'll see the dialogue that FTP Explorer has established with the server. When you see Transfer Complete, the files have been copied successfully, and you see them in the file list panel (see Figure 21.3).

That's all you need to do to publish your files, with most ISPs. You've copied them to a directory that's accessible to the Web server. When an external request is made for these files, the server will dish them out. You've gone public! You'd better do some more testing, though, to make sure everything looks good. Repeat the tests you ran on your local drive to make sure all the links are still working and that everything looks good. Don't forget to try different browsers!

 You can use FTP Explorer to manage your remote Web site. To delete an unwanted file, just select it and press Delete. To add a subdirectory, highlight the directory in which you

want the subdirectory to appear and choose New Folder from the File menu. To rename a file, highlight the file and choose Rename from the File menu.

Uploading Your Files with Your HTML Editor

If you're using an HTML editor that has built-in FTP publishing support, you may find it easier to use this program for uploading purposes rather than to use a standalone FTP program. Good HTML editors are more Web-savvy than FTP programs; for example, they may automatically detect that a page contains graphics and upload these, too.

HotDog Professional goes much further. If you create a project for all the Web pages and supporting documents that go into a site, HotDog will keep track of all the relative directory relationships and upload the files to the correct directories on your Web server automatically. The program will even create the remote directories for you, if they don't exist. This feature really comes in handy when you're creating a huge site with lots of files. You'll find it convenient, for example, to make separate directories to hold your graphics, Java classes, sounds, and other support files.

Creating a Project

If you want to take full advantage of HotDog's ability to track all the directory references in your hyperlinks when you upload, your first step is to create a project to hold your HTML files. To do so, follow these steps:

1. On the Elements toolbar, click Open the Project Manager. You'll see a blank Project Manager dialog box, shown in Figure 21.4.

2. Fill out the Details page, and click the Files tab.

3. Use the Add button to add all the files involved with this project, and click the Working Directories tab.

4. In the Working Directories panel, identify the directories where you have stored the documents, graphics files, autosave files, published files, and templates for this project. These will become the new defaults when you create any new files for this project.

5. Click Save Project to save your project.

6. Click Close to exit.

Uploading to Your Web Server

To upload one or more files, or a project, to your Web server, choose Upload to Host from the Tools menu. You'll see the Auto Upload dialog box, shown in Figure 21.5.

To upload a page or project, do the following.

1. In the Host area, type the computer address of your ISP's server.

2. In the Directory area, type the directory where you've stored your HTML files. In the Login As area, type your login name.

3. In the Password area, type your password.

4. In the Send Which Files area, choose what you want to send. If you want to upload support files (such as graphics), be sure to check this option. Check Make Remote Directories if you would like

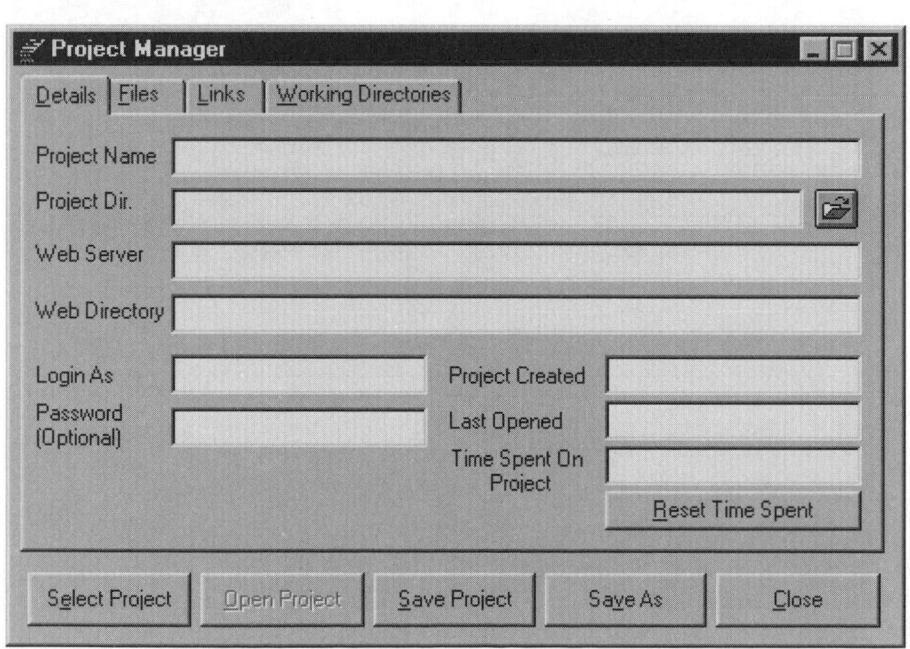

Figure 21.4 The Project Manager dialog box.

HotDog to create any necessary directories for storing support and other files on the remote server.

5. In the Transfer Options area, leave the defaults unless your ISP tells you to change them.

6. Click Add Files to start adding files to the upload list.

7. Click Send Files to send the files.

Direct Publicity

The marketers who send unsolicited snail mail know that people like to get mail—it makes them feel loved. Knowing this, they flood mailboxes with flyers and brochures, hoping that some of the people they spam with junk

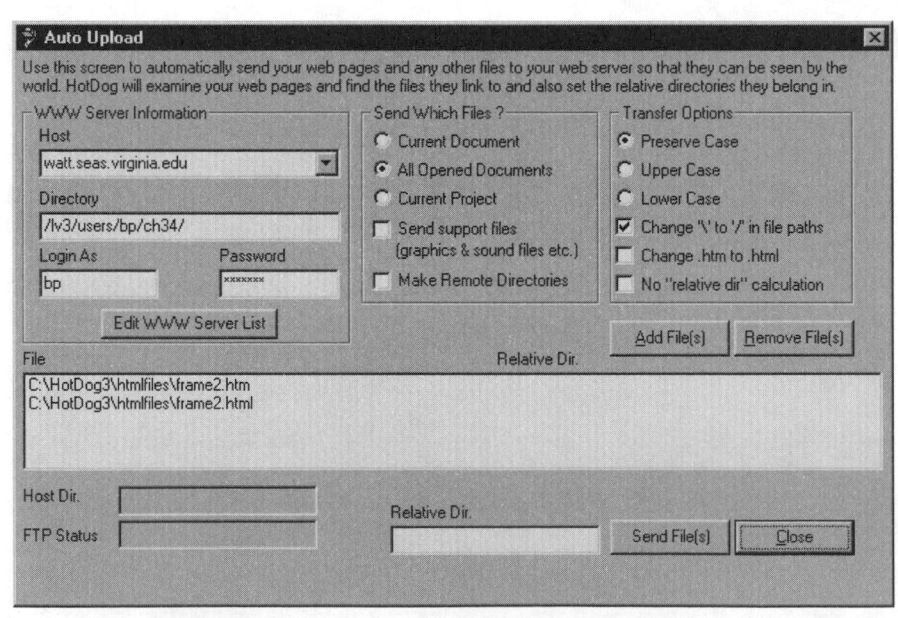

Figure 21.5 HotDog's Auto Upload dialog box offers incredible flexibility for uploading Web pages.

mail will be persuaded to buy a product or service from them. Direct marketers have found that direct mailings have a much higher response rate than less targeted advertising, such as radio and television commercials.

You don't need to approach the advertising of your newly created site quite so cynically, but you can take a hint from junk mailers and know that by sending information about your product (your site) to the people for whom it's designed, you stand a better chance of winning attention for it than if you rely entirely on broadcast advertising. Your site will certainly gain more attention if you advertise it carefully than if you don't advertise at all and count on word-of-mouth and happenstance to garner attention for your site.

You should have identified your audience by now—so you should know how to reach its members, too. Take advantage of this fact and bring the news of your site directly to the people it's designed to interest. Write to them directly, if you can, or do the next best thing and post to a mailing list or Usenet newsgroup. This section deals with some of the ways in which you might be able to gain access to the electronic mailboxes of the people you want to use your Web resource.

Tell Your Friends

It sounds simplistic and decidedly low-tech, but an old-fashioned invitation to friends to visit your site can improve traffic there tremendously. Your friends are also likely to include links to your site on their pages, making it more likely that casual Web surfers will happen across your resource. This is one way webs grow—with one friend linking to another's site, and so on.

It's also likely that at least some of your friends have interests similar to yours, so the links from their site can help draw more people from your target group to your resource.

Post to Mailing Lists

Though they're harder to find than Usenet newsgroups, mailing lists are second only to direct personal mail as an advertising medium. They get your message into the electronic mailboxes of the people you want to know about your site, forcing them to pay attention to your message for at least long enough to read your name and the subject header.

Since members of your target audience may *only* read your name and subject header before deleting your announcement, make sure you're descriptive in your choice of words. Something like "NEW RESEARCH

AID" probably won't get much attention, but something like "BOTA-NISTS: Web Guide to Orchid Species Available" will at least merit a read from those interested in orchid taxonomy. Remember, the Web and Internet are different from television, radio, and other broadcast media because few people use the Web and Net just for fun—they're usually doing something related to their work. Assume that the people who read your mailing-list posting are in a hurry: explain the resource, give the URL (on a separate line so it's easy to copy and paste), and let the site speak for itself to whomever decided to give it a visit.

To locate lists of people interested in the subject of your site, visit the various search facilities on the Web (Infoseek, Lycos, WebCrawler, and so forth) and hunt for words related to your site's topic. Very often, mailing list moderators will include a mention of their lists on their home pages, so a full-text searching engine like WebCrawler may be your best bet, in case the moderator mentions the list near the bottom of his or her home page.

It's possible that the mailing lists you most want to advertise on are closed lists—you must be invited to join, or there's some sort of screening process. Often, the screening process is perfunctory, and consists entirely of a check to see if you're on a list of people who disrupted the list in the past. If the screening process is more severe, as in the case of lists that require members to be college professors or other recognized experts in a field, send a message to the moderator or another individual on the list. Explain how you think members of the list will benefit by knowing about your resource, and ask the person to forward your material to the list.

Post to Usenet Newsgroups

Usenet newsgroups are not as good a place to advertise your new site as mailing lists and direct electronic mail for two reasons:

1. Usenet postings do not directly enter people's electronic mailboxes. It's easy for potential users of your site to miss your information because they chose not to read Usenet postings during the time your advertisement was posted.

2. Many fewer people use Usenet than use electronic mail. Those newsreaders that are easy to install (tin and trn, especially) are hard to understand, and those that are easy to understand (such as Free Agent and WinVN) are difficult to install. For these reasons, many people shun Usenet and stick with relatively easy-to-understand electronic mail.

To circumvent these potential problems, don't rely on Usenet totally. Instead, post notices to mailing lists and try some of the advertising methods suggested in the "Indirect Publicity" section of this chapter. The more places you make your site known, the more attention it will get.

When you do post to Usenet, follow general Usenet etiquette and frame your post carefully to ensure maximum impact:

- Keep your header brief and descriptive. Make sure that it says your post is about a new Web resource, and what that resource is for.

- Post your message several times—once a week for three weeks, say. This helps ensure that people hear about your site even if they missed your first posting because they were away or for some other reason were not using Usenet. Don't post too much to one group, though. Your site is only new for so long, and if you post the same message repeatedly, you'll annoy more people than you inform.

- Don't spam—post your announcement to two or three relevant newsgroups only. Resist the urge to post a copy of your message to every newsgroup with a topic tangentially related to that of your site. It's really bad netiquette to stray from the topic of a discussion group, especially when you're not a regular participant in that group.

INDIRECT PUBLICITY

The whole point of carefully identifying your audience before getting into the specifics of planning and building your site was to decide who you wanted to make your site appeal to. Still, you should spread the word of your site to the general Web community, if for no other reason than to showcase cool HTML techniques in your site and give others ideas for how they might incorporate your organizational techniques into a site specializing in another topic.

Most of the people who peruse the resources described in this chapter have an interest in the Web for the Web's sake. They want to see neat HTML tricks and clever organizational techniques. Using the techniques described in this section probably won't bring in many more members of your target audience, but it will bring in some Webmasters, who may choose to tell friends interested in your subject about your site.

Solutions

Getting Your Site Into the Search Engines

To raise your chances of getting your site into search engines and subject directories such as Excite, AltaVista, or Yahoo, spend some time getting to know these services. If you want to get your site into a directory, figure out where it should go. What's the best category and subcategory? The more you can save them some work and thought, the greater the likelihood that they'll use your submission. Leave this key information out, or submit it incompetently, and it goes directly to /dev/null (the cybernetic equivalent of the round file).

Here's a list of URLs for adding your pages to the leading search engines and directories:

- **AltaVista**   altavista.digital.com; follow the link to Add URL
- **Excite!**   www.excite.com/Info/add_url.html
- **Infoseek**   www.infoseek.com/AddUrl
- **WebCrawler**   www.webcrawler.com/WebCrawler/SubmitURLS.html
- **Yahoo!**   www.yahoo.com/bin/add

Search Engines

Some search engines, including the very popular Lycos search engine, have forms that allow you to add the URL of your site to the search engine's database. Adding your site to the database ensures that anyone who searches for the subject of your site—at least in the way you describe it on the submission form—will see the URL for your site.

Here's a great site with links for publicizing your site: Resources for Publicizing Your Web Site. You'll find it at www.citycom.com/links/linklinks.html.

Submit It!

Of the various ways in which you can obtain indirect publicity for your new page, arguably the best is a service called Submit It! (www.submit-it.com/). You can choose your level of service:

- **Free** Submit It's freebie service send notices of your new page to about twenty search engines and subject directories. Included (currently) are What's New on the Internet, Infoseek, WebCrawler, Apollo, Starting Point, ComFind, InfoSpace, Yellow Pages Online, What's New Too, LinkStar, Pronett, BizWiz, WebDirect, New Rider's WWW Yellow Pages, Nerd World Media, AltaVista, Mall Park, and AAA Matilda.

- **Commercial** The commercial service gets the word out to an impressive 300 search engines and directories, including hundreds that are topically focused in such fields as building/construction, travel and tourism, and many more. Prices start at $60 for two URLs.

 An alternative to Submit It is QwikLaunch (www.qwiklaunch.com), which offers an impressive free service (they notify Yahoo, Lycos, Open Text and others, for a total of 15 services).

FROM HERE

- By now, you've built a Web page and have made it known to the Web community. Now it's time to jazz up your page with multimedia—the graphics, sounds, and video clips that make the Web stand out from the rest of the Internet. Chapter 22 deals with collecting multimedia with scanners, microphones, and camcorders.

File Edit View Favorites Help

Address: http//www

Part IV

PRODUCING

DYNAMIC

CONTENT

Chapter
22

Capturing
Multimedia Material

Scanners, Microphones, and
Camcorders

This chapter deals with the mechanics of acquiring multimedia information for inclusion in your Web publication. Discussions of scanners, sound hardware, and video hardware, as well as supporting software, are included in the following sections. This chapter does not purport to be an exhaustive authority on capturing still images, sound, and video. Entire books—indeed, entire college-level courses of study—are devoted to these topics. It is intended to give you a general overview of what is involved in collecting nontextual information. The ability to handle multimedia information is one of the Web's strong points; you'd be foolish not to take advantage of it.

Chapters 23, 24, and 25 deal with what to do with multimedia material once you've acquired it, since raw images, sounds, and video "footage" (the word, which stems from linear feet of film, is now technically obsolete) require editing before they can be used with full effect. Chapter 23 deals with still graphics production, Chapter 24 with sound production, and Chapter 25 with video production. Chapter 26 explains how to use Adobe Acrobat software to incorporate documents with formatting beyond the capabilities of HTML into your Web site.

For the Time-Challenged

♦ Scanners are used to translate printed images into digital information in the form of graphics files.

♦ Scanners are operated with a special scanning program or a special routine in a large image-editing program like Adobe Photoshop.

♦ Before selecting an image, sound, or video clip for inclusion in your Web site, you should make sure the image or clip isn't copyrighted. You can get into serious legal trouble if you use copyrighted information, especially for profit-making purposes.

♦ Any multimedia item that you include in your site should be small, both dimensionally and in terms of storage required. Big multimedia files render your site unusable because they vastly increase the time required for downloading.

♦ To record sounds, you need a microphone and a sound card with a jack to accept the microphone. You'll also need a recording program such as Sound Recorder, which is bundled with Microsoft Windows 95.

♦ If you need to record sounds in the field, away from your computer, you can record them on a cassette deck, then later feed the output of the cassette deck into the Line In jack of the sound card.

♦ To capture video images for inclusion in Web publications, you need a camcorder and a video capture card, as well as video capture software. You can use any camcorder, but a professional model with interchangeable lenses and advanced editing features will give better results.

SCANNERS

You've probably seen a scanner—the big flat thing on the desk of the desktop publishing guru at the office, or in the little computer room at Kinko's Copies. It's likely, though, that you've never used one. You know scanners are used to translate printed graphics into a form the computer can use, but you don't know the specifics. Now you want to include graphics in your Web publication and it seems you need to use a scanner in order to do that. This section explains the rudiments of translating printed images into machine-readable graphics files.

What's a Scanner?

A scanner is any device that interprets visual information in a way that makes it useful to computers. Under this definition, the bar-code readers and automatic door sensors at the supermarket are scanners, just like the flatbed scanners that translate printed information into digitized data. The scanners used to encode graphical data for the Web are flatbed scanners—those with glass panels like copier machines—or hand-held scanners, which you drag manually across material to be scanned.

Scanners are also distinguished by their ability to handle color information. Though grayscale scanners exist and are somewhat less expensive than color-capable scanners, the price difference isn't significant and color graphics are *de rigueur* on the Web. Color scanners are distinguished primarily by the color depths they handle. The best scanners have 24-bit color depth—they record each pixel of an image with 24 bits of data. Other scanners, which are entirely adequate for most Web work, have color depths of 8 bits. They assign 8 bits of data to record the color information for each pixel.

Resolution is a measure of the sharpness of images generated by a scanner. There are two kinds of resolution: hardware and interpolated. Hardware resolution is a real measure of a scanner's quality, since it is determined by the number of charge-coupled devices (the electronic devices that sense light reflected from the image to be scanned) in the scan head and the speed of the stepper motor that moves the scan head across the image. 300 dot by 600 line hardware resolution is good; 600 by 600 resolution is great; 600 by 1200 is excellent. Interpolated resolution, which uses a software algorithm to fill in extra pixels between those actually scanned, should be 600 by 1200 or better.

How much can you expect to pay for a scanner? As with a lot of things, you generally get what you pay for. A low-end hand-held scanner with 8-bit color depth and 300 by 300 resolution can be had for $250 or so, but you can expect to pay between $600 and $1000 for much nicer—and much more versatile—flatbed scanners.

Scanning Software

A scanner isn't much good without software to support it by handling file management tasks and basic image cropping and editing duties. Though your scanner may come bundled with a rudimentary scanning software package, a better program is almost certainly worth the extra investment. Good scanning software makes scanning images and preparing them for publication much easier.

What should you look for in scanning software? There's only so much to be done by software in the scanning process itself, and many programs handle the necessary tasks well. Make sure the program you choose allows you to adjust the color depth and resolution of the graphics file output and allows you to save the files in a variety of different formats. Also—this sounds silly, but it's vital—make sure your scanning software works with your scanner. Sometimes special libraries of code are needed to make programs work with certain hardware.

Scanning, in fact, is often an ancillary function of image-editing software. Programs like Adobe Photoshop, which are designed mainly to modify graphics files, can support scanning. Photoshop or a similar graphics-editing package is probably your best bet for scanner software.

Selecting Graphics for Scanning

The biggest concern when selecting graphics for scanning and subsequent inclusion in your Web publication is not the range of colors included in a graphic or the difference between its darkest colors and its lightest ones, though those criteria are important. The overriding concern in picking images to be scanned is copyright: whether the image you want to scan is in the public domain or if someone owns the rights to it and can prohibit you from reproducing it.

All corporate logos fall into the protected category—if your name is Alice Teresa Thompson you can't legally put an AT&T logo on your site just to be cute. Most photographs in newspapers and magazines are copyrighted either by the publisher or the photographer, so you can't legally scan and republish them. A good rule of thumb is to assume that an image is copyrighted unless an authoritative source—such as a note on the case for a CD-ROM disc full of images—says otherwise.

 **My site is already loaded with images that are probably copyrighted! How much trouble am I in?**
You're in violation of the law, to be sure, but don't expect FBI agents to knock on your door any time soon. If you're using the images in a way that neither earns money for you nor detracts from the income of someone else, the worst you can expect is a letter from a lawyer warning you of possible legal action and telling you to take the images off the Web.

Corporations actually face something of a dilemma concerning use of copyrighted information on the Web: If somebody uses a copyrighted image to promote a product or company, are they harming the company or doing it a favor? Time will show the ways in which copyright law will change in the age of the Web. Chapter 29 offers a more in-depth discussion of Web copyright issues.

Once you've established that an image is not copyrighted and may be used in your Web publication, evaluate it for its technical suitability. Make sure the graphic is small, since giant pictures make sites take forever to download. Also, make sure the image has a good range of colors and a strong contrast between its dark portions and its light portions. You're ready to move on to actually scanning the image for modification in a graphics-editing program.

Scanning and Cropping

Place the image to be scanned on the glass deck of a flatbed scanner (or lay it on a flat surface for scanning with a hand-held scanner) and start your scanning software. The program you use probably gives you the option to set the scan resolution and adjust the color depth. Remember, scanners are designed to digitize images for printing on laser printers, which are capable of much higher resolutions and color depths than any monitor on which your Web publication will be viewed. Avoid setting the scanner for its greatest resolution and color depth, since those settings will result in a giant graphics file that will effectively go to waste on the Web, where its fineness cannot be seen.

Make sure to use the preview feature of your scanning program. Most scanning programs allow you to make a preliminary scan of an image, designate the part of it you want to include in the output file, and scan only that portion of the document in detail. Use the preview feature to save yourself trouble later—by using it, you'll save the hassle of having to trim unwanted parts of the image during the editing process (described in Chapter 23). Figure 22.1 shows a scanned image in Adobe Photoshop.

Graphics Libraries

The best way to obtain graphics for use on the Web is from a graphics library. Graphics libraries are CD-ROM discs packed with images of all sorts: photographs, line art, and graphical elements such as rules and boxes. There are several advantages to using graphics libraries:

- There's no need to buy a scanner or elaborate, expensive editing software. All the scanning and editing is done for you.

- You can rest assured (if the library comes from a reputable manufacturer) that there are no legal strings attached to the artwork. You won't have to worry about getting a call from an angry photographer's lawyer demanding that you pay royalties.

- You're absolved of the need to develop artistic talent. Usually, professional graphic artists create the images included in graphics

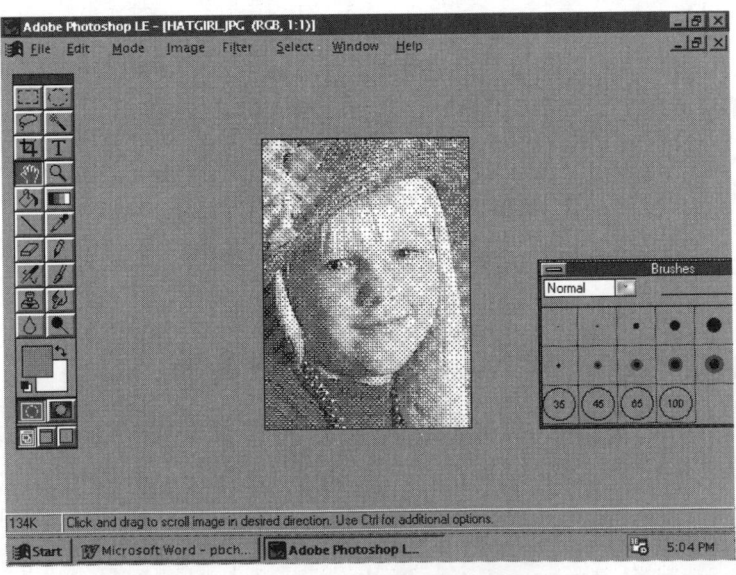

Figure 22.1   A scanned image in Adobe Photoshop.

libraries and their work is of high quality (though there's a large variation in quality among collections of artwork).

What Do I Do Now?

Now that you've acquired, by whatever means, a graphic image in computer-readable format, what do you do with it? Chances are, the image could use some tweaking before you're happy with releasing it to the Web. Chapter 23 is for you. In that chapter, you'll learn how to use image-editing software to modify graphics to your (and your audience's) liking.

DIGITAL CAMERAS

There is an alternative to scanning: Take the picture yourself, with a digital camera. For real estate agents, corporate personnel directory specialists, and others who need to get lots of pics online with a minimum of fuss, this is the way to go.

A digital camera generates a computer-readable digital image that you can view on your computer. Nothing more than toys just a couple of years ago, digital cameras have matured technologically—and what's more, their prices have come down. The Epson PhotoPC 500, for example, sells currently for $499, a price that's competitive with high-quality nondigital cameras, and is nicely designed for computer use: The camera captures 24-bit color images at 640×480 resolution. Software that comes with the camera enables you to convert files to JPEG format for Web publishing.

If you need to take many photographs, digital cameras offer a huge economic incentive: low cost. Instead of having to shell out significant money for film and processing, you record your images in the camera's memory, which is erasable, of course. You can shoot a scene over and over until you have it right. How can you tell? Some digital cameras come with a small LCD output monitor, which enables you to view the results immediately.

This isn't all fun and games, of course. After you shoot the pictures, you need to download them to your PC. A variety of methods have been tried to make this work smoothly, but none of them is entirely successful. Some cameras use PCMCIA cards, which force you to download first to your notebook computer—you *do* have a notebook computer, don't you?—and then to your PC. The best choice is a plain old RS232-C serial port connection, although that's a hassle if you've already used up all of your computer's serial ports for various other gadgets.

Solutions
How to Scan for Publishing on the Web

Scanning for the Web is a different proposition than scanning for, say, desktop publishing. The bottom line? You're producing media for low-resolution devices. Macs display 72 dots per inch (dpi), while PCs can display 96 dpi. It's best to plan for the lowest common denominator; if you assume that your graphics will be viewed on a PC display, you may find that your graphic scrolls off the screen when viewed on a Macintosh. So peg it at 72 dpi. If you publish your material at a higher resolution than 72 dpi, you're needlessly increasing downloading time.

But that doesn't mean that you should *scan* at 72 dpi—far from it. On the contrary, it's much better to scan at a very high resolution and maximum color depth. In fact, scan at double size (200%). The theory here is to try to *capture* as much information as possible. Subsequently, you'll bring the file into an image editor (see Chapter 23) and reduce the color depth and save to the appropriate format (JPEG for photographs and other continuous-tone images, GIF for graphics with areas of solid color).

Because you'll be opening your graphic subsequently in an image-editing program, you can worry about the file format later. Choose a graphics format that saves the maximum amount of information, such as TIFF or PICT, and don't worry about compression or file size for now.

When you open the scanned graphic in an image editor program, such as Adobe Photoshop or Paint Shop Pro, you'll do the following:

- Adjust the brightness and contrast.

- If the image editor has filters, try increasing the edge sharpness.

- Resave the graphic to JPEG format, using a color depth of 256 colors. Size the graphic so that it's small enough to display appropriately on a Web page. Choose medium (good) compression.

- If the graphic has many areas of solid color, resave the graphic again to GIF format. Try reducing the color depth to 16 colors, which gives the smallest possible file size. If this produces unwanted effects, use a color depth of 256 colors.

Should the chemical-based photo industry worry about these gadgets? In the short run, I'd say no, because it's still a hassle to download the images from the camera and it's even more of a hassle to print them with anything approaching photographic quality. There's a new breed of digital video printers that are designed to print beautiful, high-resolution images on 4 inch by 6 inch paper, but guess what? The paper's about as expensive as standard film processing and printing.

In the long run, though, it's obvious that digital camera technology is going to supplant its predecessor, just as digital audio has supplanted the analog world of vinyl records and magnetic tape. Sure, there are purists who will tell you that real photographs require film, darkrooms, and a craftsperson's touch—and I heartily agree. For Web publishing, though, especially considering that your images are limited to 72 dpi resolution on-screen, that type of artistry is pretty much irrelevant. The digital camera is a great tool for any Web publisher to have around.

MICROPHONES

Your Web presentation won't be complete without sounds, although sound is, compared to text and graphics, new to the stable of options Web authors have for communicating their messages. In fact, many people don't think of a presentation as employing "multimedia" if it uses only text and still graphics. You need sound (and video) if you really want to get the attention of Web surfers raised on radio and television.

Many books have been written on communicating messages with sound (radio is a field of study in itself), and this section does not aim to compete with them. Here, you'll learn the basics of collecting sounds for use on the Web, as well as some essential information about sound-recording software and sound file formats.

Audio Hardware

Unlike new Macintosh computers, PCs don't come with built-in sound support and require you to add a sound card that supports recording sounds. Look for a sound card that supports 16-bit sound resolution (resolution is a measure of the fidelity of a digitized sound) and a 44.1 KHz sampling rate. A good sound card, such as the Sound Blaster Awe/32, costs about $100.

The actual conversion of sound waves into electrical impulses is handled by a microphone. You can plug a $10 microphone from the local electronics or stereo store into your sound card, but you'll get better sound quality if you use a better microphone that costs $30 to $50. You can drop several thousand dollars on a studio-quality microphone, but it's unlikely (unless your site is targeted at recording professionals) that visitors to your site will have the playback equipment to appreciate the improved quality.

Audio Software

You'll need software that enables you to control your sound card and microphone. Microsoft Windows 95 includes Sound Recorder, an applet that is adequate for recording sounds to be published on the Web. Sound Recorder saves sound files in .WAV format only. Sound Recorder, with an open file, is shown in Figure 22.2.

If you need more flexibility in recording (and editing) sounds, use Waveform Hold and Modify (WHAM). WHAM handles a variety of sound formats and can be used as a helper application for your Web browser too.

A relatively new innovation in Web sound recording is RealAudio, a product of Progressive Networks. The advantage of RealAudio is that it begins playing *before* the audio file completely downloads. Several news operations, including National Public Radio and ABC News, post their radio news reports to the Web several times a day.

To record your own information in RealAudio, you'll need a copy of RealAudio Studio, which you can download from the Progressive Networks RealAudio Studio page (http://www.prognet.com/products/studio.html). RealAudio Studio comes with RealAudio Encoder, which converts audio files of several types to RealAudio format.

Figure 22.2   Microsoft Windows 95 Sound Recorder with a .WAV file open.

Recording in the Field

It's hard to record digitized sounds directly if they exist away from your computer. Bird calls, for example, or the sound of warning bells at a railroad grade crossing are hard to capture, as they require you to travel to a location remote from your computer and work in an area in which there is no electricity. Unless you have access to a high-end portable computer (recording-capable notebooks can cost $5000 or more) you're stuck with having to dub sounds taped on a traditional cassette.

To digitize a taped sound, connect the Line Out jack of your tape deck with the Line In jack of your sound card. Play the cassette and record the signals coming into the Line In jack as if it were connected to a microphone. Though sound will be fine if you work with good-quality analog cassettes, you'll have better luck with digital audio tapes (DATs), which record with near-CD quality.

Prerecorded Sound Clips

As with graphics, your safest bet in terms of copyright law, technical quality, and artistic merit is a collection of prerecorded sound files. Collections are available from several manufacturers. You can modify the sounds, which are licensed to be used by anyone who pays for them, as much as you wish, and chances are good you'll find a high-quality sound that matches your needs. Though the hardware and software required for sound collecting and editing is not as elaborate as that needed for still graphics or videos, recording sounds that cannot be heard within a few feet of your desktop is a chore, and it's probably worth it to invest in a library of prerecorded sounds.

What Do I Do Now?

After acquiring sounds, you need to modify and combine them before publishing them on your Web site. Chapter 24 teaches the technical and artistic aspects of sound editing.

CAMCORDERS

Video adds a lot to a Web publication. It draws viewers' attention because it is a moving picture in an environment that otherwise consists of static pictures. The production costs of video, both in terms of time and money, are greater than those of other media, and the cost prohibits many Web publishers from using video. If you can afford the cost, though, video will virtually guarantee that your site gets visited more often than sites without motion pictures.

This section deals with capturing live-action video, as opposed to animation, which can be done entirely with a standard computer system. Here, you'll learn how to capture video in the real world and transfer it to your computer.

Selecting a Camcorder and Tape

A camcorder senses light reflected from a subject and converts that sensed light into an electrical signal that it records on a magnetic tape. All camcorders serve that purpose, but there is considerable variation among camcorders in the quality and versatility with which they perform that task.

What kind of camcorder do you need to capture video images for Web publishing? Again, it depends on your needs. If you're just shooting one clip of the company president promoting the company's stock, you can probably get by with the VHS camcorder you bought to tape your kid's birthday party. If you have a more elaborate project in mind, you'll want a fancier camcorder. The Canon L2 offers interchangeable lenses, autofocus capability, and a variety of other attractive features that make it the camera of choice among videographers who don't want to invest in studio-quality equipment. Even the L2 will probably cost more than the rest of your computer system, so it's not an investment to be made unless you plan to do a lot of videotaping, for the Web or for traditional tape publication.

Buy top-quality tapes for your camcorder. Standard 8-millimeter tape will work, but Hi-8 tapes are better because there is very little degradation in image quality from one generation to the next and the tape maintains high resolution even after extensive editing. High-quality tapes also promise not to break or jam—which cheap tapes often seem to do at critical times in a taping session.

Other Video Hardware

In addition to the camcorder, you'll need a video capture card to convert analog video signals (either from the camera or from a recorded tape) into digital files that can be read by the computer. Video capture cards, such as the MICROVIDEO DC30, plug into your computer's expansion bus and have ports that accommodate input from a VCR or camcorder. A home version costs $359.

You'll also need a strong video adapter (the card that connects to your monitor). Make sure the card you choose has a 64- or 128-bit data bus and at least 2 MB of VRAM. Motion video puts gigantic demands on graphics hardware, so make sure your monitor is of high quality too. You'll pay $400 to $1200 for a video card and $800 to $1500 for a good monitor.

Video-Editing Software

You'll need a program to control your video hardware—and the Intel Smart Video Recorder Pro comes with an ideal one: Asymetrix Software's Digital Video Producer Capture. DVP Capture is designed to monitor the flow of video information into the video capture board and convert it to MPEG format, in which form you can edit it with Asymetrix's Digital Video Producer software (also bundled with the Intel capture board), Adobe Premiere, or another video-editing software package.

Camera, Lighting, and Sound Technique

You can spend years in school learning about how to record moving subjects on videotape, and even then you need to spend years accumulating experience before you're considered any sort of an expert. This book can't begin to cover the details of good videotaping technique, but there are a few things you should keep in mind:

- Don't overuse your camera's zoom feature. It's best to cut directly from a wide-angle shot to a close-up, without the bore of watching the camera zoom in. Worst of all is zooming in and out on a static subject in a futile attempt to make it appear more exciting.

- Use some kind of stabilizer. Put your camcorder on a tripod or monopod, or just brace it against something stable while shooting. This will prevent "the wobblies"—an annoying characteristic of amateur video.

- Light your subject carefully. Bright sunlight isn't the best lighting for video, since it creates harsh shadows. Learn to use filler lights to soften shadows and bring out detail.

- Don't rely on the little microphone that's built into your camcorder. Instead, get a microphone that can be placed close to the sound source or clipped to the speaker's clothing.

- Shoot efficiently to minimize the need for editing later. If you can avoid shooting useless material, you won't have to waste time cutting it out.

Prerecorded Video Clips

As with still graphics and sounds, libraries of video clips are available. It is less likely these clips will be useful to you, though, since you probably want a video of a specific thing, such as your company president speaking or a salesman pitching your company's product. A generic video of a bear cub running around or a sailboat floating in a harbor probably won't solve all your video needs, but such clips might be useful as parts of a larger video presentation. And remember, clips on video libraries published by reputable manufacturers are royalty-free.

What Do I Do Now?

Capturing motion pictures for use in a presentation is just the beginning. You'll want to edit the files you've created, add titles, and include special effects. You might want to add voice-over narration or integrate animation with your live-action video. Chapter 25 covers all these topics in some depth.

FROM HERE

- The next three chapters teach you what to do with the material you learned how to capture in this chapter. You'll learn how to prepare still images for the Web by cutting out the extraneous parts and giving them, where appropriate, a transparent background. You'll learn how to alter sound files by adding special effects. And you'll learn how to edit videos and add titles to them.

Chapter 23

Producing Web Graphics

The age of text-based interfaces for personal computers ended in 1988 with the wide adoption of Microsoft Windows 3.0, DesqView, and other graphical user interfaces. Text-based interfaces survived on the Internet, however, until the Web made them obsolete in 1992 or so. The ability to embed graphics in text is one of the main reasons the Web caught on initially, and one of the reasons it remains the fastest-growing portion of the Internet today. Though it's neat to embed sound, video, and other special files in Web publications, no media but text and still graphics display automatically, without a helper application. You can't beat still graphics in terms of impressiveness per unit of time invested.

This chapter teaches you how to prepare graphics for publication on the Web. In Chapter 22, you learned how to capture printed images with a scanner. This chapter shows you how to alter those images so they suit your site visitors'—and your own—needs. Among other things, this chapter shows

---

For the Time-Challenged

♦ You can characterize Web graphics by their resolution (sharpness), color depth (the number of colors they contain), and the amount of memory they occupy.

♦ GIF images have poor compression (they usually take up a lot of storage space), but they can have transparent backgrounds. They're well suited to making icons, rules, and other small elements.

♦ JPEG images have good compression, but lower image quality and no transparency capability. JPEG images are good for large graphics, such as photographs.

♦ Create transparent GIFs so that your graphics blend with background colors.

♦ Try to cut down on file size by reducing color depth.

♦ GIF animations are easy to create and do not require special software to view.

♦ Try to keep your Web images simple, small, and repetitive. By doing so, you'll save visitors to your site from having to wait while big images download. You'll also allow them to learn what certain icons and buttons mean—something they could not do if you didn't use the same images repeatedly throughout your site.

---

you how to make GIF image files with transparent backgrounds, which can make your site look very clean and professional. You'll also learn how to make GIF animations, which can really jazz up your site. Remember, though, that graphics is a giant field—lots of people make a living in it—and this section is merely an introduction to basic Web graphics skills.

A BRIEF INTRODUCTION TO IMAGE FILE FORMATS

Image file formats are the ways in which your computer encodes the information that defines an image in a machine-readable format. Image file formats take the color, brightness, and contrast values that make images appear as they do and convert them into bits of data. Several image file formats exist, and each has strong points and shortcomings.

Before learning about the various file formats, though, you need to understand some basic facts about computer graphics. Some important terms:

- **Resolution**   The sharpness of a graphic. Usually, you describe resolution in terms of dots per inch (dpi). Unless you're planning for visitors to your site to print your graphics out, you can get away with lower resolutions than in paper publications, since monitor resolutions fall far short of laser printer resolutions. Most monitors display 72 dpi, maximum.

- **Color depth**   The number of colors in a graphic. You describe color depth in terms of the number of bits used to encode each pixel, as in "24-bit graphics" or "4-bit GIF." A 4-bit image, though it can cost much more than 50 cents, contains only 16 colors and fits into a small file. An 8-bit image has 256 colors. A 24-bit image, in contrast, features more than 16.7 million colors—more than the human eye can distinguish—and requires a lot of storage space. Generally, keep your color depths low to avoid overloading your server with requests for giant files.

- **Compression**   The ability of an image file format to fit a lot of graphics data into a small file. Compression varies from one file format to another, and often there's some kind of trade-off for high compression, such as a slight loss of color depth.

Although there are lots of image file formats, only two matter to those using a Windows PC to publish on the Web. Read about GIF graphics and the JPEG format in the sections that follow. In the future, PNG graphics may play a role.

GIF Images

The Graphics Interchange Format (GIF) has been on the Web since its earliest days. Every major graphical Web browser displays GIF images without a helper application, and lots of shareware GIF editors exist to make creating and modifying images easy.

Transparent GIFs

Of most interest to Web publishers is GIF version 89a, which allows the use of a transparent "color"—a code, treated just like codes for red and blue, that makes pixels tagged with it assume the color of the background behind the image. You'll learn how to make GIF images with transparent backgrounds later in this chapter.

Do I have to pay a royalty for using a GIF image?
Although GIF images use a patented compression technique, you don't need to worry about getting a call from an attorney if you use a GIF image. A royalty must be paid, though, by companies that make software capable of creating and storing images in the GIF format.

Interlaced GIFs

Another attractive feature of the latest GIF format (89a) is its support for *interlaced* files. Briefly, an interlaced GIF downloads a rough, out-of-focus approximation of the graphic very quickly (Figure 23.1) and then fills in the

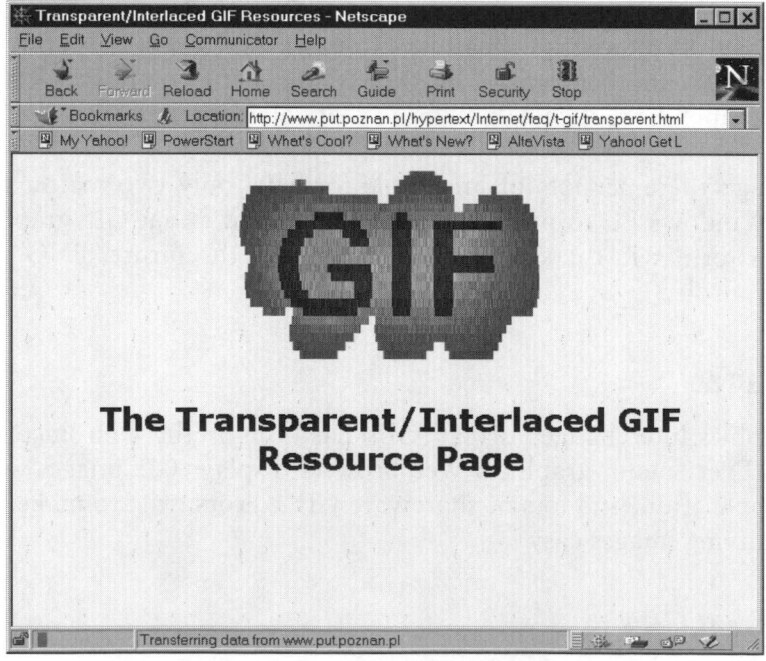

Figure 23.1   Interlaced GIF at beginning of download.

details gradually (Figure 23.2). On your Web page, the effect is appealing to viewers; they don't have to wait for the whole image to download to get an idea of its content. Interlacing is a function of the file format, not HTML; with most graphics programs, you can open any graphic and save it as a GIF interlaced file.

Animated GIFs

Yet another very cool feature of the GIF format is built-in animation. The wonderful thing about animated GIFs is that recent browsers (including both Internet Explorer and Netscape Navigator) can play these animations without requiring a plug-in or helper application. Briefly, GIF animations consist of a single GIF file that, in reality, contains as many as a dozen or more separate images. Also included in the file is a list of the images, indicating the order in which they should be played. When your browser plays the images, the result is an illusion of movement. This isn't space-age animation, folks—it's strictly herky-jerky and low-res—but it's still possible to create small, eye-catching animations that attract attention to a certain part of your page.

Figure 23.2 Interlaced GIF at end of download.

 Use the GIF file format for graphics that have areas of solid color. GIFs of these graphics will download more quickly than JPEGs.

JPEG Images

Developed by the Joint Photographic Experts Group (JPEG) of the International Standards Organization, the JPEG image file format employs an ingenious compression scheme with which it can pack huge images into fairly small files. The compression scheme relies upon tricking the brain by taking advantage of the fact that it can perceive differences in color less readily than differences in brightness. The JPEG format throws out some color information in order to conserve storage space—that's why it's said to use *lossy compression*—and keeps brightness information, which it uses to distinguish among different areas that once were of slightly different colors.

Most graphical Web browsers support JPEG images without a helper application now, so it's safe to include them in your Web publication. The JPEG format doesn't support transparent backgrounds (as GIF images do), so JPEG images aren't useful as icons or other small elements, but because of the format's superior compression, it's preferred for large images.

 Use the JPEG file format for any image that has fine color gradations, such as a photograph.

PNG Graphics

PNG graphics (short for Portable Network Graphics) are designed to provide the ideal graphics format for the Web. Endorsed by the World Wide Web consortium as the official graphics format for the Web, PNG is a patents-free format; that's not of concern to users, but it's very much of concern to software developers, who must pay royalties to the holders of the compression formats used in GIF files. The PNG graphics standard is intended to replace GIF. Like GIF, it offers lossless compression. Unlike GIF, it offers 24-bit color (called truecolor) as well as a 256-color palette and grayscale.

The PNG format has been slow to gain acceptance because it's so new, and because the standard wasn't released in time for inclusion in Netscape

3.0 and Microsoft Internet Explorer 3.0. However, use is expected to increase gradually. Because PNG doesn't include facilities for animation at present, I don't expect the format to displace GIF entirely.

COLOR AND THE WEB

When you're publishing GIF graphics on the Web, it's important to bear in mind that people will be looking at your graphics on a variety of hardware platforms, including the Macintosh, Windows, and UNIX. A graphic that looks pretty on your monitor might not look so hot on another one. You'd be wise to consider color choices carefully.

Introducing Color Palettes

Color choices come into play when you're creating graphics using a fixed color palette, such as the 256-color palette that most GIF paint programs enable you to use. These colors are expressed in three ways:

- **Name** These aren't standardized, and they aren't very helpful, either, unless you've spent most of your life selling tubes of paint in an art supply store. It's best not to specify colors by name.

- **RGB Value** This is a code that specifies the amount of red, green, and blue in the color. For example, white is specified as 255 255 255.

- **Hexadecimal Value** This is a hexadecimal (base 16) version of the RGB code. This is the code you use when you type in your color choices in an HTML page. For example, white is specified as FF FF FF (FF is the hexadecimal equivalent of 255).

For a list of color codes, see Appendix C.

How Computers Display Color

When you're displaying a graphic using a fixed color palette, the computer's video card tries to match the color code in the graphic with one of the computer's built-in colors (*system colors*), usually 256 in number. If it finds a match, it displays the color, and the color looks good.

What happens if the color isn't matched by one of the system colors? The video card uses *dithering*. Dithering is required when a particular color isn't in the computer's color palette. To create a semblance of the color, the computer's video card fakes it by combining tiny dots of other colors. The result might look something like the original color, but it might vary much more than you'd like.

The 216-Color Palette

Is there a way to avoid dithering? If you assume that your viewers are using Netscape and Microsoft Internet Explorer, the answer is—maybe.

Netscape's and Internet Explorer's color palettes for Microsoft Windows and the Macintosh include 216 colors that do not require dithering. If you restrict your palette to the 216 colors that Netscape can display without dithering, you can be assured that—at least on these systems—the colors will display pretty much as you hope they will. Using other colors will require dithering, with results that you may not like.

To see the non-dithering Netscape colors in action, check out Victor Engel's No-Dither Netscape Color Palette (http://www.onr.com/user/lights/netcol.html). If this site is down, try the Web Color Chart (www.webplaces.com/html/colors.htm).

Appendix C contains an alphabetized list of the 216 non-dithering colors.

I can't get rid of the speckles on this graphic!
Does your graphic look like somebody hit it with a spray can, real lightly, so that there are specks on all or parts of the graphic? Chances are this results from dithering.

Reduce, Reduce, Reduce

If you've (wisely) restricted your color choices to the 216-color palette favored by the most popular browsers, your graphics will probably look good. To make sure that your graphics files are as compact as possible, be sure to reduce the color palette to the absolute minimum that's required to display the colors you've chosen.

TOOLS FOR PRODUCING WEB GRAPHICS

You'll find dozens of freeware, shareware, and commercial products for graphics creation, management, and publishing. Here are just a few of my favorites.

Adobe Photoshop

Photoshop is the premiere graphics application that's in daily use in the world's top design workshops. If you have artistic and design ability and you'd like to create your own high-quality graphics for your Web site, this is the program of choice. But be forewarned: It's expensive and difficult to learn. This is commercial software (www.adobe.com/proindex/photoshop/main.html).

 Be sure to get version 4.0, which (finally) supports popular Web graphics formats, including GIF, PNG, Progressive JPEG, and PDF files.

GIF Construction Set for Windows (Alchemy Mindworks)

GIF Construction Set enables you to create transparent, interlaced, and animated GIF graphics for your Web site. It's just the ticket for working with existing GIFs so that they're optimized for Web publication. Among the other extremely neat things it can do: Convert AVI video streams to animated GIFs, create and edit comment blocks, compress GIFs for fast downloading, and create looping animations. Registration is currently $20 (www.mindworks.com/alchemy/).

Figure 23.3 shows the control script for a GIF animation; these are the commands that tell a browser how to play the animation. You don't have to learn how to write these scripts by hand; GIF Construction Set writes the script for you.

 GIF Construction Set's animation wizard makes this the hands-down winner in the ease-of-use sweepstakes. If you want to create animated GIFs, this is the program to use.

Graphics Workshop for Windows (Alchemy Mindworks)

Graphics Workshop is perhaps the ideal program for managing large quantities of graphics for a Web site. You can create and display thumbnails (see

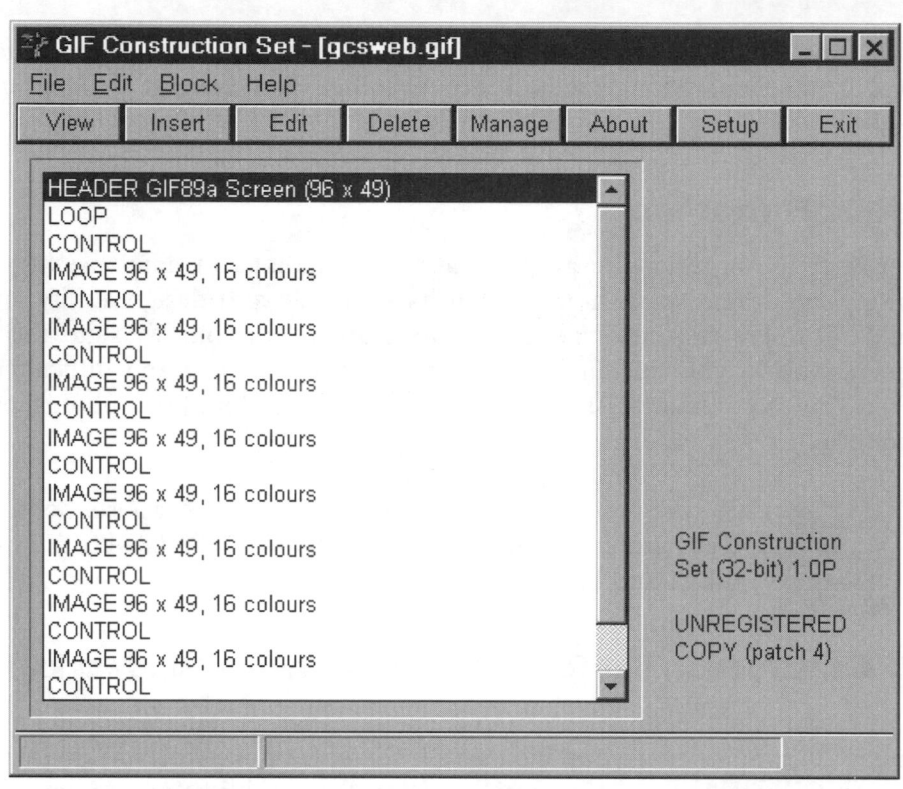

Figure 23.3   GIF Construction Set is just the ticket for Webbifying GIFs.

Figure 23.4), modify images in various ways (including changing color depth and applying filters), and create catalogs of graphics. Registration is currently $40 (www.mindworks.com/alchemy/).

Paint Shop Pro (Jasc, Inc.)

Paint Shop Pro (Figure 23.5) is a great program for creating and modifying graphics in all imaginable file formats, including PNG. A variety of special effects rival some of those included in the much pricier Adobe Photoshop. This is the program of choice if you'd like to create some of your own graphics but don't want to fork over the dough for Adobe Photoshop. To obtain Paint Shop Pro, see www.jasc.com. Registration is $69.

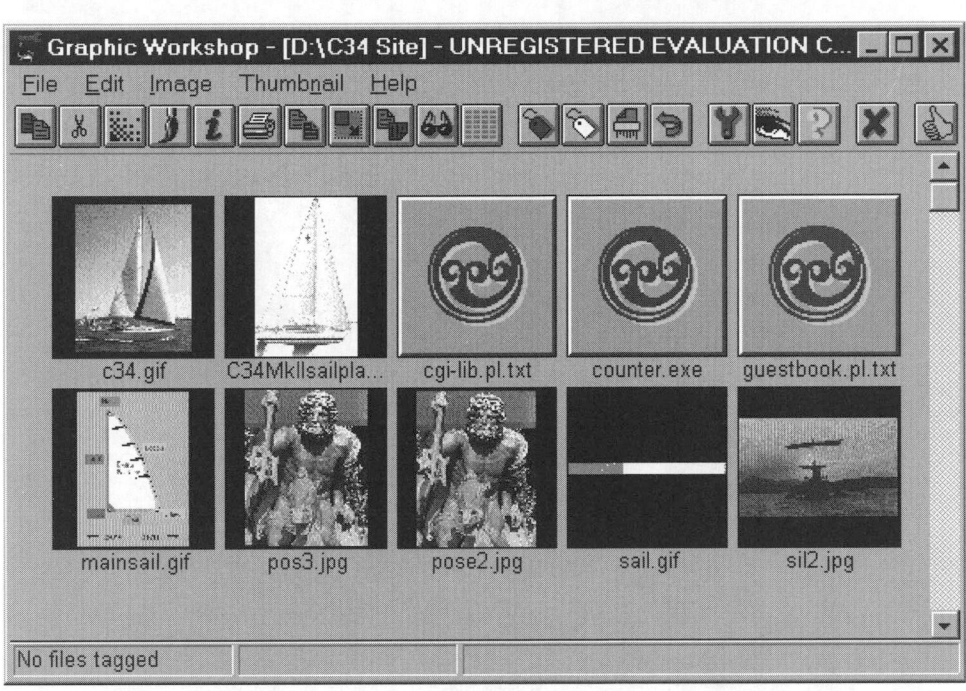

Figure 23.4 Thumbnail images viewed in Graphics Workshop for Windows.

 Paint Shop Pro is my choice for manipulating file formats, changing color depth, and managing graphics files via thumbnails. It's expensive, though.

WebPaint

WebPaint is a great program for creating spiffy-looking GIFs for your Web page (Figure 23.6). You can add yellow tool tip boxes, 3D buttons, drop shadows, shadow text, and other special effects. A GIF animation tool enables you to create neat-looking GIF animations easily. To learn more about WebPaint, access www.barentsnett.no/WebPaint. Registration is 300 Kroner (approximately $42.36, at today's exchange rate).

Figure 23.5   Paint Shop Pro.

These are just a few of the graphics programs you can use. For the tasks discussed in this chapter, they're very handy.

CREATING A TRANSPARENT GIF

What's a transparent GIF? It's not really transparent; it's a GIF graphic in which the background color of the graphic has been set to a special *trans-*

Figure 23.6 WebPaint isn't as expensive as Paint Shop Pro but does many of the same things.

parency color. You can choose any color in the 256-color GIF palette to serve as the transparency color.

Why is a transparent GIF needed? Take a look at Figure 23.7. The C34 logo doesn't look that good, does it? That background is *ugly,* all the more so because Netscape has dithered it, with random results. After making this background transparent, it will look white and blend in with the page background. The result is that the GIF "floats" on the background as if it were an integral part of the page design.

Creating a Transparent GIF with Paint Shop Pro

To create a transparent GIF with Paint Shop Pro, do the following:

1. Open and save the graphic as a Version 89a Interlaced file.
2. Click on the dropper tool.

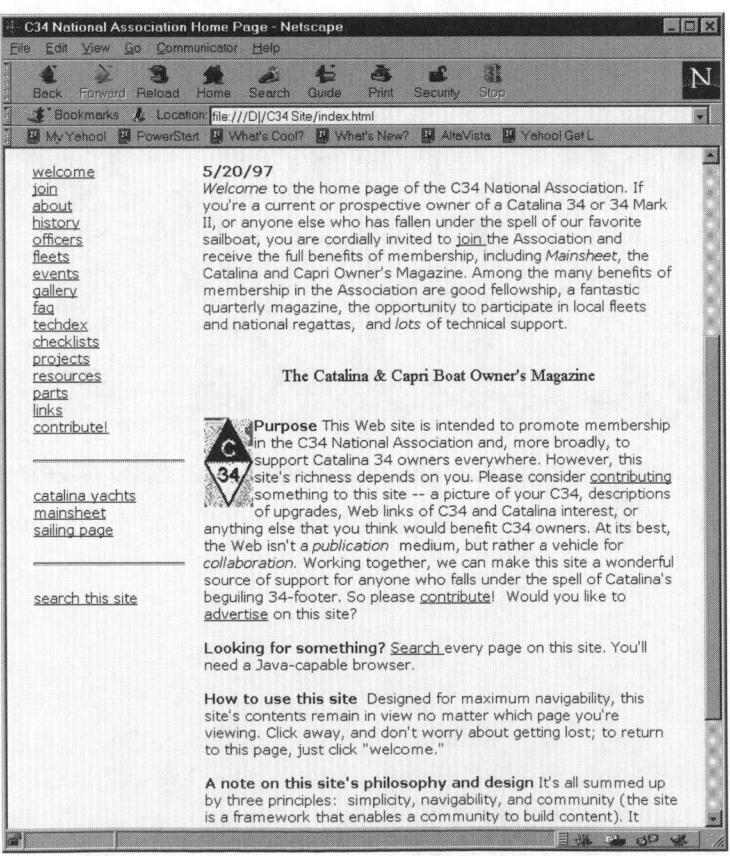

Figure 23.7   Graphic with a nontransparent background.

3. Move the pointer to the background color of the graphic, and click the *right* mouse button. You've made the background color the active color.

4. From the Selections menu, choose Modify, and then choose Transparency color.

5. In the Transparent Color Select dialog box, choose Background Color from the Transparent Color list box, and click OK.

6. Click the Save button.

Creating a Transparent GIF with GIF Construction Set

To create a transparent GIF with GIF Construction Set, do the following:

1. Open your GIF file. In the GIF Construction Set window, you'll see a Header block and an Image block.

2. Click on the Header block.

3. Click Insert. You'll see the Insert Object dialog box.

4. Click Control. Now you see CONTROL in the middle of the list.

5. Double-click Control. You'll see the Edit Control Block dialog box.

6. Select Transparent color.

7. Click the eyedropper tool. You'll see your graphic. Click the color that you want to be transparent.

8. In the Remove By list box, choose Background.

9. Click OK.

10. From the File menu, choose Save.

CREATING INTERLACED GIFs

It's a cinch to transform any GIF (or a graphic from most other file formats, for that matter) into an interlaced GIF. Just open it in one of the graphics packages described in this chapter, such as Paint Shop Pro, and save the file as a GIF 89a Interlaced file.

REDUCING COLOR DEPTH

If you're planning to publish a graphic with only two or three colors in it (such as the C34 logo in Figure 23.7), there's no point in saving the file with a 256-color palette. You can reduce the color palette to see whether you can live with the colors that your application substitutes. Try it.

In WebPaint, you can reduce the color depth by choosing Palettes from the Options menu, and choosing 16 Colors.

In Paint Shop Pro, choose Decrease Color Depth from the Colors menu, and choose 16 Colors (or 2 Colors).

CREATING ANIMATED GIFs

You can easily transform a series of GIFs into an animation using GIF Construction Set, WebPaint, or other applications that are designed to do this. In this section, I'll show you how to use GIF Construction Set's cool animation wizard.

Before you create your animation, you'll need the raw materials—at least three or four separate GIF files that show some gradation of action from one file to another. You don't have to be a Great Artiste to do this. I'm going to make an easy GIF animation of my C34 logo that fades in and out. I'll do this by saving several versions of the file with varying degrees of fade.

Here's how to create an animated GIF, once you have the files that make up the animation:

1. In GIF Construction Set, choose Start Animation Wizard from the File menu. You'll see the welcome page. Click Next. You'll see a page asking whether you want to create a graphic for a Web page.

2. Click Yes to create a Web graphic, and click Next. You'll see a page asking whether you want the animation to loop or to play once and stop. Your choice. Click Next. You'll see a series of options about the type of image that you're animating (Photorealistic, Drawn, Drawn in sixteen colors, or Matched to first palette).

3. Choose the image type that seems right for your image, and click Next. You'll see a list of delay options, ranging from .001 second to 5 seconds. Try the default setting, and click Next. You'll see the page that enables you to choose the files to incorporate into your animation.

4. Click Select, and choose the first file. After you click Open, the dialog box springs back again, enabling you to choose the second file. Continue choosing files until you've chosen them all, and then click Cancel to close the Open dialog box.

5. Click Next, and Done. You'll see a window showing the controls you've created, as seen in Figure 23.8. Click Exit, and then save your file.

 You can edit the settings by opening the file again, selecting the Control block that comes before each file, and choosing settings. In this way, you can vary the amount of time that each frame displays.

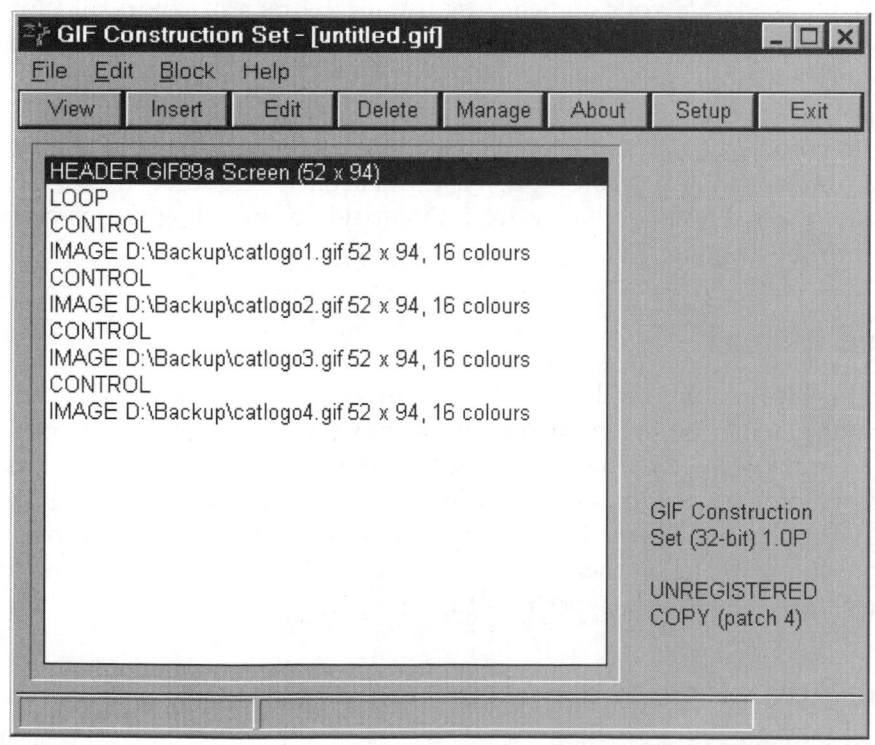

Figure 23.8 Controls for an animated GIF.

GRAPHICS PRODUCTION HINTS

Again, this book isn't large enough to include all the information that deserves to be in this section. Since the days of the first cave-dweller who scratched a picture of his dinner on the wall of his home, human beings have tried to understand what makes one picture appealing and another picture repulsive. This book doesn't purport to be a textbook for students of the visual arts.

This section includes a few hints about how to make your graphics look good on the Web, a publication venue that's still foreign to many graphic artists. Between the hints here and the expertise of someone with some artistic skill and design sense, you should be able to generate some good-looking still graphics that take advantage of the Web's unique characteristics.

Keep It Simple

Don't try to dazzle your audience by using hundreds of colors and lots of elaborate shapes, especially when designing icons, rules, and buttons. Often, you can achieve great impact with simple color schemes and basic, unadorned shapes—less is often more on the Web. Also, by sticking to a simple color scheme, you prevent the problem of having a site visitor get some unseemly blob where your beautiful icon is supposed to be, simply because the site visitor's hardware isn't capable of handling the colors you put into the graphic.

Keep It Small

Big graphics require big bandwidth. Small graphics add flavor to your site without placing too much burden on your visitors' connections. If you load your site up with giant, high-resolution images, your pages will take forever to download, especially if lots of other busy sites use the same server. Keep your graphics small—or, if your subject requires large photographs or other graphics, put them on their own pages and warn visitors about download time before they follow hyperlinks to those pages.

Take Advantage of the Cache: Repeat Images

When a Web browser downloads an image for use in displaying a Web document, it stores it in a cache. It can draw on images in the cache if they're called for again. When designing your site, make sure you repeatedly use the same graphics. Not only does this give your site a consistent look (visitors quickly learn what the various icons mean and what various buttons do), it reduces the load on your visitors' connections to the Web. Their Web browsers need only download the repeated images once, then retrieve them from the cache.

FROM HERE

- Now that you've learned how to create transparent and animated GIFs, try your hand at imagemaps (Chapter 24).

- Create sounds for your site (Chapter 25) and add video too (Chapter 26).

Chapter
24

Creating Imagemaps

An imagemap (also called a clickable map) is a graphic that contains two or more hyperlinks, each tied to a particular region of the image. The linkage of graphic region and URLs is accomplished by means of a *map* file, a text file that contains the definitions of the various clickable areas on the graphic, along with their associated URLs. The definitions consist of specific areas that are delineated in terms of the mouse's position within the graphic. When someone accessing your site views a clickable graphic and clicks part of it, the browser detects the mouse's position.

What happens next depends on which kind of imagemap you're creating. *Server-side imagemaps* require scripts to process the information. The newest wrinkle in imagemaps is *client-side imagemaps,* which require browsers capable of processing the imagemap information. The newer versions of the leading browsers can do this (Netscape 2.0 and higher, Microsoft Internet Explorer [all versions], and Spyglass Mosaic 2.0 and higher).

For the Time-Challenged

♦ Not all graphics are suitable as clickable maps. You must be able to mark squares, rectangles, circles, ellipses, or polygons within the graphic, and assign these shapes to URLs.

♦ Imagemap editors enable you to define these shapes on-screen with a mouse, and also enable you to link each shape with a URL. Finally, the imagemap editor creates the .MAP file, which the imagemap script uses to link mouse coordinates with specific Web documents.

Thanks to client-side imagemaps, any reader of this book can include imagemaps on his or her pages. Just remember that you'll be excluding a small proportion of viewers who are using older browsers, as well as people who have switched graphics off. Prepare an alternative menu of text-only navigation links or consider offering a text-only version of your site.

Imagemaps solve one of the most persistent problems of Web document design: The need to gain control over your presentation's graphical appearance without sacrificing the interactivity of HTML. Most of today's hottest new sites present a welcome page that includes an imagemap marquee, like the one shown in Figure 24.1. The use of imagemaps in this way permits Web designers to kill two birds with one stone: You can establish a consistent look for your pages at the same time that you provide navigation buttons.

CREATING THE GRAPHIC

Not every graphic is suitable for use as an imagemap. You need to be able to identify clickable regions that have the following geometric shapes:

• Squares

• Rectangles

- Circles

- Ellipses (Ovals)

- Polygons

Figure 24.2 displays an example of the simple shapes that enable you to easily assign URLs to shapes: All the clickable regions are rectangular.

INTRODUCING IMAGEMAP EDITORS

An indispensable tool for making imagemaps is an *imagemap editor*. Imagemap editors enable you to define these shapes on-screen with a mouse, and also enable you to link each shape with a URL. Finally, the imagemap editor creates the .MAP file, which the imagemap script uses to link mouse coordinates with specific Web documents.

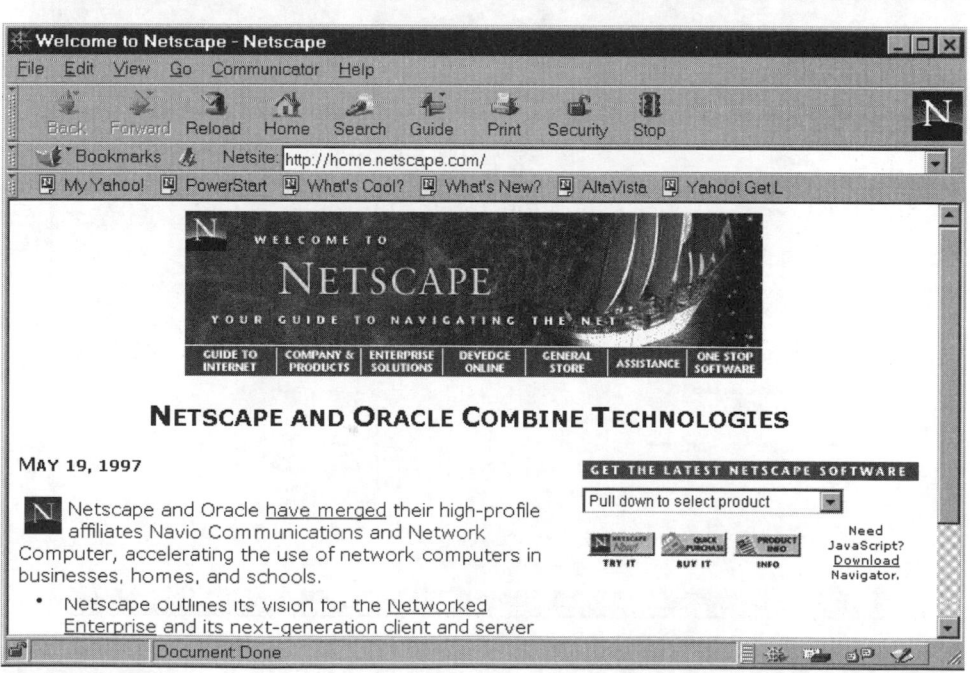

Figure 24.1   Imagemap as marquee.

There are a number of imagemap editors available, but this chapter focuses on one of them that I find particularly easy to use: Mapedit (www.boutell.com/mapedit). This site offers lots of information concerning Mapedit, including online registration using a secure server. You can use the evaluation version of the program for free for 30 days; subsequently, registration is $25.

GETTING STARTED

To create an imagemap for your Web page, you need to begin with a draft of the page that includes the graphic. (For information on creating graphics, see Chapter 23, "Producing Web Graphics."). Remember that your graphic should contain regular shapes so that the user can see what should be clicked (see Figure 24.2).

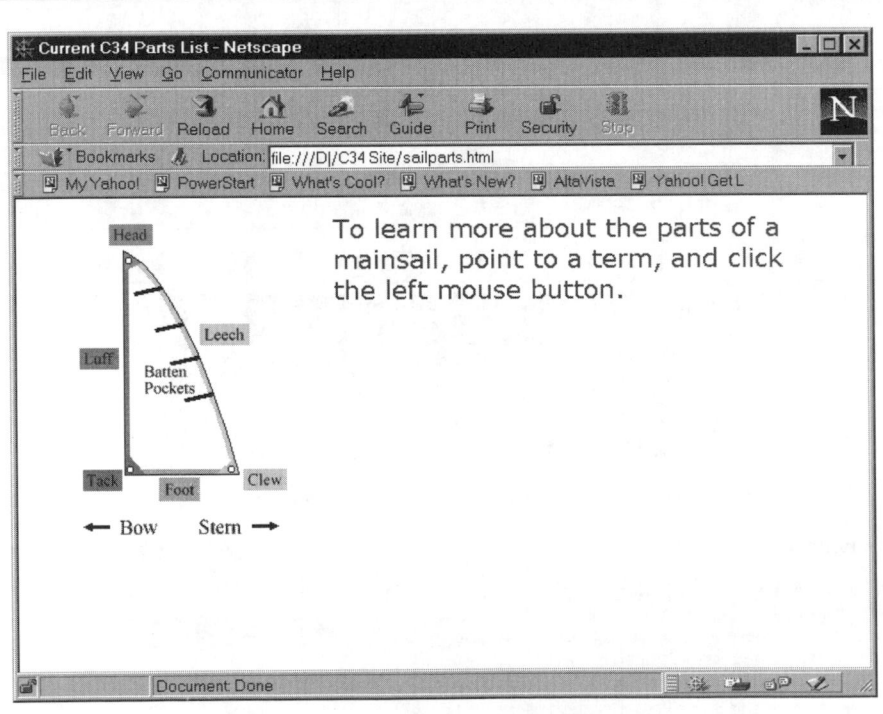

Figure 24.2　A draft of a Web page that's ready for markup with an imagemap editor.

Telling the Imagemap Editor Which Files to Use

Once you've created a draft of your page with a graphic, it's time to start the imagemap editor and tell the program which file you're using. With Mapedit, you see the dialog box shown in Figure 24.3. Here, you specify the location of the file and the name of the graphic that you want to use as an imagemap. Since you're creating a client-side imagemap, it doesn't matter whether you choose NCSA or CERN.

After you've identified the files you want to use, you'll see your graphic in the map editor's window. Most map editors give you a variety of tools to work with. Mapedit includes tools for rectangles, polygons, and circles.

CREATING YOUR IMAGEMAP

It's easy to create your imagemap—if, that is, you created your graphic with regular shapes.

Planning the Links

Before you spend a lot of time marking up your imagemap, take a moment to think about how you want to organize the various files on your server. If

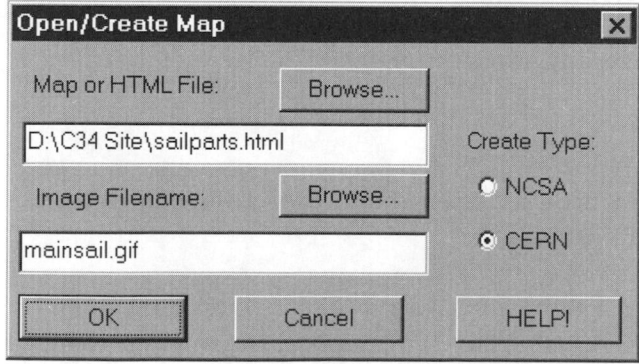

Figure 24.3 To get started creating your imagemap, you tell the editor which files to use.

they're all in one directory (this is the easiest way), or in a directory beneath the one in which the imagemap document is stored, you can use relative URLs (URLs that include nothing but the file name, such as "sail.html"). Otherwise, you'd be wise to use absolute URLs. This is particularly true if you think you'll someday move the imagemap document to a different directory location without also moving the linked files.

 I strongly recommend that you simply keep all your files in one directory. This is much less confusing, unless you're planning to create a really huge site. Another plus: You can create and test all the necessary files on your local system, without even being connected to the Internet. Just place the imagemap file, the graphics, and all the linked files in one directory. You can later upload them to your server, as explained in Chapter 21.

Once you've decided how you're going to organize your files on the server, make a list of the exact file names of all the URLs you want to include in the imagemap. You'll need to type these precisely.

Marking a Shape

To mark a shape, select the tool you want to use, and drag over the graphic. When you're finished dragging, click the button again. You'll see a dialog box asking you to identify the URL you want to use (see Figure 24.4). Type the URL. Be sure to include alternate text for the benefit of people who aren't browsing with graphics turned on.

Continue adding shapes and URLs until you've linked to all the files you want to include, and save your work.

Testing Your Work

Switch to your browser, open the imagemap document, and test the links you've created. Cool, huh?

 **There's a horrible border around my graphic!**
When you view your imagemap document with your browser, you'll find that there's a big (probably blue) border around it. Looks ugly, doesn't it? This is automatically supplied by your browser, which has detected hyperlinks within the graphic. To get rid of the border, edit the underlying

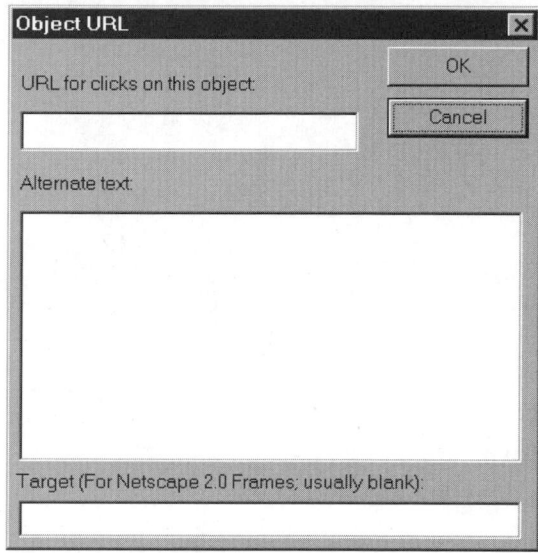

Figure 24.4   Specify the URL for the area you've marked.

HTML and add a BORDER=0 attribute to the <IMG> tag that references your imagemap.

Editing the Imagemap

Should you discover an error in a URL you've assigned to a shape, switch back to your imagemap editor. Generally, there's a way you can edit the URL. In Mapedit, choose Test + Edit from the Tools menu, and double-click the region that contains the erroneous URL.

FROM HERE

- If you get tired of doing all that HTML coding by hand (and who doesn't?), check out an HTML editor. You'll find an introduction to HotDog in Chapter 20.

Chapter 25

Producing Audio

Y ou learned about the HTML aspects of embedding sounds in your Web documents when you read Chapter 25, but you're probably still wondering about what those hyperlinks should connect to. You're probably not a sound engineer, and the last of your artistic inclination may have perished when you went back to school for that advanced degree. Yet you still need to produce attractive and technically slick sound files for your Web site.

What's the answer? This chapter. While a single chapter of a book can't teach you even the most rudimentary basics of sound production, and certainly can't endow you with creative talent, a chapter of a book can teach you enough to get sounds onto the Web. You learned about capturing audio—recording sounds with a microphone—in Chapter 22. This chapter gives you some idea of what you do after you've collected material. You'll

---

For the Time-Challenged

♦ Sounds come in a variety of sound file formats. It's important to use a popular format, such as .WAV or .AU, so visitors to your site won't have to find a helper application before they can play your files.

♦ Waveform Hold and Modify (WHAM) is a shareware sound editor that is available all over the Web. NetEdge has WHAM—its URL is http://www.netedge.com/pages/utilities.html. Be aware that WHAM doesn't always work well with Microsoft Windows 95.

♦ In WHAM, you can adjust the sampling rate and resolution with which you record sounds. A sampling rate of 44,100 Hz and a resolution of 16 bits guarantees a high-fidelity file, but at a cost of lots of memory.

♦ WHAM supports cutting and pasting portions of sound, just like a word processing program supports cutting and pasting text.

♦ There are two "Play" buttons in WHAM. The leftmost Play button on the button bar plays the entire sound file. The second play button plays only the selected portion of the sound file, if you've made a selection, or the portion of the sound file to the right of the cursor.

♦ Adjust the size of a selection by dragging the triangular markers just above the time scale at the bottom of the screen.

♦ Generally, keep your sound files small to save bandwidth.

♦ Make sure all the files on your pages play at about the same volume, to keep visitors to your site from having to adjust their speaker controls repeatedly.

---

learn about various sound formats, as well as how to edit sounds and modify them to produce a variety of special effects.

This chapter focuses on Waveform Hold and Modify (WHAM), a shareware program written by Andrew Bulhak of Ferntree Gully, Australia. I chose to write about WHAM because it's a great program that handles all the basic tasks of producing sounds for the Web and its registration fee is, at most, $30. (In the About box, Bulhak asks you to send "$20–30" to his address—but he doesn't specify what country's dollars he wants). Other good Windows sound editors exist, to be sure. Check out Cool Edit and Gold Wave too (both Cool Edit and Gold Wave are shareware).

A GUIDE TO SOUND FILE FORMATS

On the Web, you'll encounter sounds encoded in a variety of ways. Each of these file formats has its advantages and disadvantages. Some of the common sound file formats are listed below:

.AU	The file format generated by Sun and NeXT workstations
.WAV	Windows' favorite file format
.RA	The RealAudio format that allows you to start playing a sound before it downloads entirely
.MID	The MIDI format, designed to simulate musical instruments
.AIFF	A format used mainly by Amiga and Macintosh computers
.VOC	A fairly obscure file format developed by Creative Labs

Put your sounds in a common format. If you don't, you run a serious risk of having your site's visitors download a sound only to find that they don't have the proper helper application for playing it, so they move on to friendlier sites. Generally, .WAV is your best bet, but .AU is widely supported, too. Use RealAudio format when your clips are long—several sites use that format for half-hour recordings of radio broadcasts—but be aware that the sound quality supported by RealAudio files is rather poor.

Sounds in a given file format may have a variety of *resolutions* and *sampling rates*. Essentially, resolution and sampling rates are measures of the quality of a sound—sampling rate describes the number of times a sound was measured each second, and resolution describes the number of bits assigned to record each sample. A sampling rate of 44.1 Hz corresponds to compact-disc quality sound; lower sampling rates indicate correspondingly lower sound quality. 16-bit resolution is superb; 12-bit resolution works for everything but music; you should avoid 8-bit resolution for all but the simplest sounds (such as beeps and whistles). Remember, though, that higher sampling rates and resolutions yield larger sound files, so use the lowest values you can. It may be worthwhile to include poor-quality sound files that site visitors can download and evaluate before deciding to download a better-quality file.

 For an in-depth discussion of sound file formats, sampling rates, resolutions, and all the other technical aspects of sound recording and reproduction, look at the Audio File Formats FAQ assembled by Guido van Rossum. Part 1, the body of the document, appears at

> http://www.cis.ohio-state.edu/hypertext/faq/usenet/
> audio-fmts/part1/faq.html

Part 2, the appendices, is at

> http://www.cis.ohio-state.edu/hypertext/faq/usenet/
> audio-fmts/part2/faq.html

ACQUIRING WAVEFORM HOLD AND MODIFY (WHAM)

If you know the Web well at all you can skip this section—it's a brief set of instructions on how to find WHAM. You'll learn where I got my copy, but you'll also see that it's probably best for you to use a search engine and find the WHAM repository closest to you. Be sure to read "A Word of Warning" below, though, if you're running Microsoft Windows 95.

Finding WHAM on the Web

WHAM appears all over the Web, so finding a copy isn't hard. I got my copy from NetEdge, at http://www.netedge.com/pages/utilities.html. There's nothing special about getting WHAM from that site, though. Just visit a search facility such as InfoSeek or Lycos, run a search for WHAM, and head to the listed site closest to you.

A Word of Warning

WHAM's creator, Andrew Bulhak, had not ported WHAM to Windows 95 as of this writing. The 16-bit version of the program isn't especially stable under Windows 95, and requires you to perform some odd rituals. For example, to maximize WHAM when there's no sound file loaded, you have to right-click the WHAM icon on the taskbar and choose Maximize from the control menu, instead of just clicking the icon. Generally, work slowly and deliberately with WHAM under Windows 95 so as not to provoke problems. Do not taunt WHAM under Windows 95.

RECORDING SOUNDS WITH WHAM

This section covers the mechanics of controlling your microphone and sound card with WHAM (Chapter 22 covered sound cards and microphones themselves).

When you're ready to record a sound with WHAM, choose Record New from the File menu. The Record Sound dialog box (Figure 25.1) will appear. If you want to use WHAM's default sampling and resolution options (8-bit resolution and 22,050 Hz sampling rate), move directly to the "Recording a Sound" section. The next section describes how to adjust the sampling rate and resolution.

Setting Resolution and Sample Rate

To adjust the resolution and sampling rate, click the Options button to expand the dialog box (Figure 25.2). You can choose between sampling rates of 44,100 Hz (CD quality) and 22,050 Hz (approximately FM radio quality). You can choose either 8-bit or 12-bit resolution. Don't forget that by using the higher sampling rate, you'll create a giant sound file and may have trouble getting your computer to record. For example, my computer is powerful—a 90 MHz Pentium with 16 MB of RAM—but it still required some tweaking before it would record with 16-bit resolution and a 44,100 Hz sampling rate.

Figure 25.1   The WHAM Record Sound dialog box.

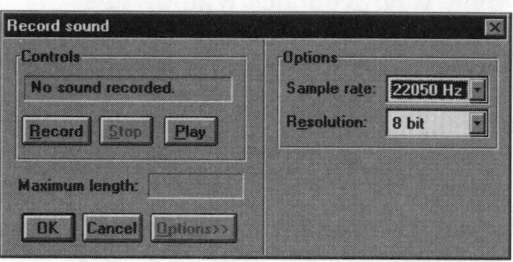

Figure 25.2   The WHAM Record Sound dialog box after clicking the Options button.

If you can't record with a sampling rate of 44,100 Hz, make sure your sound card supports that sampling rate—many cards do not.

Recording a Sound

Recording a sound with WHAM is just like recording a sound on a traditional tape recorder. You click the Record button, wait until WHAM decides memory allocation issues, then record the sound you want with your microphone. Click the Stop button to end recording.

If you think you captured the sound you want, click OK to close the Record Sound dialog box and return to the main editing window. In the main editing window, you can fine-tune the recorded sound until it meets your needs. The next section covers editing sounds.

MODIFYING SOUNDS WITH WHAM

If you found a sound on the Web that has some redeeming portion but is otherwise loaded with useless chaff, you'll need to use WHAM to trim out the unwanted portions. Likewise if you recorded a sound yourself and want to, um, cut out the, uh, parts you don't, you know, want.

When you open a sound in WHAM (or record one and close the Record Sound dialog box), you'll see a graphic representation of the sound in the main editing window (Figure 25.3). The graphic representation of the sound (you can choose from among several versions under the View menu) isn't

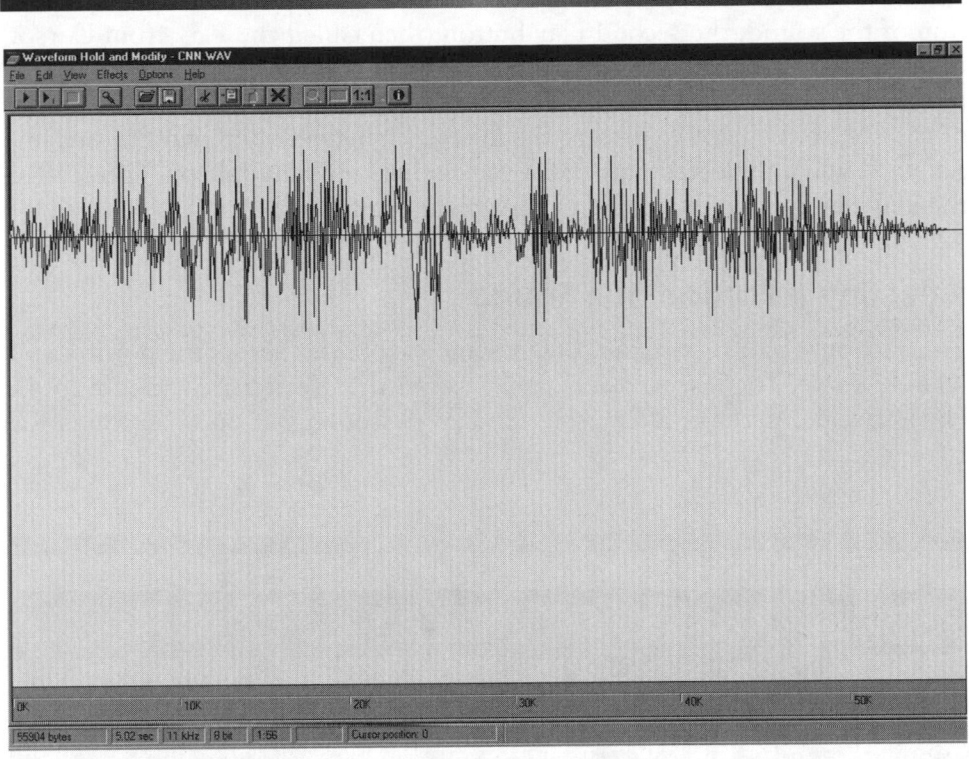

Figure 25.3 WHAM's main editing window.

terribly useful unless you have a lot of experience with sound editing or your sound is made up of distinct parts with silence between them (such as a series of gunshots), but by placing the cursor at various points in the graphic representation, you can isolate the portion of the sound with which you want to work.

The Two Play Buttons

Before you edit a sound by cutting, pasting, and adding effects, you need to identify the portion of the sound with which you want to work. To do this, you need to understand the functions of WHAM's two Play buttons. The first (the leftmost button on the button bar) plays the entire sound file from beginning to end, regardless of the placement of the cursor or any portion of the file you've selected. The second Play button (the second button from the left on the button bar) does one of two things. If you haven't selected a portion of the sound, the second Play button (then called the Play from Cursor button) will play from the cursor to the end of the file. (Click the graphical representation of the sound to place the cursor, which sits at the beginning of the file, so it's hard to discern the difference between the two buttons initially.) If you've selected part of the file, the second Play button (then called the Play Selection button) will play only the selected part.

Selecting a Portion of a Sound

To select only part of a sound, drag the mouse pointer across the portion you want to select. You'll see a black highlight over the selected area (Figure 25.4). If you decide, perhaps after using the Play Selection button to examine the

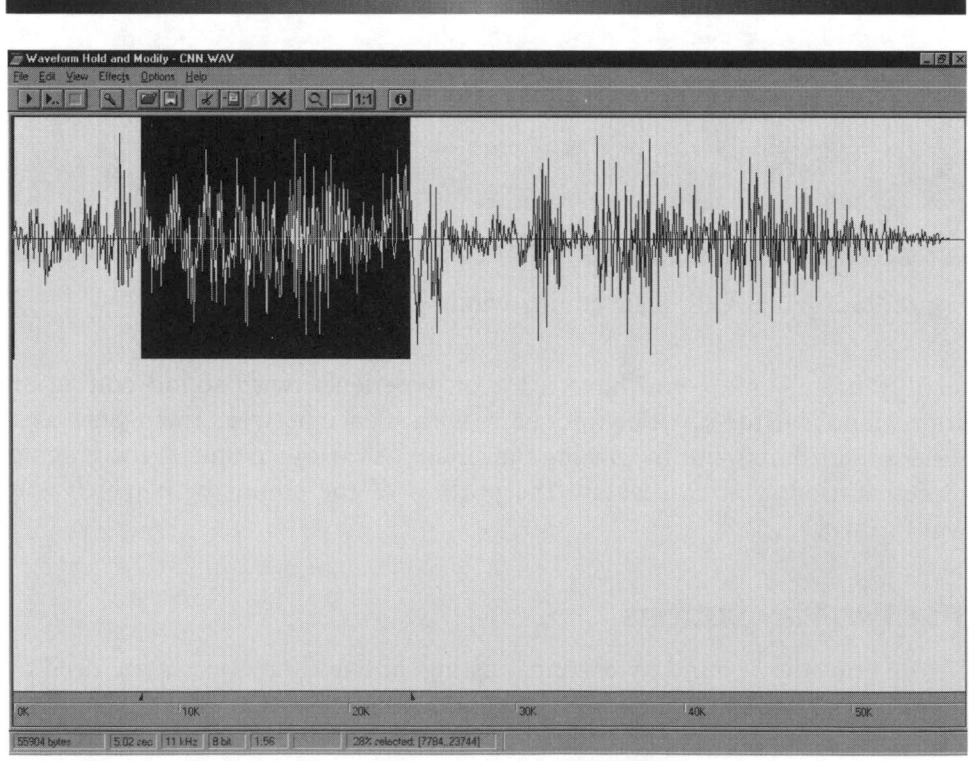

Figure 25.4 A selection in WHAM.

selected portion, that the selection is not the right length, you can relocate either end of the selection. Do this by dragging the triangular markers just above the time scale at the bottom of the screen. As you drag the pointers, you'll see a vertical line intersecting the graphical representation of the sound file. Drag the marker until the vertical line intersects the file at what you feel to be the proper point, then let the marker go. Test your selection with the Play Selection button, and keep adjusting the markers as needed.

Cutting and Pasting

You can cut and paste portions of sounds in WHAM just like you can cut and paste passages of text in your word processing program. Just highlight a selection and choose Cut or Copy from the Edit menu (or click the corresponding button on the button bar). Then, to insert the clipped sound into the same (or another) sound file, choose Paste from the File menu or click the Paste button on the button bar. WHAM shows you a dialog box that gives you the option of replacing the entire open sound file with the material to be pasted, adding the clip to the end of the open file, adding the clip at the beginning of the file, or inserting the clip at the cursor. If you have selected a portion of the sound, it offers to replace the selection with the sound on the Clipboard. Choose the option you want and click OK.

Changing the Volume

If you recorded a sound at the wrong volume level or you've found a sound that's much louder or softer than the other sounds on your Web publication, you'll need to adjust the volume. WHAM makes it easy to increase or decrease the volume of an entire sound file, or just a portion of one. Be careful about increasing the volume of a sound file—too much volume quickly leads to distortion.

To double the volume of an entire file, place the cursor anywhere in the graphical representation of the file and choose Volume from the Effects menu, then pick Increase (200%) from the menu that flies out to the right. To halve the volume of an entire file, follow the same procedure but choose Decrease (50%) from the fly-out menu. If you've made a selection before changing the volume, the volume change will affect only the selected portion.

If you want to increase or decrease the volume by a specific percentage, choose Change from the fly-out menu and enter the percentage change you want. One hundred percent represents no change, 120% indicates a 20% increase, and 80% indicates a 20% decrease.

Other Effects

For weird effects, you can choose Stretch/Shrink from the Effects menu and distort the sound file to fit into a longer or shorter time frame. Enter a percentage of stretch or shrinkage—remember that percentages greater than 100% represent stretching (sounds are slower), and percentages less than 100% represent shrinking (for Chipmunk-like effects). You can also choose Playback Rate from the Effects menu and adjust the rate at which the program plays back samples to accomplish the same effects.

WHAM provides a facility for reversing sound files—the same thing as spinning LP records backwards with your finger to hear deviant messages from recording artists. Choose Reverse from the Effects menu, and the entire file reverses. You can reverse individual selections, too.

Important note to Windows 95 users: The Microsoft Sound, when played backwards, does not reveal subliminal messages from Bill Gates. Sorry. I checked.

HINTS FOR SUCCESSFUL SOUND PRODUCTION

This section attempts to distill some basic wisdom about sound production into a few key points. Obviously, this isn't all there is to sound production, since working with sound is an art and a science that requires years of education and experience to master. Still, this is a start, and if you follow these hints, you'll be ahead of many Web publishers in terms of sound quality.

Keep It Short

Often, you can bring to mind an entire piece of music (or the television show or movie with which it's associated) with just a short clip. All that's necessary to bring to mind all the cultural baggage associated with *Star Trek* is the "These are the voyages of the Starship *Enterprise*" portion of the show's intro. You can suggest either American patriotism or baseball with the first few bars of *The Star-Spangled Banner*—there's no reason to reproduce the whole song.

Keep It Small

This follows from the previous paragraph, but with the added consideration of resolution and sampling rate. There's no need to record simple beeps and buzzes at 16-bit resolution with a 44.1 Hz sampling rate—that creates huge files and wastes bandwidth. Instead, use high resolutions and sampling rates for music and other applications in which sound quality figures prominently and stick with 8-bit resolution and 22,050 Hz sampling rate for less quality-critical situations.

Keep the Volume Consistent

Nothing is more annoying than having one sound on a site be very loud and the next one barely audible. Don't make visitors to your site adjust their volume settings repeatedly—make all your sounds audible but not overpowering at a common speaker-volume setting. You should do volume adjustments in the production phase—your site visitors shouldn't do them while surfing.

Remember the Visitor's Hardware

Don't put CD-quality sounds on your site if members of your audience typically use their computers' internal speakers. Likewise, don't put sounds with 8-bit resolution and 11,000 Hz sampling rates on a site designed for people with direct, high-speed network connections and fancy sound hardware. Pay attention to the planning you did before building your site.

FROM HERE

- Sounds are cool, but by themselves they're so...*1935*. Flip to the next chapter and get into the really cuspy stuff—video production.

Chapter
26

Producing Video

U ntil relatively inexpensive videocassette recorders became available in the early 1980s, home video involved great expenditure and technical challenge. If you wanted to watch recorded movies at home on demand, you had to invest in what amounted to a small television production studio, complete with a skilled technician—and that enabled you only to tape video from television and play it back later. Those dark ages of home video parallel the state of personal-computer video production today.

It's *possible* to produce video on your personal computer, but only by the same token that it's possible to run all your household utility functions with your computer, too. Video production requires, at minimum, a top-of-the-line 90 MHz Pentium machine with a fast video card and 16 MB of RAM— and that only allows you to edit video. If you want to capture your own material (and you probably do, since stock footage of a caribou grazing or a bicycle whizzing by probably won't convey your persuasive or artistic message), you'll need a camcorder, a VCR, and a video capture card—an investment that can easily total more than $10,000. Take a look at Chapter 22 for a more complete discussion of videotaping real-world action.

In short, true taping-to-broadcast video production is not within the capabilities of most Web publishers. If it's what you want to do, several fine books on the topic exist—this chapter doesn't pretend to compete with them. Here, you'll find a brief, basics-only introduction to video editing with Adobe Premiere, a program widely considered the finest desktop video editor ever published. After reading this chapter, you'll be able to modify video clips to fit your needs—whether you find the clips on the Web, hire a professional to tape them for you, or tape them yourself.

A Brief Introduction to Video File Formats

Like all information encoded for use by a computer, video clips are translated into digital datastreams that can be stored in RAM or on a hard disk. Several schemes exist for doing this, though, and each scheme requires a particular kind of player. When publishing video clips to the Web, you have to be careful to use the video file format that best suits the needs of you and your audience.

Fortunately (because there's less to get confused about) or unfortunately (because other formats might offer better characteristics than the ones that exist now), there are only a few video file formats in widespread use. These include the following:

- **.AVI** The Microsoft Video for Windows format. Microsoft designed this format to work well with Windows machines. Video for Windows files employ a special scheme for synchronizing audio with video—AVI stands for "Audio-Video Interleaved." Windows 95 users can play .AVI files with Media Player, included with Windows 95.

- **.MOV** The QuickTime format supported at the System level of all recent Macintosh computers. A utility called QuickTime for Windows enables Windows machines to play .MOV files—but without the system-level elegance with which Macs play them.

For the Time-Challenged

◆ Several video file formats exist. The most common formats are .AVI (Video for Windows), .MOV (QuickTime, native to the Macintosh), and .MPEG (used for big video files and other large-scale applications, such as satellite television).

◆ Adobe Premiere is a very powerful video-editing program. If you can't afford professional video editing, Premiere makes it possible (even easy, sometimes) to assemble video presentations on your home computer.

◆ Premiere uses a timeline analogy in the Construction window to help you understand how various components of your presentations fit together. You drag parts of your presentation onto the timeline from the Project window.

◆ To bring a clip (audio, video, or still graphic) into the Project window, choose Import, File from the menu bar and select the clip you want.

◆ You can put transitions between clips by dragging them from the Transitions window to the transitions track between two video tracks. Don't go crazy with transitions, though—too many will spoil the show.

◆ Create titles (such as credits) by choosing New, Title from the menu bar and using the tools as if they were part of a presentation graphics program. The "T" tool allows you to add text to the title window.

◆ When you're done editing your presentation, choose Make, Make Movie from the menu bar. Give your movie a filename, then click the Output Options button. In the Project Output Options window, choose Entire Project from the Output drop-down list box in the upper left corner and choose the file format you want from the drop-down list box in the upper right corner. Click OK, then click OK in the Make Movie box. You'll see a bar graph showing Premiere's progress in assembling your movie. When it completes compilation, it will show the first frame of your movie in a window; click the right-pointing arrow at the bottom of the window to view your movie.

◆ If Premiere overwhelms you or you lack creativity, consider hiring a professional video producer to do editing for you (check the Web search engines for videographers' home pages). If that's beyond your means, see if your local vocational-technical school will do the editing as part of a class project.

- **.MPEG (or .MPG)**   A lossy compression scheme used mainly for professional transmissions of video information, such as from a remote camera installation to a studio, or from a communications satellite to a dish antenna on Earth. MPEG employs *lossy compression*—that is, it's a digitization scheme that sacrifices some image quality for a reduction in file size. Several versions of MPEG exist (MPEG 1, MPEG 2, and MPEG 4, there's no MPEG 3). Later versions have better image quality and compression.

- **.FLI or .FLC**   A fairly rare animation format designed by AutoDesk and used in their popular Animator software, which performs morphs, distortions, and other special effects.

Which format should you use? If your production is to be five minutes or fewer in length, you'll probably want to use .AVI, since it's designed to work with Windows and viewers can be had all over the place. Use the .MPEG format for longer clips. Remember, though, that even a "short" video clip can occupy several megabytes of memory, so you can quickly get into download times of 15 minutes or more if you're not careful.

Using Adobe Premiere

Widely acclaimed as a program that simultaneously offers power and ease of use, Adobe Premiere is in the toolkit of nearly every serious producer of personal-computer video. Though it's not as powerful as the Video Toaster software found in television production studios, it's more than adequate for most Web publishers' needs. It handles editing—including insertion of spiffy transitions and picture-in-picture insets—and supports elaborate titling effects and frame-by-frame tweaking. Basically, if you can't learn to do some task with Premiere, the task is probably so complex as to require a professional anyway.

Expert videographers (which I am not) have written entire books about desktop video production and Adobe Premiere—and most of those books enable you to sit three inches taller when you're not reading them. This section offers only a taste of what Premiere can do—read the program's documentation or a book dedicated to Premiere's details if you want a more in-depth look at this powerful program.

Understanding the Timeline Analogy

Think back to grade school. Remember when the teacher gave you a long strip of paper, and told you to write "Fort Sumter—April 12, 1861" at one end, "Appomattox—April 9, 1865" at the other, and a couple of dozen other Civil War dates in between? That was a timeline, and it helped you understand the way historical events fit together in a continuum. Premiere uses the same analogy to help you organize your video presentations.

Instead of having just one timeline, though, Premiere's default configuration has seven. It calls them "tracks": two for video, one for transitions between the two video tracks, one for titles and other overlays, and three for audio. All seven of these tracks appear in the Construction window (Figure 26.1), in which you'll do most of your work in Premiere. If you need more than seven tracks, you can add up to 98 more audio or video tracks. You'll learn how to add clips to the Construction window in the next section.

When Premiere assembles a movie from the various clips you've placed in the Construction window, it starts at the left edge of the window and moves

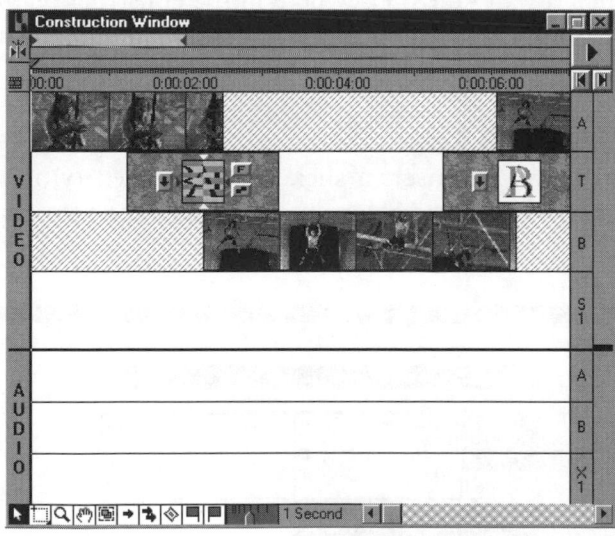

Figure 26.1 Clips and transitions arranged in the Construction window.

to the right, looking at all the tracks simultaneously and compiling the contents of all of them into a single video file. This way, you can overlay one video image with another, or play a music clip as a nature scene occupies the screen. The timeline analogy makes it easy to keep track of the logical flow of your presentation.

Placing Clips in the Construction Window

The timeline analogy's great, but you need to put clips into it before it's at all useful. Importing clips into Premiere involves another window: the Project window (Figure 26.2). To bring a clip into the Project window, bring the Project window to the foreground by clicking it, then choose File, Import, File from the menu bar. You'll see a mostly standard Windows Open dialog box. Find the file you want, highlight it (note that you can see a preview of the clip at the right of the dialog box), and click OK.

When the clip's information block (including the first frame of the clip and some data about the clip) appears in the Project window, you can move it to the Construction window. Click the information block, hold down the mouse button, and drag the block to the appropriate track in the Construction window. You can slide the clip back and forth in its track to properly coordinate it with other clips (of all kinds) elsewhere in the construction window. Refer back to Figure 26.1 to see clips arranged in the Construction window.

Using Transitions

Premiere makes it easy to insert a slick effect between two video clips. To put a transition effect (such as a wipe or fade) between two clips, make sure

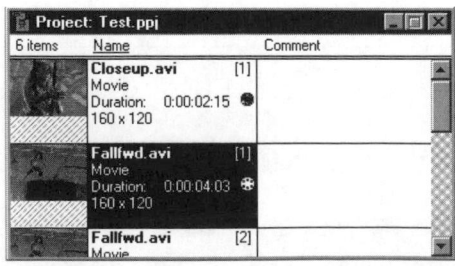

Figure 26.2   The Project window.

the clips are on different tracks and the transition track is between the two. Then bring the Transitions window (Figure 26.3) to the foreground, select the transition you want (aren't the animated illustrations helpful?) and drag it to the transition track in the Construction window. Now when you tell Premiere to compile your movie (as you'll learn to do later in this section), it won't just cut abruptly from one clip to the next; it will insert the effect you selected between them.

Some common attractive transitions include Additive Dissolve, in which the old clip fades and the new clip appears; Center Merge, in which the old clip shrinks into a tiny box in the center of the new clip and disappears; and Page Peel, in which the old clip "lifts away" from the new clip to simulate turning the pages of a book. Premiere also supports some weird transitions, including Curtain, in which the old image splits in the middle and lifts up like a theater curtain, and Tumble Away, in which the old image shrinks and spins to reveal the new image.

 Don't overdo it with fancy transitions—you don't want your editing to draw attention away from your subject. Use simple splices (sometimes called "cuts") and unobtrusive fades instead of bizarre circular wipes and other novelty effects. Just as desktop publishing software and laser printers spawned newsletters with a dozen fonts or more on each page, desktop video-editing software makes everyone think they're an effect-happy Spielberg. Resist the temptation—don't load your videos with unusual effects.

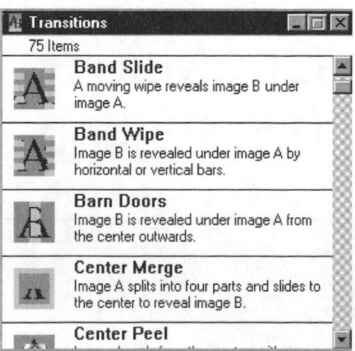

Figure 26.3   The Transitions window.

Titling

At the very least, you'll want to give yourself credit for your editing efforts, and that means you'll want to make your printed name part of the video file. Video experts call this *titling*. To create a title for your presentation, choose File, New, Title from the menu bar. You'll see the Title window (Figure 26.4). The Title window looks a lot like a slide-creation window in a presentation graphics program (the Title window and such programs serve the same purpose, after all). You can select the text tool (marked with a "T"), position the cursor on the blank area, and type your title. Then, save your title by choosing File, Save from the menu bar and typing a name for your title in the Save dialog box.

To bring the newly created title into the editing window, choose Import, File from the Menu bar and pick your title from the files listed in the dialog box. The title will then appear in the Project window, from which you can drag it to the overlays track (labeled S1) in the Construction window.

Compiling Your Presentation

When you're happy with the way you've arranged clips in the Construction window, you're ready to assemble the contents of the various timelines into

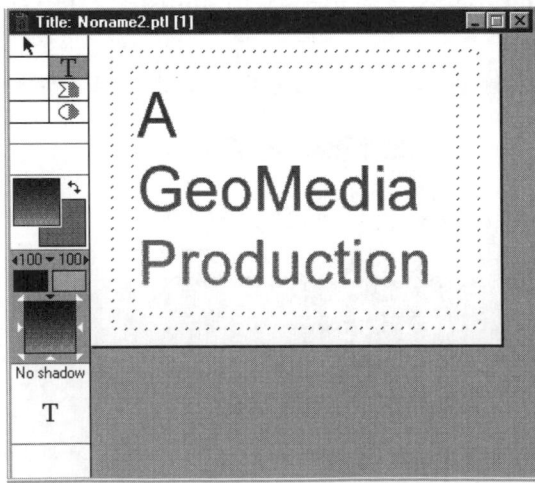

Figure 26.4   The Title window.

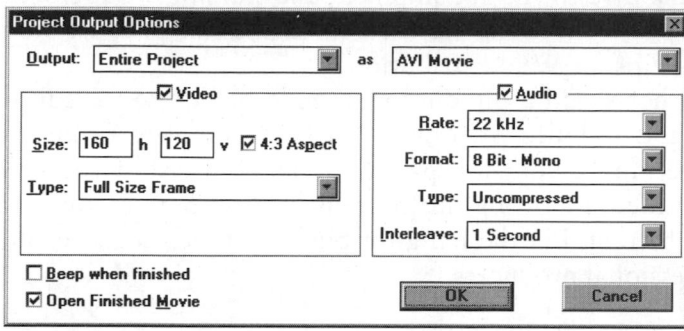

Figure 26.5 Project Output Options dialog box.

a movie. To do this, choose Make, Make Movie from the menu bar. You'll see the Make Movie box, in which you type a filename and select the directory in which Premiere should save your movie.

Before clicking OK, click the Output Options button. In the Project Output Options dialog box that appears (Figure 26.5), choose Entire Project from the Output drop-down list box in the upper left corner and choose the file format you want from the drop-down list box in the upper right corner. Click OK, then click OK in the Make Movie box. You'll see a bar graph showing Premiere's progress in assembling your movie. When it completes compilation, it will show the first frame of your movie in a window; click the right-pointing arrow at the bottom of the window to view your movie.

VIDEO PRODUCTION HINTS

You learned a lot about video production in Chapter 22, and the Webmaster tip in the last section is probably the single most important piece of advice you can heed as you begin working with Premiere and other video-editing tools.

Consider Farming It Out

This doesn't sound like much of a tip, but it's probably good advice. Video production involves such a high degree of specialized skill and so much expensive equipment that, unless you'll be doing enough video production to justify a big investment in equipment and training, you're better off leaving it to the pros. Check the Web search engines for production houses that specialize in clips for Web distribution.

You need not spend a bundle to get good-quality video editing, though. Vocational and technical schools often have complete production studios and will often make your job part of a class exercise if you provide some supplies. Granted, following this route is like stopping by the barber school for a cheap haircut, but the bang-for-buck of student editing often exceeds that of professional producers.

Keep It Short

This tip appears in every multimedia chapter in this book, and that's because it's very important. Especially with video, it's easy to create enormous files that will choke even powerful server computers. Considering that most people access the Web, at least part of the time, via a 14,000 bps connection, you can't ask them to download a giant video clip—it could take hours. With that in mind, use video in small doses, or at least warn site visitors before they commit to downloading a 5 MB video file.

FROM HERE

- Now you know how to produce still graphics, audio, and video. What about text layouts that exceed the capabilities of HTML? The next chapter explains how to use Adobe Acrobat and the Portable Document Format to publish complex documents on the Web.

Chapter
27

Producing Adobe Acrobat Documents

INTRODUCING ADOBE ACROBAT

Adobe Acrobat 2.0 provides computer users with a means of creating and interpreting *portable documents*—documents that appear the same on different machines running different software. Acrobat isn't one program, but rather a package of several programs designed to work together.

The Need for Adobe Acrobat

Before portable documents came about—and Acrobat is not the first portable-document software package—computer publishers spent hours carefully laying out and formatting documents, but were unsure what their products would look like when they were transmitted electronically to a viewer.

This uncertainty led publishers to cling to paper, printer, and facsimile technology for applications in which appearance was key, because it enabled them to know exactly what document recipients would see.

For applications in which page layouts, typefaces, and graphics were not important, exchange standards such as ASCII and Microsoft's Rich Text Format (RTF) were (and are) adequate. Such standards support the sharing of alphanumeric characters but cannot support the fancy formatting that is essential to business communication and that word processing program users have grown accustomed to.

With the growth of the World Wide Web and the corresponding growth in businesses' interest in publishing there, the need for a portable document format became apparent. The limited formatting capabilities of HTML and the omnipresent need for a consistent corporate look conflicted, and Web publishers began to look for a way to make their publications appear the same to both their creators and their consumers. Also, faxing documents to every Web user who visited a site would be impractical and would defeat every advantage of the Web.

Although several companies, including WordPerfect, have published portable document solutions, Acrobat seems to have been anointed the standard for Web publishing.

Adobe Acrobat Reader

One of the main reasons for Acrobat's success is Acrobat Reader, a program distributed free of charge on the Internet and many bulletin board systems. Most sites that offer PDF documents, in fact, can also download Acrobat Reader.

Reader is a read-only interpreter—it enables you to look at PDF documents but does not allow you to modify them or create new ones. If you plan to use Reader to view documents downloaded from the Web, you can configure Reader as a helper application that automatically displays any PDF file you download.

Adobe Acrobat

Acrobat is not one program, but rather a package of programs that extend a user's abilities to work with PDF files. The Acrobat package contains Acrobat Reader as well as the following:

Acrobat Exchange	Allows you to modify PDF documents by adding text, annotations, security restrictions, and hyperlinks.

Acrobat PDF Writer	Lets you direct print output from a word processing or page layout program to a PDF file instead of a printer.
Acrobat Search	Enables you to look for words in PDF documents indexed with Adobe Acrobat Catalog software, which is not part of the Acrobat package.

For the Time-Challenged

♦ The various Adobe Acrobat products enable you to use documents in Portable Document Format (PDF), which ensures that they look the same on all computers equipped with Acrobat software.

♦ Acrobat Reader—which enables you to look at PDF documents, but not alter them—is distributed free of charge and can be configured to act as a helper application to a Web browser.

♦ Navigate around an Acrobat document by following hyperlinks, by selecting a particular page from the outline or thumbnails on the left side of your screen, or by choosing to go to a page by clicking the page indicator (the one that says "Page 3 of 34" or something like that) in the lower-left corner of your screen.

♦ Acrobat Distiller is used to convert Encapsulated PostScript (EPS) files to PDF.

♦ PDF Writer works just like a printer driver. When you want to make a file (such as a word processing document or desktop publishing layout) into a PDF file, select PDF Writer from the list of printers available, follow your program's print procedure, and respond to the dialog boxes that appear. Your word processing file will be saved as a PDF file.

♦ You can create a hyperlink from one part of a document to another by clicking the link button on the toolbar (the one with the links of chain on it), adjusting the settings in the Create Link dialog box, moving to the view to which you want the link to lead, and clicking Set Link.

♦ You can make text items into "articles"—easy-to-follow units of text—by choosing Article from the Tools menu and dragging rectangles around each block of text. When you've surrounded the last piece of text, click the End Article button at the bottom of the screen.

♦ Axcess Magazine's experimental PDF edition (available for downloading from http://www.internex.net/axcess/) is the best example of Acrobat use on the Web. Take a look.

Adobe Acrobat Pro

The standard Adobe Acrobat package is fine for most applications, but those Acrobat users with *legacy documents*—documents written and published before Acrobat technology came into being—need a way to convert old files into PDF form. Adobe Acrobat Pro, with its Acrobat Distiller component, is the way to do this.

Acrobat Distiller converts Encapsulated PostScript (EPS) files, word processing files, page layout files, and images to PDF. It enables you to convert an archive of correspondence, documentation, personnel reports, or resumes to a common form. Acrobat Catalog, sold independently and as part of the Adobe Acrobat for Workgroups package (which includes ten licensed copies of all the programs in the Adobe Acrobat package, as well as copies of Acrobat Catalog and Acrobat Distiller), lets you prepare the converted archive for full-text searching with Acrobat Search.

The prospect of keeping business records in a common, searchable format is exciting. Imagine you're a human resources expert. Each day you receive dozens of resumes, even when there are no jobs available. Instead of trashing them or filing them away to be forgotten, you could scan them and convert the resulting word processor files to PDF format. Then, when a job opens, you can search the stored documents for keywords, such as "B.A. in English" or "PageMaker 6.0." Re-engineering opportunities like this exist in many fields, so think about how Acrobat and other technologies can make your work easier.

READING ADOBE ACROBAT DOCUMENTS

Adobe has done all it can to ensure that before long, you'll be faced with the need to read a PDF document. By making the format open and providing Acrobat Reader software free of charge, the company has made PDF an appealing option for those who wish to put formatting-rich documents on the Web.

But how do you read PDF documents? Both Acrobat Reader and Acrobat Exchange enable reading, and both use the same interface. This section walks you through opening and navigating PDF documents—the instructions apply to both applications.

Opening a Document

To open a PDF document for viewing, choose Open from the File menu and, in the Open dialog box, select the file you want to see. Double-click its filename or highlight its filename and click OK.

Modifying the Display

The Reader or Exchange window, after you have opened a document, is divided in two (Figure 27.1). To the left of the vertical dividing bar is a guide—an outline or a set of thumbnail icons (you can choose which, or eliminate the guide portion of the screen altogether by choosing among the buttons in the leftmost cluster of buttons on the toolbar). To the right of the dividing bar is one page of the document itself.

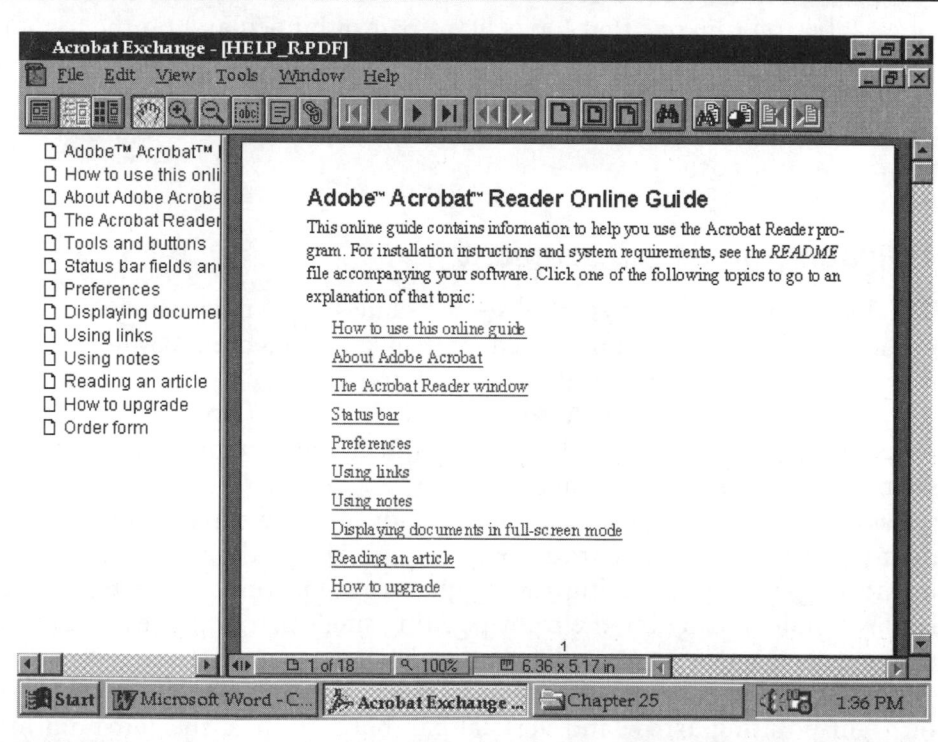

Figure 27.1 Adobe Acrobat Reader or Exchange window.

Chances are, you can't see the entire page in the portion of the window Reader or Exchange has allocated for document display. There are three ways to adjust how the document is shown:

1. You can click the Zoom Out button (the magnifying glass with a minus sign in it), then click the document. You can click several times with the Zoom Out tool to make the document appear even smaller, but the on-screen representation quickly becomes too small to use.

2. You can use the grabber hand to move the document around your screen. Use the grabber hand by clicking the hand button on the toolbar, then dragging the document up and down and from side to side with the hand-shaped pointer that results. Note that when you drag the document, the hand pointer turns into a fist that, if you have a strong imagination, looks like it's holding onto the document and pulling it around.

3. You can use the three buttons immediately to the left of the Search button (the one that looks like a pair of binoculars) on the toolbar. These buttons, which contain rectangular icons of various sizes, automatically adjust the document to fit into a space of a specific size. Try clicking each of the buttons to find the size that best suits your needs.

Navigating within a Document

PDF documents support hyperlinks—the same sort of navigation employed on the World Wide Web. Embedded hyperlinks, which are red, allow you to move from one location in a document to another quickly and without losing your train of thought. Acrobat software also supports hyperlinks to URLs on the World Wide Web—it will launch your browser automatically when you click such a hyperlink.

   Aside from using hyperlinks, you can move among the pages of a document in several ways. The traditional way is to view the pages of the document sequentially, by using the single-arrow buttons at the top of the display window. Clicking the right-pointing single arrow moves you to the next page of a document; clicking the left-pointing single arrow moves you to the previous page. To move to the last page of a document, click the right-pointing-arrow-and-vertical-bar button; click the left-pointing-arrow-and-vertical-bar button to move back to the first page of a document.

You can also navigate within a document by clicking in the guide area to the left of the vertical dividing bar. Click an outline entry or thumbnail representation of a page to move to that page. Or you can click the page indicator in the lower-left corner of your screen (it says something like "Page 1 of 5") and enter the number of the page to which you want to move.

CREATING ADOBE ACROBAT DOCUMENTS

Chances are, you won't want simply to read PDF documents. If you're a Web publisher or a member of a workgroup that needs to share documents, you'll need to create PDF documents yourself. The Adobe Acrobat package provides an easy way to create PDF documents, and Adobe Acrobat Pro includes two.

Creating Documents with PDF Writer

The easiest way to create a document to be stored as a PDF file is to use your word processing program. Create a document in that program just as you would for any other purpose, but follow this special printing procedure:

1. When you choose Print from the File menu and see the Print dialog box, choose PDF Writer from the list of available printer drivers (you may have to choose Print Setup to see this list). Click OK.

2. Acrobat Writer will prompt you for the name of the PDF file it will create (Figure 27.2). Be sure to provide the complete path along with the filename if the default path is not correct.

If you want, you can click the View PDF File check box to bring up Acrobat Reader after you print to the file so that you can examine your work. You can also click the Prompt for Document Info check box, which will bring up another dialog box in which you can enter information about the document, such as the author's name and a brief summary of the document's contents.

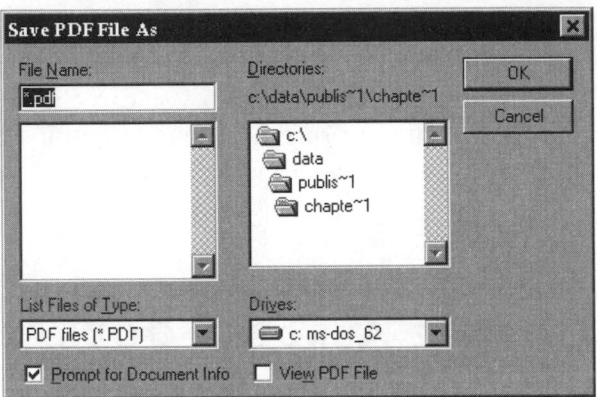

Figure 27.2   Creating a PDF document in Acrobat Writer.

Creating Documents with Acrobat Distiller

Acrobat Distiller converts Encapsulated PostScript (EPS) files to PDF format. You can use Distiller in three ways:

1. The most intuitive way is to choose Open from the Distiller File menu and choose the PostScript file you wish to convert. Double-click the PostScript document's filename, or select it and choose OK. Distiller will prompt you for the name and path of the PDF file it will generate. Click OK and watch the progress of the bar graph as Distiller does its work (Figure 27.3).

2. If you don't want to open a file in Distiller, you can put the Encapsulated PostScript file to be converted to PDF into the "In" folder under the folder in which you store Distiller. Distiller monitors that folder (Adobe calls it a "watched folder") and converts any PostScript files stored there. After converting the files, Distiller places them in the "Out" folder under the folder containing Distiller.

3. Perhaps the easiest way to convert a PostScript document—if you're using OS/2 or Windows 95—is to place the Distiller icon on the Desktop and drag PostScript file icons to it. Distiller converts the files to PDF and saves them in its "Out" folder.

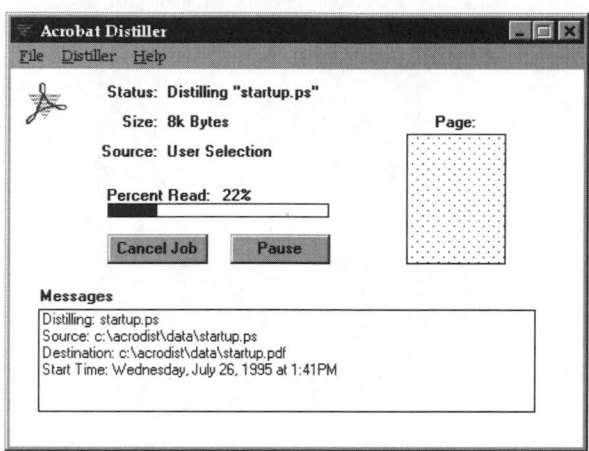

Figure 27.3 Acrobat Distiller.

ADDING INTERNAL HYPERLINKS IN AN ADOBE ACROBAT DOCUMENT

One of the appealing features of PDF documents is their ability to contain hyperlinks from one piece of data to another. This feature enables you to create documents that are not necessarily linear in flow, as traditional documents, such as books and letters, are. Hypertext documents—as the Web illustrates—can convey the precise information a reader needs without requiring the reader to waste time reading through extraneous information.

Creating a Hyperlink

Adobe Exchange uses a process of mouse-dragging and dialog-box adjustment to establish hyperlinks between portions of a document. To create a hyperlink, make sure the area of the document you want to link *from* is visible, and click the link button—the interlocked links of chain—on the toolbar. The mouse pointer will turn from an arrowhead into crosshairs. Drag the crosshairs around the area you wish to link. The Create Link dialog box (Figure 27.4) will appear as soon as you release the mouse button.

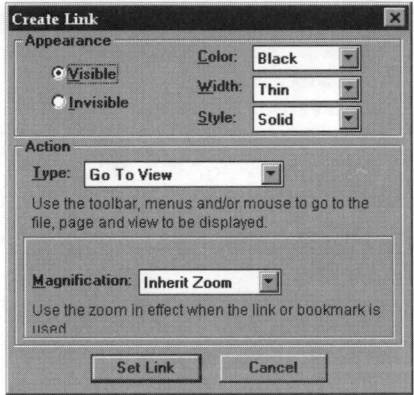

Figure 27.4   Create Link dialog box.

In the Create Link dialog box, set the Appearance options to your liking (unless you have a reason to do otherwise, make all your hyperlinks a consistent style). Choose Go To View from the Type list box, and choose Inherit Zoom from the Magnification list box (if you don't choose Inherit Zoom, you run the risk of confusing your reader with unpredictable variations in zoom).

Using the scroll bars or navigation aids, move to the view to which you want to link. When you have the view you want, click Set Link in the Create Link dialog box. The link is established, and you can test it by clicking in the area you defined at the beginning of the linking process.

COLUMNS AND ARTICLES

A real shortcoming of HTML is its inability to handle page layouts that involve columns. Skilled HTML programmers can use the column-creation tags included in the Netscape extensions of HTML, but with only limited flexibility. With Acrobat, you can use the column features of your word processing program, print it to a PDF file, and use Acrobat Exchange's article-creation tools to define the order in which Acrobat Reader will guide viewers through columnar text.

It's important to distinguish between columns and articles. *Columns*, which you create with tools in your word processing program, are a feature of text formatting. You might choose to have two side-by-side columns on a page, or a single column of text on each page. Creating columns is not a function of any Acrobat product.

Instead, Acrobat Exchange defines *articles*—the way in which related text flows through a document. If you define articles, viewers using Acrobat Reader will be able to follow a piece of writing from its beginning to its end, without having to worry about finding the continuation each time a page ends or the story, for some other reason, ends on one page and continues on another.

Defining Articles in Acrobat

To create an article, first open a PDF document by choosing Open from the File menu and selecting a file. Double-click its filename or select its filename and click OK.

Using the navigation tools in Exchange, find the beginning of the article you wish to define. Choose Article from the Tools menu; the mouse pointer will change from an arrowhead to a set of crosshairs.

Drag the crosshairs from the top-left corner of the first column of the article to the lower-right corner of the same column. Repeat the procedure with each subsequent column. The first column will be labeled (in Article view only) as "X-1," where X is the number of the article. If this is the first article in a document you've identified, the first column will be labeled "1-1."

When you reach the lower-right corner of the last portion of the article, click the End Article button at the bottom of the screen. Exchange will prompt you for information about the article—the author and title, for example. Fill in this information if you want, then click OK.

Now when a reader looks at your document and begins to read some text that's been defined as an article, he or she can simply click on a screenful of text and automatically see the next screenful—even if the text continues on another page. Article definition is a powerful tool that can significantly improve the readability of articles stored in PDF.

AN ACROBAT SAMPLER

Acrobat is a fairly new technology and isn't nearly as widespread on the Web as older document types, such as GIF graphics or AU sounds. Still, some site designers have seen the suitability of PDF to the Web and have incorporated it into their products.

Only one implementation of PDF is examined here because it outshines all others by a giant margin. Though many sites make use of PDF's formatting-retention features for a variety of good reasons (the Desktop Publishing Glossary at the University of Pennsylvania's Wharton School of Business is a great example), only one site makes use of Acrobat's capabilities for both technical and aesthetic reasons. Examine this document, and you'll learn a great deal.

Axcess Magazine

The coolest implementation of Acrobat technology on the Web is an experimental issue of Axcess Magazine, available for download at http://www.internex.net/axcess/. An electronic variety publication that specializes in alternative music and Internet culture, Axcess' experiment defines the capabilities of Acrobat publishing and sets a standard for others. The magazine's only shortcoming is its size—it's 99 graphics-laden pages long. Once you download the 2.5 megabyte PDF document and start browsing, though, you'll understand the potential of PDF publishing.

My Web browser doesn't know how to handle PDF files!
Okay, you need to configure your browser to use Acrobat Reader or Acrobat Exchange as a *helper application*—a program that handles particular kinds of files. In most browsers, the dialog box that tells you the file type is unrecognized offers to let you configure a helper application. Choose that option, and either type the path and filename of the program you want to use (Reader or Exchange) or choose Browse and find it in the graphical representation of your hard disk. Now that application will start automatically whenever you download a PDF document.

If you don't have a copy of Reader or Exchange, the chances are good that any site offering PDF files for download has Reader available too.

Axcess' welcome screen (Figure 27.5) exemplifies the high-quality layout and illustration to be found inside the magazine. The welcome screen makes good, intuitive use of hyperlinks (you click the magazine's logo to proceed to the table of contents), and it takes advantage of the ease with which Acrobat can assign a hyperlink to only part of a graphic—the same task in HTML would be a difficult undertaking.

The magazine's main table of contents (Figure 27.6) exploits the fact that, since hyperlinks in Acrobat are assigned to areas of documents and not to

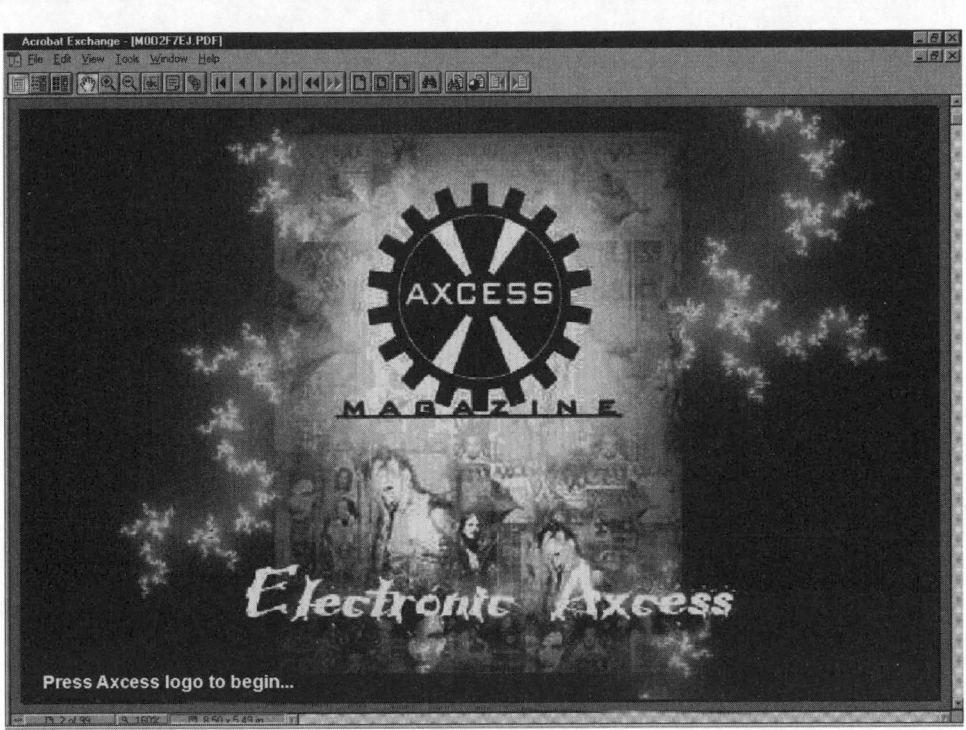

Figure 27.5 Axcess Magazine's welcome screen.

passages of text, page designers can make buttons visually appealing—there's no need to use a standard dialog-box button or to slog through tedious imagemap coding procedures.

The table of contents to the Music section (Figure 27.7) is a marvel of attractive design and intuitive functionality. Clicking the Tori Amos button on the Music guide takes you to a story that shows how attractive design can be incorporated with text and stored in the PDF format (Figure 27.8). When combined with good reporting and decent writing, as the Amos layout is, good graphic design can allow a PDF publication to compete with the finest print magazines.

Aside from its large size, Axcess falls short in its failure to use Acrobat's article-definition features. The magazine's designers went to great lengths to include hyperlinked navigation buttons on each page of each article, but they neglected to take advantage of the fact that Acrobat will guide readers through articles

Figure 27.6   Axcess' main table of contents.

Figure 27.7   Table of contents for Axcess Magazine's Music section.

Figure 27.8 An example of good graphic design in a PDF publication.

automatically. Their means of guiding readers is entirely adequate, but a reader experienced with Acrobat might want to follow an article without moving his mouse, and be disappointed that none of Axcess' stories are defined as articles.

Overall, though, Axcess' experimental PDF publication—the magazine's publishers are taking mail now to see if there's enough interest in continued PDF publication—is a superb example of the power of PDF. If you're even slightly interested in publishing in this format, visit the Axcess site and examine the experimental issue.

FROM HERE

- By this point, you understand the technical aspects of planning your Web site, coding its HTML, and producing multimedia to add spice. The rest of this book deals with issues affecting Web publishers. Read on to learn about security, copyright, and standardization issues in Part V.

Part V

WEB PUBLISHING ISSUES

Chapter
28

Security

A revolution in Web commerce is about to happen. The spark for the revolution will not be a riot or an invasion; it will be secure transaction capability for the Internet and the Web. Such capability exists today, but there is no single standard used by all server and browser manufacturers. When a standard is adopted—and one will be adopted within the next year or so, experts say—consumers will be able to send vendors their credit card numbers via the Internet without being concerned about someone intercepting and using them illegally.

This chapter provides you with an introduction to Web security issues and technologies. These subjects are interesting and central to the future expansion of the Web, but this chapter is not an exhaustive treatment of security issues as they apply to Web publishers. Entire books have been written about creating a secure Web site and carrying on secure commerce on the Web.

WHAT IS "SECURITY"?

In the computer world, *security* has three distinct shades of meaning: *authentication, confidentiality,* and *integrity,* as the following sections discuss. Of greatest interest to you, as a potential provider of commercial Web services, are confidentiality and integrity.

Authentication

In brief, *authentication* ensures that you are really who you say you are when you log on to a server.

Most Web servers demand no authentication at all—they just let you in. However, virtually all Web servers support simple protection by password: You must type a login name (user name) and password to access the service.

An example of a Web service that requires password authentication is Hot-Wired, the online version of *Wired* magazine.

When you access HotWired for the first time, you're asked to create a login name and password and to supply your e-mail address. You then receive an automatically generated e-mail message that includes an authorization number. You must then supply this authorization number to access the system. What's gained from this? A modicum of assurance that you aren't accessing the site with someone else's name and e-mail address.

Confidentiality

Confidentiality refers to the protection of information while it is en route to its destination. It's not nice to think about, but none of the information you are transmitting via the Web is free from prying eyes. Hackers, criminals, or investigators can easily intercept, record, and print all the information you transmit.

Integrity

Integrity refers to the exact preservation of the transmitted data so that it reaches its destination without any alteration, accidental or deliberate. As with confidentiality, the Web provides absolutely no means of ensuring the integrity of transmitted data. It could be altered while en route, either by chance or deliberate interference, and the receiving computer would have no way of knowing.

THE NEED FOR ENCRYPTION

The solution to the Web's confidentiality and security problems lies in the use of *encryption*. In essence, encryption is the process of converting a *plaintext* message (a message that could be read by anyone) into an unreadable *ciphertext* by means of a *key* (a method of transforming the message so that it appears to be gibberish). The message can be read only by the intended recipient, who possesses the key and uses it (in a process called *decryption*) to make the text readable again. A simple encryption technique is ROT-13, which "rotates" all letters 13 characters to the right in the alphabet. The ciphertext looks like gibberish, but it is easily decrypted by rotating the letters 13 characters left. Encryption ensures integrity as well as confidentiality;

if anyone or anything has altered the message en route, it won't decode 100% correctly, so you'll know that something has gone wrong.

ROT-13 is a poor encryption technique because its key is so simple. In fact, it's used on Usenet only to keep adult-oriented material away from the eyes of children or those who would rather not see such material. More complicated keys are needed to ensure confidentiality and integrity. With more complicated keys, though, another problem arises: How to transmit the key to the recipient. Traditionally, this has been done by courier, but this is costly and time-consuming. Military strategists in ancient Rome lamented the "messenger problem"—the challenge of getting a key to its intended recipient and running the risk that the messenger carrying it would be captured or, worse, bribed into revealing the key.

A new cryptographic method called *public key cryptography* eliminates the need to deliver the key and raises the possibility that people who have never previously exchanged messages could send encrypted messages to each other, which could not be intercepted by a third party. In public key cryptography, there are two different keys, an encryption key and a decryption key:

- **Public encryption key**   You make your encryption key public; people use it to send an encrypted message to you.

- **Decryption key**   This key is kept private. You use it to decode the messages sent to you. Nobody else can read the message without this key.

With public key cryptography, there is no need to establish a secure channel to exchange the decryption key; the person who wishes to send an encrypted message to you merely obtains the public encryption key, encrypts the message, and sends it to you. Nobody along the way can decode the message, even if they have intercepted the encryption key; they need the decryption key, and you keep that secret. Rightfully, public key encryption has been described as a revolution in cryptography. It makes cryptography available to ordinary people.

Introducing the Secure Socket Layer (SSL) Security Protocol

To provide secure transactions via the World Wide Web, Netscape Communications Corporation has proposed a standard called the Secure Socket Layer

(SSL) protocol. This proposed Internet standard seeks to provide secure public key encryption capabilities so that people can exchange information securely via any established Internet protocol, including not only the Web but also Gopher, FTP, Telnet, and others. What is more, SSL seeks to do this without placing undue demands on users; much or all of the SSL processing goes on in the background, without requiring any intervention from the user.

An SSL session begins when an SSL-capable client (such as Netscape Navigator) contacts an SSL-capable server (such as Netscape's secure Web servers). A brief exchange of public keys occurs; from that point on, the client and server can exchange secure, encrypted messages and no third party can intercept them. In addition, SSL includes integrity-checking features that assure both parties that the message has not been tampered with or altered during its transmission.

WHAT ABOUT STANDARDS?

As of this book's writing, there is no "official" standard for the secure transmission of sensitive data on the World Wide Web. In an effort to gain acceptance for its SSL protocol as the standard security protocol for the Web, Netscape has published SSL's specifications and made the technology widely available. However, competing firms are attempting to do the same. The worst-case scenario is that two or more competing but incompatible security standards will exist. If this happens, the Web's budding commercial ventures could die on the vine; a user of Netscape would be able to access only Netscape-friendly secure sites, while users of Spyglass's Enhanced NSCA Mosaic would be able to access only those sites conforming to Spyglass's protocol.

The most likely outcome of this struggle, in the short run, is that two or three competing security standards will exist and Web servers will have to recognize them all. Netscape has announced its plans to support both its own SSL and S-HTTP, a competing security protocol, in both Netscape Navigator and its server products. In the long run, it seems likely that the Web community will be able to agree on a single standard for secure Web transactions. Most likely, it will include many features from SSL plus additional ones from Netscape's competitors. The *Wall Street Journal* recently reported that Netscape Communications had invested in Terisa Systems, which is developing a Web security standard that would unify all the competing security technologies. A solution to the standardization dilemma may be very near.

Is My Customers' Information Really Safe?

Public key encryption protects information from being intercepted or altered while it is transmitted. Does that mean customers' credit card information is safe? With a secure connection on the Web, you can be assured that nobody can obtain credit card numbers by "tapping" your Internet connection. But sending a credit card number via a secure link is very much like giving it to somebody over the telephone: Customers are still dependent on the honesty and integrity of vendors. In the end, ordering on the Web won't be any safer than any other form of mail order.

If you're thinking about ordering something by credit card on the Web, use all the common-sense rules that you would when ordering by telephone or mail. Order from well-established firms with good reputations. Make sure you fully understand the firm's policies regarding the delivery of ordered goods, returns and exchanges, and refunds. If you're selling things via the Web, handle credit card information with the utmost care, and make sure your customers know they can trust you. You're ahead of the game if your company is well known and has a good reputation. If you're new, you have to establish credibility with customers before others entrust their credit card information to you.

From Here

- Concerned about issues of copyright as well as security? Take a look at the next chapter.

Chapter
29

Copyright

I f you've been using the Web and other Internet features, such as mailing lists and Usenet newsgroups, for more than a few weeks, you've probably seen some kind of discussion about copyrights and copyright law. These topics are perennial favorite discussion topics of Internet users, and it makes sense: the Web and the rest of the Internet are designed to make information easy to find and use, while copyright law is supposed to, in one sense, restrict the flow of information. The purposes of information technology and copyright law often conflict, so it follows that users of information technology are concerned about how copyright law applies to them.

This chapter provides a basic introduction to the concepts of copyright. It's not complete: You can go to law school for years and not fully comprehend the vagaries of copyright law, and no one's entirely sure how traditional copyright ideas apply to relatively new electronic publishing media, anyway. Take a look at this chapter for a general idea of how copyright law applies to your Web publication—but consult a lawyer if you're in copyright trouble or have very specific questions.

WHAT IS COPYRIGHT LAW?

Copyright law is a collection of laws that protect the expression of those who engage in creative work. Originally put into practice in the time of Queen Elizabeth I of England, copyright law is designed to enable novelists, poets, songwriters, and other artists to profit from their work.

What Does Copyright Law Do?

In the United States, copyright law ensures that the creator of a piece of creative work, such as a play, a painting, a photograph, or a poem, can control what is done with that piece of creative work. Typically, the creator reserves the right to:

- Make and sell copies of the work (this is why book authors get royalties on each copy of their books that publishers sell).

- Perform or display the work publicly.

- Adapt the work to a new medium (to convert a novel into a screenplay, for example).

- Receive recognition as author when the work is used or cited by another creator (this is why students should be careful to attribute quoted material in their papers to its original authors).

It's important to note that copyright law covers only the expression of an idea, not the idea itself. Otherwise, two reporters, each from a different newspaper, would be violating copyright law if they wrote news stories about the same event. For this reason, it's easier to violate a copyright on fictional material than on nonfiction material. Virtually everything a novelist puts into a novel is a product of his or her imagination (the ideas are the novelist's), while an engineer might draw heavily on the decidedly uncopyrighted laws of physics in a professional paper.

For the Time-Challenged

♦ Copyright law protects the right of those who produce creative work to profit from that work.

♦ For works created in the United States after 1978, the copyright period ends 50 years after the death of the creator.

♦ You have a copyright on anything you create. However, you cannot sue for copyright infringement unless you register your copyright with the U.S. Copyright Office.

♦ Material not protected by copyright is said to be in the public domain and may be used by anyone, for any purpose, including making a profit.

♦ You can use copyrighted material with permission from the copyright holder or, in small quantities, under the "fair use" rules of copyright law.

♦ The Web and other new information technologies will probably soon cause an upheaval in copyright law.

Though there have been many changes in the rules regarding how long copyright protection lasts, the general rule for works created after 1978 is that copyright protection of a piece of creative work lasts until 50 years after the creator's death. Earlier laws required copyright holders to renew their copyright claims every few years; that rule is generally obsolete. Talk to a lawyer about the specific duration rules that apply in your case.

How Do I Get a Copyright on Material I've Created?

If you created a piece of work, you automatically have the copyright on that piece of work. You no longer need to register your claim to the work with the U.S. Copyright Office or to include any sort of copyright notice on the work itself in order to have a copyright. There are, however, some good reasons to register your creation and to include a copyright notice on it anyway.

Most important, you cannot sue someone for infringing on your copyright unless your claim is registered with the Copyright Office. You can register as soon as you see an infringement and want to sue, but it's better to register ahead of time for the following reasons:

- A rush registration, which you would need if you had to complete registration before a court date, costs $200, while a standard registration costs $20.

- You may be eligible for a larger award from the court, including attorney's fees, if you register before an infringement takes place.

You should also include a copyright notice on your work. A copyright notice consists of the © symbol, your name, and the date on which the creative work was completed. By including a copyright notice on your work, you reduce the possibility that someone you sue for infringement will argue ignorance—that he or she didn't know your work was copyrighted—and thereby reduce the penalty.

My computer won't make the © symbol! Is (c) good enough? No. At least, probably not, and you're better off figuring out how to make the © symbol than finding out in court that a substitute wasn't good enough. Copyright law in the United States gives you three options for indicating that a work is copyrighted: the © symbol, the word "copyright," and the abbreviation "Copr." International copyright law recognizes only the © symbol. Avoid trouble: use a circle-c copyright symbol.

Who Enforces Copyright Law?

You may be loathe to comply with copyright regulations, and something along the lines of, "What's going to happen? Are the copyright police going to come get me?" may have passed your lips. The answer to your question is, yes, if you remain in violation of copyright laws long enough, a court can issue an order that law enforcement officers can uphold. Don't panic, though, if your copyright violation is minor or unintentional. If you have copyrighted material on your site and you're not making money from it or detracting from the profits of the copyright's owner, the worst you can reasonably expect is a nasty letter from the copyright owner's lawyer, telling you to take the material off the Web. If you comply with the lawyer's request, you'll be okay.

If you ignore the letter and leave the material up, the copyright holder can sue you for infringing on his or her copyright. The result of such a trial, assuming there is no doubt about the copyright holder's right to the material, could be a court order making you pay damages to the copyright holder or making you stop using the copyrighted material, or both. If you ignore a court order, police can confront you and make you comply with it.

WHAT DOES "PUBLIC DOMAIN" MEAN?

Copyrighted material may only be legally used by the copyright holder; public domain material may be used by anyone in any way they wish. Think of it in terms of the land in a city: Anyone can use the public parks for any purpose they wish, as long as that purpose is within the limits of the city's laws. Private land, in contrast, may only be used by its owners or by people given special permission by its owners. Information is the same. No one can successfully sue for copyright infringement on public domain information.

That's not to say you can't sell public domain information. If you go to the trouble of assembling census data for all the states onto a CD-ROM disc, you can sell it. Likewise, if you print *Hamlet* as a paperback book, you can sell that book. In these cases, though, the product you're selling isn't the information—it's available free of charge to anyone who wishes to compile it—it's the packaging. By putting the census data on CD-ROM or printing *Hamlet* in a readable typeface, you're adding value to the information.

How Does Information Enter the Public Domain?

There are several ways a piece of creative work can enter the public domain. Once it's in the public domain, a work cannot be copyrighted again.

- The most common way is expiration of copyright—the creator's rights to a creative work have been lost because of the passage of time. The rules on copyright terms have changed over the years, but the current rule in the United States is that a copyright expires 50 years after the creator's death. Expired copyrights explain why classical music is used so frequently in advertisements—advertisers need not pay royalties to the creator of a 200-year-old composition.

- Any information created by the U.S. government (such as census data) is automatically public domain, since the government cannot claim copyright on any of its creative products. Before you amble over to the Pentagon and ask to see the public domain plans for the Seawolf submarine, though, remember that there are lots of other ways the government can protect its creative products.

- Certain creative products, such as brief slogans or words, cannot be copyrighted (though they may be trademarked; trademark law offers similar protection). In a neat example of this rule, General Motors had to use the word "Flxible" (without an e) to describe a line of buses because "flexible" is a common word.

- Copyright holders can abandon or forfeit their copyrights in a variety of legally technical ways.

Can I Use Information That Is Not in the Public Domain?

Yes, you can use copyrighted information in either of two ways: by asking and receiving permission from the copyright holder or by making "fair use" of the material.

Asking permission is straightforward. You go to the holder of a copyright and ask for the right to use the copyrighted material in a particular way. If you're granted permission, you can use the material in a particular way, and if permission is refused, you cannot use the material. It's a good idea to get this permission in writing, as a written document will stand up in court should the copyright holder later claim that permission was not given.

Fair use is a little more complex, but it also makes logical sense. The fair use clauses of copyright laws say that you can use small parts of copyrighted material for certain purposes. These purposes include, among others:

- Including quotes from a speech or presentation in a news article.

- Including quotes from a novel or nonfiction work in a review or critique.

- Reproducing copyrighted material, in small quantities, for instructional purposes.

- Parodying a copyrighted work.

The thing to remember about fair use is that you can't make money from it, and you can only use small portions of a work. Courts recognize that reproducing and sharing copyrighted work is part of the law's purpose.

HOW HAS INFORMATION TECHNOLOGY CHANGED COPYRIGHT LAW?

In brief, it hasn't. Aside from recognizing that computer programs and other electronic media can be copyrighted since they represent creative work, the ideas behind copyright law haven't changed much in the last 400 years. This is partly due to the inherent conservatism of courts (it took the United States Supreme Court 40 years to conclude that motion pictures are covered by the First Amendment), but it's also due to the totally new nature of many things on the Web. Movies were thought of as a new form of theater, and music recordings were considered a derivative of live concert performance, but there's nothing to which to compare the Web adequately. It will probably be some time before the courts sort out the issues of copyright facing the Web and the Internet. This section lists some of the questions courts will have to deal with as Web publication grows more popular.

What Constitutes a Web Publication?

Does copyright law cover only the HTML code used to create a Web page, or does it cover the way that code appears when interpreted by a browser? Are multimedia clips hyperlinked to a Web page part of that page, or are they separate entities? What about other Web pages, written and maintained by other people?

Who's the Author of a Web Publication?

Is the HTML programmer the sole creator of a Web publication? Or is the person who configures their browser to interpret the HTML code in a certain way an author too? Perhaps the people who developed HTML itself, and therefore made all other Web publications possible, should get some credit for every Web page ever created. If a program, such as a search engine, builds a Web page, is that program an author? Can it receive credit for what it created?

FROM HERE

- This chapter examined the legal issues that govern (or soon will govern) Web publishing. The next chapter describes the technological trends that will change Web publishing in the near future.

Chapter
30

Standardization Issues

I n the beginning, there was Standard Generalized Markup Language (SGML), a set of codes used to attach format descriptions to academic papers published on the Internet. When the Web came along, an SGML Document Type Description (DTD) was developed to describe HyperText Markup Language (HTML). The HTML DTDs (one exists for each of the several versions of HTML) describe the function of each HTML tag and give parsers—Web browsers—suggestions about what to do with text attached to each tag.

That's what the DTDs do—they give suggestions about formatting. Browsers can be configured by programmers or even their users to do many different things with text attached to particular tags. Most browsers have a setup dialog box of some sort in which users can specify how big various headers should be, what color text should be, and in what typeface different

For the Time-Challenged

♦   There are two camps on the subject of standardizing the way HTML code is interpreted by browsers: the faction that says the interpretation should be standardized, and the faction that says it should not.

♦   Those who favor standardization say standardization would guarantee an HTML developer the ability to know how his or her code would appear when finally interpreted for the use of a viewer. They also say commercial applications of the Web, in which image is key, demand a standardization of HTML to handle such things as corporate logos and slogans.

♦   Those who oppose standardization of HTML interpretation say that standardization is contrary to the spirit of the Web—that HTML was designed to give flexibility to producers and consumers of information alike, and that standardizing interpretation makes the Web too much like television or radio. They also say that people will be shut out from the Web community if they can't see the small typefaces publishers using HTML with standard interpretations are sure to use.

types of text appear. This flexibility was cited as one of the big advantages of HTML in its early days. People could make their text extra large if they didn't see well, or could put body text in a sans serif font it that pleased them.

Now, though, as commercial enterprise gains a foothold on the Web, customization has come to be seen by some as more of a liability than an advantage. Commercial site publishers want their efforts to look the same to everyone, no matter what kind of equipment viewers use (just like television). If viewers have the ability to alter the appearance of sites at their will, commercial Web publishers have no way of knowing how their sites will appear—and are afraid they'll look bad.

And so a debate rages about the extent to which the interpretation of HTML should be standardized, if at all. This chapter explains both sides of the debate and leaves it to you to determine which side's points appeal to you the most.

THE CASE FOR STANDARDIZATION

Arguments in favor of standardization are put forward mainly by business people who want their site to appear the same to everyone who views it. Among publishers of Web newspapers and magazines, it's primarily those who came to Web publishing after a career in traditional paper-based publishing that want to make HTML into a new desktop publishing tool with strict typographic controls. Their arguments are few but potent.

Better Typographic Control

The appeal of desktop publishing programs like PageMaker and Quark Xpress is that they allow you to place text and graphics in a precise position on a page. They allow you to decide everything from how big a document's margins are to how close to a graphic words and numbers approach. They offer extensive support for color matching and allow you to manipulate the appearance of graphics in dozens of ways.

HTML offers little typographical control. To format a paragraph as body text, you tag it with the <P> tag, instead of defining it as 12-point Times New Roman with 14 points of leading, a 10-pica initial indent, and ragged-right formatting, as you would in a desktop publishing program. The way a particular browser interprets a particular tag is not known to the person coding a document in HTML—and it's possible that a document that looks great on one browser will look terrible on another.

People have devised tricks to circumvent the typographic limitations of HTML. One of the more creative solutions is to use lots of single-pixel transparent GIF files to space text and graphic elements properly—but solutions like these are far from being standard HTML. An HTML standard that is more compatible with traditional ideas of typography and page design is favored by those who want their documents to appear the same to everyone.

Documents Look Good on All Browsers

The truth is, few people actually go into their browsers' configuration dialog box and adjust the way their browsers interpret HTML tags. They assume that the people at the software development house that published the browser knew what they were doing, and unless they have a special need, they don't alter the factory settings (people with special needs are one of the main arguments against standardizing HTML interpretation—see below). Still, several different software houses publish Web browsers, and they all interpret tags slightly differently. Hyperlinks, for example, are green in NCSA Mosaic and blue in Netscape Navigator.

Standardizing the way HTML is interpreted would eliminate the discrepancies in document appearance among different browsers. It would absolve Web publishers of the need to test their publications on several browsers.

Consistent Corporate Image

It's hard to market a corporation and its products nowadays without a consistent corporate image—and in our society, corporate image rests on visual cues. What would you think if you saw a New York Times whose flag (the words "The New York Times" on the front page) was in Helvetica Light? What if you saw a can of Coca-Cola that was blue, with black Courier lettering on it? You'd probably decide the products were fakes—cheap, illegal Malaysian knockoffs or something. You wouldn't buy them.

That's the problem with putting material that's central to corporate image on the Web. Depending on how viewers have their browsers configured, they can make HTML material appear however they wish. There's no room for corporate consistency in standard HTML. Of course, corporate HTML developers can use graphics or other formatting tricks to get their material to look right all the time, but then they're meddling with issues of reducing flexibility and wasting bandwidth.

THE CASE AGAINST STANDARDIZATION

Others, who seem to be in the minority on the Web now, argue that markup languages' flexibility is their appeal. To try to give HTML a standard appearance in every browser, the opponents of appearance standardization say, is to defeat the main point of HTML. Standardization of HTML interpretation makes the Web just another variation on newspapers and television, in which media producers decide how things appear to consumers and the consumers themselves have no real input.

Contrary to Spirit of Markup Language

Markup languages, HTML purists say, are not supposed to be about consistent appearance. They're supposed to be about transmitting basic formatting information from a document creator to a document consumer as efficiently as possible. Creativity and flexibility are due to the consumer of the document as much as they're due to its producer, and the ability to modify the appearance of HTML documents makes the consumer feel more involved in the information-exchange process.

Taking the ability to adjust the appearance of HTML documents away from the consumer is to force them into a passive absorption of data that is contrary to the spirit of the Web. The Web, supporters of this point say, is supposed to promote *exchange*, not just *distribution*, of information.

Less Flexibility for Users

Opponents of the standardization of the way HTML code is interpreted also say that standardizing appearance cuts out people who *need* their information to appear a certain way. Under traditional HTML rules, people who have poor eyesight or who have trouble distinguishing dark text against a dark background can adjust the display of text to their liking. Standardized HTML interpretation puts the power with the producers of information, who, as demonstrated by television and newspapers, will present information in a way that appeals to most, but not all, people. Those with special needs, who don't have to be ignored by the Web (since it's easy to customize Web information, unlike printed or televised information), should not be left out because of a desire for corporate consistency and appearance standardization.

FROM HERE

- This is the last chapter in *Publish it on the Web!* You're well prepared to go to your computer and begin producing Web documents that include formatted text, graphics, sound, and video. You also have a good understanding of the intricacies of HTML code, the coming trends in Web design, and the issues that face Web publishers. If you have questions about particular HTML tags, you can refer to Appendix A. Happy publishing!

Part VI

APPENDICES

Appendix
A

HTML 3.2 Quick Reference Guide

This reference guide emphasizes practical HTML—that is, the tags that are recognized and correctly interpreted by the leading browsers, Netscape Navigator and Microsoft Internet Explorer. For this reason, this appendix does not include many little-used HTML tags. However, it does include some nonstandard tags that are not in general use. Nonstandard tags are flagged with a Netscape (N) or Microsoft Internet Explorer (I) icon, or both, to indicate which browser supports them. Italicized words indicate variables.

Comment

Task	Tag	Notes
Insert a nonprinting comment.	<!-->...<-->	Browsers ignore anything inside these tags.

Head

Task	Tag	Notes
Define the overall HTML environment.	<HTML>...</HTML>	Always nest your entire HTML document within these tags.
Create the head environment.	<HEAD>...</HEAD>	Nested within <HTML>. In most documents, the only tag that goes within the head is <TITLE>.
Define a title.	<TITLE>...</TITLE>	The title text appears on the browser's title bar, not in the document. Use an <H1> tag to define what appears to be a title within the document.
Automatically take viewer to a different site.	<META HTTP-EQUIV=refresh CONTENT="*seconds*" URL="*URL*">	Try 5 seconds.
Indicate the author's name for search engine retrieval.	<META NAME= "author" CONTENT="*name*">	Type your name for "*name.*"
Indicate keywords for search engine retrieval.	<META NAME="keywords" CONTENT="*word1, word2, word3*">	Type as many words as you'd like, separated by commas.
Give a brief abstract for display by a search engine.	<META NAME= "description" COTENT="*abstract*"	Type a brief summary for "*abstract.*"

Body

Task	Tag	Notes
Create the body element without any special attributes.	<BODY>...</BODY>	Nested within <HTML>, and below <BODY>.
Create the body element with a background color.	<BODY BGCOLOR="*color code*">	For a list of color codes, see Appendix C.
Create the body element with a background graphic.	<BODY BACKGROUND="*filename*">	You can use a JPEG graphic for a background.
Create the body element with a text color.	<BODY TEXT="*color code*">	For a list of color codes, see Appendix C.
Create the body element with a link color.	<BODY LINK="*color code*">	For a list of color codes, see Appendix C.
Create the body element with a visited link color.	<BODY VLINK="*color code*">	See Appendix C for a list of color codes.

Task	Tag	Notes
Create the body element with an active link color.	<BODY ALINK=*"color code"*>	See Appendix C for a list of color codes.
Create the body element and define the base font size.	<BODY BASEFONT SIZE=*number*>	Type a number from 1 to 7; the default base font size is 3.

Style Sheets

Task	Tag	Notes
Create a style definition.	<STYLE>...</STYLE>	If placed before the <BODY> tag, this defines the style for the whole document.
Define an element.	<STYLE *tag* {*definition*}>...<STYLE>	For *tag*, use any valid element, such as BODY or H1. See below for *definitions*, which are enclosed in braces.
Define the typeface.	{font-family: *"name"*}	Add one or more font names, separated by commas. The browser will try to use the first one, then the second, and so on. You can also use the generic names serif, sans serif, cursive fantasy, or monospace.
Define the font size.	{font: *size*}	Enter the size in points (such as 12pt), inches (in), centimeters (cm), or pixels (px).
Define the font color.	{font: color: *colorname*}	Enter a color name or code. You can use the following names: black, silver, gray, white, maroon, red, purple, fuchsia, green, lime, olive, yellow, navy, blue, teal, aqua.
Define the font weight.	{font-weight: *weight*}	Options include extra-light, light, demi-light, medium, demi-bold, bold, and extra-bold.
Define the font style.	{font-style: *style*}	Use normal or italic.
Define the line height.	{line-height: *height*}	Enter a line height in points, such as 12pt.
Define the left margin.	{margin-left: *distance*}	Enter the distance in points, inches, centimeters, or pixels.
Define the right margin.	{margin-right: *distance*}	Enter the distance in points, inches, centimeters, or pixels.
Define the top margin.	{margin-top: *distance*}	Enter the distance in points, inches, centimeters, or pixels.
Align the text.	{text-align: *alignment*}	Choose from left, center, or right.
Indent the text.	{text-indent: *distance*}	Enter the distance in points, inches, centimeters, or pixels.

Task	Tag	Notes
Add a background color to the element.	{background: *color code*}	Use one of the color codes listed in Appendix C.
Add a background graphic to the element.	{background: *URL*}	Specify the graphic's location.

Line and Paragraph Breaks

Task	Tag	Notes
Start a new line without leaving a blank line.	 	This tag doesn't leave a blank line.
Instruct the browser to leave the text formatted as you've typed it (with the same line breaks).	<PRE>...</PRE>	Preserves line breaks and spacing.
N I Prevent line breaks within the enclosed text.	<NOBR>...</NOBR>	Prevents a line break.
N Show where to break a line optionally within text defined with the <NOBR> tag.	<WBR>	Shows where to break a word, should the browser need to break a lengthy word or expression.
Insert white space so that the next text appears below a graphic, not to the side of it.	<BR CLEAR=*option*>	If you've inserted a graphic flush left, use <BR CLEAR=LEFT> to insert white space so that the next text appears below the graphic. If you've inserted a graphic flush right, use <BR CLEAR=RIGHT> to insert white space so that the next text appears below the graphic. If you've used more than one graphic, use <BR CLEAR=ALL>.

Alignment

Task	Tag	Notes
Align text in a block	<DIV ALIGN="*aliment*">...</DIV>	Options are LEFT, RIGHT, or CENTER.
Center text	<CENTER>...</CENTER>	
Control the alignment of body text (flush left, center, or flush right).	<P ALIGN=*option*>...</P>	Choose LEFT, RIGHT, or CENTER.

Rules and Borders

Task	Tag	Notes
Insert a vertical rule.	<HR>	
Align the rule.	<HR ALIGN=*alignment*>	You can align the rule left, right, or center.
Define the rule's thickness.	<HR SIZE=*pixels*>	Supply a number in pixels.
Control the rule's width.	<HR WIDTH=*pixels* or *percent*>	Supply a number in pixels or type a percentage of page width. To make sure the rule always spans the window, use <HR WIDTH=100%>.
Remove the three-dimensional effect of a rule.	<HR NOSHADE>	This option omits the 3-D look.

Headings and Subheadings

Task	Tag	Notes
Define a level one heading.	<H1>...</H1>	Use this tag for the apparent title of the document (the <TITLE> text appears on the title bar).
Define a level two heading.	<H2>...</H2>	This is a good tag to use for what appear to be first-level headings within your document (the <H1> tag looks like a title).
Define a level three heading.	<H3>...</H3>	Use only if you've also used an <H> heading; use a minimum of two <H3> subheadings under each <H2> tag.
Define a level four heading.	<H4>...</H4>	Not normally used. Too many subheadings are confusing. If necessary, use only if you've already used <H2> and <H3>, and use a minimum of two <H4> subheadings under each <H3> tag.
Define a level five heading.	<H5>...</H5>	Not normally used. See notes for <H4> tag.
Define a level six heading.	<H6>...</H6>	Not normally used. See notes for <H4> tag.
Align the heading in the center of the page.	<H*n* ALIGN=*option*>	Use with any of the heading tags. You can use LEFT, CENTER, or RIGHT.

Emphasis

Task	Tag	Notes
Call attention to particularly important text, but enable the browser to decide how to format it.	\<STRONG>...\</STRONG>	Usually displayed as bold.
Emphasize the text, but enable the browser to decide how to format it.	\<EM>...\</EM> or \<DFN>...\</DFN>	Usually displayed as italic.
Format a bibliographic citation.	\<CITE>...\</CITE>	Usually displayed in italics.
Boldface text.	\<B>...\</B>	
Italicize text.	\<I>...\</I>	
Underline text.	\<U>...\</U>	This can confuse the reader because hyperlinks are underlined.
Format the text with strikeout, as in a legal document.	\<S>...\</S>	
Format the text so that it looks like typewritten text.	\<TT >...\</TT >	Displayed in a monospace font.
Format the text using a fixed-width font, so that it looks like computer code.	\<CODE >...\</CODE > or \<SAMP>...\</SAMP> or \<LISTING>...\</LISTING> or \<KBD>...\</KBD> or \<VAR>...\</VAR>	These tags overlap in function and are not consistently implemented. Most browsers format these tags using a fixed-width font.
Code the text so that it blinks.	\<BLINK>...\</BLINK>	Use sparingly—or avoid altogether. Please?
Format the text so that everything within it appears in the browser, even HTML tags.	\<PLAINTEXT>.. \</PLAINTEXT>	This tag is obsolete. Use \<PRE> instead.

Fonts

Task	Tag	Notes
Define the document's base font.	\<BASEFONT SIZE=*number*>	Use a number between 1 and 7. The default basefont size is 3.
Change the base font size for a unit of text by increasing or decreasing the base font size.	\<FONT SIZE=+*n*>...\</FONT> or \<FONT SIZE= –*n*>... \</FONT>	Use a number between 1 and 7. If the base font is 3, typing +4 raises the font size to 7, the maximum. If the base font is 5, typing –3 lowers the font size to 2.
Change the font size for a unit of text by typing an absolute font size number.	\<FONT SIZE=*n*>... \</FONT>	Use a number between 1 and 7.

Task	Tag	Notes
Color the text a specified color.	<FONT COLOR= "colr-code">	See Appendix C for a list of color codes.
Format the text using the specified font.	<FONT FACE= "name">	Type a font name, such as ARIAL or TIMES ROMAN. .
Increase the font size by one relative size.	<BIG>...</BIG>	
Decrease the font size by one relative size.	<SMALL>...</SMALL>	

Paragraph Formats

Task	Tag	Notes
Type an extended quotation, set apart from the body text in an indented quote.	<BLOCKQUOTE>... </BLOCKQUOTE>	
Distinctively format a contact person's name	<ADDRESS>...</ADDRESS>	The address is usually displayed in italics.

Lists

Task	Tag	Notes
Create a list of items without bullets.	<MENU> <LI>*Item 1* <LI>*Item 2...* </MENU>	Be sure to place <LI> before each item in the list.
Create a bulleted list.	<UL> <LI>*Item 1* <LI>*Item 2* </UL>	Be sure to place <LI> before each item in the list.
Define the bullet type.	<UL TYPE=*option*> <LI>*Item 1* <LI>*Item 2* </UL>	Choose from BULLET, CIRCLE, or SQUARE.
Create a numbered list.	<OL> <LI>*Item 1* <LI>*Item 2...* </OL>	Be sure to place <LI> before each item in the list. Don't add numbers before items; your browser will do this automatically.
Specify the starting number in a numbered list.	<OL START=*number*> <LI>*Item 1* <LI>*Item 2...* </OL>	Type the beginning number.
Choose the style of the numbered list.	<OL TYPE=*option*> <LI>*Item 1* <LI>*Item 2...* </OL>	Choose from A (capital letters), a (lowercase letters), I (uppercase Roman numerals), i (lowercase Roman numerals), and 1 (Arabic numbers, the default).

Task	Tag	Notes
Create a list of definitions, with the terms in the left column and the definition in the right.	<DL> <DT>*term*<DD>*definition 1* <DT>*term*<DD>*definition 2...* </DL>	
Add a definition item within a definition list	<DD>...</DD>	This tag indents the definition.
Create a directory list.	<DIR> <LI>*Item 1* <LI>*Item 2* </DIR>	Not often used. Most browsers format this as a bulleted list.

Hyperlinks

Task	Tag	Notes
Link to an external URL.	<A HREF="*URL*">*Text to appear on-screen*</A>	Don't forget the quote marks and the closing </A> tag.
Link to a local file in the same directory.	<A HREF="*filename*">*Text to appear on-screen*</A>	To link to a file one directory up from the HTML file's location, use the parent directory symbol, as follows: "*/../filename*". To link to a file one directory down from the HTML file's location, use the subdirectory name. To link to a file in the DOCS directory, for example, use this: "*/DOCS/filename*".
Define a link to a target that you've defined within the same document.	<A HREF="#*target name*">*Text to appear on-screen*</A >	Don't forget the pound sign before the target name.

Graphics

Task	Tag	Notes
Insert a graphic that's located in the same directory as the HTML document.	<IMG SRC="*filename*">	
Insert a graphic that's located at the specified URL.	<IMG SRC="*URL*">	This is not recommended. What if the author of the remote site removes the URL from the Web? Also, using this tag places a heavy load on the remote site's server.
Align the graphic vertically.	<IMG VALIGN=*option* SRC="*filename*">	Choose from TOP, MIDDLE, or BOTTOM.
Align the graphic horizontally.	<IMG ALIGN=*option* SRC="*filename*">	Choose from LEFT, RIGHT, or CENTER.

Task	Tag	Notes
Specify text to use for display in nongraphical browsers.	<IMG ALT="*text*" SRC="*filename*">	It's considerate to include this.
Specify the border width.	<IMG BORDER=*pixels* SRC="*filename*">	To make sure that the graphic has no border, including a blue border if the graphic is defined as a hyperlink, use BORDER=0.
Specify the width of the graphic in screen pixels.	<IMG WIDTH=*pixels* SRC="*filename*">	Since most browsers preserve aspect ratio when sizing graphics, you can control graphic size by using this attribute alone.
Specify the height of the graphic in screen pixels.	<IMG HEIGHT=*pixels* SRC="*filename*">	
Specify the width of the frame in which the graphic is situated.	<IMG HSPACE=*pixels* SRC="*filename*">	By default, no additional space is set aside for the frame width.
Specify the height of the frame in which the graphic is situated.	<IMG VSPACE=*pixels* SRC="*filename*">	By default, no additional space is set aside for the frame height.
Specify that the graphic is a server-side imagemap.	<IMG ISMAP SRC="*filename*">	
Link the graphic to an external URL.	<A HREF= "*URL*"> <IMG BORDER=0 SRC="*filename*"></A>	Use the BORDER=0 attribute to hide the blue border around the graphic.

Sounds and Movies

Task	Tag	Notes
Insert a sound.	<A HREF="*filename*">*Text to appear on-screen*</A>	Be sure to inform your readers of the sound's size. The sound must be in the same directory as the HTML document.
Insert a movie.	<A HREF="*filename*">*Text to appear on-screen*</A>	Be sure to inform your readers of the movie's size. The video must be in the same directory as the HTML document.
Embed a plug-in	<EMBED>...</EMBED>	
Specify the location of a video clip or VRML world to be displayed.	<IMG DYNSRC="*filename*">	This is an Internet Explorer tag and may not work with other browsers.

Task	Tag	Notes
Display a set of VCR-like controls for a movie or animation.	<IMG DYNSRC="*filename*" CONTROLS>	
Control the number of times that a video or animation loops.	<IMG DYNSRC="*filename*" LOOP=*number*>	To loop the video or animation infinitely, type INFINITE instead of a number.
Specify when the video or animation starts playing.	<IMG DYNSRC="*filename*" START=*option*>	Choose from FILEOPEN (when the file is opened) or MOUSEOVER (when the user passes the mouse pointer over the video or animation).
Specify a sound to play automatically when the document is accessed.	<BGSOUND SRC="*filename*">	You can use MIDI, *.au, or *.wav sounds. Use the LOOP attribute to control looping.

Forms for User Input

Task	Tag	Notes
Enable the user to send an e-mail reply to you (requires a mail-capable browser).	<A HREF="mailto: *e-mail address*"> *Text to appear on-screen*</A>	Type your e-mail address as the text to appear on-screen. This tag does not require a script.
Create the environment for a form.	<FORM ADDRESS="*URL*" METHOD=*option*> ...</FORM>	Note that forms require server-side scripts. The ADDRESS attribute identifies the location of the script. The METHOD attribute enables you to select the GET or POST methods; POST is preferred for most servers.
Create an input field.	<INPUT TYPE=*option* NAME="*name*">	Choose from CHECKBOX, HIDDEN, IMAGE, PASSWORD, RADIO, RESET, SUBMIT, TEXT, or TEXTAREA. Define a name for the control by using the NAME attribute.
Control the position of the next line of text with respect to the input field's location.	<INPUT TYPE=*option* NAME="*name*" ALIGN=*option*>	Choose TOP, MIDDLE, or BOTTOM.
Create a checkbox.	<INPUT TYPE=CHECKBOX NAME="*name*" CHECKED=*option*>	For CHECKED, choose TRUE (checked) or FALSE (unchecked).
Create a radio button.	<INPUT TYPE=RADIO NAME="*name*" CHECKED=*option*>	For CHECKED, choose TRUE (checked) or FALSE (unchecked).

Task	Tag	Notes
Create a single-line text entry box.	<INPUT TYPE=TEXT NAME="*name*" SIZE=*characters* MAX-LENGTH=*characters*>	For SIZE, indicate the width of the text box in characters. For MAXLENGTH, indicate the maximum number of characters the user can enter. If MAXLENGTH exceeds SIZE, the text box will scroll to enable input.
Create a multiple-line text entry box.	<INPUT TYPE=TEXT AREA NAME= "*name*" SIZE= *characters, lines*>	For SIZE, type the width of the text box in characters, followed by a comma and the height of the text box in lines.
Create a password entry box, in which the text the user types is not displayed on-screen.	<INPUT TYPE=PASSWORD NAME= "*name*" SIZE= *characters* MAXLENGTH= *characters*>	For SIZE, indicate the width of the text box in characters. For MAXLENGTH, indicate the maximum number of characters the user can enter. If MAXLENGTH exceeds SIZE, the text box will scroll to enable input.
Define the default text to appear in a text box.	<INPUT TYPE=TEXT NAME="*name*" SIZE=*characters* VALUE="*text*">	The text you type in for the TEXT attribute will appear in the text box. The user can erase it or edit it.
Create a button that resets the form with the default values.	<INPUT TYPE="RESET" VALUE="*text*">	For VALUE, type the text that you want to appear on the button's face (normally "Reset").
Create a button that sends the form data to the server.	<INPUT TYPE="SUBMIT" VALUE="*text*">	For VALUE, type the text that you want to appear on the button's face (normally "Submit" or "Send").
Create an environment for a drop-down list box.	<SELECT NAME="*name*"> ...</SELECT>	To define the options in the list box, use the <OPTION> tag.
Indicate that more than one option can be selected in a list box.	<SELECT NAME="*name*" MULTIPLE> ...</SELECT>	If you don't use the MULTIPLE attribute, the user can select only one item.
Specify the height of the drop-down list box's text box.	<SELECT NAME="*name*" SIZE=*lines*>	By default, the list box is one line high.
Define an option to appear in the list box.	<SELECT NAME= "*name*"> <OPTION VALUE="*text*"> *Text to appear in list box* <OPTION VALUE="*text*"> *Text to appear in list box...* </SELECT>	For VALUE, type the text that you want the browser to send to the server when the user chooses this item.
Select one of the items in a list box by default.	<OPTION SELECTED VALUE="*text*">*Text to appear in the list box*	If you don't select one of the items, the first one will be selected by default.

Tables

Task	Tag	Notes
Define the table environment.	<TABLE>...</TABLE>	
Create a title (caption) for the table.	<TABLE <CAPTION="*text to appear on-screen*">	
Align the table on the page.	<TABLE ALIGN=*option*>... </TABLE>	Choose LEFT or RIGHT. Most browsers will float text so that it appears side by side with a table that doesn't span the entire page width.
Define the table border.	<TABLE BORDER=*piels*>... </TABLE>	To delete the table border, use BORDER=0.
Define the table border's color.	<TABLE BORDER-COLOR="*color number*"> ... </TABLE>	For a list of color codes, see Appendix C.
Define the table's background color.	<TABLE BGCOLOR="*color number*">... </TABLE>	For a list of color codes, see Appendix C.
Define the spacing between table cells.	<TABLE CELLSPACING=*pixels*>... </TABLE>	
Insert white space within the table cell.	<TABLE CELLPADDING=*pixels*>... </TABLE>	
Define the table's width by typing the width in pixels.	<TABLE WIDTH=*pixels*>... </TABLE>	
Define the table's width by typing the width as a percentage of screen width.	<TABLE WIDTH=*percentage*> ... </TABLE>	
Define a table header.	<TABLE> <TH> *Text to appear on-screen*</TH> </TABLE>	Shown bold and centered with most browsers.
Control the table header alignment.	<TABLE> <TH ALIGN=*option* VALIGN=*option*>Text to appear on-screen</TH> </TABLE>	For ALIGN, choose from LEFT, RIGHT, or CENTER. For VALIGN, choose TOP, MIDDLE, or BOTTOM.
Control the table header width by typing the number of pixels.	<TABLE> <TH WIDTH=*pixels*>Text to appear on-screen</TH> </TABLE>	
Control the table header width by typing a percentage of screen width.	<TABLE> <TH WIDTH=*percentage*>Text to appear on-screen</TH> </TABLE>	

Task	Tag	Notes
Create a header that spans the table columns.	<TABLE> <TH COLSPAN=*number of columns to span*>*Text to appear on-screen*</TH> </TABLE>	If your table has three columns, type 3 to span all three of the columns.
Define a table row.	<TABLE> <TR>...</TR> <TR>...</TR>... </TABLE>	To place items within each row, use <TD>.
Define a table data item.	<TABLE> <TR> <TD>item 1</TD> <TD>item 2 </TD> </TR > </TABLE >	To create more than one column, use two or more <TD>...</TD> tags within each table row (<TR>).
Create a column that spans two or more rows.	<TABLE> <TR ROWSPAN=*number of columns to span*> <TD>*item 1*</TD> </TR> </TABLE>	
Control the alignment of individual table rows.	<TR ALIGN=*option* VALIGN=*option*>... </TR>	For ALIGN, choose from LEFT, RIGHT, or CENTER. For VALIGN, choose TOP, MIDDLE, or BOTTOM.
Control the alignment of individual table cells.	<TD ALIGN=*option* VALIGN=*option*>	See previous note for ALIGN options.
Choose a color for a table row.	<TR BGCOLOR=*"color name"*></TR>	For a list of color codes, see Appendix C.
Choose a color for a table cell.	<TD BGCOLOR=*"color name"*></TD>	For a list of color codes, see Appendix C.

Frames

Task	Tag	Notes
Create body for frames.	<FRAMESET>... </FRAMESET>	These tags replace the <BODY>... </BODY> tags.
Establish the number of columns.	<FRAMESET COUMNS= *"column specification"*>... </FRAMESET>	To specify the number and size of columns, type a fixed size in pixels or a percentage value between 1 to 100, and separate each size with a comma. For example, COLUMNS=10%, 40%,30%,20%. You may also use an asterisk to let the browser give the frame all available space.

Task	Tag	Notes
Establish the number of rows.	`<FRAMESET ROWS="`*row specification*`">` `</FRAMESET>`	To specify the number and size of rows, type a fixed size in pixels or a percentage value between 1 to 100, and separate each size with a comma. For example, ROWS=10%,40%,30%, 20%. For each row, include a `<FRAME >` tag.
Place a document into a frame.	`<FRAME= "`*URL*`">`	
Specify a margin width for a frame.	`<FRAME= "`*URL*`" MARGINWIDTH="`*number of pixels*`">`	
Specify a margin height for a frame.	`<FRAME= "`*URL*`" MARGINHEIGHT="`*number of pixels*`">`	
Specify scrolling options for a frame.	`<FRAME= "`*URL*`" SCROLLING="`*option*`">`	The options are YES (scrollbar displayed), NO (no scrollbar displayed), or AUTO (scrollbar displayed if the user chooses a window size that is smaller than the frame contents.
Prevent the user from resizing the frame.	`<FRAME NORESIZE>`	
☐I☐ Control width of frame border.	`<FRAMESET FRAMEBORDER="`*number of pixels* `>`	Internet Explorer 3.0 only.
Give the frame a name so that it can be targeted.	`<FRAME NAME="`*name*`">`	The frame name must begin with an alphanumeric character.
Set the frame's margin width.	`<FRAME MARGINWIDTH="`*number*`">`	Specify the margin width in pixels.
Set the frame's margin height.	`<FRAME MARGINHEIGHT="`*number*`">`	Specify the margin height in pixels.
☐N☐☐I☐ Display a message if the user's browser can't display frames	`<NOFRAMES>...` `</NOFRAMES>`	Type the message between these tags.

Java and JavaScript

Task	Tag	Notes
Insert a Java applet.	`<APPLET CODEBASE="URL">` `...</APPLET>`	These tags replace the `<BODY>...` `</BODY>` tags that you would normally use.
Define an applet's operating parameters.	`<PARAM NAME= "`*name*`" VALUE= "`*value*`">`	Consult the applet's documentation to determine which parameters you can customize.
Include a script.	`<SCRIPT LANGUAGE="`*language*`">...<SCRIPT>`	Specify the script's language, such as JavaScript

Appendix

B

ISO Latin-1 Special Characters

Various Useful Symbols

To create this character:		Insert this code in your document:
&	Ampersand	&amp;
<<	Angle quotation mark, left	&laquo;
>>	Angle quotation mark, right	&raquo;
|	Broken vertical bar	&brkbar;
¢	Cent sign	&cent;
®	Circled R registered sign	&reg;
©	Copyright sign	&copy;
¤	Currency sign	&curren;
°	Degree sign	&deg;
ª	Feminine ordinal indicator	&ordf;

To create this character:		Insert this code in your document:
$\frac{1}{2}$	Fraction $\frac{1}{2}$	&frac12;
$\frac{1}{4}$	Fraction $\frac{1}{4}$	&frac14;
$\frac{3}{4}$	Fraction $\frac{3}{4}$	&frac34;
>	Greater than sign	&gt;
¡	Inverted exclamation mark	&iexcl;
<	Less than sign	&lt;
º	Masculine ordinal indicator	&ordm;
μ	Micro sign	&micro;
·	Middle dot	&middot;
¬	Negation sign	&not;
	Nonbreaking space	
¶	Paragraph sign	&para;
±	Plus-or-minus sign	&plusmn;
£	Pound sign	&pound;
"	Quotation mark	&quot;
§	Section sign	&sect;
-	Soft hyphen	&shy;
´	Spacing acute	&acute;
¸	Spacing cedilla	&cedil;
¨	Spacing dieresis	&uml;
¯	Spacing macron	&hibar;
^{1}	Superscript 1	&sup1;
^{2}	Superscript 2	&sup2;
^{3}	Superscript 3	&sup3;
¥	Yen sign	&yen;

Foreign Language Characters

To create this character:		Insert this code in your document:
Á	Capital A, acute accent	&Aacute;
À	Capital A, grave accent	&Agrave;
Â	Capital A, circumflex accent	&Acirc;
Ã	Capital A, tilde	&Atilde;
Å	Capital A, ring	&Aring;
Ä	Capital A, dieresis or umlaut mark	&Auml;

To create this character:		Insert this code in your document:
Æ	Capital AE dipthong	&AElig;
Ç	Capital C, cedilla	&Ccedil;
É	Capital E, acute accent	&Eacute;
È	Capital E, grave accent	&Egrave;
Ê	Capital E, circumflex accent	&Ecirc;
Ë	Capital E, dieresis or umlaut mark	&Euml;
Í	Capital I, acute accent	&Iacute;
Ì	Capital I, grave accent	&Igrave;
Î	Capital I, circumflex accent	&Icirc;
Ï	Capital I, dieresis or umlaut mark	&Iuml;
	Capital Eth, Icelandic	&ETH;
Ñ	Capital N, tilde	&Ntilde;
Ó	Capital O, acute accent	&Oacute;
Ò	Capital O, grave accent	&Ograve;
Ô	Capital O, circumflex accent	&Ocirc;
Õ	Capital O, tilde	&Otilde;
Ö	Capital O, dieresis or umlaut mark	&Ouml;
Ø	Capital O, slash	&Oslash;
Ú	Capital U, acute accent	&Uacute;
Ù	Capital U, grave accent	&Ugrave;
Û	Capital U, circumflex accent	&Ucirc;
Ü	Capital U, dieresis or umlaut mark	&Uuml;
Ý	Capital Y, acute accent	&Yacute;
	Capital Thorn, Icelandic	&THORN;
ß	Small sharp s, German	&szlig;
á	Small a, acute accent	&aacute;
à	Small a, grave accent	&agrave;
â	Small a, circumflex accent	&acirc;
ã	Small a, tilde	&atilde;
å	Small a, ring	&aring;

To create this character:		**Insert this code in your document:**
ä	Small a, dieresis or umlaut mark	&auml;
æ	Small ae dipthong	&aelig;
ç	Small c, cedilla	&ccedil;
é	Small e, acute accent	&eacute;
è	Small e, grave accent	&egrave;
ê	Small e, circumflex accent	&ecirc;
ë	Small e, dieresis or umlaut mark	&euml;
í	Small i, acute accent	&iacute;
ì	Small i, grave accent	&igrave;
î	Small i, circumflex accent	&icirc;
ï	Small i, dieresis or umlaut mark	&iuml;
	Small eth, Icelandic	&eth;
ñ	Small n, tilde	&ntilde;
ó	Small o, acute accent	&oacute;
ò	Small o, grave accent	&ograve;
ô	Small o, circumflex accent	&ocirc;
õ	Small o, tilde	&otilde;
ö	Small o, dieresis or umlaut mark	&ouml;
ø	Small o, slash	&oslash;
ú	Small u, acute accent	&uacute;
ù	Small u, grave accent	&ugrave;
û	Small u, circumflex accent	&ucirc;
ü	Small u, dieresis or umlaut mark	&uuml;
ý	Small y, acute accent	&yacute;
	Small thorn, Icelandic	&thorn;
ÿ	Small y, dieresis or umlaut mark	&yuml;

Appendix

C

Non-Dithering Color Codes

Color Name	RGB Code	Hexadecimal Code
AliceBlue	240 248 255	F0 F8 FF
AntiqueWhite	250 235 215	FA EB D7
AntiqueWhite1	255 239 219	FF EF DB
AntiqueWhite2	238 223 204	EE DF CC
AntiqueWhite3	205 192 176	CD C0 B0
AntiqueWhite4	139 131 120	8B 83 78
Aquamarine	127 255 212	7F FF D4
Aquamarine1	127 255 212	7F FF D4
Aquamarine2	118 238 198	76 EE C6
Aquamarine3	102 205 170	66 CD AA
Aquamarine4	69 139 116	45 8B 74
Azure	240 255 255	F0 FF FF
Azure1	240 255 255	F0 FF FF
Azure2	224 238 238	E0 EE EE
Azure3	193 205 205	C1 CD CD
Azure4	131 139 139	83 8B 8B
Beige	245 245 220	F5 F5 DC
Bisque	255 228 196	FF E4 C4
Bisque1	255 228 196	FF E4 C4
Bisque2	238 213 183	EE D5 B7
Bisque3	205 183 158	CD B7 9E
Bisque4	139 125 107	8B 7D 6B
Black	0 0 0	00 00 00

Color Name	RGB Code	Hexadecimal Code
BlanchedAlmond	255 235 205	FF EB CD
Blue	0 0 255	00 00 FF
Blue1	0 0 255	00 00 FF
Blue2	0 0 238	00 00 EE
Blue3	0 0 205	00 00 CD
Blue4	0 0 139	00 00 8B
BlueViolet	138 43 226	8A 2B E2
Brown	165 42 42	A5 2A 2A
Brown1	255 64 64	FF 40 40
Brown2	238 59 59	EE 3B 3B
Brown3	205 51 51	CD 33 33
Brown4	139 35 35	8B 23 23
Burlywood	222 184 135	DE B8 87
Burlywood1	255 211 155	FF D3 9B
Burlywood2	238 197 145	EE C5 91
Burlywood3	205 170 125	CD AA 7D
Burlywood4	139 115 85	8B 73 55
CadetBlue	95 158 160	5F 9E A0
CadetBlue1	152 245 255	98 F5 FF
CadetBlue2	142 229 238	8E E5 EE
CadetBlue3	122 197 205	7A C5 CD
CadetBlue4	83 134 139	53 86 8B
Chartreuse	127 255 0	7F FF 00
Chartreuse1	127 255 0	7F FF 00
Chartreuse2	118 238 0	76 EE 00
Chartreuse3	102 205 0	66 CD 00
Chartreuse4	69 139 0	45 8B 00
Chocolate	210 105 30	D2 69 1E
Chocolate1	255 127 36	FF 7F 24
Chocolate2	238 118 33	EE 76 21
Chocolate3	205 102 29	CD 66 1D
Chocolate4	139 69 19	8B 45 13
Coral	255 127 80	FF 7F 50
Coral1	255 114 86	FF 72 56
Coral2	238 106 80	EE 6A 50
Coral3	205 91 69	CD 5B 45
Coral4	139 62 47	8B 3E 2F
CornflowerBlue	100 149 237	64 95 ED
Cornsilk	255 248 220	FF F8 DC
Cornsilk1	255 248 220	FF F8 DC
Cornsilk2	238 232 205	EE E8 CD
Cornsilk3	205 200 177	CD C8 B1
Cornsilk4	139 136 120	8B 88 78
Cyan	0 255 255	00 FF FF
Cyan1	0 255 255	00 FF FF
Cyan2	0 238 238	00 EE EE
Cyan3	0 205 205	00 CD CD
Cyan4	0 139 139	00 8B 8B

Color Name	RGB Code	Hexadecimal Code
DarkBlue	0 0 139	00 00 8B
DarkCyan	0 139 139	00 8B 8B
DarkGoldenrod	184 134 11	B8 86 0B
DarkGoldenrod1	255 185 15	FF B9 0F
DarkGoldenrod2	238 173 14	EE AD 0E
DarkGoldenrod3	205 149 12	CD 95 0C
DarkGoldenrod4	139 101 8	8B 65 8B
DarkGreen	0 100 0	00 64 00
DarkGrey	169 169 169	A9 A9 A9
DarkKhaki	189 183 107	BD B7 6B
DarkMagenta	139 0 139	8B 00 8B
DarkOliveGreen	85 107 47	55 6B 2F
DarkOliveGreen1	202 255 112	CA FF 70
DarkOliveGreen2	188 238 104	BC EE 68
DarkOliveGreen3	162 205 90	A2 CD 5A
DarkOliveGreen4	110 139 61	6E 8B 3D
DarkOrange	255 140 0	FF 8C 00
DarkOrange1	255 127 0	FF 7F 00
DarkOrange2	238 118 0	EE 76 00
DarkOrange3	205 102 0	CD 66 00
DarkOrange4	139 69 0	8B 45 00
DarkOrchid	153 50 204	99 32 CC
DarkOrchid1	191 62 255	BF 3E FF
DarkOrchid2	178 58 238	B2 3A EE
DarkOrchid3	154 50 205	9A 32 CD
DarkOrchid4	104 34 139	68 22 8B
DarkRed	139 0 0	8B 00 00
DarkSalmon	233 150 122	E9 96 7A
DarkSeaGreen	143 188 143	8F BC 8F
DarkSeaGreen1	193 255 193	C1 FF C1
DarkSeaGreen2	180 238 180	B4 EE B4
DarkSeaGreen3	155 205 155	9B CD 9B
DarkSeaGreen4	105 139 105	69 8B 69
DarkSlateBlue	72 61 139	48 3D 8B
DarkSlateGray	47 79 79	2F 4F 4F
DarkSlateGray1	151 255 255	97 FF FF
DarkSlateGray2	141 238 238	8D EE EE
DarkSlateGray3	121 205 205	79 CD CD
DarkSlateGray4	82 139 139	52 8B 8B
DarkTurquoise	0 206 209	00 CE D1
DarkViolet	148 0 211	94 00 D3
DeepPink	255 20 147	FF 14 93
DeepPink1	255 20 147	FF 14 93
DeepPink2	238 18 137	EE 12 89
DeepPink3	205 16 118	CD 10 76
DeepPink4	139 10 80	8B 0A 50
DeepSkyBlue	0 191 255	00 BF FF
DeepSkyBlue1	0 191 255	00 BF FF

Color Name	RGB Code	Hexadecimal Code
DeepSkyBlue2	0 178 238	00 B2 EE
DeepSkyBlue3	0 154 205	00 9A CD
DeepSkyBlue4	0 104 139	00 68 8B
DimGrey	105 105 105	69 69 69
DodgerBlue	30 144 255	1E 90 FF
DodgerBlue1	30 144 255	1E 90 FF
DodgerBlue2	28 134 238	1C 86 EE
DodgerBlue3	24 116 205	18 74 CD
DodgerBlue4	16 78 139	10 4E 8B
Firebrick	178 34 34	B2 22 22
Firebrick1	255 48 48	FF 30 30
Firebrick2	238 44 44	EE 2C 2C
Firebrick3	205 38 38	CD 26 26
Firebrick4	139 26 26	8B 1A 1A
FloralWhite	255 250 240	FF FA F0
ForestGreen	34 139 34	22 8B 22
Gainsboro	220 220 220	DC DC DC
GhostWhite	248 248 255	F8 F8 FF
Gold	255 215 0	FF D7 00
Gold1	255 215 0	FF D7 00
Gold2	238 201 0	EE C9 00
Gold3	205 173 0	CD AD 00
Gold4	139 117 0	8B 75 00
goldenrod	218 165 32	DA A5 20
Goldenrod1	255 193 37	FF C1 25
Goldenrod2	238 180 34	EE B4 22
Goldenrod3	205 155 29	CD 9B 1D
Goldenrod4	139 105 20	8B 69 14
gray81	207 207 207	CF CF CF
gray91	232 232 232	E8 E8 E8
Green	0 255 0	00 FF 00
Green1	0 255 0	00 FF 00
Green2	0 238 0	00 EE 00
Green3	0 205 0	00 CD 00
Green4	0 139 0	00 8B 00
GreenYellow	173 255 47	AD FF 2F
Grey	190 190 190	BE BE BE
grey11	28 28 28	1C 1C 1C
grey21	54 54 54	36 36 36
grey31	79 79 79	4F 4F 4F
grey41	105 105 105	69 69 69
grey51	130 130 130	82 82 82
grey61	156 156 156	9C 9C 9C
grey71	181 181 181	B5 B5 B5
Honeydew	240 255 240	F0 FF F0
Honeydew1	240 255 240	F0 FF F0
Honeydew2	224 238 224	E0 EE E0
Honeydew3	193 205 193	C1 CD C1

Color Name	RGB Code	Hexadecimal Code
Honeydew4	131 139 131	83 8B 83
HotPink	255 105 180	FF 69 B4
HotPink1	255 110 180	FF 6E B4
HotPink2	238 106 167	EE 6A A7
HotPink3	205 96 144	CD 60 90
HotPink4	139 58 98	8B 3A 62
IndianRed	205 92 92	CD 5C 5C
IndianRed1	255 106 106	FF 6A 6A
IndianRed2	238 99 99	EE 63 63
IndianRed3	205 85 85	CD 55 55
IndianRed4	139 58 58	8B 3A 3A
Ivory	255 255 240	FF FF F0
Ivory1	255 255 240	FF FF F0
Ivory2	238 238 224	EE EE E0
Ivory3	205 205 193	CD CD C1
Ivory4	139 139 131	8B 8B 83
Khaki1	255 246 143	FF F6 8F
Khaki2	238 230 133	EE E6 85
Khaki3	205 198 115	CD C6 73
Khaki4	139 134 78	8B 86 4E
lavender	230 230 250	E6 E6 FA
LavenderBlush	255 240 245	FF F0 F5
LavenderBlush1	255 240 245	FF F0 F5
LavenderBlush2	238 224 229	EE E0 E5
LavenderBlush3	205 193 197	CD C1 C5
LavenderBlush4	139 131 134	8B 83 86
LawnGreen	124 252 0	7C FC 00
LemonChiffon	255 250 205	FF FA CD
LemonChiffon1	255 250 205	FF FA CD
LemonChiffon2	238 233 191	EE E9 BF
LemonChiffon3	205 201 165	CD C9 A5
LemonChiffon4	139 137 112	8B 89 70
LightBlue	173 216 230	AD D8 E6
LightBlue1	191 239 255	BF EF FF
LightBlue2	178 223 238	B2 DF EE
LightBlue3	154 192 205	9A C0 CD
LightBlue4	104 131 139	68 83 8B
LightCoral	240 128 128	F0 80 80
LightCyan	224 255 255	E0 FF FF
LightCyan1	224 255 255	E0 FF FF
LightCyan2	209 238 238	D1 EE EE
LightCyan3	180 205 205	B4 CD CD
LightCyan4	122 139 139	7A 8B 8B
LightGoldenrod	238 221 130	EE DD 82
LightGoldenrod1	255 236 139	FF EC 8B
LightGoldenrod2	238 220 130	EE DC 82
LightGoldenrod3	205 190 112	CD BE 70
LightGoldenrod4	139 129 76	8B 81 4C

Color Name	RGB Code	Hexadecimal Code
LightGray	211 211 211	D3 D3 D3
LightGreen	144 238 144	90 EE 90
LightPink	255 182 193	FF B6 C1
LightPink1	255 174 185	FF AE B9
LightPink2	238 162 173	EE A2 AD
LightPink3	205 140 149	CD 8C 95
LightPink4	139 95 101	8B 5F 65
LightSalmon	255 160 122	FF A0 7A
LightSalmon1	255 160 122	FF A0 7A
LightSalmon2	238 149 114	EE 95 72
LightSalmon3	205 129 98	CD 81 62
LightSalmon4	139 87 66	8B 57 42
LightSeaGreen	32 178 170	20 B2 AA
LightSkyBlue	135 206 250	87 CE FA
LightSkyBlue1	176 226 255	B0 E2 FF
LightSkyBlue2	164 211 238	A4 D3 EE
LightSkyBlue3	141 182 205	8D B6 CD
LightSkyBlue4	96 123 139	60 7B 8B
LightSlateBlue	132 112 255	84 70 FF
LightSlateGray	119 136 153	77 88 99
LightSteelBlue	176 196 222	B0 C4 DE
LightSteelBlue1	202 225 255	CA E1 FF
LightSteelBlue2	188 210 238	BC D2 EE
LightSteelBlue3	162 181 205	A2 B5 CD
LightSteelBlue4	110 123 139	6E 7B 8B
LightYellow	255 255 224	FF FF E0
LightYellow1	255 255 224	FF FF E0
LightYellow2	238 238 209	EE EE D1
LightYellow3	205 205 180	CD CD B4
LightYellow4	139 139 122	8B 8B 7A
LimeGreen	50 205 50	32 CD 32
Linen	250 240 230	FA F0 E6
LtGoldenrodYello	250 250 210	FA FA D2
Magenta	255 0 255	FF 00 FF
Magenta1	255 0 255	FF 00 FF
Magenta2	238 0 238	EE 00 EE
Magenta3	205 0 205	CD 00 CD
Magenta4	139 0 139	8B 00 8B
Maroon	176 48 96	B0 30 60
Maroon1	255 52 179	FF 34 B3
Maroon2	238 48 167	EE 30 A7
Maroon3	205 41 144	CD 29 90
Maroon4	139 28 98	8B 1C 62
MediumAquamarine	102 205 170	66 CD AA
MediumBlue	0 0 205	00 00 CD
MediumOrchid	186 85 211	BA 55 D3
MediumOrchid1	224 102 255	E0 66 FF
MediumOrchid2	209 95 238	D1 5F EE

Color Name	RGB Code	Hexadecimal Code
MediumOrchid3	180 82 205	B4 52 CD
MediumOrchid4	122 55 139	7A 37 8B
MediumPurple	147 112 219	93 70 DB
MediumPurple1	171 130 255	AB 82 FF
MediumPurple2	159 121 238	9F 79 EE
MediumPurple3	137 104 205	89 68 CD
MediumPurple4	93 71 139	5D 47 8B
MediumSeaGreen	60 179 113	3C B3 71
MediumSlateBlue	123 104 238	7B 68 EE
MediumTurquoise	72 209 204	48 D1 CC
MediumVioletRed	199 21 133	C7 15 85
MedSpringGreen	0 250 154	00 FA 9A
MidnightBlue	25 25 112	19 19 70
MintCream	245 255 250	F5 FF FA
MistyRose	255 228 225	FF E4 E1
MistyRose1	255 228 225	FF E4 E1
MistyRose2	238 213 210	EE D5 D2
MistyRose3	205 183 181	CD B7 B5
MistyRose4	139 125 123	8B 7D 7B
Moccasin	255 228 181	FF E4 B5
NavajoWhite	255 222 173	FF DE AD
NavajoWhite1	255 222 173	FF DE AD
NavajoWhite2	238 207 161	EE CF A1
NavajoWhite3	205 179 139	CD B3 8B
NavajoWhite4	139 121 94	8B 79 5E
NavyBlue	0 0 128	00 00 80
OldLace	253 245 230	FD F5 E6
OliveDrab	107 142 35	6B 8E 23
OliveDrab1	192 255 62	C0 FF 3E
OliveDrab2	179 238 58	B3 EE 3A
OliveDrab3	154 205 50	9A CD 32
OliveDrab4	105 139 34	69 8B 22
Orange	255 165 0	FF A5 00
Orange1	255 165 0	FF A5 00
Orange2	238 154 0	EE 9A 00
Orange3	205 133 0	CD 85 00
Orange4	139 90 0	8B 5A 00
OrangeRed	255 69 0	FF 45 00
OrangeRed1	255 69 0	FF 45 00
OrangeRed2	238 64 0	EE 40 00
OrangeRed3	205 55 0	CD 37 00
OrangeRed4	139 37 0	8B 25 00
Orchid	218 112 214	DA 70 D6
Orchid1	255 131 250	FF 83 FA
Orchid2	238 122 233	EE 7A E9
Orchid3	205 105 201	CD 69 C9
Orchid4	139 71 137	8B 47 89
PaleGoldenrod	238 232 170	EE E8 AA

Color Name	RGB Code	Hexadecimal Code
PaleGreen	152 251 152	98 FB 98
PaleGreen1	154 255 154	9A FF 9A
PaleGreen2	144 238 144	90 EE 90
PaleGreen3	124 205 124	7C CD 7C
PaleGreen4	84 139 84	54 8B 54
PaleTurquoise	175 238 238	AF EE EE
PaleTurquoise1	187 255 255	BB FF FF
PaleTurquoise2	174 238 238	AE EE EE
PaleTurquoise3	150 205 205	96 CD CD
PaleTurquoise4	102 139 139	66 8B 8B
PaleVioletRed	219 112 147	DB 70 93
PaleVioletRed1	255 130 171	FF 82 AB
PaleVioletRed2	238 121 159	EE 79 9F
PaleVioletRed3	205 104 137	CD 68 89
PaleVioletRed4	139 71 93	8B 47 5D
PapayaWhip	255 239 213	FF EF D5
PeachPuff	255 218 185	FF DA B9
PeachPuff1	255 218 185	FF DA B9
PeachPuff2	238 203 173	EE CB AD
PeachPuff3	205 175 149	CD AF 95
PeachPuff4	139 119 101	8B 77 65
Peru	205 133 63	CD 85 3F
Pink	255 192 203	FF C0 CB
Pink1	255 181 197	FF B5 C5
Pink2	238 169 184	EE A9 B8
Pink3	205 145 158	CD 91 9E
Pink4	139 99 108	8B 63 6C
Plum	221 160 221	DD A0 DD
Plum1	255 187 255	FF BB FF
Plum2	238 174 238	EE AE EE
Plum3	205 150 205	CD 96 CD
Plum4	139 102 139	8B 66 8B
PowderBlue	176 224 230	B0 E0 E6
Purple	160 32 240	A0 20 F0
Purple1	155 48 255	9B 30 FF
Purple2	145 44 238	91 2C EE
Purple3	125 38 205	7D 26 CD
Purple4	85 26 139	55 1A 8B
Red	255 0 0	FF 00 00
Red1	255 0 0	FF 00 00
Red2	238 0 0	EE 00 00
Red3	205 0 0	CD 00 00
Red4	139 0 0	8B 00 00
RosyBrown	188 143 143	BC 8F 8F
RosyBrown1	255 193 193	FF C1 C1
RosyBrown2	238 180 180	EE B4 B4
RosyBrown3	205 155 155	CD 9B 9B
RosyBrown4	139 105 105	8B 69 69

Color Name	RGB Code	Hexadecimal Code
RoyalBlue	65 105 225	41 69 E1
RoyalBlue1	72 118 255	48 76 FF
RoyalBlue2	67 110 238	43 6E EE
RoyalBlue3	58 95 205	3A 5F CD
RoyalBlue4	39 64 139	27 40 8B
SaddleBrown	139 69 19	8B 45 13
Salmon	250 128 114	FA 80 72
Salmon1	255 140 105	FF 8C 69
Salmon2	238 130 98	EE 82 62
Salmon3	205 112 84	CD 70 54
Salmon4	139 76 57	8B 4C 39
SandyBrown	244 164 96	F4 A4 60
SeaGreen	46 139 87	2E 8B 57
SeaGreen1	84 255 159	54 FF 9F
SeaGreen2	78 238 148	4E EE 94
SeaGreen3	67 205 128	43 CD 80
SeaGreen4	46 139 87	2E 8B 57
Seashell	255 245 238	FF F5 EE
Seashell1	255 245 238	FF F5 EE
Seashell2	238 229 222	EE E5 DE
Seashell3	205 197 191	CD C5 BF
Seashell4	139 134 130	8B 86 82
Sienna	160 82 45	A0 52 2D
Sienna1	255 130 71	FF 82 47
Sienna2	238 121 66	EE 79 42
Sienna3	205 104 57	CD 68 39
Sienna4	139 71 38	8B 47 26
SkyBlue	135 206 235	87 CE EB
SkyBlue1	135 206 255	87 CE FF
SkyBlue2	126 192 238	7E C0 EE
SkyBlue3	108 166 205	6C A6 CD
SkyBlue4	74 112 139	4A 70 8B
SlateBlue	106 90 205	6A 5A CD
SlateBlue1	131 111 255	83 6F FF
SlateBlue2	122 103 238	7A 67 EE
SlateBlue3	105 89 205	69 59 CD
SlateBlue4	71 60 139	47 3C 8B
SlateGray1	198 226 255	C6 E2 FF
SlateGray2	185 211 238	B9 D3 EE
SlateGray3	159 182 205	9F B6 CD
SlateGray4	108 123 139	6C 7B 8B
SlateGrey	112 128 144	70 80 90
Snow	255 250 250	FF FA FA
Snow1	255 250 250	FF FA FA
Snow2	238 233 233	EE E9 E9
Snow3	205 201 201	CD C9 C9
Snow4	139 137 137	8B 89 89
SpringGreen	0 255 127	00 FF 7F

Color Name	RGB Code	Hexadecimal Code
SpringGreen1	0 255 127	00 FF 7F
SpringGreen2	0 238 118	00 EE 76
SpringGreen3	0 205 102	00 CD 66
SpringGreen4	0 139 69	00 8B 45
SteelBlue	70 130 180	46 82 B4
SteelBlue1	99 184 255	63 B8 FF
SteelBlue2	92 172 238	5C AC EE
SteelBlue3	79 148 205	4F 94 CD
SteelBlue4	54 100 139	36 64 8B
Tan	210 180 140	D2 B4 8C
Tan1	255 165 79	FF A5 4F
Tan2	238 154 73	EE 9A 49
Tan3	205 133 63	CD 85 3F
Tan4	139 90 43	8B 5A 2B
Thistle	216 191 216	D8 BF D8
Thistle1	255 225 255	FF E1 FF
Thistle2	238 210 238	EE D2 EE
Thistle3	205 181 205	CD B5 CD
Thistle4	139 123 139	8B 7B 8B
Tomato	255 99 71	FF 63 47
Tomato1	255 99 71	FF 63 47
Tomato2	238 92 66	EE 5C 42
Tomato3	205 79 57	CD 4F 39
Tomato4	139 54 38	8B 36 26
Turquoise	64 224 208	40 E0 D0
Turquoise1	0 245 255	00 F5 FF
Turquoise2	0 229 238	00 E5 EE
Turquoise3	0 197 205	00 C5 CD
Turquoise4	0 134 139	00 86 8B
Violet	238 130 238	EE 82 EE
VioletRed	208 32 144	D0 20 90
VioletRed1	255 62 150	FF 3E 96
VioletRed2	238 58 140	EE 3A 8C
VioletRed3	205 50 120	CD 32 78
VioletRed4	139 34 82	8B 22 52
Wheat	245 222 179	F5 DE B3
Wheat1	255 231 186	FF E7 BA
Wheat2	238 216 174	EE D8 AE
Wheat3	205 186 150	CD BA 96
Wheat4	139 126 102	8B 7E 66
White	255 255 255	FF FF FF
WhiteSmoke	245 245 245	F5 F5 F5
Yellow	255 255 0	FF FF 00
Yellow1	255 255 0	FF FF 0
Yellow2	238 238 0	EE EE 00
Yellow3	205 205 0	CD CD 00
Yellow4	139 139 0	8B 8B 00
YellowGreen	154 205 50	9A CD 32

Appendix
D

About the CD-ROM

The CD-ROM accompanying this book contains a superb library of software covering every aspect of Web publishing. Please note that there is no single installation or setup program for the entire disc; you choose the programs you wish to install, and use File Manager (Windows 3.1) or My Computer (Windows 95/NT) to locate and run the setup utility.

To use this appendix, do the following:

1. Turn to the section entitled "Guide to Your Web Publishing Toolkit," to see what you can do with the programs on the enclosed disc.

2. When you find a program you like, check to see whether it's available for the version of Windows you're using. Some

programs are available in two versions, one for Windows 3.1 (16-bit), and another for Windows 95/NT (32-bit). In general, Windows 95 users can run 16-bit Windows 3.1 programs, but Windows NT users cannot. Also, Windows 3.1 users cannot run programs created for Windows 95/NT.

3. Once you've selected a program that you want to try, turn to the List of Programs to determine where the installation or setup utility is located.

4. Use File Manager or My Computer to locate and double-click the setup program. Note that in each program's directory, the software is organized into folders named 32-bit (Windows 95/NT version) and 16-bit (Windows 3.1 version). If only one of these folders is present, then that's the only version available.

5. Please register the program if you wish to continue using it after the evaluation period has expired.

I don't know how to use File Manager to run a setup program!
There are quite a few variations on this, including—I'm not kidding—"I'm not sure which side of the CD-ROM disc to insert!" *Please* do not contact your poor beleaguered author, or the hapless personnel of AP PROFESSIONAL, with questions about *anything* having to do with this CD-ROM disc. This is provided for your convenience only; we don't possess the resources to support dozens of people, provide elementary training in Microsoft Windows, or to deal with the gazillions of things that can go wrong when complex programs interact with complex, user-modified computer systems. As much as I'd like to help, I'll ignore any e-mail about this disc. If you want help with the programs, there's a very simple solution: Register your software, and get technical support from the program's publisher.

THE SHAREWARE CONCEPT

Shareware publishers distribute their products on a "try before you buy" basis, and you're the beneficiary. You can try the program before you purchase it. You, and not some salesperson or magazine ad, can determine whether the program meets your needs!

After you've tried the program for a specified evaluation period, you are required to register the program by accessing the program's home page (see List of Programs, later in this chapter), or you must delete the program from your computer.

What do you get for registration? It depends on the specific program. In general, you get free technical support and upgrade notifications. Most publishers will give you a break on the registration fee for the next major upgrade. Most of all, you make the next major upgrade possible!

GUIDE TO YOUR WEB PUBLISHING TOOLKIT

If you would like to:	Try this program:
View animations	mBed, ShockWave
Keep logs of Web visitors for analysis and advertising purposes	Site Sleuth
Create scrolling or rotating advertising banners	Banner Show
Automate forms processing with CGI scripts	CGI StarPro
Automate forms processing with client-side scripts	WebForms
Add convenient graphics file management commands to Windows pop-up menus	PicaView 32, PicaView 16
Create and save graphics to 256-color palette and add features such as shadow text and yellow tool tips	WebPaint
Create stunning visual effects with filters for Paint Shop Pro or Adobe Photoshop	Eye Candy
View and manage graphics files	ACDSee32, ACDSee16
Create awesome three-dimensional shapes and effects for your Web page	Pixel3D
Create a guestbook for your site	Guestbook Star
Create a cool-looking HTML page quickly with a non-WYSIWYG editor, including nifty JavaScripts and backgrounds	CoffeeCup HTML Editor
Use a non-WYSIWYG HTML editor with tables, built-in spelling checker, preview panel, and help with hard-to-enter tags such as forms, applets, and targets	Aardvark Pro
Create client-side or server-side imagemaps from a graphic	Mapedit
Configure ready-to-use Java applets for animated logos, scrolling banners, color-cycling bullets, charts, imagemaps, and icons	AppletAce

Software Support

If you have problems installing or using any of these programs, *please do not contact the author or AP PROFESSIONAL.* These programs are provided for your convenience; neither the author nor AP PROFESSIONAL possesses the staff or the technical expertise to deal with every conceivable problem that can arise when you try to install or run this software. *To get technical support on these products, contact the software publisher and pay the registration fee.* The author regrets that he is unable to respond to requests for assistance for any of the material on this CD-ROM.

List of Programs

Table D.1 lists what's on the CD-ROM, including a brief description of the program, the version number, the hardware requirements, the cost, and ordering information, including the program's home page.

Note: The following information was correct at the time of this book's publication. Since then, new versions may have appeared, fees and terms may have changed, and Web sites may have moved. To see whether a new version of the program is available, please access the program's home page.

Table D.1   Programs Included on the CD-ROM

Program Name and Version Number	Description	Requires	Cost[*]	Program Home Page and Registration Information
Aardvark Pro	HTML Editor	Win 95/NT or Win 3.1	$75	**Location and name of setup file on CD-ROM:** \aardvark\32-bit\av32_242.exe or \aardvark\16-bit\
				Program home page: www.tmgnet.com/aardvark/
				Secure online ordering: Access www.tmgnet.com/aardvark/ and follow the links
				Fax order: (410) 820-9322
				Snail mail: Aardvark Registrations TMG 111 Franklin Street Denton, MD 21629-1207 Please make check payable to The Martin Group.

Table D.1 *Continued*

Program Name and Version Number	Description	Requires	Cost*	Program Home Page and Registration Information
ACDSee32 1.0 and ACDSee16 1.5	Graphics management	Win 95/NT or Win 3.1	$30	**Location and name of setup program on CD-ROM:** \acdsee\32-bit\ acdsee3221.exe or \acdsee\ 16-bit\acds1615.exe **Program home page:** www.acdsystems.com **Toll-free phone order:** In the USA call 1-800-414-2237 or call (250) 361-8962 (order 24 hours a day, 7 days a week; VISA or MasterCard). **Fax order:** In the USA fax 1-800-819-2207 or (250) 382-7099 (print out and complete the supplied order form accessible from www.acdsystems.com). **Online ordering with CompuServe:** GO SWREG and follow the links. **Snail mail:** Send completed order form (print out from www.acdsystems.com) with your check, in US funds, or money order to: ACD Systems Ltd. 177 Telegraph Road, #591 Bellingham, WA 98226 USA
AppletAce	Configure some very cool (supplied) Java applets, including animated logos, banners, color-cycling bullets, charts, imagemaps, and icons	Win 95/NT	Free	**Location and name of setup program on CD-ROM:** \appace\32-bit\appace.exe
Banner Show 2.1	Creates scrolling or rotating banners for site advertising	Win 95/NT	$29	**Location and name of setup program on CD-ROM:** \banner\32-bit\bs32.exe

Table D.1   *Continued*

Program Name and Version Number	Description	Requires	Cost*	Program Home Page and Registration Information
				Program home page: www.webgenie/com/software/
				Online ordering: www/webgenie/com, and follow the links to Register Software.
				Snail mail: WebGenie Software Pty Ltd PO Box 149 Rundle Mall, SA 5000 Australia
				Fax ordering: +61 8 8303 4355
CGI Star	Creates CGI scripts for forms processing, without requiring programming knowledge	Win 95/NT	$99	**Location and name of setup program on CD-ROM:** \cgi-star\32-bit\csp32.exe
				Program home page: www.webgenie/com/software/
				Online ordering: www/webgenie/com, and follow the links to Register Software.
				Snail mail: WebGenie Software Pty Ltd PO Box 149 Rundle Mall, SA 5000 Australia
				Fax ordering: +61 8 8303 4355
CoffeeCup HTML Editor 4.0	HTML Editor with built-in browser, tables, Java Scripts, image previewer, and backgrounds	Windows 95/NT	$30	**Setup program location on CD-ROM:** \coffee\32-bit\
				Program home page: www.coffeecup.com
				Secure on-line ordering: www.coffeecup.com, and follow links to order.
				Phone orders: (512) 887-7778

Table D.1 *Continued*

Program Name and Version Number	Description	Requires	Cost*	Program Home Page and Registration Information
				Mail orders: Send a check to: CoffeeCup Software 801 Elizabeth Street Corpus Christi, Texas 78404
Eye Candy 3.0	Filters for Adobe Photoshop and Paint Shop Pro		$199	**Location and name of setup program on CD-ROM:** \eyecandy\32-bit\ EC30demo.exe
FTP Explorer 1.00.09	FTP client for uploading Web pages to Web servers	Win 95/NT	Free for individual use; $30 for businesses	**Location and name of setup file on CD-ROM:** \fptex\32-bit\setup.exe
				Program home page: www.ftpx.com
				Secure online registration Access www.ftpx.com, and follow the links.
				Fax orders: Access the form at www.ftpx.com, and send it to (405) 348-4753.
				Snail mail: Print the form at www.ftpx.com/order.html, and send it to: FTP Explorer PO Box 20574 Oklahoma City, OK 73156-0574
Guestbook Star	Creates a guestbook for your site; CGI scripts are required unless you have WebGenie host your guestbook (3 months free with registration)	Win 95/NT	$29	**Location and name of setup program on CD-ROM:** \guest\32-bit\gs32.exe **Program home page:** www.webgenie/com/software/ **Online ordering:** www/webgenie/com, and follow the links to Register Software.

Table D.1   *Continued*

Program Name and Version Number	Description	Requires	Cost*	Program Home Page and Registration Information
				Snail mail: 　WebGenie Software Pty Ltd 　PO Box 149 　Rundle Mall, SA 5000 　Australia **Fax ordering:**　+61 8 8303 4355
Macromedia Flash2 (2.0)	Creates animated, interactive Web interfaces, advertising banners, navigation buttons, panels, logos and cartoons, with synchronized sound; Flash2 plug-in required to view these effects	Win 95/NT	$199	**Location and name of setup program on CD-ROM:** \flash2\flash2trial.EXE **Program home page:** www.macromedia.com
Mapedit	Create server-side or client-side imagemaps		$25	**Location and name of setup program on CD-ROM:** mapedit32-bitmap32dst.exe or mapedit16-bitmapdst.exe **Program home page:** www.boutell.com/mapedit/ **Secure online ordering:** www.boutell.com/mapedit/, and follow the links. **Phone orders:**　+1 206 325 3009 **Snail mail:** 　Boutell.Com, Inc. 　PO Box 20837 　Seattle, WA 98102
m-BED	Plug-in for Interactor animations with synchronized sound	Win 95/NT or Win 3.1	Free	**Location and name of setup file on CD-ROM:** \mbed\32-bit\setup.exe or \mbed\16-bit\setup.exe

Table D.1 *Continued*

Program Name and Version Number	Description	Requires	Cost*	Program Home Page and Registration Information
				Program home page: www.mbed.com
Paint Shop Pro 4.21	Full-featured paint program for creating Web graphics	Win 95/NT and Win 3.1	$69	**Location and name of setup program on CD-ROM:** \pspro\32-bit\setup.exe or \pspro\16-bit\setup.exe
				Program home page: www.jasc.com
				Secure online ordering: Access www.jasc.com, and follow the links to the ordering page.
				Phone orders: (800) 622-2793
				Fax orders: (612) 930-9172
PicaView32 1.0 and PicaView16 1.3	Adds very convenient commands to File Manager or pop-up menus for graphics file management	Win 95/NT or Win 3.1	$20	**Location and name of setup program on CD-ROM:** \picaview\32-bit\ pvu3210.exe or \picaview\ 16-bit\pvu1613.exe
				Program home page: www.acdsystems.com
				Toll-free phone order: In the USA call 1-800-414-2237 or call (250) 361-8962 (order 24 hours a day, 7 days a week; VISA or MasterCard).
				Fax order: In the USA fax: 1-800-819-2207 or to (250) 382-7099 (print out and complete the supplied order form accessible from www.acdsystems.com).
				Online ordering with CompuServe: GO SWREG and follow the links.

Table D.1 *Continued*

Program Name and Version Number	Description	Requires	Cost*	Program Home Page and Registration Information
				Snail mail: Send completed order form (print out from www.acdsystems.com) with your check, in US funds, or money order to: ACD Systems Ltd. 177 Telegraph Road, #591 Bellingham, WA 98226 USA
Pixel 3D	Create awesome 3-D graphics for your Web pages	Win 95/NT and Win 3.11 (16-bit program)	$64.95	**Location and name of setup file on CD-ROM:** \pixel3d\16-bit\setup.exe **Program home page:** www2.wavetech.net/~pixelboy/ **Phone order:** 612-702-0811 **Fax order:** 612-578-1934 **Snail mail:** Forward Design 2258 Cypress Drive Woodbury, MN 55125
Shockwave	Plug-in for Netscape and Netscape-compatible browsers	Win 95/NT and Win 3.1	Free	**Location and name of setup program on CD-ROM:** \shock\32-bit\shockwave_installer.exe or \shock\16-bit\SWWorks.exe
Site Sleuth		Win 95/NT	$50	**Location and name of setup program on CD-ROM:** guest32-bit **Program home page:** www.webgenie/com/software/ **Online ordering:** www/webgenie/com, and follow the links to Register Software. **Snail mail:** WebGenie Software Pty Ltd PO Box 149 Rundle Mall, SA 5000 Australia

Table D.1 *Continued*

Program Name and Version Number	Description	Requires	Cost*	Program Home Page and Registration Information
				Fax ordering: +61 8 8303 4355
				Program home page: www.webgenie/com/software/
TextPad 2.3 (shareware)	Text editor with spell checking (replaces Windows NotePad utility); many foreign language dictionaries available	Win 95/NT; Win 3.1	$27	**Location and name of setup program on CD-ROM:** \textpad\32-bit\setup.exe or \textpad\16-bit\setup.exe
				Program home page: www.textpad.com
				Secure online ordering: www.textpad.com, and follow links to order.
				CompuServe: GO SWREG and follow the online instructions. The registration ID number is 3938.
WebPaint 3.3	Paint program with many features designed for Web publishing, including yellow tool tips and 256-color palette	Win 95/NT	300 Kr. (Nor-weigian)	**Location and name of setup program on CD-ROM:** \webpaint\32-bit\setup.exe
				Program home page: alpha.barentsnett.no/webpaint/
				Online ordering: alpha.barentsnett.no/webpaint/ (follow links to Order Page)

Table D.1 *Continued*

Program Name and Version Number	Description	Requires	Cost*	Program Home Page and Registration Information
WebForms	Process interactive forms with or without CGI	Win 95/NT	WebForms Standard, $21.95; WebForms Pro, $34.95	**Program home page:** www.q-d.com **Phone order:** Call PsL (Public Software Library) at (800)242-4775 or (713)524-6394. **Fax order:** Fill out the online form, print it, and fax it to (908)626-9224.

*Quoted price is for individual users only. For use on more than one computer or for site license fees, please contact the publisher.

Index

A

AAA Matilda, 423

Aardvark Pro, 188

absolute URLs, 278, 412, 466

<ABSTRACT> tag, 233, 247, 262–263

access statistics, 103

ACTION attribute, 297

ActiveX, 46, 47, 49–50, 64, 364–367

Add a Resource page, 146

<ADDRESS> tag, 197, 222–223, 293

Adobe Acrobat

   Acrobat Exchange, 492, 494–497,
     500–501

   Acrobat Search, 493, 494

   to add hyperlinks, 499–500

   articles in, 493, 501

   capabilities of, 491

   columns, 500–501

   to create documents, 497, 498

   history of, 491–492

   to navigate in, 493, 496–497

   PDF Writer, 493, 497

   Reader, 492, 493, 494–497, 500

Adobe Acrobat Catalog, 493, 494

Adobe Acrobat for Workgroups, 494

Adobe Acrobat Pro, 494, 498

Adobe Photoshop, 126

   logo creation, 151

   plug-in architecture of, 358

Related Titles from AP PROFESSIONAL

VAUGHAN-NICHOLS, *Intranets*

WATKINS/MARENKA, *The Internet Edge in Business*

WAYNER, *Agents at Large*

WAYNER, *Digital Cash, Second Edition*

WAYNER, *Disappearing Cryptography*

WAYNER, *Java and JavaScript Programming*

Ask your local bookseller, computer store, or librarian for any of these AP PROFESSIONAL titles, or contact us directly.

Ordering Information

 **AP** PROFESSIONAL
An Imprint of ACADEMIC PRESS
A Division of HARCOURT BRACE & COMPANY

In the USA and Canada

AP PROFESSIONAL
Order Fulfillment Department
6277 Sea Harbor Drive
Orlando, FL 32821-9816

Call Toll Free: 1-800-3131-APP
Fax: 1-800-874-6418
E-mail: app@acad.com

In the U.K., Europe, Africa, and the Middle East

Academic Press, Ltd.
24–28 Oval Road
London NW1 7DX
United Kingdom

Phone: +44 (0) 181 300 3322
Fax: +44 (0) 171 267 0362
E-mail: app@apuk.co.uk

For All Other International Orders

AP PROFESSIONAL
Order Fulfillment Department
6277 Sea Harbor Drive
Orlando, FL 32821-9816

Phone: 1-407-345-3800
Fax: 1-407-345-4060
E-mail: app@acad.com

Editorial: 1300 Boylston St., Chestnut Hill, MA 02167; (617) 232-0500

Web: http://www.apnet.com/approfessional